Human Capital and Institutions
A Long Run View

Human Capital and Institutions is concerned with human capital in its many dimensions and brings to the fore the role of political, social, and economic institutions in human capital formation and economic growth. Written by leading economic historians, including pioneers in historical research on human capital, the chapters in this text offer a broad-based view of human capital in economic development. The issues they address range from nutrition in premodern societies to twentieth-century advances in medical care; from the social institutions that provided temporary relief to workers in the middle and lower ranges of the wage scale to the factors that affected the performance of those who reached the pinnacle in business and art; and from political systems that stifled the advance of literacy to those that promoted public and higher education. Just as human capital has been a key to economic growth, so has the emergence of appropriate institutions been a key to the growth of human capital.

David Eltis is Robert W. Woodruff Professor of History at Emory University and has held visiting appointments at Harvard and Yale universities. He is author of *The Rise of African Slavery in the Americas,* co-compiler of *The Transatlantic Slave Trade: A Database on CD-ROM* and its successor at www.slavevoyages.org, co-editor of *Extending the Frontiers: Essays on the New Transatlantic Slave Trade Database* (with David Richardson), co-editor of *Slavery in the Development of the Americas* (with Frank Lewis and Kenneth Sokoloff), and editor of *Coerced and Free Migrations: Global Perspectives.* He is also author and co-author of numerous articles on slavery, migration, and abolition, most recently in the *American Historical Review* and the *William and Mary Quarterly.*

Frank D. Lewis is Professor of Economics at Queen's University, Kingston, Canada. He has written on historical issues involving agriculture, land settlement, transportation, Native American history, war, and slavery. His work has appeared in a variety of publications that include leading economic history and economics journals. Articles on the North American fur trade of the eighteenth century (with Ann Carlos) have been awarded prizes by the Canadian Economic Association and the Library Company of Philadelphia. Some of his more recent papers have appeared in the *Economic History Review,* the *Journal of Economic History,* and *Explorations in Economic History.*

Kenneth L. Sokoloff (1953–2007) was Professor of Economics at the University of California, Los Angeles, and research associate at the National Bureau of Economic Research.

Human Capital and Institutions

A Long Run View

Edited by

DAVID ELTIS

Emory University

FRANK D. LEWIS

Queen's University, Canada

KENNETH L. SOKOLOFF

University of California, Los Angeles

CAMBRIDGE
UNIVERSITY PRESS

CAMBRIDGE UNIVERSITY PRESS
Cambridge, New York, Melbourne, Madrid, Cape Town, Singapore, São Paulo, Delhi

Cambridge University Press
32 Avenue of the Americas, New York, NY 10013-2473, USA

www.cambridge.org
Information on this title: www.cambridge.org/9780521769587

First published 2009

Printed in the United States of America

A catalog record for this publication is available from the British Library.

Library of Congress Cataloging in Publication data

Human capital and institutions : a long run view / edited by David Eltis, Frank Lewis,
Kenneth L. Sokoloff.
p.   cm.
Includes bibliographical references and index.
ISBN 978-0-521-76958-7 (hardback)
1. Human capital.   2. Economic development.   3. Business and education.
I. Eltis, David, 1940–   II. Lewis, Frank, 1947–   III. Sokoloff, Kenneth Lee.   IV. Title.
HD4904.7.H8583   2009
306 – dc22   2009020208

ISBN   978-0-521-76958-7 hardback

Contents

In Memoriam: Kenneth L. Sokoloff

Kenneth L. Sokoloff, who was a close collaborator of Stanley Engerman, passed away prematurely on May 21, 2007. This volume is an occasion to also acknowledge his contributions.

It seems particularly fitting to evoke Sokoloff's work on endowments and institutions because he began it as part of a dissertation completed under the supervision of Robert Fogel at Harvard in 1982. This part of his research was closest to that pursued by Engerman, a co-author and close collaborator of Fogel's, and what had been a long-running conversation blossomed into full-fledged collaboration in the 1990s.

Much of Sokoloff's research has focused on the interaction between the expansion of markets and productivity growth. In his early work on industrialization he emphasized the importance of market forces in spurring firms to reorganize their modes of production. This theme recurred in his work on the relationship between agricultural seasonality and the adoption of capital intensive methods of manufacturing. He also reprised this approach in his work on patenting and invention, in which he showed that patenting rates were much higher in counties traversed by navigable waterways and that repeat inventors were likely to move to such counties as they pursued the returns to their discoveries. Over time, however, Sokoloff became more deeply concerned with understanding how endowments and institutions co-evolved, rather than simply attributing primacy in economic outcomes to one or the other. It was this latter set of interests that brought him to work closely with Engerman.

In a 1997 jointly authored paper, "Factor Endowments: Institutions, and Differential Paths of Growth Among New World Economies: A View from Economic Historians of the United States," Engerman and Sokoloff turned to a fundamental puzzle of American economic history. Why was it that those areas that were the most economically successful before 1800 have generally fared poorly in the period after 1850? They argued that the endowments Europeans found on arrival played a far more critical role in shaping early institutions than the colonists' political, religious, or legal backgrounds. On the one hand, where slave-based agriculture took root, institutions hardened over time to ensure the continued unequal distribution of economic and political rights. These institutions did not prove much of a hindrance to prosperity for staple export economies, but they made the transition to the higher income afforded by modern economic growth virtually impossible. On the other hand, where slave-based agriculture was not profitable, institutions developed that allowed easy immigration, access to land, and relatively open political rights, enabling these countries to benefit from the opportunities that industrial development later presented. Sokoloff and Engerman emphasized that a variety of institutional arrangements were tried in each ecological zone but that economies quickly adjusted to take advantage of their endowments. After the publication of their original article, Sokoloff, Engerman, and their co-authors would pen nearly a dozen papers that provided detailed empirical evidence for their argument. These articles have been massively cited and helped persuade economists of the importance of history to understanding economic outcomes.

Our discipline has lost a leader. His personal generosity, intellectual openness, and dedication to the careful gathering of empirical evidence were unparalleled. His commitment to uncovering the sources of long-term economic growth lives on in his students, colleagues, and, we hope, the discipline.

Naomi R. Lamoreaux, UCLA
Jean-Laurent Rosenthal, Caltech

Contributors

George R. Boyer, Cornell University

Michael Edelstein, Queens College and The Graduate School, CUNY

Stanley L. Engerman, University of Rochester

Robert W. Fogel, The University of Chicago Graduate School of Business

David W. Galenson, University of Chicago

Claudia Goldin, Harvard University

Robert Jensen, University of Kentucky

Lawrence F. Katz, Harvard University

Elisa V. Mariscal, LECG

Hugh Rockoff, Rutgers University

Kenneth L. Sokoloff, University of California, Los Angeles

Richard H. Steckel, Ohio State University

Robert J. Steinfeld, University at Buffalo Law School

Peter Temin, Massachusetts Institute of Technology

Introduction

Stanley Engerman and Kenneth Sokoloff have been leaders in renewing interest in institutions and their impact on economic development. The papers in this volume are concerned with human capital in its many dimensions, and bring to fore the role of political, social, and economic institutions in human capital formation and economic growth. The papers address a broad range of issues, from nutrition in pre-modern societies to twentieth-century advances in medical care, from the institutions that concerned workers in the middle and lower ranges of the wage scale to the factors that affected the performance of those who reached the pinnacle in business and art, and from political systems that stifled the advance of literacy to those that promoted public and higher education. Just as human capital has been a key to economic growth, so has the emergence of appropriate institutions been a key to human capital formation. It is this theme that underlies the papers in this volume.

Along with Stan Engerman, Robert Fogel pioneered the use of anthropometric evidence to study economic growth, and helped expand our view of human capital. Formal schooling, apprenticeship programs, specialized job training in the workplace, and learning-by-doing all raise productivity, but other forms of human capital investment are also important. The notion that health and physical size and strength can affect labor productivity is not new, but Fogel has brought these forms of human capital to center stage. Indeed, if we are to explain economic performance even in modern times, it is important that we not ignore those issues of diet, disease, sanitation, and health care that are at the foundation of Fogel's work.

In Chapter 1 Fogel addresses the relation between mortality and measures of health status, such as height and body mass index. Since the eighteenth century, health in the West has improved remarkably, although the estimates of life expectancy suggest that the gains have been by no means continuous. As Fogel documents, improved nutrition and sanitation accounted for much of the advance up to World War II, but since then expenditures on medical care have played an increasingly important role, especially in reducing mortality of the elderly. To the extent that such investments in health are directed to those who have left the labor force, they have little effect on output, but as Fogel emphasizes they have a great impact on welfare. The high income elasticities of demand for health care that Fogel reports suggest that as economies advance, and workers retire earlier and live longer, the benefits of economic growth will become increasingly tied to health status. Fogel argues a greater investment in medical care for the old as well as the young is the appropriate market and social response.

Richard Steckel has been at the forefront of exciting work involving the use of skeletal remains to infer the health status of pre-modern populations. In Chapter 2, Steckel describes the approach and discusses some of the methodological issues, including both the weaknesses and the promise of this unique form of evidence. He, Jerome Rose, and Paul Sciulli have developed a health index for the pre-Columbian period based on the skeletons of 4,078 individuals who lived at 23 localities in North, Central, and South America. Steckel uses the index to compare the health status of hunter–gatherers with those who lived in villages and urban areas. Larger settlements led systematically to poorer health and the effect was large. Those not living in fixed settlements averaged in the top 15 percent of the health distribution in contrast to the urban dwellers who were in the bottom 20 percent. Although diseases related to crowding were less of a factor than in Europe, the scarcity of meat and fish and the lack of protein-rich grains were likely more serious problems. Over the long period from 6,000 BC to Columbus, the trend in health was downward, reflecting the shift from the mobile lifestyle associated with hunting–gathering to fixed settlements. Steckel is in the tradition of those who are finding that the progress associated with the transition to settled agriculture came with a human cost.

A healthy, physically able workforce has been the basis of successful economies and was a key element of eighteenth- and nineteenth-century industrialization. George Boyer points out, however, that the economic advances that increased wages also brought greater insecurity. Unemployment or illness of the main breadwinner could be devastating to even relatively high-income families. Important to workers in Britain and elsewhere was the emergence of institutions that provided protection to those experiencing a temporary decline in income. In Chapter 3 Boyer explores how Britain responded. Over the period from 1830 to the eve of the First World War, workers throughout the wage distribution faced serious income insecurity. In response, Britain introduced various forms of insurance, both private and public. Public relief provided through the Poor Laws was directed at those in the bottom third of the wage distribution, but higher income workers demanded protection as well. For many of these workers, friendly societies became an important source of income during periods of illness or unemployment. In the latter part of the nineteenth century, this insurance role was gradually taken over by labor unions, and early in the twentieth century social programs such the Old Age Pension and health and unemployment insurance superseded public relief. Like other forms of capital, the returns to human capital are uncertain; and because, for most workers in the nineteenth century, labor earnings were the only source of income, it was important that insurance mechanisms emerge. These mechanisms raised welfare by smoothing consumption, and made possible the entry of workers into occupations with high wage variability. Construction, for example, was characterized by high but variable wages. Thus insurance of the type examined by Boyer contributed to greater overall productivity by promoting entry into this and similar occupations.

Stanley Engerman and Kenneth Sokoloff have done influential work on how factor endowments can help shape the institutions so important to economic growth. In Chapter 4, also characteristic of the new institutional economics to which they have been leading contributors, Engerman, Elisa Mariscal, and Sokoloff explore the development of schooling institutions in the Americas. Until 1800, the center of economic activity in the Americas was outside mainland North America. It was the sugar-based slave economies of Brazil and the West Indies that produced the highest levels of income per capita and generated by far the most trade with Europe. But during the nineteenth century, the economies of these regions stagnated, falling far behind the United States and Canada. With their early emphasis on primary education, the United States and Canada had in 1800 perhaps the most literate populations in the world. And beginning in the 1820s their lead in education increased as the common school movement took hold. This experience contrasts with the rest of the Americas where public schooling was rare.

What explains the different education paths? Engerman, Mariscal, and Sokoloff itemize the possible candidates: religion, ethnicity, form of government, and resources; but in the end they argue that extreme inequality in Latin America both in income and political power, rooted ultimately in factor endowments, was the cause of their poor educational outcomes. They arrive at this conclusion partly by examining the record within Latin America, where there were differences across countries in the distribution of income and the timing of the suffrage. Argentina and Chile invested more in education than the other parts of Latin America, and it was there that income and political power were much more equally distributed. By describing and explaining cross-country differences in human capital investment, Engerman, Mariscal, and Sokoloff further our understanding of how institutions affect relative economic performance.

Focusing mainly on the United States, Claudia Goldin and Lawrence Katz have written extensively on the history of education, where prominent is their finding that investment in education there has been much greater than in similarly developed countries. In Chapter 5 they ask why this was true in the period 1910 to 1940. Their focus is on high school enrollment and on the numbers graduating from high school. The United States stands out in terms of both measures. From 1910 to 1940, the proportion graduating from high school increased from 10 percent to 50 percent; and, in 1955, 80 percent were enrolled full time in high school. By contrast, the full-time enrollment rate in the highest enrollment European country, Sweden, was just 25 percent. Goldin and Katz use state-level cross-section comparisons of high school participation to shed light on the exceptional United States performance. Quite a number of factors influenced enrollment, but what especially distinguished the United States from Europe was its much greater reliance on local financing of public schools. This approach to funding made possible returns-to-scale not present in a private system while at the same time promoting public school systems that reflected the educational demands of the people within each local area. This matching of public schools to the costs and benefits of education in each community promoted much higher levels of investment than the centralized European model. Goldin and Katz argue as well that public investment in U.S. colleges and universities, by increasing the potential return from completing high school, further raised high school enrollment and graduation rates.

While Chapters 4 and 5 are concerned with international comparisons of access to and quality of general education, Michael Edelstein (Chapter 6) focuses on education of a more specific kind. Using a unique data set, he explores graduation rates from engineering schools in New York State over a period of 150 years. During much of the nineteenth century, few in the United States who described themselves as engineers were graduates of university or technical programs. But after 1870, a year when only 10 percent of engineers had a higher degree, there was a burgeoning in formal engineering education. By 1910 the share of engineers with degrees had increased to more than a third and, in 1940, 57 percent of the nation's nearly 300,000 engineers had four or more years of higher education.

New York State, which includes among the earliest American institutions of higher education, collected comprehensive data on college and university degrees beginning in the late eighteenth century. From 1823 to 1953 the annual number of higher degrees per 100,000 population increased from about 100 to nearly 3,000, an average growth of 30 percent per decade. And, during the late nineteenth and early twentieth centuries, the number of engineering degrees grew even faster. The peak was in the 1910s when 15 percent of graduates were from engineering programs. Underpinning these broad aggregates is Edelstein's detailed accounting of the number of engineering graduates at institutions throughout the state. In addition to presenting a remarkably full picture of the pattern of engineering graduation, Edelstein makes the case that the rapidly increasing share of professional engineers in the workforce was a significant element in America's industrial success.

Research on human capital typically deals with average or expected results. In their study of genius in the world of art, David Galenson and Robert Jensen (Chapter 7) look at outliers, focusing on whether great painters produced their most highly regarded work as the result of a long process of human capital accumulation, or whether their best work was produced early in their careers. From their survey of art history and their analysis of art auctions, Galenson and Jensen identify a clear distinction between those artists whose contribution resulted from what they describe as the experimental approach, typified by the paintings of Rembrandt, Cézanne, and Pollock; and artists whose genius has been regarded as conceptual, among them, Raphael and Picasso. They find that artists such as Cézanne, whose work is regarded as experimental, continued to add to their human capital throughout their lifetime, producing paintings of increasing importance and financial value. On the other hand conceptual artists, such as Picasso, made their greatest impact early in their careers. The lesser importance of their later work suggests a gradual depreciation of their human capital. Galenson and Jensen present an intriguing hypothesis about the life cycle of artists, and show how an analysis of markets, in this case art market, can contribute to our understanding of, not just artistic genius, but also the overall process of human capital accumulation.

Another approach to the tail of the human capital distribution is presented in Chapter 8. Peter Temin discusses of the proportion of Jews in the Forbes 400, a list of the wealthiest Americans, focusing on the role of networks and information flows among small ethnic, religious, or other minority groups. Jews have comprised about 2 percent of the U.S. population; yet, in 1982, 15 percent of those on the Forbes 400 list were Jewish, and in 1998 the proportion was 20 percent. Such a disparity cannot be explained by a difference in levels of schooling; nor, Temin argues, does discrimination against Jews account for their economic success. According the latter view, because Jews were prevented from becoming part of the business elite, they disproportionately became small entrepreneurs, some of whom were spectacularly successful. Temin points out that Jews were in fact present among the business elites throughout the twentieth century, and argues that, by limiting their opportunities, discrimination more likely reduced the chance a Jew could acquire great wealth.

Jews have been over-represented among the richest 400 Americans, according to Temin, because they have had the advantage of being part of a social network. Each financially successful Jew tended to promote the success of other Jews through business and social contacts to a degree not seen in the general population. Notwithstanding the recent troubles of the company that they founded, the experience of Marcus Goldman and Samuel Sachs illustrates how contacts with other Jews, including Julius Rosenwald head of Sears, Roebuck and Jacob Werthein of United Cigar Manufacturers, led to the emergence of a major financial firm. And the concentration of the richest Jews in particular industries, notably apparel and cosmetics, and banking finance, is further evidence of the power of network effects.

Incentives are essential if a worker's human capital is to translate into high productivity. This message of the principal-agent literature has underlying it a model where employers design contracts to elicit effort from workers. In modern economies the range of contracts is circumscribed. Unlike the case of slavery, where employers use violence and threats of violence, in addition to positive incentives, to increase the productivity of workers, employers in modern economies are (appropriately) restricted in the degree to which their workers can be coerced. Robert Steinfeld (Chapter 9) points out, however, that, as late as the nineteenth century, employers in England had available to them tools that, while not as draconian as those associated with slavery, allowed for severe punishment of nominally free workers. By invoking Master and Servant acts, employers might convince a court to fine and even imprison at hard labor a worker found to have violated a labor contract.

Such penalties, which were commonly applied to indentured workers and apprentices, protected employers. They also provided a mechanism for these workers to pre-commit to the terms of their contracts. The cost of hiring and training new workers could be considerable, and to the extent that employers bore the cost, they wanted to be assured that they would earn a return on that investment. The Master and Servant acts helped provide that assurance. Especially after 1860, British labor groups campaigned vigorously against the Master and Servant acts, and in 1875, eight years after the suffrage had been greatly expanded and political power shifted from business interests to workers, the acts were repealed.

In Chapter 10 Hugh Rockoff presents a wide-ranging analysis and review of usury laws. Usury laws, which date back at least to Biblical times, typically specified a maximum lending rate where the penalty for violating the law was a fine based on the amount of the interest and principal. Adam Smith, who recognized the benefits of loans above the usual market interest rate, still argued for some interest rate ceiling. He wrote that money borrowed at high rates would go to "prodigals and projectors"; prodigals who would dissipate the money on their own consumption, and projectors who would invest in improbable schemes. Jeremy Bentham took a contrary view; and his *Defense of Usury* became influential on both sides of the Atlantic.

The United States and some European countries were greatly affected by British thinking on usury laws, which Britain, in the nineteenth century, was liberalizing. In 1833 Britain eliminated usury limits on bills of exchange with less than three months to maturity, and in 1854 all Britain's usury laws were repealed. In the United States the maximum interest rate and the penalty varied by state, but, despite some differences in approach, the overall trend was toward relaxing interest rate restrictions and reducing penalties. By 1881, seventeen states had repealed their usury laws. There were attempts to control the interest rate charged by national banks, but the

Congress ultimately gave them more flexibility than even the state banks. Rockoff points out that, by limiting interest rates, usury laws could affect many forms of investment, including investment in human capital.

Eight of these papers were presented at a conference in Rochester that honored Stanley Engerman. One of the organizers of that conference was Kenneth Sokoloff, who is also a co-author of one the chapters. Ken took the lead in bringing these papers together, but he was unable to see the project to completion. We dedicate this book to his memory.

PART I

HEALTH AND LIVING STANDARDS

Biotechnology and the Burden of Age-Related Diseases

Robert W. Fogel

During the past two decades, there have been a number of major advances in constructing time series on the decline in mortality in Western Europe, Japan, and the United States. The data for these time series were obtained from a variety of archives. Both the retrieval and the processing of the data were made possible by the remarkable advances in computer technology that not only permitted the creation of the time series but enabled linkage to a variety of variables aimed at explaining the improvement in health and longevity over the past three centuries. In this chapter, I focus first on England and France, for which the longest time series exist, but will make use of data from several other countries including Sweden, Norway, the Netherlands, the United States, and Japan.

Figure 1.1 shows time series for the decline in mortality rates going back to the 1540s in England and to the 1740s in France. These diagrams present the annual crude mortality rates for each country as a scatter of points. The heavy dark line in the center of each scatter shows the underlying trend in the mortality rate.

Figure 1.1 shows that in both England and France, crude mortality rates were much higher in the eighteenth century than they are today – on the order of three to four times higher. A second feature is the much greater volatility of mortality rates in the past than today, with annual death rates sometimes exceeding the secular trend by as much as 50 to 100 percent. It was these mortality crises that initially caught the attention of demographers who were focused on the data of particular localities. They argued that mortality crises accounted for a large part of total mortality during the seventeenth and eighteenth centuries, and that the decline in mortality rates after about 1750 was due largely to the elimination of these crises. The elimination of crisis mortality was, in turn, attributed to the elimination of periodic famines. However, when the nationwide time series shown in Figure 1.1 were partitioned, it turned out that in both the French and the British cases the elimination of crisis mortality, whether related to famines

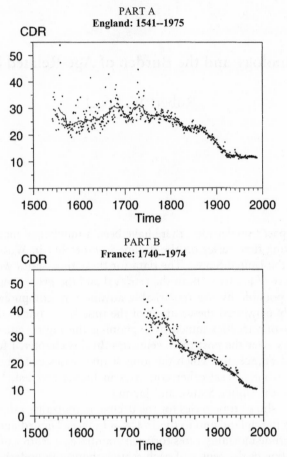

FIGURE 1.1. The Secular Trends in Mortality Rates in England and France. *Note:* Each diagram shows the scatter of annual death rates around a 25-year moving average. *Source:* Fogel (1992).

or not, accounted for only a small fraction of the secular decline in mortality rates. About 90 percent of the drop was due to the reduction in the "normal" levels of mortality.

Still another feature of Figure 1.1 is the repeated interruption of downward trends in mortality and their reversal. Substantial interruptions and reversals in the downward trend have also been demonstrated during the nineteenth century for the United States, Sweden, and Hungary. Such interruptions and reversals lasted several decades and prevented even the keenest contemporary observers from appreciating that the growing control of the environment had the capacity to transform human physiology. It was not until World War I that biodemographers and epidemiologists recognized that they were in the midst of a long-term reduction in mortality rates that had not yet run its course.

Just how remarkable the change has been during the past three centuries is summarized by three key figures on life expectancy at birth. In France and England at the beginning of the eighteenth century, and in a few other OECD nations for which some measurement is possible, life expectancy at birth was about 30 years. Today it is in the neighborhood of 76 to 80 years for the high-income nations of the OECD. The lowest long-term life expectancy rate at which *Homo sapiens* can survive is about 20 years. Hence, over the roughly 200,000 year history of the species, life expectancy at birth has so far increased by about 60 years, and five-sixths of this increase has occurred since 1700. Half of the increase occurred during the past 100 years.

Attempts to explain the remarkable decline in mortality rates since 1700 and the concurrent improvement in health, especially over the past century, have produced significant advances in knowledge. Although many of the new findings are still tentative, they suggest a new theory of evolution that Dora Costa (an economist and biodemographer at UCLA) and I call *technophysio evolution*.

Technophysio evolution is the result of a synergism between technological and physiological improvements that has produced a form of human evolution that is biological (but not genetic), rapid, culturally transmitted, and not necessarily stable. This process is still ongoing in both rich and developing countries. Unlike the genetic theory of evolution through natural selection, which applies to the whole history of life on earth, technophysio evolution applies only to the last 300 years of human history, and particularly to the last century.

Human beings have gained an unprecedented degree of control over their environment – a degree of control so great that it sets them apart not only from all other species, but also from all previous generations of *Homo sapiens*. This new degree of control has enabled *Homo sapiens* to increase its average body size by over 50 percent, to increase its average longevity by more than 100 percent, and to improve greatly the robustness and capacity of vital organ systems.

Figure 1.2 shows how dramatic the change in the control of the environment after 1700 has been. During its first 200,000 years or so, *Homo sapiens* increased at an exceedingly slow rate. The discovery of agriculture about 11,000 years ago broke the tight constraint on the food supply imposed by a hunting and gathering technology, making it possible to release between 10 and 20 percent of the labor force from the direct production of food, and also giving rise to the first cities. The new technology of food production was so superior to the old one that it was possible to support a much higher rate of population increase than had been the case prior to c. 9000 B.C. Yet the advances in the technology of food production after the *second* Agricultural Revolution (which began about 1700 A.D.) were far more

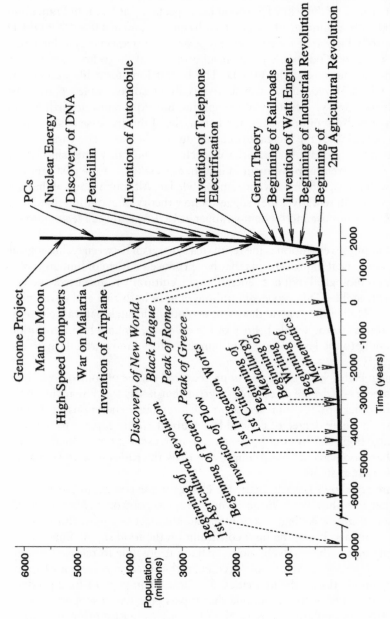

FIGURE 1.2. The Growth of the World Population and Some Major Events in the History of Technology. *Source:* Fogel (2004).

dramatic than the earlier breakthrough, since they permitted population to increase at so high a rate that the line representing population appears to explode, rising almost vertically. The new technological breakthroughs in manufacturing, transportation, trade, communications, energy production, leisure-time services, and medical services were in many respects even more striking than those in agriculture. The twentieth century witnessed a huge acceleration in both population and technological change. The increase in world population between 1900 and 1990 was four times as great as the increase during the whole previous history of humankind. Not only has technological change accelerated dramatically since 1700, but the diffusion of modern technology has also accelerated greatly over the past two centuries.

The most important aspect of technophysio evolution is the continuing conquest of chronic malnutrition due mainly to a severe deficiency in dietary energy, which was virtually universal three centuries ago. In rich countries today, some 1,800 to 2,000 kcal of energy are available daily for work by a typical adult male aged 20–39. During the eighteenth century, however, France produced less than one-third the current amount of energy for work, and England was not much better off. One implication of these estimates of caloric availability is that mature European adults of the eighteenth and much of the nineteenth century must have been very small and less active by current standards.

Recent studies have established the predictive power of height and weight at early ages with respect to onset of diseases and premature mortality at middle and late ages. Figures 1.3 and 1.4 summarize data showing the connection of height and weight to the risk of dying in American and Norwegian cohorts of males. The American cohort turned age 65 around 1910 and the Norwegian cohort turned age 65 about 1980. The two cohorts thus span most of the improvements in health and longevity over the twentieth century. Yet the functions relating height and the body mass index (BMI) to the risk of dying are quite similar. BMI is a measure of weight controlled for height.

Variations in height and weight are associated with variations in the chemical composition of the tissues that make up vital organs, in the quality of the electrical transmission across membranes, and in the functioning of the endocrine system and other vital systems. Nutritional status, as represented by height and weight, thus appears to be a critical link connecting improvements in mortality to improvements in human physiology.

So far I have focused on the contribution of technological change to physiological improvements. The process has been synergistic, however, with improvement in nutrition and physiology contributing significantly to the process of economic growth and technological progress along the lines that I have described elsewhere (Fogel 2004). Here I merely want to point out the main conclusion. Technophysio evolution appears to account for about half of the economic growth in Europe over the past two centuries.

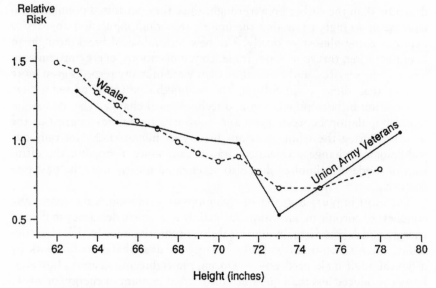

FIGURE 1.3. Relative Mortality Risk among Union Army Veterans and among Norwegian Males.

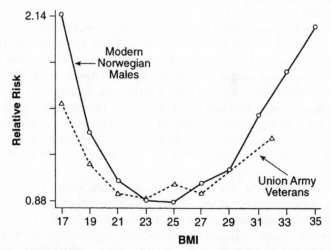

FIGURE 1.4. Relative Mortality Risk by BMI among Men 50 Years of Age, Union Army Veterans around 1900, and Modern Norwegians. *Note:* In the Norwegian data, BMI for 79,084 men was measured at ages 45–49, and the period of risk was seven years. BMI of 550 Union Army veterans was measured at ages 45–64, and the observation period was 25 years. *Source:* Costa and Steckel (1997) with permission from the University of Chicago Press. Copyright 1997 by the National Bureau of Economic Research.

Much of this gain was due to the improvement in human thermodynamic efficiency. The rate of converting human energy input into work output appears to have increased by about 50 percent since 1790.

THE DECLINE IN THE BURDEN OF HEALTH CARE

Both environmental improvements and advances in biomedical technology have contributed to a striking decline in prevalence rates of chronic conditions in high-income countries during the course of the twentieth century. This development is illustrated for the United States by Table 1.1, which compares prevalence rates of Civil War veterans (who were 65 years or older around 1910) and veterans of WWII (who were the same ages in the mid-1980s). Even before the impact of alleviating medical intervention is considered, Table 1.1 shows that prevalence rates were down by 29 to 52 percent over the course of the seven and a half decades separating the elderly veterans of the two wars. But for two of the disorders, genital–urinary conditions and central nervous and related diseases, prevalence rates were higher in the mid-1980s than in 1910.

Medical intervention reduced prevalence rates for all six disorders. Such interventions were especially effective in chronic digestive and genito–urinary disorders, where prevalence rates were cut 60 percent and 70 percent, respectively. In the cases of musculoskeletal, circulatory, and respiratory disorders, the main impact of medical intervention has been to reduce the severity of the conditions rather than to eliminate them. For example, intervention reduced the prevalence rate of circulatory disorders from 42.9 percent to 40.0 percent, whereas digestive disorders were reduced from 49 percent to 18 percent. Whether various medical interventions cured disorders or merely attenuated them, they usually contributed to extending the duration of chronic conditions by postponing death. In other words, medical intervention appears to have had the ironic effect of increasing the duration of some disorders.

It is not yet certain whether environmental improvements and medical interventions have reduced or increased the overall average duration of chronic diseases over the course of the twentieth century. Preliminary analysis indicates that the average age of onset of chronic disorders among veterans of the Union Army may have begun about five years earlier than among veterans of WWII. But this effect is partly offset by an extension in life expectancy at age 50 of about three years for the WWII veterans.

Nevertheless, the combined effect of improvements in the environment and in biomedical interventions over the past century has greatly improved the health of the population at middle and late ages. This proposition is supported by Table 1.2, which shows the capacity of Union Army veterans c. 1900 to engage in manual labor. By ages 60–64, capacity had declined to about a third of what it had been at its peak, which is about half the

TABLE 1.1. *Comparison of the Prevalence Rates of Selected Chronic Conditions among Union Army Veterans in 1910 and World War II Veterans in the Mid-1980s (in percent)*

Disorders	1 Union Army Veterans	2 World War II Veterans before Alleviating Intervention	3 Annual Rate of Decline in Prevalence Rates before Alleviating Intervention	4 World War II Veterans after Alleviating Intervention	5 Annual Rate of Decline in Prevalence Rates after Alleviating Intervention
Musculoskeletal	67.7	47.9	0.4	42.5	0.6
Digestive	84.0	49.0	0.7	18.0	2.0
Genito-urinary	27.3	36.3	+0.4	8.9	1.5
Central nervous, endocrine, metabolic, or blood	24.2	29.9	+0.3	12.6	0.9
Circulatory	90.1	42.9	1.0	40.0	1.1
Respiratory	42.2	29.8	0.5	26.5	0.6

Note: + indicates an increase in prevalence rates. The term "before alleviating intervention" in Column 2 refers to interventions that alleviated existing chronic conditions, not interventions that prevented chronic conditions from occurring, as in the use of penicillin to prevent rheumatic heart disease from occurring.

Source: Fogel (2000).

TABLE 1.2. *The Long-Term Trend in the Structure of Expanded Consumption and the Implied Income Elasticities of Several Consumption Categories*

Consumption Class	Distribution of Expanded Consumption (%)		Long-Term Income Elasticities
	1875	1995	
Food	49	5	0.2
Clothing	12	2	0.3
Shelter	13	5	0.7
Health care	1	9	1.6
Education	1	5	1.6
Other	6	7	1.1
Leisure	18	68*	1.4

* Percentages do not equal 100 due to rounding.
Source: Fogel (2000).

proportions shown by current age-earnings profiles. It is also worth noting that peak earnings were reached at about age 35, which is about 15 years earlier than today.

Partitioning the decline in prevalence rates into environmental effects and medical intervention effects is quite complex because of the long reach of nutritional and other biomedical insults at earlier ages on the odds of developing chronic diseases at middle and late ages. Although such lifecycle effects have long been suspected in particular diseases, it is only recently that a substantial body of evidence bearing on the interconnections has been amassed. Longitudinal studies connecting chronic diseases at maturity, middle ages, and late ages to conditions *in utero* and infancy were reported with increasing frequency beginning in the 1980s and extending through the 1990s. The exact mechanisms by which malnutrition and trauma at early ages affect waiting time to the onset of chronic diseases are still unclear, but it seems reasonable to infer that environmental insults during the period when cell growth is rapid could lead to long-lasting impairments of vital organs.

The connections of alcoholic consumption and smoking during pregnancy to the damaging of the central nervous system of fetuses were established by the early 1980s. Although suggested as early as 1968, evidence confirming that protein–calorie malnutrition (PCM) could cause permanent impairment of central nervous system function accumulated in the 1990s. New evidence also indicated that iodine deficiency *in utero* and severe to moderate iron deficiency during infancy could also cause permanent neurological damage.

Perhaps the most far-reaching studies connecting early age insults and chronic conditions at later ages were those undertaken by the Environmental Epidemiological Unit of the British Medical Research Council at the University of Southampton. Based on studies of a large sample of birth records linked to medical records at middle and late ages, they reported that such conditions as coronary heart disease, hypertension, stroke, type II diabetes, and autoimmune thyroiditis began *in utero* or in infancy, but did not become apparent until mid-adult or later ages. Although numerous questions were raised about the validity of these findings during the first half of the 1990s, the second half of the decade witnessed a substantial expansion of research into the connection between characteristics before age one and the later onset of chronic diseases (or premature mortality). The strongest evidence for such links that has emerged thus far pertains to hypertension, coronary heart disease (CHD), and type II diabetes. A review of 32 papers dealing with the relationship between birth weight and hypertension concluded that there was a significant tendency for blood pressure at middle ages to increase as birth weight declined. Evidence of a connection between anthropometric measures of the neonate and later coronary heart disease has been found by investigators in Finland, India, and Sweden.

The theory of a nexus between environmental insults *in utero* or at early ages and the onset of chronic diseases at later ages suggests that the rapid advances in public health technology between 1890 and 1950 should contribute to a continuing decline in the prevalence rates of chronic diseases and perhaps even to an acceleration of this decline. The first half of the twentieth century witnessed an avalanche of new technologies that improved the environment, including the cleaning up of the water supply, the cleaning up of the milk supply, the widespread draining of swamps, the improvement of garbage disposal and sewage systems, the rapid reduction in the use of animals (especially in cities) for transportation, the switch to electricity and to fuels with a lower carbon content than had been used previously, and the rapid advance in obstetric technology and neonatal care. This period also witnessed significant improvements in the diversity of the food supply throughout the year and the beginnings of dietary supplements that improved year-round consumption of vitamins and other trace elements.

Evidence indicating that these improvements had an effect on longevity during middle and late ages is contained in a recent study undertaken at the Max Planck Institute for Demographics Research in Rospock, Germany. This study found strong correlations between month of birth and longevity samples of middle-aged men from Austria, Denmark, and Australia (Doblhammer 1999). The connection appears to be related to the relatively poor quality of the diet available to mothers during winter months for the first third of the twentieth century. Using correlation analysis and other statistical techniques, the study concludes that approximately one-third of the variance in longevity after age 50 was due to environmental influences during the months following conception. Very similar results have been found for the Union Army veterans who were born two generations earlier.

Evidence that the rate of decline in chronic and disabling conditions may be accelerating has been reported by the investigators at the Center for Demographic Studies at Duke University, who have made use of data obtained from National Long Term Care Surveys conducted between 1982 and 1999 (Manton et al. 1997). This study reported an average annual decline of about 1.7 percent in disability rates during the 17-year period. However, when this period was broken into three parts, there was a statistically significant acceleration in the rate of decline during the second and third parts of the period as compared with the first part. The study attributes the acceleration to a variety of health and socio-economic factors, including the level of education, which increased markedly and rapidly during the first half of the twentieth century.

Does the mounting evidence of the long-term decline in the prevalence rate of chronic diseases, and what also may be an acceleration in the long-term rate of decline, mean that the "supply" of treatable chronic diseases is declining? I use the word *supply* in order to distinguish the physiological burden of health care from the demand for health care services that may rise even if the physiological burden remains constant or declines. Moreover, I use a different definition of the burden of disease than that employed by the World Health Organization and the World Bank. They treat death as the maximum burden of disease, as it should be from an ethical standpoint. However, from a financial standpoint, death terminates health care expenditures on a particular individual. Consequently, to address the question of whether declines in physiological prevalence rates will relieve current fiscal pressures on the health care systems of OECD nations, it is necessary to weigh the existence of a particular chronic disease by the cost of treating that condition, which generally increases with age.

Such an index is shown in Figure 1.5. In this figure the burden of per capita health care costs, which is based on U.S. data, is standardized at 100 for ages 50–54. Figure 1.5 shows that the financial burden of health care per capita rises slowly in the fifties, accelerates in the sixties, accelerates again in the seventies, and accelerates even more rapidly after the mid-eighties. The financial per capita burden at age 85 and over is nearly six times as high as the burden at ages 50–54. Notice that the financial burden of health care for ages 85 and over is over 75 percent higher per capita than at ages 75–79. However, the physiological prevalence rate (number of conditions per person) is roughly constant at ages 80 and over.

Costs rise, even though the number of conditions per person remains constant, because the severity of the conditions increases or because the cost of preventing further deterioration, or even partially reversing deterioration, increases with age. It should be kept in mind that standard prevalence rates merely count the number of conditions, neglecting both the increasing physiological deterioration with age and the rising cost of treatment per condition. Figure 1.5 indicates that to forecast the future financial burden of health care, it is necessary to make use of a function of the age-specific cost of health care, such as that shown in Figure 1.5.

What, then, can be said about the likely movements in the curve of the relative burden of health care costs at ages 50 and over during the next

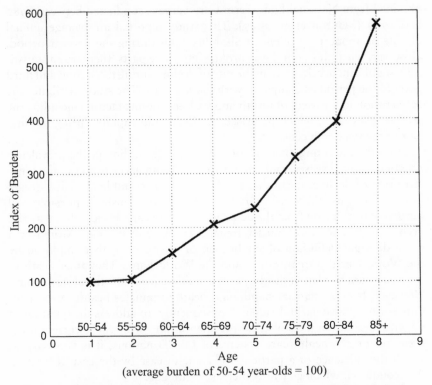

FIGURE 1.5. Relative Burden of Health Care by Age, U.S. Data circa 1996. *Sources:* Fogel 2000, Table 5d.1 and Federal Interagency Forum on Aging-Related Statistics 2000, Table 26B.

generation? Figure 1.6 lays out three possibilities. The first possibility is that there will be a proportional downward shift in the curve (Case A). This is the curve implied by using the change in the average prevalence rate, which implies a shift downward at a constant average rate at all ages. The example shown in Figure 1.6 implies a decline in average prevalence rates of 1.2 percent per annum, which locates all of the points in Case A at about two-thirds of the previous level. If I had used 1.5 percent, the points on the Case A curve would all be located at about 60 percent of the original level.

A second alternative, shown as Case B in Figure 1.6, is that the curve of disease burden by age will shift to the right. The Case B curve was constructed on the assumption that over the course of a generation, the average age of onset of chronic conditions is delayed by about five years. This assumption is supported by a number of epidemiological studies in the Netherlands, Britain, the United States, and elsewhere. This forecast is based partly on the evidence that the average age of the onset of chronic disabilities has been declining since the start of the twentieth century.

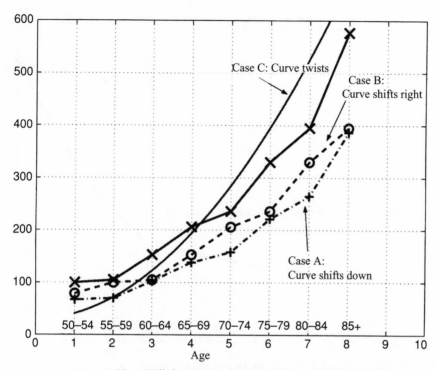

FIGURE 1.6. How Will the Curve of Relative Disease Burden Shift?

It is also based on studies of the relative cost of health care by years before death. These studies have produced the curve shown in Figure 1.7, which is standardized on the average costs of health care for all persons age 65 and over in the U.S. Medicare program. Figure 1.7 shows that five years before the year of death, annual health cost is virtually the same as all annual Medicare costs per capita. By the second year before death, the cost has risen by about 60 percent, and in the year of death the annual cost exceeds the average by over four times. Indeed, expenditure on persons during their last two years of life accounts for 40 percent of all Medicare expenditures.

The pattern portrayed in Figure 1.7 has not changed significantly over the past two decades. The relative constancy in health care costs by years before death supports Case B in Figure 1.6, since it implies that no matter how far to the right the health care curve shifts, age-specific costs will eventually rise sharply as the proportion of persons who die in any given age category increases.

Figure 1.6 shows a third possibility, Case C. In that case, the curve of age-specific health costs twists. At ages 50 through 64 the curve shifts downward, while at ages above 65 the curve rises. The downward shift before age 65 is due to a presumed acceleration in the delay in the onset of chronic disease

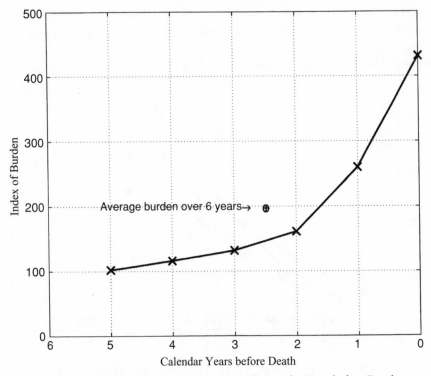

FIGURE 1.7. Index of Average Annual Health Care by Year before Death.

and an initially slower rate of deterioration. The sharper rise after age 65 is partly due to a diffusion of the most expensive interventions and partly to the assumption that the more effective interventions of the future will also be more expensive.

FORECASTING TRENDS IN THE DEMAND FOR HEALTH CARE SERVICES

So far I have focused purely on the economic burden of treatable chronic conditions. Figures 1.5 and 1.6 focused on the cost-adjusted supply of treatable conditions. I now want to consider the likely trend in the demand for health care services by consumers. Table 1.2 presents the change in the structure of consumption in the United States between 1875 and 1995. The trend in the structure of consumption in other OECD nations has been quite similar. The term "expanded consumption" takes account of the fact that as income has increased, consumers have preferred to take an increasing share of their real income in the form of leisure, rather than in purchasing more commodities as would be possible if they did not reduce their hours of work.

One notable feature of Table 1.2 is the change in the share of income spent on food, clothing, and shelter, which has declined from 75 percent of expanded consumption to just 15 percent over the 120-year period. Another striking change is the share of income spent on health care, which has increased nine-fold, from one percent of expenditures to nine percent.

For purposes of forecasting, the most important feature of Table 1.2 is the last column, which presents the long-term income elasticities for each category of expenditures. The income elasticity is defined as the percentage increase in expenditures on a given commodity that will occur with a one-percent increase in income. Notice that the income elasticities for food and clothing are quite low, which means that the share of these items in total consumption will continue to decline. An income elasticity of one means that the share of a given item in total consumption will remain constant. Notice that shelter, which includes most consumer durables, is closer to, but still below, one. On the other hand, the income elasticities for health care, education, and leisure are all well above one. The income elasticity of 1.6 means that, if per capital income increases at 2 percent per year, income expenditures on health care in the United States are likely to rise from a current level of about 14 percent of GDP to about 21 percent of GDP in 2040.

Is that bad? Should such a development be avoided? Should governments seek to thwart consumer demand for health care services? Such a policy would be necessary only if OECD nations lacked the resources to provide that much health care. However, the growth in productivity of traditional commodities, including food, clothing, shelter, and consumer durables, will release the resources required to provide expanded health care. In the United States a century ago, it took about 1,700 hours of work to purchase the annual food supply for a family. Today, it requires just 260 hours. If agriculture productivity grows at just two-thirds of its recent rates, then by 2040 a family's annual food supply may be purchased with about 160 hours of labor.

A recent study of the role of the change in the benefits and costs of health care conducted by investigators at the National Bureau of Economic Research (NBER) concluded that the benefits of health care services over the past 40 years have more than justified their costs. They suggest a fundamental repositioning of the public debate about medical care, from how governments can limit spending to how to get the most out of the spending that is undertaken. NBER investigators have also suggested changing the methods of health care financing so that the consumer demand for increasingly effective services is not unnecessarily thwarted.

Bibliography

Allen R.C. 1992. *Enclosure and the Yeoman: The Agricultural Development of the South Midlands 1450–1850*. Oxford: Oxford University Press.

Allen R.C. 1994. Agriculture during the industrial revolution. In *The Economic History of Britain since 1700, Volume 1, 1700–1860*, ed. R. Floud, D. McCloskey, 96–122. Cambridge: Cambridge University Press.

Cipolla C.M. 1974. *The Economic History of World Population*. Middlesex: Penguin Books.

Clark J.G.D. 1961. *World Prehistory: An Outline*. Cambridge: Cambridge University Press.

Costa D.L., Steckel R.H. 1997. Long-term trends in health, welfare, and economic growth in the United States. In *Health and Welfare during Industrialization*, ed. R.H. Steckel, R. Floud, 47–89. Chicago: University of Chicago Press.

Derry T.K., Williams T.I. 1960. *A Short History of Technology*. London: Oxford University Press.

Doblhammer G. 1999. Longevity and month of birth: Evidence from Austria and Denmark. *Demographic Research* 1: Article 3.

Fagan B.M. 1977. *People of the Earth*. Boston: Little Brown and Company.

Federal Interagency Forum on Aging-Related Statistics. 2000. *Older Americans 2000: Key Indicators of Well-Being*. Washington, DC: U.S. Government Printing Office.

Fogel R.W. 1992. Second thoughts on the European escape from hunger: Famines, chronic malnutrition, and mortality rates. In *Nutrition and Poverty*, ed. S.R. Osmani, 243–86. Oxford: Clarendon Press.

Fogel R.W. 2000. *The Fourth Great Awakening and the Future of Egalitarianism*. Chicago: University of Chicago Press.

Fogel R.W. 2004. *The Escape from Hunger and Premature Death*, 1700–2100. Cambridge: Cambridge University Press.

Fogel R.W., Costa D.L., Kim J.M. 1993. Secular trends in the distribution of chronic conditions and disabilities at young adult and late ages, 1860–1988: Some preliminary findings. Presented at the NBER Summer Institute Economics of Aging Program, Cambridge, MA.

Manton K.G., Corder L., Stallard E. 1997. Chronic disability trends in elderly United States populations: 1982–1994. *Proceedings of the National Academy of Sciences USA* 94: 2593–98.

McNeill W. 1971. *A World History*. New York: Oxford University Press.

Piggott S. 1965. *Ancient Europe from the Beginnings of Agriculture to Classical Antiquity*. Chicago: Aldine.

Slicher van Bath B.H. 1963. *The Agrarian History of Western Europe A.D. 500–1850*. Trans. O. Ordish. London: Edward Arnold.

Trewartha G.T. 1969. *A Geography of Population: World Patterns*. New York: John Wiley & Sons.

Wrigley E.A. 1987. Urban growth and agricultural change: England and the Continent in the early modern period. In *People, Cities, and Wealth: The Transformation of Traditional Society*, 157–93. Oxford: Blackwell.

2

Extending the Reach of Anthropometric History to the Distant Past

Richard H. Steckel

Economic historians have long been familiar with the challenges posed by meager economic data. The constraint is acute for many developed countries in the early and middle phases of industrialization, when information on real Gross National Product per capita is unavailable or at best crudely estimated. Although useful income statistics are available for many countries for much of the nineteenth century, as a whole these series lack both annual and regional detail that is important for appraising the causes and consequences of long-run economic growth (Maddison 1995).

Over the past quarter century scholars have used anthropometric measures such as average stature in part to address this problem. Constructed from individual level data from military records and other sources for birth cohorts beginning in the eighteenth century, various height series have added important new information on the welfare aspects of industrialization. Sometimes oversold as "the" biological standard of living, heights are a measure of net nutrition during the growing years, and capture an important aspect of the quality of life that has entered debates between optimists and pessimists. Height series for several countries show that both groups can claim at least partial victory (Steckel and Floud 1997).

This paper vastly extends the chronological reach of anthropometric history by illustrating how skeletal remains can be used to depict important aspects of wellbeing over the millennia. The approach, then, embraces human activities from the era of hunter-gatherers onward to settled agriculture, the rise of cities, global exploration and colonization, and eventual industrialization. Skeletons are widely available for study in many parts of the globe, and unlike heights, they depict health over the life cycle. As a package the skeletal measures provide age- and source-specific detail on biological stress from early childhood through old age. The remains also exist for women and for children, two groups often excluded from more familiar historical sources such as tax documents, muster rolls, and wage records. Thus, skeletons provide a more extensive and complete picture of community health than available from historical records on stature. Trends and differences in skeletal health can be analyzed when combined with data from archaeology, historical documents, climate history, Geographic Information Systems (GIS) databases, and other sources.

MOTIVATION

Before considering the methodology, it is appropriate to ask why a millennial perspective on health may be interesting and useful. What is the point of placing the modern era (the past couple of centuries) in very long-term perspective? For some, it is the pure satisfaction in knowing more about the long, complicated path that humanity has taken from the Neolithic era to modern times; but the study of skeletons can satisfy far more than natural intellectual curiosity about the contours of the human past. Not only a basic ingredient in the quality of life, health is intertwined with demographic, social, economic, and political change and with the outcomes of wars and other conflicts. Health affects work capacity and the incentives to invest in skills that contribute to economic growth. Economists, historians, and political scientists have identified not only inequality in income or wealth, but also disparities in health and nutrition, as a driving force in social, political, and economic change. Thus, health has played a central role in human history, both as an agent of change and as an outcome measure indicating the quality of life.

Skeletons also inform us about human adaptation to changing climate, a topic inspired by growing concerns over global warming. Using tree rings, ice cores, lake sediments, and other sources, climate historians have made considerable progress in measuring important aspects of climate over many thousands of years (Fagan 2000). Economists such as Jeffrey Sachs have engaged in the debate over the natural environment and economic performance, and climate historians such as Peter deMenocal have used the new evidence to link climate change to the fall of the Maya (deMenocal 2001; Sachs 2001). The fall of civilizations, however, is a rough measure of social performance. By linking skeletal health with new climate data as well as information from archaeological sources and historical records it will be possible to measure the connection between climate and human welfare with greater precision.

Sampling issues inevitably arise in the comparative study of skeletons and there are ambiguities in interpreting this biological evidence. Confidence in the approach is bolstered, however, by comparing results with patterns of health that are well established from other sources.

WHAT CAN BE LEARNED FROM SKELETONS?

It is useful to begin with a general discussion of skeletal manifestations of stress.[1] Unlike dental enamel, bones are living tissues that receive blood and adapt to mechanical and physiological stress. Habitual physical activity that requires exertion leads to a readily visible expansion of the related muscle attachments on the skeleton. If the action is repetitive in a particular direction, the bones adapt to the load by thickening in the direction of the plane of motion (Larsen 1997). Hunter–gatherers who walked long distances, for example, had oval-shaped femurs but these bones are nearly circular among settled agriculturalists who had diverse activity patterns. Similarly, professional athletes such as tennis players and baseball pitchers develop extensive muscles, tendons, and bones in the shoulders and arms on the side that they use.

Net nutrition has been an effective concept for understanding the environmental factors that influence human growth. The body is a biological machine that requires fuel for basal metabolism, to perform work, and to combat infection, all of which claim dietary intake (Tanner 1978; Steckel 1995). If net nutrition is insufficient and the deprivation is chronic and severe, growth slows or ceases, and linear growth of the skeleton is stunted.

In principle, anthropologists could use any bone to estimate stature, but the femur is most widely used because it is often well preserved and is easily measured. It also has the greatest correlation with stature, in part because it comprises about one quarter of standing height. Seeking information useful in forensics, Mildred Trotter and Goldine Gleser estimated the relationship between the two variables using femur lengths of the deceased whose living height was known from muster rolls or other sources (Trotter and Gleser 1952). The equations vary somewhat by sex (females are a few centimeters shorter than males for a given femur length), and accurate height estimates require anthropologists to draw upon sexually dimorphic characteristics of the pelvis and the skull that appear in adolescence.[2]

As a group, physical anthropologists collect hundreds of skeletal measures, including various metrics that are used to determine sex and age at death. Many of these measures are very specialized and some reflect rare or unusual forms of physiological stress (Buikstra and Ubelaker 1994). In designing a study of community health involving a large number of contributors, it is important to select general health indicators that are understood and widely reported by physical anthropologists, regardless of specialty. Richard Steckel and Jerome Rose organized an effort loosely called the

---

[1] For discussion and references to the literature, see Larsen (1997); Goodman and Martin (2002).

[2] Growth plates obfuscate the bone lengths of juveniles, and height estimates are correspondingly problematic until the bony components of the femur fuse late in the teenage years.

Western Hemisphere project, in which all contributors agreed on the importance of utilizing numerous indicators of skeletal health. The database per-
tained to the past several thousand years and contained estimates of sex and
age at death along with three indicators of health during childhood (stature,
linear enamel defects, and skeletal signs of anemia), two measures of decline
among adults (dental decay and degenerative joint disease), and two that
could affect any age group, but are more prevalent among older children
and adults (skeletal infections and trauma) (Steckel and Rose 2002a). Stature
has already been discussed as a child health indicator, and the others are
briefly explained below.[3]

Enamel Hypoplasias (linear enamel defects)

Hypoplasias are lines or pits of enamel deficiency commonly found in the
teeth (especially incisors and canines) of people whose childhood was bio-
logically stressful. They are caused by disruption to the cells (ameloblasts)
that form the enamel. The disruption is usually environmental, commonly
due to either poor nutrition or infectious disease or a combination of both.
Although nonspecific, hypoplasias are informative about physiological stress
in childhood in archaeological settings.

Indicators of Iron Deficiency Anemia (porotic hyperostosis and cribra orbitalia)

Iron is essential for many body functions, such as oxygen transport to the
body's tissues. In circumstances where iron is deficient – owing to nutritional
deprivation, low body weight, chronic diarrhea, parasite infection, and other
factors – the body attempts to compensate by increasing red blood cell production. The skeletal manifestations appear in those areas where red blood
cell production occurs, such as in the flat bones of the cranium. The associated pathological conditions are sieve-like lesions called porotic hyperostosis
and cribra orbitalia for the cranial vault and eye orbits, respectively. The
lesions can also be caused by other factors, but iron deficiency is among
the most common causes. In infancy and childhood, iron deficiency anemia
is associated with impaired growth and delays in behavioral and cognitive
development. In adulthood, the condition is associated with limited work
capacity and physical activity.

Dental Health

Dental health is an important indicator both of oral and general health.
Dental health in archaeological skeletons is assessed from dental caries,
antemortem tooth loss, and abscesses. Dental caries is a disease process

---

[3] For more information, see Larsen (1997); White (2000).

characterized by the focal demineralization of dental hard tissues by organic acids produced by bacterial fermentation of dietary carbohydrates, especially sugars. In the modern era, the introduction and general availability of refined sugar caused a huge increase in dental decay. In the more distant past, the adoption of agriculture led to a general increase in tooth decay, especially from the introduction of maize. The agricultural shift and the later use of increasingly refined foods have resulted in an increase in periodontal disease, caries, tooth loss, and abscesses.

Degenerative Joint Disease

Degenerative joint disease (DJD) is commonly caused by the mechanical wear and tear on the joints of the skeleton due to physical activity. Generally speaking, populations engaged in habitual activities that are physically demanding have more DJD (especially buildup of bone along joint margins and deterioration of bone on articular joint surfaces) than populations that are relatively sedentary. Studies of DJD have been valuable in documenting levels and patterns of activity in past populations.

Skeletal Infections (osteoperiostitis)

Skeletal lesions of infectious origin, which commonly appear on the major long bones (especially the tibia), have been documented worldwide. Most of these lesions are found as plaque-like deposits from periosteal inflammation, swollen shafts, and irregular elevations on bone surfaces. Most lesions are nonspecific but they often originate with *Staphylococcus* or *Streptococcus* organisms. These lesions have proven very informative about patterns and levels of community health in the human past.

Trauma

Fractures, weapon wounds, and other skeletal injuries provide a record of accidents or violence. Accidental injuries, such as ankle and wrist fractures, reflect difficulty of terrain and the hazards of specific occupations. Injuries caused by violence, such as weapon wounds or parry fractures of the forearm, provide a barometer of domestic strife, social unrest, and warfare.

MEASURING COMMUNITY HEALTH

Health has two important elements: length of life and morbidity. The methodology for measuring the first, using life expectancy at birth (and at other ages), was refined during the nineteenth century but much less agreement exists on principles for the second. While death is well defined, morbidity is much less precise. The incidence of various chronic diseases, days lost from school or work, and assessments of physical capacity are used, but all have conceptual limitations. Moreover, gathering reasonably comprehensive and accurate morbidity information often requires time-consuming and expensive personal interviews or health exams. Significant progress on the problem may be made eventually by using devices that transmit information from receptors implanted in or on the body.[4]

How effective are skeletons in capturing the two elements of health, mortality and morbidity? At most localities or burial sites, a useful but incomplete picture is available for morbidity based on lesions found on bones and teeth. Mortality, however, is more complicated. Estimates of mortality rates are currently limited by the quality of age-at-death estimates, for which confidence intervals are relatively large at older ages (especially above 50). These will be improved by newly developed techniques of aging skeletons but these have been applied to only a small subset of archaeological remains. Even with these techniques, estimating life tables (from age-specific mortality rates) requires some knowledge of the denominator – the population at risk by age. Such inferences can be made from population growth rates, potentially derivable from contextual information available in archaeological and/or historical sources. Lack of information on life expectancy is less damaging than it might appear for the study of health, however. To the extent that morbidity and mortality are positively correlated, as much evidence suggests, health can still be indexed or ranked across sites by using morbidity indicators from skeletons.

Skeletons are good at summarizing several types of chronic morbidity, with the exception of various soft-tissue conditions such as hernias or torn ligaments. Degenerative joint disease and dental decay often develop over many years, and both have adverse functional consequences. DJD is painful and limits mobility, whereas dental decay limits the ability to chew and digest a coarse diet, which impairs net nutrition, weakens the immune system, and increases vulnerability to illness. Signs of anemia (cribra orbitalia and porotic hyperostosis) usually appear early in childhood and the adverse environmental conditions that created these bony malformations tend to persist thereafter. Skeletal infections are often painful and signal a weakened immune system that can lead to illness and functional loss. Broken bones and weapon wounds are painful and require time to heal, and the loss of mobility or dexterity associated with them can be permanent if they heal in a misaligned fashion.

---

[4] The next great research frontier will likely use nano-size biosensors to measure brain activity and assay biochemicals in a search for patterns and determinants of well-being, happiness, and important aspects of morbidity or loss of functional capacity. For example, miniature total analysis systems, commonly called lab-on-a-chip devices, contain all the necessary elements for analyzing minuscule amounts of bodily fluids, including intake, transport, mixing, separation, and measuring results (Focus 2006; Whitesides 2006; Steckel 2008).

Stunting and linear enamel hypoplasias (LEH for short, which refers to enamel deformities in teeth) have generic causes linked to poor net nutrition in childhood, and are not direct measures of morbidity, but they signal a loss of functional capacity. Hunger is painful and limits physical activity in the fashion of anemia, and hypoplasias are usually the direct result of severe bouts of disease or malnutrition in early childhood. These skeletal lesions therefore index various types of morbidity.

Qualifications

Research on life expectancy from skeletons is limited by reliable estimates of age at death at advanced ages. The ages of children and young adults can be accurately determined from dental development and from the age-related pattern of fusion in various growth plates, but the chronological sequence of skeletal changes is more subtle at older ages, and sometimes these changes are obscured by poor skeletal preservation following burial. Using techniques such as systematic changes in the pubic bone, some physical anthropologists lump ages beyond 50 into a single category. Others believe that the pattern of cranial suture closures provides useful information at advanced ages. From one point of view, this limitation is modest because few people were likely to have survived beyond age 50 in most premodern societies. On the other hand, death rates rise rapidly at older ages, and the lack of reliable ages in this range significantly constrains the information available for estimating model life tables, thereby increasing confidence intervals.[5] The outlook is promising, however, because new techniques based on annual rings in tooth cementum (a hard tissue that covers the external surface of tooth roots) can provide highly accurate estimates of ages, even for very old adults (Wittwer-Backofen, Gampe et al. 2004).

Physical anthropologists know that the bones of infants and very young children are soft and frequently deteriorate after burial. Careful excavation is required to recount the deaths at these ages. Sometimes more limiting is the geographic dispersion of burials, so that excavations associated with new roads, buildings, and other development projects recover only a portion of the deaths in any society. This is not a problem if burial was random, but it is an issue if infants or young children were buried in separate locations.

Population growth rates were probably small in pre-modern times for areas as large as continents and their major sub-regions, and on this scale the assumption of a stationary population is plausible. In a stationary population

---

[5] There is also the problem of selecting a suitable model life table, which is complicated by lack of detailed information on age patterns of death in ancient populations. One can make informed conjectures but this adds to the uncertainty of results.

life expectancy simply equals the average age at death, which can be determined if all burials of a society are recovered and accurately aged. Any particular society, however, may have grown or shrunk from fluctuations in fertility or mortality relative to the regional or continental average. High birth rates, for example, increase the relative number of deaths at young ages. Compensation for these effects can be made if archaeological or other information is available as an ingredient to estimating fertility rates. While this is a new area of paleodemography, it is likely that considerable information gaps will remain for many burial sites.

One may reasonably suppose that life expectancy ranged from approximately 20 to 40 years for most societies prior to the late nineteenth century. Populations close to 20 years were highly stressed and would have vanished quickly without high fertility, which would have been unlikely under the environmentally stressful conditions that produced high mortality. Life expectancy in excess of 40 years is rarely observed without good nutrition or, in its absence, aspects of the health revolution such as improved sanitation or other practices inspired by the germ theory of disease. With complete excavation of a society's burial sites, along with accurate age estimates and considerable archaeological information, it is reasonable to hope that life expectancy could be reliably placed into one of three categories: low-to-mid 20s, high 20s to low 30s, and mid-to-high 30s. Although imprecise, this information is very useful for understanding the quality of life in the past.

Sampling Issues

Physical anthropologists may have little control over the location and extent of an excavation if it is the result of a development project that clears a small area of ground. With the exception of the removal of entire cemeteries containing reasonably closed populations, one can seldom argue that skeletons represent an entire society. Many burial sites in Europe, for example, are revealed by construction projects that are numerous in urban relative to rural areas.

This constraint is a hindrance but far from disabling. In formulating a large comparative project involving numerous sites, stratified sampling can provide adequate representation from rural and urban areas. Weighting samples is a second option. As discussed below in connection with the health index, one may sidestep age bias by converting information to age-specific rates if the age distribution of deaths has been skewed by fertility, migration, or excavation.

A Health Index

To assist with comparative analysis, is useful to summarize the diverse health information available from skeletons into a single number. This process

TABLE 2.1. *Scoring Pathological Conditions*

Variable	Type
Stature	continuous
Hypoplasias	3 categories
Anemia	3 categories
Dental Health	
Teeth (75%)	continuous
Abscesses (25%)	3 categories
Infections	4 categories
Degenerative joint disease	2, 4 or 5 categories, depending on joint
Trauma	2 categories

Note: Two categories denotes present or absent; three categories denotes absent, moderate and severe; and so forth.

Source: Steckel, Sciulli et al. (2002).

requires numerous simplifying assumptions and approximations.[6] Ideally both life expectancy and morbidity would be incorporated into the measure of health, as done for example, by quality-adjusted life years. Unfortunately life expectancy is simply not available or is otherwise unreliable for most archaeological sites. Therefore the health index discussed here includes only morbidity as expressed in the frequency and severity of skeletal lesions by age at death, but the index could be modified to incorporate length of life (Steckel, Sciulli et al. 2002). As noted above, a positive correlation between morbidity and mortality is likely, which mitigates the lack of data on life expectancy in ranking values of the health index across sites or localities.

For each individual, the seven skeletal measures discussed above are graded in categories indicated by Table 2.1. Some measures, such as stature are expressed as a continuous variable relative to modern height standards, and others such as hypoplasias are graded in categories: present or absent, absent, mild or severe. All components or attributes are then converted to a scale of 0 (most severe expression) to 100 (no lesion or deficiency). For example, the transformed hypoplasia scores become 0 (severe), 50 (moderate), or 100 (absent). Similarly, the transformed trauma scores are either 0 or 100, such that the end result (average for the population or site) is simply the percentage of individuals who did not have trauma.

Age-specific rates of morbidity pertaining to the health indicators during childhood (stature, LEH, and anemia) are calculated by assuming that the indicators reflected conditions that persisted from birth to death – an assumption justified by knowledge that childhood deprivation is correlated

---

[6] A short paper necessarily conveys only a flavor of the methodology; for additional details and justification, see Steckel, Sciulli et al. (2002). Presumably future research will lead to more appropriate assumptions and an improved health index.

TABLE 2.2. *Age Categories and Relative Weights for the Health Index*

Age Category	Relative Weight
0–4	0.123
5–14	0.202
15–24	0.183
25–34	0.157
35–44	0.128
45+	0.207

Source: Steckel, Sciulli et al. (2002).

with adverse health as an adult.[7] The duration of morbidity prior to death is, however, unknown for the remaining four components (infections, trauma, DJD, and oral health) and is the subject of ongoing research. It is known that these chronic conditions ordinarily accumulate slowly, or otherwise limit functional capacity over a period of many years. A decline in oral health, expressed in caries and abscesses, typically begins soon after permanent teeth emerge. Similarly hard physical labor and repetitive motions lead to gradual erosion of cartilage and eventually bony formations (spicules) at the joints that are characteristic of degenerative joint disease. In the extreme, the cartilage is eroded to the point that bone rubs against bone to create polishing or ebernation of the articular surfaces.

As a rough approximation, here it is assumed that conditions observed at death persisted for ten years prior to death. For example, if a person had a particular level or grade of degenerative joint disease observed at age 38 (death), it is assumed this condition persisted from age 28 onward. It is then possible to calculate the number of person-years and the specific ages at which the individual had functional disability from this condition. In the example, the degenerative joint condition existed for seven person-years in the age category 25–34 and three years in the age category 35–44. To calculate the health index, results are then grouped into six age categories as shown in Table 2.2.

Next, the scores for a particular attribute are combined across individuals to form age-specific rates. An example illustrates. If the person discussed above, who died at age 38, had moderate degenerative joint disease that translated into a score of 50, then it is presumed that the condition (and thus the score) persisted from age 28 to 38. This person contributes seven person-years, at a score of 50, to the age category 25–34, and three years (at the same score) to the age category of 35–44. Other individuals, who died

---

[7] The effect of fetal and early childhood health on adult health is sometimes called the Barker hypothesis, which is discussed in (Barker 1998). For an additional discussion, see Fogel and Costa (1997).

at various ages and with various scores for degenerative joint disease, are treated accordingly. For the site or locality as a whole, the denominator of the rate in any age category is the number of person-years lived in the age category with a measurable score. Conditions existed prior to ten years before death, but they are not measurable or observable according to the methodology. The numerator is the sum of person-year scores on that attribute within that age group across individuals at the site or locality. These types of calculations apply to each of the six age categories, from 0–4 to 45+.

The age-specific rates for each skeletal attribute are then weighted by the relative number of person-years lived in a reference population that is believed to roughly agree with pre-Columbian mortality conditions in the Western Hemisphere, as shown in Table 2.2. Note that this step imposes the same life table or age-pattern of mortality on every site, and thus strips the health index of any influences that genuine differences in life expectancy may have contributed to health. This step is of course regrettable, but is required by the knowledge that mortality rates (and thus life tables) cannot be accurately estimated at the level of the site in many if not most archaeological settings.

Finally, the results are multiplied by life expectancy in the reference population and expressed as a percent of the maximum attainable, which corresponds to a complete lack of skeletal defects or lesions.[8] The seven components of the index are then weighted equally to obtain the overall index.

Numerous assumptions underlying the index can be challenged, modified, and refined, which cannot be pursued in a brief paper. It would be appropriate to weight the elements of the index, such as dental decay and trauma, by their functional consequences but this is complicated by the nature of the social safety net, medical technology, and other factors that vary in unknown ways across societies. Thus, equal weighting is questionable but it is also difficult to justify an alternative scheme given the present state of knowledge. In addition, the index is an additive measure that ignores interactions, but having both a skeletal infection and trauma could have been worse than the sum of their independent effects on health.

SOME RESULTS

Comparing results with patterns well established in historical studies is a useful technique for assessing the health index as a work in progress.[9] Settlement size is a suitable category of analysis; demographers widely report that

---

[8] The reference is a Model West level 4 population, which has a life expectancy at birth of 26.4 years and roughly corresponds to what was likely to have prevailed in the pre-Columbian era. For a discussion of model life tables, see Coale and Demeny (1966).

[9] Various types of sensitivity analysis and formulation of standard errors are also planned, following public reaction to the methodology of the health index.

mortality rates were higher in urban as opposed to rural areas prior to the adoption of public health measures inspired by the germ theory of disease.

Because European exploration and colonization distorted Native American mortality patterns in ways that could have obscured the effects of settlement size, comparisons are limited to pre-Columbian sites, which include skeletons of 4,078 individuals who lived at 23 localities in North, Central, and South America. Steckel and Rose used archaeological evidence to arrange the settlements into three types: mobile (essentially hunter-gatherers); village, or settled but dispersed populations; and town or paramount urban center (roughly, populations of 10,000 or more). The estimated regression of the health index on settlement type is:

$$\text{HI} = 78.98 - 8.71(\text{Village}) - 14.91(\text{Urban}) \quad N = 23 \quad R^2 = 0.42$$
$$\phantom{\text{HI} = }(0.000) (0.021) (0.001)$$

where significance levels of the coefficients (on the null hypothesis that the coefficient equals zero) are given in parentheses, and the mean and standard deviation of the dependent variable are 70.5 and 8.0, respectively (Steckel and Rose 2002b, p. 564).

The health index systematically declined by nearly 15 points (roughly two standard deviations) as settlement size increased from the omitted class (hunter-gatherer) to urban. This is welcome news for the methodology because such a relationship between health and size of settlement has been widely observed prior to the advent of public health founded on the germ theory of disease. The index has passed an important preliminary test, suggesting it is credible even in its crude form. Presumably refinements in the methodology will sharpen the quantification of important aspects of health.

The lower health index in villages and urban areas in the pre-Columbian world is consistent with other historical studies (United Nations 1973), but the mechanisms by which this relationship operated in this Western Hemisphere environment remain to be established.[10] A prime suspect is rates of exposure to pathogens that increased with community size. Even though many notable contagious European diseases such as smallpox and typhoid were not evident in the Western Hemisphere prior to the late 1400s, other crowd diseases may have played the same role. On the other hand, natives of the Western Hemisphere may have been less afflicted by crowd diseases because they had few livestock, which was the original source of several contagious viruses that evolved to plague humans. In the absence of written records, useful clues might be found in the analysis of ancient DNA found in skeletal remains.

---

[10] Lower health in the cities raises the interesting question of why the transition was made. There must have been some amenities to urban life. Because rates of deliberate trauma were much lower in cities than among hunter-gatherers, one important amenity was probably a reduction in violence (Steckel and Wallis 2007).

If crowd diseases were less prevalent in pre-Columbian America than in Europe, another candidate for poor health in the cities is socio-economic inequality that led to differences in diet and/or work effort. These differences could have been imposed by a caste system or rigid social structure that left little opportunity for upward (or downward) mobility. Moreover, market forces could have led to a similar result if in-migration consisted largely of the disadvantaged from the countryside. Except for llamas, which were largely used as pack animals or sources of fiber, there was little meat protein available in the form of livestock. Similarly, protein-rich small grains familiar in European or Mediterranean agriculture were also lacking. Marine sources might have been exploited but many large urban areas were located away from the coast. Maize, beans, and squash can provide a complete protein if consumed in the right proportions, but urban inequality could have thwarted this balance. Study of burial artifacts, which is underway, may provide opportunities to quantify the degree of inequality in the pre-Columbian cities.

Pre-Columbian Time Trend

A fascinating temporal trend emerges by arranging the pre-Columbian sites in order of chronological development. Figure 2.1 shows a scatter diagram of health-index values for 23 pre-Columbian (pre-1492) sites where all

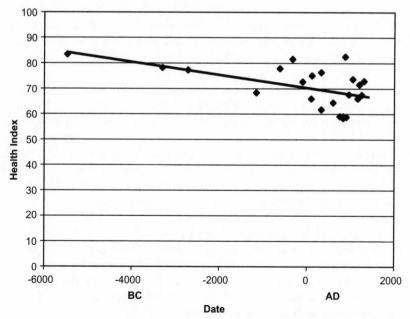

FIGURE 2.1. Time Trend in Pre-Columbian Health. *Source:* Steckel and Rose (2002).

attributes were reported by the different research teams. The downward trend is quite obvious, and is statistically significant ($R^2 = 0.53$), corresponding to a decline of 2.5 points per millennium. The trend agrees with the results of a compendium of studies on the health consequences of the transition to settled agriculture (Cohen and Armelagos 1984). Regrettably, few sites are concentrated in the early pre-Columbian period, which complicates the interpretation of the time trend. There are only three data points before approximately 1000 BC. The chronological concentration therefore makes it important to consider possible environmental changes that contributed to the decline.

The trend can be analyzed by regressing the health index on various aspects of the ecological environment in which the sites were situated, such as terrain, vegetation, whether people consumed domesticated plants, and the nature of the settlement (whether dispersed, village, or urban). As noted above, urban living was deleterious for health. All effects noted below are statistically significant.

Diet was closely related to the change in the health index, with performance being nearly 12 points lower under the triad of corn, beans, and squash compared with the more diverse diet of hunter–gatherer groups. Because the transition to settled agriculture usually occurred with the rise of large communities, it is difficult to obtain precise measures of their separate effects on health.

Among the other environmental conditions that systematically affected health (as measured by the health index) was elevation. People who lived above 300 meters scored about 15 points lower in the index. The exact mechanism for this relationship is unknown, but it is likely that a richer array of foods was available (with less work effort) at lower elevations.

Vegetation surrounding the site may have affected health via the type and availability of resources for food and shelter. Forests, for example, provide materials for the diet, fuel, and housing, and also sheltered animals that could have been used for food. Semi-deserts posed challenges for the food supply relative to more lush forests or grasslands, but the dry climate might have inhibited the transmission of some diseases. The net effect of these forces favored forests and semi-deserts as opposed to open forests and grasslands, where the health index was about 9 points lower.

Flood plain or coastal living provided easy access to aquatic sources of food and enabled trade compared with more remote, interior areas, but trade may have promoted the spread of disease. Uneven terrain found in hilly or mountainous areas may have provided advantages for defense, but could have led to more accidents and fractures. Apparently the net benefit to health favored coastal areas, where the health index was about 8 points higher compared with non-coastal regions.

Breaking the sample into two chronological periods, pre– and post–1500 years before the present, and considering the ecological conditions typical of each period, one observes that over time people increasingly lived in less healthy ecological environments. We do not yet know why this may have happened, but one possibility is that population growth may have directed settlement into less desirable areas, where greater work effort was required to provide food. Another possibility is that over time, more complex, hierarchical societies emerged, leading to greater biological inequality. Both possible explanations will be considered in future research.

The availability of hemisphere-wide data on the health of earlier human populations opens up many exciting new possibilities for studying the ecological correlates of disease patterns. It is clear that a complete explanation of any group's health status can be obtained only through a detailed site-specific analysis of local cultural practices and living conditions. Nevertheless, a surprising amount of variability in the health index can be accounted for by a few key ecological variables with far-reaching health-related consequences. For example, there is a relationship between health status and local environmental variables available from the Geographic Information System (GIS), which contains site-specific ecological information from satellite telemetry and other sources. Among the variables are measures of topographical relief, vegetation pattern, and seasonal variation in local primary productivity. Multiple regression analysis reveals a number of interesting correlations between environmental variables and health status. About 40% of the variance in the health index can be accounted for by a model that includes the following variables: elevation, plant domestication, and measures of seasonal variation in green-leaf biomass. In particular, populations living in deserts and areas of high green-leaf biomass had the lowest health index values. These are populations with a dependence on agriculture whose living conditions exposed them to a diversity of disease-causing microorganisms. In another analysis, statistically significant correlations were found between the presence of both cribra orbitalia and porotic hyperostosis (skeletal lesions traditionally associated with childhood anemia) and environmental variables including altitude, the Normalized Differential Vegetation Index (a measure of primary plant productivity), and topographical relief (maximum slope) in the vicinity of the site. Studies such as these clearly have great potential to shed light on the relative significance of the complex set of local cultural and environmental variables that influence a group's health status.

The transition to agriculture has been widely considered a benchmark development for humanity, laying the groundwork for "civilization" and all of its elements, such as democracy, learning, art, literature, architecture, and so forth. From this perspective, humans underwent a transition from a lifeway that, as described by Hobbes, was "nasty, brutish, and short," to a lifestyle brimming with leisure and excess. The findings from the Western

TABLE 2.3. *Summary of Adult Male Height Trends in Northern Europe*

Era*	Place	Average Heights (cm)
9–11th Cent.	N. Europe	173.4
12–14th Cent.	N. Europe	171.5
Middle Ages	N. Europe	171.4
17–18th Cent.	N. Europe	167.5
18th Cent.	N. Europe	166.2
17–19th Cent.	N. Europe	169.8
Late 19th Cent.	Sweden, Netherlands, Britain	169.7
1930	Sweden, Netherlands	172.5

*There is some overlap in categories due to the use of different published sources.
Source: Steckel (2004).

Hemisphere project argue that in fact the reverse was closer to reality. This is not to say that life went from rosy and healthy to bleak and unhealthy but the finding does clash with public perceptions of the past.

Long-Term Height Cycle in Europe

A central concern of economic history is the related set of questions on when, why, and where modern industrial societies became rich and healthy. With regard to income, we know that several generations ago our ancestors did not live this way, based on rates of modern economic growth extrapolated backward in time from early estimates of GDP per capita. Within a few generations the implied levels of GDP per capita would have been insufficient to sustain life. The technological basis for a high material standard of living simply did not exist prior to industrialization.

The same technique, however, cannot be applied to life expectancy or health. In the absence of information, economic historians have tended to agree with Hobbes. Thus, the major works on the European escape from hunger begin the story of dramatic improvement in the nineteenth century (Fogel 2004).

Direct evidence from skeletal remains tell a very different story, at least for northern Europe (Steckel 2004; Steckel 2005). An assemblage of evidence given in Table 2.3 shows that standing height estimated from femur lengths for northern European men who lived in the early Middle Ages averaged about 173 centimeters, a height not attained again until the early twentieth century. Moreover, the course of average height followed a large U-shape with a downturn beginning near the fifteenth century and a minimum reached sometime near the seventeenth century.[11] Thus research on

[11] The data collected to date do not permit a more precise estimate. Within a few years much more will be known about the cycle from the European project described near the end of the paper.

the modern period has viewed only the upturn in health, extrapolating it backward or assuming it was constant at some minimum floor needed for a population's survival.

We do not yet know why men of the early Middle Ages were so tall, or why height declined. But ingredients of an explanation will likely include some combination of the following:

1. *Climate change.* The Medieval warm period was good for crop production and extractive industries; the Little Ice Age that began in the 1400s reached its extreme in the seventeenth century and did not fully end until the 1800s;

2. *Population density* was low in the 800s and 900s and tended to increase thereafter, with the exception of reversals associated with epidemics such as the Black Death;

3. *Growth of cities and towns* became significant by the thirteenth century, spreading communicable diseases;

4. *The revival of trade and colonization* also spread diseases on a large scale;

5. *Growing inequality* accompanied the end of the Middle Ages, based on the course of prices for commodities purchased by the rich and by the poor;

6. *Wars over state-building and religion* began in the late 1400s and a long period of peace did not begin until 1815.

Ultimately heights and several others measures of health obtained from skeletal remains will be linked with contextual data obtained from sources in climate history, archaeology, and historical documents. Such a database will permit the description and analysis of health changes in pre-industrial Europe.

EXTENSIONS

The frequency and severity of skeletal lesions in the Western Hemisphere database correlates with a variety of ecological or environmental variables such as settlement size, elevation, topography, and subsistence patterns. The responsiveness or sensitivity of health to the environment in these data suggested there would be great potential for understanding the long-term evolution of human health by gathering and analyzing skeletal and environmental data from numerous parts of the world.

A new project on Europe substantially exceeds the Western Hemisphere effort in size, scope, and complexity (Steckel 2003). By creating several large databases, investigators will be able to reinterpret the history of human health from the late Paleolithic era to the early twentieth century. With a transatlantic network of collaborators, the project will undertake large-scale comparative studies of the causes and health consequences of these and other dramatic changes in arrangements for work, living, and human interaction.

The project is also ambitious in gathering environmental or ecological information from sources commonly used in archaeology, climate history, history, and geography – all fields that have witnessed substantial expansions of knowledge over the past half century. Climate history, for example, has been greatly enriched by the analysis of ice cores, lake sediments, and tree rings. Historians have unearthed an enormous amount of information from parish records, shipping records, wage rates, prices of various commodities, monastic records, censuses, harvest dates, wine yields, tax receipts, military records, royal archives, and so forth. Similarly, geographers and other scientists now make extensive use of GIS (Geographic Information Systems) databases. Skeletal lesions have little comparative value if studied in isolation; their context is essential for exploratory analysis of trends and patterns in health.

References

Barker, D. J. P. 1998. *Mothers, Babies, and Health in Later Life*. Edinburgh, New York: Churchill Livingstone.

Buikstra, Jane E. and Douglas H. Ubelaker. 1994. *Standards for Data Collection from Human Skeletal Remains*. Fayetteville, AR: Arkansas Archeological Survey.

Coale, Ansley J. and Paul George Demeny. 1966. *Regional Model Life Tables and Stable Populations*. Princeton: Princeton University Press.

Cohen, Mark Nathan and George J. Armelagos. 1984. *Paleopathology at the Origins of Agriculture*. New York: Academic Press.

Demenocal, Peter B. 2001. "Cultural Responses to Climate Change During the Late Holocene." *Science* 292(5517): 667–73.

Fagan, Brian M. 2000. *The Little Ice Age: How Climate Made History*, 1300–1850. New York, NY: Basic Books.

Focus. 2006. "Labs-on-a-Chip: Origin, Highlights and Future Perspectives on the Occasion of the 10th Mtas Conference." *Lab on a Chip* 6(10): 1266–73.

Fogel, Robert W. and Dora L. Costa. 1997. "A Theory of Technophysio Evolution, with Some Implications for Forecasting Population, Health Care Costs, and Pension Costs." *Demography* 34(1): 49–66.

Fogel, Robert William. 2004. *The Escape from Hunger and Premature Death, 1700–2100: Europe, America, and the Third World*. New York: Cambridge University Press.

Goodman, Alan S. and Debra L. Martin. 2002. Reconstructing Health Profiles from Skeletal Remains. In *The Backbone of History: Health and Nutrition in the Western Hemisphere*, R. H. Steckel and J. C. Rose, eds., 11–60. New York: Cambridge University Press.

Larsen, Clark Spencer. 1997. *Bioarchaeology: Interpreting Behavior from the Human Skeleton*. New York: Cambridge University Press.

Maddison, Angus. 1995. *Monitoring the World Economy*, 1820–1992. Paris: OECD.

Sachs, Jeffrey D. 2001. *Tropical Underdevelopment.* Cambridge, MA: National Bureau of Economic Research, working paper No. 8119.

Steckel, Richard H. 1995. "Stature and the Standard of Living." *Journal of Economic Literature* 33(4): 1903–40.

Steckel, Richard H. 2003. "A History of Health in Europe from the Late Paleolithic Era to the Present: A Research Project." *Economics and Human Biology* 1(1): 139–42.

Steckel, Richard H. 2004. "New Light on the 'Dark Ages': The Remarkably Tall Stature of European Men During the Medieval Era." *Social Science History* 28: 211–29.

Steckel, Richard H. 2005. Health and Nutrition in the Pre-Industrial Era: Insights from a Millennium of Average Heights in Northern Europe. In *Living Standards in the Past: New Perspectives on Well-Being in Asia and Europe*, R. C. Allen, T. Bengtsson and M. Dribe, eds., 227–53. Oxford: Oxford University Press.

Steckel, Richard H. 2008. "Biological Measures of the Standard of Living." *Journal of Economic Perspectives* 22: 129–52.

Steckel, Richard H. and Roderick Floud. 1997. *Health and Welfare During Industrialization.* Chicago: University of Chicago Press.

Steckel, Richard H. and Jerome C. Rose, Eds. 2002a. *The Backbone of History: Health and Nutrition in the Western Hemisphere.* Cambridge; New York: Cambridge University Press.

Steckel, Richard H. and Jerome C. Rose. 2002b. Patterns of Health in the Western Hemisphere. In *The Backbone of History: Health and Nutrition in the Western Hemisphere*, R. H. Steckel and J. C. Rose, eds., 563–79. New York: Cambridge University Press.

Steckel, Richard H., Paul W. Sciulli, et al. 2002. A Health Index from Skeletal Remains. In *The Backbone of History: Health and Nutrition in the Western Hemisphere*, R. H. Steckel and J. C. Rose, eds., 61–93. New York: Cambridge University Press.

Steckel, Richard H. and John Wallis. 2007. Stones, Bones, Cities and States: A New Interpretation of the Neolithic Revolution. Columbus, OH.

Tanner, J. M. 1978. *Foetus into Man: Physical Growth from Conception to Maturity.* Cambridge, MA: Harvard University Press.

Trotter, Mildred and Goldine C. Gleser. 1952. "Estimation of Stature from Long Bones of American Whites and Negroes." *American Journal of Physical Anthropology* 10(4): 463–514.

United Nations. 1973. *The Determinants and Consequences of Population Trends: New Summary of Findings on Interaction of Demographic, Economic and Social Factors.* New York: United Nations.

White, Tim D. 2000. *Human Osteology.* San Diego: Academic Press.

Whitesides, George M. 2006. "The Origins and the Future of Microfluidics." *Nature Reviews Neuroscience* 442(27): 368–73.

Wittwer-Backofen, Ursula, Jutta Gampe, and James Vaupel (2004). "Tooth Cementum Annulation for Age Estimation: Results from a Large Known-Age Study." *American Journal of Physical Anthropology* 123(2): 119–29.

3

Insecurity, Safety Nets, and Self-Help in Victorian and Edwardian Britain

George R. Boyer

The main need of the English working classes is Security.... The meshes of our safety net are only adapted to subscribers [to friendly societies and trade unions], & all those who are not found on any of those innumerable lists go smashing down on the pavement. It is this very class, the residue,... for whom no provision exists in our English machinery, who have neither the character nor the resources to make provision for themselves, who require the aid of the state.

(Winston Churchill to A. Wilson Fox, January 4, 1908)[1]

Workers' insecurity of income has not been given the attention it deserves in the standard of living debate.[2] Despite steady improvements in material living standards from 1830 to the First World War, as measured by average full-time wages or earnings, a large share of manual workers in Britain continued to experience "acute financial" distress at some point in their lives (Johnson 1985, 3). The examination of long-term trends in wage rates masks workers' income losses due to unemployment and sickness, and it tells us little about their ability to cope with these periodic losses of income.[3]

Workers dealt with financial insecurity by saving, by insuring themselves against income loss through membership in friendly societies and trade unions, and by applying for public and private assistance when necessary. The relative importance of these coping strategies changed significantly from 1830 to the eve of the First World War. Prior to the passage of the Poor

---

[1] The quote can be found in Churchill (1969, 759).

[2] Stan Engerman has made significant contributions to the British standard of living debate. See, in particular, Engerman (1994; 1997); Hartwell and Engerman (1975).

[3] Some historians have stressed the importance of insecurity in workers' lives. Hobsbawm (1975, 221) wrote that the mid-nineteenth-century British worker "was rarely more than a hair's breadth removed from the pauper, and insecurity was therefore constant and real." See also Floud (1997, Chapter 2). Keyssar (1986) provides a detailed examination of the uncertainly associated with unemployment in Massachusetts in the nineteenth century.

Law Amendment Act in 1834, workers relied heavily on the Poor Law for financial assistance during hard times. The New Poor Law reduced the availability, and generosity, of poor relief for able-bodied males, and many workers responded by increasing their saving and by joining friendly societies. The Crusade Against Outrelief in the 1870s led to a further decline in relief expenditures, and to a sharp increase in the share of paupers relieved in workhouses. Partly in response to the decline in outdoor relief, membership in friendly societies and in trade unions providing mutual insurance policies increased greatly after 1870.

By the beginning of the twentieth century, a large share of skilled and semi-skilled manual workers belonged to friendly societies or to trade unions that offered mutual insurance benefits. These workers were afforded some protection against income loss when sick or unemployed, although the benefits needed to be combined with other sources of income and savings. The situation was very different for unskilled workers, few of whom were members of friendly societies paying sickness benefits or of unions providing anything more than funeral benefits. The low-skilled remained quite vulnerable to unexpected income loss until Parliament's adoption of the Liberal welfare reforms in the decade before the First World War.

This paper examines workers' insecurity of income from 1830 to 1914, the rise of working class self-help during the Victorian era, and the fall and rise of social transfer spending from the passage of the Poor Law Amendment Act in 1834 to the adoption of the Liberal welfare reforms in 1906–11. The paper is divided into three parts. Part I examines income instability for manual workers in Victorian Britain. Unemployment and sickness were distributed unevenly among the working class. The majority of workers were neither unemployed nor sick within a calendar year, but many lost a month or more of work each year because of sickness or unemployment. Moreover, while elderly working-class males continued to work for as long as they could, a large share was unable to earn enough to support themselves.

Part II discusses the changing methods used by workers in Victorian and Edwardian Britain to cope with economic insecurity. I provide quantitative estimates of movements in poor relief expenditures, working class saving, and membership in, and expenditures of, friendly societies and insurance-providing trade unions from 1830 to 1913. The estimates enable me to trace the long-term trends in the roles played by public assistance and self-help.

Part III examines the political economy of the Liberal welfare reforms of 1906–11, which included several pieces of social welfare legislation that created government programs to provide workers with sickness and unemployment insurance and old-age pensions. These programs represented an about-face in British social policy after seven decades of increasing stinginess toward the poor. I contend that the timing of the Liberal welfare reforms largely can be explained by the lesser ability of low-skilled workers to protect themselves from financial insecurity, increased middle-class knowledge of workers' economic insecurity, and the greater willingness of Parliament to increase social transfer spending.

As Lindert (2004) and Engerman and Sokoloff (2005) have argued, political voice matters, and the reforms may have resulted from the growing political influence of the working class. The Second and Third Reform Acts of 1867 and 1884 extended the franchise to working-class voters and eventually led to the rise of the Labour Party. The reforms of 1906–11, I argue, were largely an attempt by the Liberal Party to woo working class voters and slow the growing momentum of Labour.

I. INSECURITY DUE TO UNEMPLOYMENT, SICKNESS, AND OLD AGE

We forget how terribly near the margin of disaster the man, even the thrifty man, walks, who has, in ordinary normal conditions, but just enough to keep himself on.... the possibility of being from one day to the other plunged into actual want is always confronting his family. (Lady Bell, *At the Works*, 1907, 47)

However steady a man may be, however good a worker, he is never exempt from the fear of losing his job from ill-health or from other causes which are out of his control.... to the insufficiency of a low wage is added the horror that it is never secure. (Maud Pember Reeves, *Round About a Pound a Week*, 1913, 208–10)

There has been some debate over the rate of growth of earnings from 1830 to 1913, but even the more pessimistic estimates indicate that real full-time earnings more than doubled (Feinstein 1995; 1998). Fully employed workers in 1913 were much better off, in terms of the ability to purchase goods and services, than their fully employed great-grandfathers. However, a large share of workers was not fully employed, either in 1830 or in 1913. Some occupations were seasonal or casual, with workers being hired by the job, the week, or even the day. Even workers with a greater degree of job security could become unemployed during cyclical downturns or might be unable to work due to sickness, during which time they were not compensated by their employers.[4] Dudley Baxter (1868, 46–7) concluded that the average worker's annual earnings were 20% less than his full-time wage as a result of unemployment, sickness, and other causes.

Cyclical Unemployment

Boyer and Hatton (2002) have calculated estimates of industrial unemployment for 1870–1913, shown in Figure 3.1.[5] Industrial unemployment

---

[4] Keyssar (1986, Chapters 3–4 and Appendix A) provides data on unemployment rates, unemployment frequency, mean duration of unemployment spells, and seasonality of unemployment by occupation, sex, and nativity for late-nineteenth-century Massachusetts.

[5] Estimates of aggregate unemployment rates are available from 1855 onwards calculated from trade union data by the Board of Trade and revised by Feinstein (1972, T125–6). There are serious problems with the Board of Trade/Feinstein estimates, as discussed by Boyer and Hatton (2002).

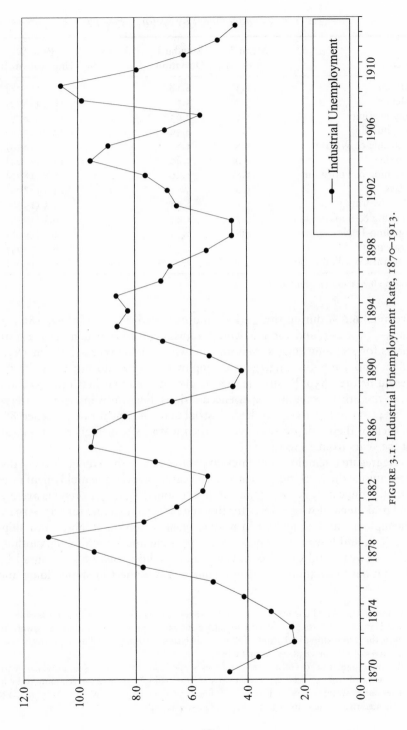

FIGURE 3.1. Industrial Unemployment Rate, 1870–1913.

TABLE 3.1. *Unemployment by Sector, 1870–1913*

Sector	Mean % 1870–1913	Standard Deviation	Years Un > 10%	Peak % Unemployment
Mining	11.3	6.18	25	27.1 (1878)
Metals	6.7	3.79	7	18.5 (1879)
Engineering	4.2	2.65	2	10.7 (1879)
Shipbuilding	8.7	6.30	14	22.7 (1908)
Carriage & Wagon	3.8	1.81	1	11.5 (1879)
Textiles	7.0	2.42	9	13.0 (1904)
Clothing & Footwear	3.8	1.20	0	7.8 (1877)
Glass	5.6	3.01	4	13.4 (1879)
Woodworking	3.1	2.03	0	9.5 (1908)
Printing & Bookbinding	3.7	1.46	0	6.3 (1912)
Building Trades	4.8	2.94	3	12.4 (1908)
Transport	6.5	1.30	0	8.6 (1893)
General Unskilled Labor	9.5	3.16	17	16.5 (1909)

Source: Boyer and Hatton (2002).

averaged 6.6% during this period, and exceeded 8% in 1878–9, 1885–7, 1893–5, 1904–5, and 1908–9. Rough adjustments to Feinstein's (1972) estimates for 1856–69 suggest that unemployment also exceeded 8% in 1858, 1862, and 1867–8.[6] Aggregate unemployment data do not exist for the period before 1856. Rostow (1948, 125) estimated that between 1830 and 1850 the British economy experienced serious downturns in 1832–3, 1837–8, 1841–3, and 1848–9.[7] If the industrial unemployment rate exceeded 8% in each of these "depression" years, then it was 8% or higher in a quarter of the years from 1830 to 1913.

Aggregate unemployment rates give some idea of the average level of distress among the working class in a given year. However, unemployment rates varied significantly across sectors of the economy. Table 3.1 presents average and peak unemployment rates for thirteen industrial sectors for 1870–1913. Unemployment was highest in mining, general unskilled labor, and shipbuilding, and lowest in woodworking, printing and bookbinding, clothing and footwear, and carriage and wagon. Absolute volatility, measured by the standard deviation of unemployment, was highest in shipbuilding and

[6] Feinstein's estimated unemployment rate for 1870–1913 is 4.5%, about two-thirds of Boyer and Hatton's estimated industrial unemployment rate. Adjusting his estimates upward to make them compatible with those of Boyer and Hatton yields industrial unemployment rates in excess of 8% for 1858, 1862, and 1867–8.

[7] Rostow (1948, 123–5) constructed a business-cycle index for 1790–1850, in which "each year is rated from 0 (deep depression) to 5 (major peak)." I defined the economy to be in a serious downturn in years Rostow rated as 0 or 1. Lindert and Williamson (1983, 15) estimated that the unemployment rate in 1842–3 was 9.4%.

mining, and lowest in clothing and footwear, transport, and printing and bookbinding. The unemployment rate in coal mining ranged from under 2% during the boom of 1872–4 to over 20% in 1877–9; it exceeded 15% in eleven years. Unemployment among shipbuilders exceeded 10% in fourteen years, and peaked at 22.7% in 1908. On the other hand, unemployment in printing and bookbinding exceeded 5.5% in only five years, and peaked at 6.3% in 1912; unemployment in clothing and footwear also exceeded 5.5% only five times, and peaked at 7.8% in 1877.[8]

Even during prosperous years, large numbers of skilled workers suffered income losses due to unemployment. Table 3.2 presents data on the distribution of unemployment among skilled workers in four trade unions. Although unemployment among engineers was very low in 1890, over one-fifth of the engineers were unemployed at some point in the year; those that were unemployed lost on average five weeks of work. For the entire period 1887–95, nearly 30% were unemployed during a calendar year, for an average of $10\frac{1}{2}$ weeks. The average unemployment rate among London Compositors for 1894–1903 was only 4.3%, and yet one-fifth of the membership was unemployed each year for an average of 10.7 weeks. The data for carpenters and woodcutting machinists are similar: in 1904–05, 43.1% of carpenters were unemployed, for an average of just over seven weeks. In sum, while the majority of workers were fully employed even during downturns, a substantial number were unemployed for a month or more every year.[9]

Unemployment-adjusted wage series for coal mining, building, shipbuilding, and unskilled workers in the Sheffield "heavy" trades for 1870–1913 are given in Figure 3.2.[10] The especially high volatility for coal miners and unskilled workers is due to annual fluctuations in nominal wages as well as unemployment. Year-to-year fluctuations in income could be quite large. Not surprisingly, unskilled workers experienced the largest fluctuations; unemployment-adjusted wage rates declined by 23% from 1883 to 1884,

---

[8] Unemployment also varied across regions. Humphrey Southall (1986, 1988) found that in the late nineteenth century unemployment rates were consistently higher in the industrial north of England than in the south and east. Some cities had extremely high unemployment rates. In April 1894, when the national unemployment rate among skilled engineers was 9.0%, it was 34.7% in North and South Shields, 23.4% in Newcastle, 21.3% in Leeds, and 17.4% in Swansea. For the same month, the unemployment rate for engineers was 7.7% in London, 6.0% in Derby, 5.5% in Bristol, and 3.4% in Coventry (Southall 1986, 277–8).

[9] In some industries workers also experienced frequent fluctuations in nominal wage rates. Wood (1901, 152) estimated that the average length of time between wage changes was about five months in iron and steel, and six months in coal mining. The frequency of wage changes was a result of agreements between workers and employers linking wages to product prices (Porter 1970; Treble 1987).

[10] Unskilled workers in the heavy trades include laborers in iron and steel works, foundries, and engineering works. Data for these workers are from Pollard (1954, 62), who reported unemployment-adjusted wage rates.

TABLE 3.2. *Distribution of Unemployment in Four Trade Unions*

	Amal. Engineers (Manchester & Leeds)			London Compositors	Carpenters & Joiners		Woodcutting Machinists	
	1890	1893	1887–95	1894–1903	1898–9	1904–5	1898	1904
Unemployment Rate	2.1	10.2	6.1	4.3	1.1	6.0	1.4	4.3
% Unemployed at some time in year	21.4	26.4	29.7	20.6	19.7	43.1	22.1	33.7
Days lost per member	6.4	31.1	18.7	14.3	3.4	18.8	4.5	13.4
Days lost per unemployed member	30.1	117.8	63.1	64.1	17.4	43.6	20.5	39.8
% Unemployed for 8 weeks or more	3.8	18.2	12.1		1.7	14.8	2.9	10.6

Sources: British and Foreign Trade and Industrial Conditions. Parliamentary Papers (1905. vol. LXXXIV; Statistics relating to England and Wales. Parliamentary Papers (1910. vol. LIII, pp. 870–6).

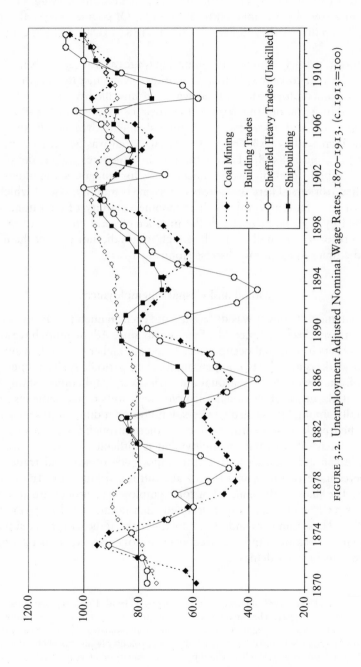

FIGURE 3.2. Unemployment Adjusted Nominal Wage Rates, 1870–1913. (c. 1913=100)

Coal Mining
Building Trades
Sheffield Heavy Trades (Unskilled)
Shipbuilding

by 29% from 1891 to 1892, by 30% from 1901 to 1902, and by 44% from 1907 to 1908. From 1883 to 1886, unemployment-adjusted wages fell three years in a row, by a combined total of 53%. Of course, wages also could increase rapidly, as they did from 1880 to 1881 (41%) and 1894 to 1895 (47%).

Figure 3.2 clearly shows that comparing wage rates at certain benchmarks masks the year-to-year volatility of workers' wage income. From 1870 to 1913 real unemployment-adjusted wages of unskilled workers in Sheffield increased by 42%, but they were below their 1870 level in 1875–80, 1884–88, 1891–94, and 1908–09. Coal miners' unemployment-adjusted wage income increased by 82% from 1870 to 1913, but was below its 1870 level in 1877–82 and 1885–86. The fluctuations in wage rates and unemployment created a high level of income uncertainty for miners, shipbuilders, and unskilled workers. There were costs to income instability, one of which was the cost of defaulting on debts. The income volatility of coal miners was matched by high fluctuations in the number of local court cases initiated for the recovery of small debts; their high wages did not protect them from periodic times of economic distress (Johnson 1993).

Seasonal and Casual Unemployment

Seasonal unemployment was different from cyclical unemployment in that it was to a large degree predictable. Economists since Adam Smith have argued that workers in seasonal occupations were paid higher wages than similarly skilled workers in order to compensate for their periodic spells of unemployment. Even if workers in seasonal industries were paid compensating wage differentials, however, seasonal unemployment still created some insecurity, especially among low-skilled workers, who found it difficult to save enough from their peak-season earnings to carry them through slack seasons.

The extent of seasonal unemployment is difficult to measure precisely, but one can get a rough idea of the importance of seasonal trades from the percentage of the workforce in agriculture, fishing, and the building trades. The share of the male labor force employed in agriculture and building was 35.8% in 1841, but it declined each decade until in 1911 it was 19.5%.[11] These numbers underestimate the share of the workforce subject to seasonality, because some manufacturing sectors also experienced seasonal fluctuations in labor demand.

---

[11] Occupational data were obtained from Lee (1979). Detailed occupational data are not available before 1841. The numbers for Britain are lower than comparable numbers for the United States. Engerman and Goldin (1994, 99) estimated that in 1850 two-thirds of the American workforce "was seasonally and involuntarily idle for about four months each year." Sokoloff and Dollar (1997) provide a comparison of agricultural seasonality in Britain and the United States in the nineteenth century.

Table 3.3 presents evidence from the early twentieth century on the extent of seasonal fluctuations in employment six non-agricultural sectors. The first two columns present indices of monthly employment in the building trades in 1907–10. Column 3 presents an index of the total amount of wages paid to building workers in each month. The magnitude of the seasonal fluctuations in wage income is larger than in employment because the workweek was slightly shorter in the winter. The wage income of construction workers was, on average, 17–24% lower from November to February than it was in May. The extent of seasonal fluctuations in labor demand varied across sections of the building trade; it was relatively low for plumbers and especially high for bricklayers and painters (Dearle 1908, 66–81).

Seasonality in mining typically was handled by reducing the number of shifts worked per week in slack seasons rather than by laying off workers. From 1897 to 1911, the average number of days worked per week varied from 5.47 in December to 4.92 in June. Employment at gas works was highly seasonal, with 11–17% fewer workers employed from March to September than in December. In the furnishing trades, unemployment varied from a low of 2.5% in April and May to over 7% in December and January; in tobacco unemployment exceeded 9% in July and August, but was 3.2% in November. Other trades experienced less pronounced seasonal fluctuations in labor demand; a 1909 Board of Trade memorandum concluded that "seasonal fluctuation is found to a more or less marked degree in nearly every industry."[12]

Systems of temporary or casual employment developed in some low-skilled occupations that were subject to sudden and irregular fluctuations in the demand for labor (Beveridge 1909, 77). Casual employment existed in many trades – Gareth Stedman Jones (1971) contends that some degree of "casualization" existed among painters and unskilled laborers in the building trades, land transport, menial services, and certain declining manufacturing trades.[13] It was especially pronounced among dock workers, due to the irregularity in the arrival and departure of ships. Dock workers were hired by the day or half day, chosen by foremen each morning and afternoon from groups of workers at calling-on stands. In his detailed study of employment at the London docks in 1891–2, Booth (1892a, 533) found that the number of workers employed in a day at the docks controlled by the joint committee varied from 3,553 to 7,781. The hourly wage rate was

---

[12] The Board of Trade memorandum was published in Royal Commission on the Poor Laws, Appendix Vol. IX, Unemployment, Parliamentary Papers, 1910, vol. XLIX, pp. 638–55. There is a good discussion of seasonality in British industry in Poyntz (1912).

[13] Jones (1971, 52–66) estimated that in London in 1891 casual workers and their families totaled about 400,000 persons, or one-tenth of the population. The extent of seasonal and casual unemployment among building trades workers at the turn of the twentieth century is vividly described in Robert Tressell's novel, *The Ragged Trousered Philanthropists*.

TABLE 3.3. *Seasonality of Employment in Six Sectors*

	Building Skilled Men Number Employed 1907–10	Building Laborers Number Employed 1907–10	Building Wage Income 1906	Coal Miners Days Worked Per Week 1897–1911	Gas Workers Number Employed 1906	Monthly Unemployment Furnishing Trades 1897–1906	Monthly Unemployment Tobacco Workers 1897–1906
January	84.4	84.0	76.2	5.20	97.2	7.9	5.8
February	89.0	87.7	82.7	5.43	93.9	6.5	6.5
March	94.5	92.5	92.6	5.39	89.1	3.3	7.4
April	96.3	95.3	97.6	5.03	85.5	2.4	7.8
May	96.3	96.2	100.0	5.23	84.2	2.5	8.3
June	94.5	95.3	96.5	4.92	83.0	3.2	8.6
July	96.3	98.1	96.6	4.98	83.6	4.1	9.3
August	100.0	100.0	98.7	4.99	84.4	4.1	9.4
September	95.4	96.2	96.3	5.35	87.8	4.2	7.3
October	89.0	90.6	91.3	5.41	92.3	4.5	5.1
November	86.2	87.7	82.6	5.39	97.2	4.9	3.2
December	80.7	82.1	78.7	5.47	100.0	7.1	4.7

Notes: The series in columns 1, 2, and 5 are indices; the index numbers show each month's employment as a percentage of the peak month's employment. The series in column 3 is an index; the index numbers show each month's wage income as a percentage of the peak month's wage income.

Sources: Columns 1 and 2: Webb (1912, 334); Column 3: Board of Trade (1910, 13); Column 4: Data for 1897–1901 from Board of Trade (1907, 5), data for 1902–11 from Board of Trade (1912, 9); Column 5: Popplewell (1912, 196); Columns 6 and 7: Poyntz (1912, 23–4).

TABLE 3.4. *Average Work Time Lost Due to Sickness, in Weeks*

Ages	Manchester Oddfellows 1866–70	Ancient Order of Foresters 1871–75	Friendly Societies' Registrar 1876–80	Manchester Oddfellows 1893–97
20–24	0.75	0.82	0.85	0.90
25–29	0.81	0.85	0.87	0.95
30–34	0.93	0.97	1.02	1.06
35–39	1.06	1.15	1.24	1.27
40–44	1.26	1.37	1.47	1.58
45–49	1.64	1.71	1.89	1.99
50–54	2.22	2.27	2.39	2.75
55–59	3.05	3.21	3.36	4.02
60–64	4.72	4.59	5.17	6.31
65–69	7.24	7.97	8.73	10.59

Source: Money (1912, 169).

relatively high, but the irregularity of employment meant that many dock workers suffered chronic distress (Beveridge 1909, 106–7).

Sickness and Old Age

There are surprisingly little data before 1914 on work time lost due to sickness. What data exist have been drawn from the records of friendly societies and trade unions paying sickness benefits. James Riley (1997, 166) estimated that, among males belonging to the Ancient Order of Foresters friendly society, the average number of work days lost due to sickness was 9 in the early 1870s, 12 from 1885 to 1900, and nearly 14 in 1911.[14] These estimates probably underestimate average work time lost for all manual laborers, as sickness rates were higher for unskilled than for skilled workers, and few low-skilled workers were members of friendly societies that paid sickness benefits (Johnson 1985, 57–63).[15]

Time lost due to sickness increased significantly with age. Table 3.4 shows the relationship between sickness and age for male friendly society members at four time periods. Workers under age 35 lost, on average, a week or less

[14] According to Riley, the increase in sickness time from the early 1870s to 1911 was caused by an increase in the average duration of sickness episodes. Increased nutrition and better health care prolonged the lives of some sick people, and some who in earlier times would have died from an illness now recovered after a prolonged period of sickness. People survived longer, but part of their additional time was spent in sickness (Riley 1997, 171–87, 269–70).

[15] On the other hand, if the existence of sickness insurance led workers to take more sick days, Riley's data might overestimate the average number of days lost due to sickness by the workforce as a whole.

work time per year due to sickness, while workers aged 50–54 lost 2.2–
2.8 weeks per year, and workers aged 60–64 lost 4.6–6.3 weeks per year.
Like unemployment, sickness affected some workers within age groups much
more than others. Southall (1988, 22) reported detailed data on the duration
of sickness among members of the Steam Engine Makers union in 1852–72.
Nearly three-quarters of workers under age 25, and slightly more than half
of workers aged 60–64, did not collect sickness benefits during a calendar
year. On the other hand, 8% of workers under 25 collected sick benefits for
at least five weeks, and 1.7% collected sick pay for more than six months.
Among workers aged 35–39, one in ten received sick pay for at least five
weeks, and 4.3% got sick pay for more than six months. Among workers
aged 60–64, nearly a quarter collected sick pay for at least five weeks, and
9.1% received sick pay for more than six months.

In 1861, 4.6% of the population of England and Wales was aged 65 and
over; in 1891, 4.7% were 65 or older (Mitchell 1988, 15). A person aged
35–9 in 1861 or 1871 had about a 50% chance of surviving to age 65, and
upon reaching 65, they could expect to live another 10–11 years.[16] A large
share of the aged lived in poverty. Table 3.5 gives estimates of pauperism
for those aged 65 and over from 1861 to 1891 (Booth 1899, 218). The
estimates in column 1 are based on day counts of the number of paupers,
and therefore underestimate the number who received poor relief at some
point over a twelve-month period. C. T. Ritchie, President of the Local
Government Board, constructed a twelve-month count of the number of
paupers from March 1891 to March 1892.[17] These data show that 29.3%
of those aged 65 and over received poor relief at some point during a one-
year period (column 2).

In contrast to the day count, which gives a good idea of the number of
"permanent" paupers, many of those in the twelve-month count received
relief only for short periods. The twelve-month count thus includes those
who were living near the margin. These elderly were able to subsist on their
own resources much of the time, but needed to apply for relief now and
then, as in winter or when they were sick.

Column 2 presents estimates of the share of persons aged 65 and over
relieved at some point during the year, calculated by assuming that the ratio
of the number relieved at some time over twelve months to the number

---

[16] This estimate was calculated by comparing the number of 35–9 year olds in 1861 (1871)
with the number of 65–9 year olds in 1891 (1901). Because most emigrants and immigrants
were younger than 35, this should provide a reasonable estimate of the probability of
surviving to age 65. Data are from Mitchell (1988, 15). The life expectancy of a 65 year
old male was 10.7 years in 1861 and 10.6 years in 1901; that of a 65 year old female was
11.6 years in 1861 and 11.8 years in 1901. Life expectancy data are from Preston, Keyfitz,
and Schoen (1972, 224, 226, 240, 242).

[17] The data collected by Ritchie are reported in the Report of the Royal Commission on the
Aged Poor, Vol. 1, Parliamentary Papers, 1895, vol. XIV, p. xii.

TABLE 3.5. *Pauperism among Those Aged 65 and Older, 1861–91*

Year	Booth % on Relief Day Count	Estimated % on Relief Year Count (a)	Estimated % on Relief Year Count (b)	Work Class % on Relief Year Count (a)	Work Class % on Relief Year Count (b)
1861	28.6	43.0	40.0	57.3	53.4
1871	28.6	43.0	40.0	57.3	53.4
1881	22.0	33.1	30.8	44.1	41.1
1891	19.5	29.3	27.3	39.1	36.4

Notes: The estimates in columns 2–5 assume that the rate of pauperism of those aged 65 and older declined at the same rate as in column 1. The estimates in columns 2 and 4, listed as (a), include those receiving only medical relief outside of a workhouse. The estimates in columns 3 and 5, listed as (b), exclude those receiving only medical relief. The estimates in columns 4 and 5 assume that the working class made up 75% of the population.
Source: Boyer and Schmidle (2009).

relieved on a particular day remained constant from 1861 to 1891. The estimates suggest that, in the 1860s, 43% of elderly individuals received poor relief at some point over a twelve-month period. Since the middle class virtually never made use of the Poor Law, and about 75% of those aged 65 and over were from the working class, it follows that as late as 1891 nearly 40% of aged working-class persons received poor relief, either in the form of a permanent pension or occasional assistance (column 4).[18]

Most men continued to work past age 65; in 1891, the labor force participation rate of males aged 65 and over was 64.8% (Quadagno 1982, 152). However, a large share of those employed worked less than full-time, and numbers employed and hours worked decreased with age. As a result, the share of aged persons who were able to support themselves declined with age, forcing an ever larger share to turn to the Poor Law, or to family and friends, for assistance. Booth (1894, 43) estimated that, in 1891–2, 20.6% of those aged 65–9 received poor relief, as compared to 31.3% of those aged 70–4, and 40.1% of those 75 and over.

This section has described unemployment and loss of employment due to sickness among the working class. Although within a calendar year a majority of workers were neither unemployed or lost days due to sickness, many were off work a month or more. Moreover, while most aged working-class males continued to work for as long as they could, a large share was unable to earn enough to support themselves. I now turn to how workers dealt with the threatened income loss.

---

[18] The estimated pauperism rates in columns 3 and 5 exclude those persons aged 65 and over who received only short-term outdoor medical relief from the Poor Law. These were only a small share of the total number relieved, and some contemporaries maintained that, because of the short average duration of their relief spells, they should not be counted as paupers.

II. COPING WITH FINANCIAL INSECURITY, 1830–1870

Wherever the Poor Laws are best administered, there the contributions of labourers to savings banks and benefit societies are the most numerous. In those districts where the most lavish payments are made from the rates, these establishments are neglected. (Ashurst Majendie, Assistant Poor Law Commissioner, 1834)

Workers in the nineteenth century coped with financial insecurity in various ways. They put aside some of their weekly pay in savings, they joined friendly societies and trade unions that paid them weekly benefits when they were unemployed or sick, and they turned for assistance to the Poor Law, private charities, and friends and relatives in times of need. The relative importance of public assistance declined throughout the period from 1830 to 1908, and the role of self-help, in the form of saving and membership in friendly societies and trade unions, increased. This section examines the shift toward self-help that began in the late 1830s, partly in response to the adoption of the Poor Law Amendment Act in 1834.

The Poor Law played the largest role of its 350-year history (from 1598 to 1948) during the first third of the nineteenth century. Real per capita relief expenditures were higher in 1818–21 than at any other time during the century, and relief expenditures as a share of GDP peaked at 2.7% in 1820–21 (Lindert 1998, 114; Boyer 2002, Table 3.1). Data on the percentage of the population that received relief are not available, but it must have exceeded 10% throughout the period 1815–30.[19] The share of relief recipients who were prime aged males also peaked during this period (King 2000). Per capita relief expenditures varied significantly across regions, and were especially high in the grain-producing south and east, where a large share of relief spending consisted of payments to seasonally unemployed agricultural laborers (Boyer 1990).

The Poor Law assisted unemployed and underemployed workers, widows, children, the sick, the elderly, and the disabled, constituting in Mark Blaug's (1964, 229) words "a welfare state in miniature." Rural and urban workers during this period were not hesitant to apply to local Poor Law authorities for assistance. They viewed poor relief as an entitlement, part of an "unwritten social contract" with employers and other middle-class taxpayers (Lees 1998; Hunt 1981, 215).

Self-help played a relatively small role before 1834, largely because workers' wages were too low to enable them to save, but perhaps also because of

---

[19] Data on the number of relief recipients exist for 1802–03 and for 1840 onwards. In 1802–03, 11.4% of the population received relief; in 1840, after the adoption of the New Poor Law, 7.7% received relief (Lindert 1998, 110; Williams 1981, 158). These numbers, based on the official head counts, underestimate, perhaps to a large degree, the number of individuals who received relief at some point during the year (Lees 1998). Given the high level of relief spending from 1815–30, it seems likely that the share on relief was at least as high as in 1802–03.

the relatively generous nature of poor relief. According to returns from local Poor Law overseers there were 925,429 members of friendly societies in England in 1815 (see Table 3.7), representing 29% of males aged 15 and over (Gorsky 1998, 493). All of these friendly societies were local organizations, and some were little more than burial clubs. Many were financially unstable (King and Tomkins 2003, 267). Probably no more than 50–60% of members were in societies that paid sickness benefits. The share of the population belonging to friendly societies was largest in Lancashire and other northern and midlands industrial counties, and lowest in southern and eastern rural counties (Gosden 1961, 22–4; Gorsky 1998, 493–7). Membership in local societies stagnated from 1815 to the early 1830s (Neave 1996, 46–7). However, this same period witnessed the rise of the national affiliated orders. The largest of these, the Independent Order of Oddfellows, Manchester Unity (IOOMU), was founded in Manchester in 1810 and by 1831 had 31,000 members. The Ancient Order of Foresters (AOF) was founded in Leeds in 1813 and claimed to have 16,510 members in 1835 (Gosden 1973, 27–30). Combining the local societies and affiliated orders, membership in friendly societies in the early 1830s probably totaled slightly less than a million, with perhaps 600,000 members (16% of adult males) in societies that paid sickness benefits.

Parliament established the Trustee Savings Banks in 1817 in part to encourage working-class saving. In 1830 these banks had 425,000 depositors, whose deposits totaled £14.6 million (see Table 3.6). In order to determine the extent of working class saving, however, it is necessary to separate workers' deposits from those of the middle class. Few if any workers had deposits greater than £50, and many of the deposits under £50 "belonged to children of prosperous parents" (Fishlow 1961, 32).[20] In 1830, 79.4% of depositors had balances less than £50, and 51.0% had balances less than £20. The upper limit of the number of working-class depositors therefore was 340,000; the actual number probably was about 280,000.[21] Depositors with balances less than £50 held 37.8% of the £14.6 million in deposits in 1830, or £5.5 million (Fishlow 1961, 32). Total working-class deposits almost certainly were less than this; a rough estimate would be that workers'

---

[20] Paul Johnson (1985, 103) considered £50 to be "an upper limit for most working-class savings bank deposits" in 1911–13. Given the large increase in working-class wages from 1830 to 1911, the upper limit for working-class savings must have been far below £50 in 1830, so that using this number as a cutoff provides an upper-bound estimate of the importance of working-class saving.

[21] If all depositors with balances below £50 were members of the working class, and all depositors with larger balances were from the middle class, then the total number of working-class depositors was 0.794 × 425,000, or 337,450. If, instead, half of the 120,700 depositors with balances between £20 and £50 were members of the middle class, then the total number of working-class depositors was 277,100.

balances totaled £3.2 million, or 22% of deposits.[22] To put the magnitude of working-class saving in 1830 in perspective, Table 3.6 shows that it represented about 57% of poor relief spending on indoor and outdoor relief.[23] In sum, before 1834 only a small minority of the working class either belonged to friendly societies offering sickness benefits or had any money in a savings bank.

The Effect of Poor Law Reform on Self-help

The relative importance of self-help and public assistance began to change after the adoption of the Poor Law Amendment Act of 1834, which recommended the abolition of outdoor relief for able-bodied workers and their families, and its replacement by relief in well-regulated workhouses. The Poor Law Commission created by the Act did not eliminate the payment of outdoor relief to the able-bodied, but it succeeded in restricting relief for able-bodied males and in reducing relief expenditures.[24] Real per capita poor relief spending fell by 45% from 1830 to 1840 and never again approached the 1830 level (Table 3.6). At the same time, there was a sharp increase in friendly society membership and private saving. Membership in the Manchester Unity Oddfellows increased from 31,000 in 1832 to 90,000 in 1838 and 259,000 in 1846; and membership in the Foresters increased from 16,500 in 1835 to nearly 77,000 in 1846 (Neave 1996, 47–9). Of the 3,074 English lodges of the IOOMU in 1875, 1,470 (48%) were established between 1835 and 1845 (Gosden 1961, 34).[25] Other, smaller, affiliated orders were also established during this period, among them the Independent Order of Rechabites and the Loyal Order of Ancient Shepherds, who together had 32,000 members in 1846 (Neave 1996, 49). There are no data on membership in local societies for the 1830s and 1840s, but it probably grew as well, albeit at a lower rate. I estimate that total friendly society membership in 1850 was

---

[22] Johnson (1985) presents evidence that about 30% of savings bank deposits were held by workers in the decades leading up to World War I. However, assuming that 30% of deposits were held by workers in 1830 gives an unreasonably large average account balance. My estimate of £3.2 million assumes that workers held all deposits under £20, that workers held half of the deposits between £20 and £50, and that the average working-class balance for this larger category of deposits was £25.

[23] Poor relief expenditures in England and Wales totaled £6.8 million in 1830. However, some of this expenditure was for administration. In 1840, expenditures on indoor and outdoor relief represented 82% of total relief expenditures. Applying this same ratio to 1830 yields an expenditure level of about £5.6 million.

[24] Williams (1981) claimed that the New Poor Law succeeded in abolishing outdoor relief for the able-bodied by 1850. However, Rose (1970), Digby (1975), and Lees (1998) have shown that the orders regulating outdoor relief largely were evaded by both rural and urban unions, many of whom continued to grant outdoor relief to unemployed and underemployed males.

[25] More than three times as many lodges were founded in 1835–45 as were founded in any other decade; 569 lodges existed in 1835.

TABLE 3.6. *Working Class Saving and Poor Relief Spending, 1830–1913*

	Trustee Savings Bank Deposits (Million £s)	Post Office Savings Bank Deposits (Million £s)	Total Savings Bank Deposits (Million £s)	Estimated Working Class Bank Deposits (Million £s)	Indoor + Outdoor Poor Relief Spending (Million £s)	Working Class Deposit/Poor Relief Spending	Real Per Capita Poor Spending	Share of Population Receiving Poor Relief
1830	14.6		14.6	3.20	5.579	0.57	100.0	
1835	17.4		17.4		4.514		87.6	
1840	23.5		23.5	5.86	3.739	1.57	54.8	
1845	30.7		30.7		4.118		65.1	
1850	28.9		28.9	7.23	4.069	1.78	62.8	12.7
1855	34.3		34.3		4.287		50.0	10.7
1860	41.3		41.3	10.33	3.775	2.74	44.2	9.0
1865	38.7	6.5	45.2		4.370		49.8	9.5
1870	38.0	15.1	53.1	15.93	5.136	3.10	53.9	9.7
1875	42.4	25.2	67.6		4.537		43.9	6.9
1880	44.0	33.7	77.7	23.31	4.469	5.22	42.7	6.5
1885	46.4	47.7	94.1		4.392		43.0	5.7
1890	43.6	67.6	111.2	33.36	4.354	7.66	41.1	5.4
1895	45.3	97.9	143.2		4.747		44.4	5.2
1900	51.5	135.5	187.0	56.10	5.246	10.69	43.4	4.6
1905	52.7	152.1	204.8		6.211		48.4	5.0
1910	52.3	168.9	221.2	66.36	6.701	9.90	47.1	4.9
1913	54.3	187.2	241.5	72.45	5.979	12.12	39.7	4.0

Sources: Columns 1 and 2: Mitchell (1988, 671–2).

Column 3: Calculated as column 1 plus column 2.

Column 4: Estimates for 1870–1913 calculated by assuming that 30% of savings banks deposits belonged to working-class accounts. See Johnson (1985, 100–05). Estimates for 1840–60 assume that 25% of deposits belonged to working-class accounts. I chose lower estimates for the percentage of the working class in 1830–60 because using 30% yielded unreasonably large average deposits per working-class account. For a discussion of how the estimate for 1830 was calculated, see text. The estimates for 1830–60 are based on a substantial amount of guesswork.

Column 5: Williams (1981, 169–71).

Column 6: Calculated as column 4 divided by column 5.

Column 7: Constructed by author, using expenditure data from column 5, cost of living estimates from Feinstein (1995), and population data from Mitchell (1988, 11–13).

Column 8: Constructed by author, following Lees (1998).

63

TABLE 3.7. *Friendly Society Membership, 1815–1911*

	Adult Males Aged 20+	Estimated Friendly Society Members	Author Est. Friendly Society Members	Registered Friendly Society Members	OFS + AFS Members	OFS + AFS Sick Benefit Members	9 Major Friendly Societies Members	4 Affiliated Friendly Societies Members
1815		925,429						45,000
1830	3,684,500	1,000,000	1,000,000					368,801
1846								368,801
1850	4,717,000	3,000,000	2,000,000					328,663
1860								524,417
1870	5,866,000							859,040
1872		4,000,000	3,500,000	1,857,896				
1875							1,039,940	1,075,864
1877				2,750,000				
1885								1,280,313
1886					3,760,000	2,845,000	1,630,972	
1887				3,600,000				
1889		4,395,160						
1891	7,516,000		4,500,000		4,110,000	3,110,000		1,464,791
1892		6,000,000		3,860,000				

Year	(1)	(2)	(3)	(4)	(5)	(6)	(7)	(8)
1896							2,004,092	1,563,466
1899				5,466,000			2,143,845	
1901	8,856,000				5,470,000	4,140,000		1,678,601
1904								
1905				6,164,000				
1910				6,623,000			2,444,632	1,688,379
1911	10,260,000				6,420,000	4,430,000		

Sources: Column 1: Mitchell (1988, 11, 15). Number for 1830 was estimated assuming that the ratio of adult males to all males was the same as in 1851.

Column 2: Estimate for 1815 from Select Committee on the Poor Laws, 1818; reported in Gosden (1961, 16); estimate for 1830 from Hopkins (1995, 24); estimate for 1849 from Perkin (1969, 381); estimate for 1872 from the Royal Commission on Friendly Societies, 1874; reported in Gosden (1961, 7); estimate for 1889 from Wilkinson (1891, 191); estimate for 1892 from Brabook; reported in Neave (1996, 49).

Column 3: Estimated by author. See text.

Column 4: Number for 1872 from Royal Commission on Friendly Societies, 1874; reported in Gosden (1961, 7); numbers for 1877 to 1910, with the exception of 1892, from Neave (1996, 61); number for 1892 from Gosden (1973, 91).

Column 5: Johnson (1985, 50, 57). OFS refers to Ordinary Friendly Societies; AFS refers to Affiliated Society Members.

Column 6: Johnson (1985, 57). Estimates for 1886 and 1891 were calculated by author assuming that the share of OFS + AFS members who were eligible for sickness benefits was roughly the same as in 1901.

Column 7: Numbers for 1872 and 1886 from Beveridge (1948, 31); number for 1896 from *Fifteenth Abstract of Labour Statistics* (1912, 256–7); numbers for 1899 and 1910 from *Seventeenth Abstract of Labour Statistics* (1915, 258–9).

Column 8: Numbers for 1846 to 1885 from Neave (1996, 49); numbers for 1891 and 1896 from *Eleventh Abstract of Labour Statistics* (1907, 180); numbers for 1901 and 1910 from *Seventeenth Abstract of Labour Statistics* (1915, 258).

at most 2 million, about 40% of adult males (see Table 3.7).[26] The number of members in societies that paid sickness benefits probably was between 1.2 and 1.35 million.[27] Thus, from 1830 to 1850, the share of adult males insured against income loss due to sickness increased from roughly 16% to 25–29% (see Table 3.8).

Private saving also increased greatly after 1834, as can be seen in Table 3.6. Deposits in Trustee Savings Banks increased by 61% from 1830 to 1840, and by a further 23% from 1840 to 1850. The number of working-class depositors grew from 280,000 in the early 1830s to 750,000 in 1850 (Table 3.8).[28] It should be stressed, however, that even with the impressive growth in private saving and friendly society membership, the majority of workers before 1850 neither had a savings account or belonged to a friendly society paying sickness benefits.

This increase in self-help must have been, at least in part, a response to the change in the administration of poor relief. The Poor Law Commission attributed much of the growth in friendly society membership after 1834 to the reform of the Poor Law. John Tidd Pratt, the barrister appointed to certify the rules of savings banks and friendly societies, stated that the founders of new lodges wrote to him that "now is the time that parties must look to themselves, as they could not receive out-door relief under the new law."[29] Pratt also attributed the increase in the number of depositors in savings banks to the reform of the Poor Law. Certainly, the rise in working-class saving and friendly society membership was not caused by a sharp increase in wage income; from 1830–32 to 1844–46, manual workers' real

[26] Supple (1974, 215) estimates that about one-half of adult males were members of friendly societies in 1850, which suggests that membership at mid-century exceeded 2.35 million. This number almost certainly is too high, in that it assumes that membership in local societies more than doubled from 1830 to 1850. Of the 1 million odd members of friendly societies in 1830, about 45,000 were members of affiliated orders and 955,000 were in local societies. Table 3.6 shows that the membership of the four largest affiliated orders in 1850 was 328,663. This suggests that there were about 2 million members of local societies in 1850. Hopkins (1995, 30) contends that "the leading affiliated orders clearly proved more attractive to many working men than the small local club with its often inadequate financial resources and uncertain future." Perkin (1969, 381) gives an estimate for total friendly society membership in 1849 of 3 million, but he gives no citation for this figure, which must be a significant overestimate.

[27] Johnson (1985, 57) estimated that in 1901 75.7% of the members of ordinary and affiliated friendly societies were in societies that paid sickness benefits. The share of local society members eligible for sickness benefits in 1850 probably was significantly below 75%. In the estimates in the text, I assume that 60–67% of all members were in societies that paid sickness benefits in 1850.

[28] The average number of accounts in Trustee Savings Banks in 1842–46 was 999,000 (Fishlow 1961, 39). I assume that 75% of these accounts were held by workers.

[29] The quote is from the Fourth Annual Report of the Poor Law Commissioners (1838, 58). The best discussion of the relationship between the friendly societies and the Poor Law is Gosden (1961, 198–210).

TABLE 3.8. *Working Class Savings Accounts and Membership in Friendly Societies with Sickness Benefits*

	Adult Males Aged 20+ (1,000s)	Working Class Savings Dep. (1,000s)	Friendly Soc. Memb. With Sick. Ben. (1,000s)	% Males with Sick. Ben. (Fr. Soc.)	Workers with Sick. Ben. (FS + TU)	% Males with Sick. Ben. (FS + TU)	Adjusted % with Sick. Ben. (FS + TU)
1830	3,685	280	600	16%			
1850	4,717	750	1,350	29			
1871	5,866	1,900	2,400	41	2,525	43%	39%
1891	7,516	4,640	3,370	45	3,950	53	47
1911	10,260	7,211	4,780	47	5,509	54	48

Sources: Column 1: From census data, reported in Mitchell (1988, 15). Number for 1830 estimated by author, assuming that the share of males aged 20 and older was the same as in 1850.

Column 2: Estimated by author from data in Fishlow (1961) and Johnson (1985, 91–3).

Column 3: Estimated by author. See text.

Column 4: Calculated as column 3 divided by column 1.

Column 5: Calculated as column 3 plus number of trade union members with sickness benefits. See text.

Column 6: Calculated as column 5 divided by column 1.

Column 7: Estimated by author, by reducing numbers in column 5 by 10% to account for duplication of policies. The adjusted estimates of individuals with sickness benefits was then divided by column 1.

earnings increased by only 10% (Feinstein 1998, 653). There is little doubt, then, that workers were devoting a larger share of their income to self-help in the 1840s than in the early 1830s.

Self-help during the Great Victorian Boom

After declining in the late 1840s, both deposits in savings banks and membership in friendly societies grew rapidly during the great Victorian boom of the 1850s and 1860s (see Tables 3.6 through 3.8). The Manchester Unity Oddfellows and the Foresters saw their combined membership increase to nearly 811,000 in 1870, a 140% increase over 1846. By 1872, the membership in registered friendly societies was about 1.86 million, and the Royal Commission on Friendly Societies (1870–4) estimated that overall friendly society membership was about 4 million. This last figure, however, is likely an overestimate; I argue that total membership was closer to 3.0–3.5 million. The number in societies that paid sickness benefits was smaller, perhaps 2.1–2.4 million, or 36–41% of the adult male population.[30]

Total friendly society expenditures are not known. Expenditure data are available for the Manchester Oddfellows and the Foresters, the two largest affiliated societies; in 1870, for example, they paid out £653,000 in sickness and funeral benefits (Neison 1877, 74–5).[31] Slightly more than one-third of friendly society members eligible for sickness benefits were in one of these two affiliated societies. If the Manchester Oddfellows and Foresters also accounted for one-third of expenditures by those societies that offered sickness benefits, then total friendly society spending in 1870 was £1.96 million, or 38% of poor relief expenditures.[32]

In 1871 the Trustee Savings Banks and the newly formed Post Office Savings Bank had between them 2.7 million depositors. Of these, likely 1.8–2.0 million were from the working class (see Table 3.8). This means there were 2.5 times as many working-class depositors in 1871 as in 1850.

[30] These estimates are based on the assumption that 75% of registered friendly society members were in societies that paid sickness benefits (see footnote 27), and that 60% of the members of non-registered or local societies were eligible for sickness benefits. If 75% of all members were in societies paying sickness benefits, then the total number eligible for sickness benefits in 1872 was 2.25–2.63 million. If, on the other hand, we assume that there were 4 million total members, and that 50% of the members of non-registered or local societies were in societies that paid sickness benefits, then the total number eligible for sickness benefits was 2.46 million.

[31] The expenditure per member on sickness and funeral benefits in 1870 was 16.1s.

[32] The above calculations are based on the assumption that the total number of members of friendly societies paying sickness benefits was 2.4 million. To calculate an upper-bound estimate of friendly society spending, suppose that membership in societies paying sickness benefits was 3 million. Then the Manchester Oddfellows and Foresters made up 27% of total membership. If they also accounted for 27% of expenditures, then total friendly society spending in 1870 was about £2.42 million, 47% of poor relief expenditures.

Meanwhile, poor relief expenditures stagnated from 1840 to 1860, then increased sharply in the 1860s. Despite this increase, real per capita relief spending in 1870 was barely half the 1830 level, and relief expenditures in 1870 were less than a third of workers' savings bank deposits (see Table 3.6).

The weekly benefits paid by friendly societies and the Poor Law were similar during the period from 1840 to 1870. The level of poor relief benefits given to an unemployed or sick worker was determined by the size of the worker's family and by the income that other family members were earning. Benefit levels were similar across towns and over time, typically 2s.–3s. for a single adult male per week, and 1s. 6d.–2s. per week for each additional family member (Rose 1965, 195–6). An unemployed man with a wife and two (three) children would receive about 8s. (10s.) per week if the family had no other sources of income, less if other family members were working. Friendly society sickness benefits varied across societies, but were on average 8s.–10s. per week in the 1850s and 1860s.[33] The median weekly wage for manual workers was about 18s. in 1860, and the upper quartile averaged 22.5s. (Bowley 1937, 46). Since most friendly society members would have been from the upper half of the income distribution, the sickness benefit likely replaced between a third and a half of their wages.

To sum up, the period from 1834 to 1870 witnessed a significant increase in self-help and a decline in public assistance, as a means of coping with financial insecurity. Nevertheless, the Poor Law continued to serve as a safety net for able-bodied males as well as for the elderly and the sick. As late as 1870, fewer than one-half of households had savings accounts or were members of friendly societies that paid sickness benefits. According to Gilbert (1966, 166–7), "friendly society membership was the badge of the skilled worker," and the same can be said about having a bank account. Few low-skilled workers were able to save, nor could they afford the premiums charged by friendly societies offering sickness benefits (Johnson 1985, 57–63).[34] When laborers lost any significant amount of work time, they were forced to turn to the Poor Law, private charity, or family and friends for assistance. Lees (1998) found that in three London parishes and six provincial towns in the years around 1850 large numbers of prime-age males continued to apply for poor relief, and that a majority of those assisted were granted outdoor relief. The Poor Law played an especially important role

---

33 Riley (1997, 281) maintains that the average friendly society benefit was 8s. per week in 1860. Hopkins (1995, 34) states that the typical weekly benefit was 8–10s.; Neave (1996, 55) maintains that the typical benefit was 10s.

34 This conclusion has been challenged by Riley (1997, 31–4), who contends that the records of individual clubs show that many poorly paid workers joined friendly societies. It is true that, by the mid 1860s, membership in the IOOMU and the AOF was spreading into the agricultural counties (Gosden 1961, 44–5). However, there seems little doubt that the share of low-skilled workers who were members of friendly societies offering sickness benefits in 1870 was small.

during cyclical downturns, since friendly societies did not pay benefits to unemployed members (Boot 1990; Boyer 2004). From 1840 to 1870, about 10% of the population of England and Wales were receiving poor relief at some point during a calendar year.[35] Given the temporary nature of most relief spells, this means that over a typical three-year period as many as 25% of the population made use of the Poor Law (Lees 1998, 180–2).

By 1870, then, there were distinct differences in the methods used by skilled and unskilled workers to cope with financial uncertainty. Skilled workers largely had accepted the Victorian ethic of respectability and self-help, and they protected themselves against income loss by saving and by joining friendly societies. Most skilled workers in mid-Victorian Britain never used the Poor Law, although some applied for poor relief during prolonged periods of unemployment or when they were elderly. For a large share of low-skilled workers, however, the Poor Law provided an important safety net that they turned to periodically. Most laborers would have preferred the strategy of self-help, but their wages were too low to make this an option.

III. COPING WITH FINANCIAL INSECURITY, 1870–1913

Simple industry and thrift will go far towards making any person of ordinary working faculty comparatively independent in his means. Even a working man may be so, provided he will carefully husband his resources. (Samuel Smiles, *Self-Help*, 1866, 254)

The last third of the nineteenth century saw a continuation of the movement toward self-help among the working class. It was spurred on by a major shift in Poor Law policy in the 1870s, known as the Crusade Against Outrelief. Encouraged by the newly formed Local Government Board (LGB), Poor Law unions throughout England and Wales sharply restricted outdoor relief for all types of paupers, in particular able-bodied males (MacKinnon 1987; Humphreys 1995). In December 1871 the LGB issued a circular claiming that the increase in expenditures on outdoor relief between 1860 and 1870 was "so great, as to excite apprehension," and that generous outdoor relief was destroying self-reliance among the poor.[36] Supporting the LGB in its desire for reform was the Charity Organization Society (COS), founded in

---

[35] Beginning in 1849, data on the number of persons receiving poor relief are available for two days a year, January 1 and July 1; the "official" estimates of the annual number relieved were constructed as the average of the number relieved on these two dates. However, studies conducted by Poor Law administrators indicate that the number recorded in the day counts was less than half the number assisted during the year. Lees's (1998, 180–1) "revised" estimates of annual relief recipients assume that the ratio of actual to counted paupers was 2.24 for 1850–1900. The share of the population receiving relief given in the text is based on Lees's revised estimates.

[36] The circular is reprinted in Rose (1971, 229–30).

1869. The COS maintained that most low-skilled workers could set aside enough income to deal with future interruptions in earnings caused by unemployment or sickness, and that any failure of workers to save was caused to a large extent by the availability of generous outdoor relief. According to the COS, restricting outdoor relief and offering the poor assistance only in workhouses would in the long run improve workers' moral and economic condition (MacKinnon 1987, 606–7).

Toward the end of the century there also was a change in the attitude of the poor toward relief. Prior to 1870, a large share of the working class treated public assistance as an entitlement. But their opinions changed, perhaps as a result of the COS. By the end of the century most workers viewed poor relief as stigmatizing (Lees 1998). This change in perception led many low-skilled workers and their families to go to great lengths to avoid applying for relief.[37] From 1870 to 1875 real per capita relief expenditures and the share of the population receiving relief fell sharply (see Table 3.6). From 1875 to 1913 the share of the population on relief continued to decline, but at a much slower pace. Real per capita expenditure also declined at first but after 1890 it increased slowly, largely because the Poor Law was providing increased amounts of medical care for the poor.

The number of accounts in the Post Office Savings Bank and Trustee Savings Banks nearly quadrupled from 1871 to 1911, by which date there were 7.2 million working-class depositors (see Table 3.8).[38] In real terms, deposits in workers' savings accounts increased by 141% from 1870 to 1890, and by another 94% from 1890 to 1913.

Membership in registered friendly societies increased from 1.86 million in 1872 to 2.75 million in 1877 and 3.6 million in 1887 (Table 3.7), although some of this increase likely represented a greater registration of existing societies. Total membership in ordinary and affiliated societies increased from 3.76 million in 1886 to 5.47 million in 1901, and 6.42 million in 1911 (see Table 3.7, column 5).[39] Following Neave (1996, 49–50), I estimate that the total number of friendly society members in 1891 was 4.5 million, and that the membership of societies paying sickness benefits probably was about 3.37 million.[40] This represented 45% of the adult male population

---

[37] As a result of the stigma attached to accepting relief, late-nineteenth century Poor Law data significantly underestimate the level of poverty, as is discussed below.

[38] There were 10.3 million savings accounts in 1911 (Johnson 1985, 91–2). Johnson (1985, 104–5) estimates that 70% of the accounts were held by members of the working class.

[39] I have not been able to determine what accounts for the discrepancies between the number of registered friendly society members in column 4 and Johnson's estimates in column 5. Johnson's figures are for registered affiliated and ordinary – those with only one office – societies. Not all friendly societies were registered. The number of unregistered members probably was relatively small; Wilkinson's (1891, 191) estimate for 1889 put total membership at 4.4 million, 7% greater than the number of registered members in 1891.

[40] I assume that the share of OFS + AFS members eligible for sickness benefits in 1891 was the same as in 1901, and that two-thirds of the 390,000 friendly society members not included

in 1891. Johnson (1985, 57) estimates that the number of friendly society members eligible for sickness benefits was 4.14 million in 1901 and 4.43 million in 1911. If we multiply his numbers by 1.08 to take account of those (relatively few) non-registered members in societies with sickness benefits, we get estimates of friendly society members eligible for sickness benefits of 4.47 million in 1901 and 4.78 million in 1911.[41] The 1911 figure represented 47% of adult males, up from 25–29% in 1850.

Annual expenditure data on benefits are available for fourteen large societies from 1886 onwards, and rough estimates can be made of total friendly society expenditures (see Table 3.9). Edward Brabrook, the Chief Registrar of Friendly Societies, estimated that in 1891 total friendly society expenditures on benefits were £4,277,000.[42] The fourteen societies for which data are available accounted for 52% of this total. If this ratio held throughout the period, then friendly society expenditures increased from £3.48 million in 1886 to £8.20 million in 1913. Friendly society spending rose from 81% of poor relief expenditures in 1886 to 104% by 1908.

Adding to this was mutual-insurance spending by trade unions. The rapid union growth after 1870 was accompanied by the spread of insurance benefits to a broad range of occupations (Webb and Webb 1897). Unions provided their members with insurance against unemployment, sickness, and accidents, pensions for retired members, and death benefits to ensure workers and their wives a proper funeral. The importance attached by workers to the insurance function of unions can be seen in the objectives listed in union rules. The Boilermakers and Iron and Steel Shipbuilders, for example, sought "to provide against a train of evils of the most serious magnitude, which evils, when they arise from any cause except sickness, are not provided for by any of the ordinary 'Benefit Societies'."[43] The benefit packages offered by unions differed markedly across occupations. In metals, engineering, shipbuilding, and the building trades, most unions provided unemployment, sickness, accident, old-age, and death benefits. Most mining and textile unions provided death benefits, and several provided unemployment benefits under certain conditions (when a mine or factory was shut down).

in ordinary or affiliated friendly societies (4.5 million – 4.11 million) were in societies that paid sickness benefits. There are two very different estimates of the total number of friendly society members in 1889–92: Wilkinson's estimate of 4.4 million members in 1889, and Brabrook's estimate of 6 million in 1892. Neave (1996, 49–50) contends that Wilkinson's estimate is much closer to the actual number, and gives his own estimate of 4.5 million for 1891.

[41] My estimates for 1891 suggest that the total number of friendly society members with sickness benefits was about 8% greater than the number of OFS + AFS members with sickness benefits.

[42] Brabrook's estimates are contained in the *Royal Commission on Labour: Minutes of Evidence*, Parliamentary Papers 1893–4, Q. 1321.

[43] The quote is from Board of Trade, *Statistical Tables and Report on Trade Unions* (1887, 7).

TABLE 3.9. *Friendly Society, Trade Union, and Poor Relief Expenditures, 1870–1913*

	14 Friendly Societies Expenditure (£s)	Est. Total Friendly Society Expenditure (£s)	Trade Union Benefit Expenditure (£s)	Friendly Society + Trade Union Expenditure (£s)	Indoor + Outdoor Relief Expenditure (£s)	Government Old Age Pension Expenditure (£s)	Friendly Soc. + Trade Union/ Poor Relief	Friendly Soc. + Trade Union/ Gov. Expend.
1870		1,960,000	250,000	2,210,000	5,136,000		0.430	0.430
1886	1,827,002	3,484,286	555,855	4,040,141	4,328,000		0.933	0.933
1892	2,310,661	4,406,675	805,969	5,212,644	4,418,000		1.180	1.180
1900	2,871,354	5,475,976	1,019,192	6,495,168	5,246,000		1.238	1.238
1908	3,531,054	6,734,094	2,339,275	9,073,369	6,467,000		1.403	1.403
1910	3,605,171	6,875,443	1,772,841	8,648,284	6,701,000	5,198,637	1.291	0.727
1913	4,301,896	8,204,172	1,879,971	10,084,143	5,979,000	8,317,912	1.687	0.705

Sources: Column 1: Data for 1886 from *Sixth Abstract of Labour Statistics* (1900, 50–7). Data for 1892 from *Eleventh Abstract of Labour Statistics* (1907, 184–5). Data for 1900 through 1913 from *Seventeenth Abstract of Labour Statistics* (1915, 260–1).

Column 2: Estimated by author. The estimates for 1886–1913 assume (following Brabrook) that the expenditures of the 14 largest friendly societies accounted for 52% of total friendly society expenditures on benefits. The estimate for 1870 assumes that total friendly society expenditures were equal to three times the expenditures of the two larges friendly societies, the Manchester Unity Oddfellows and the Foresters. See text.

Column 3: Estimated by author from various Board of Trade reports on trade unions.

Column 4: Calculated as column 2 plus column 3.

Column 5: Williams (1981, 170–1).

Column 6: *Seventeenth Abstract of Labour Statistics* (1915, 185).

Column 7: Calculated as column 2 divided by column 5.

Column 8: Calculated as column 2 divided by the sum of columns 5 and 6.

Few, however, provided sickness or old-age benefits. Unions of low-skilled workers typically provided only death and accident benefits (Boyer 1988). Unemployment insurance was the most important of the union-provided benefits, because it was not provided by friendly societies.[44]

The number of workers with trade union benefits was relatively small compared to the membership of friendly societies. In 1892, 728,000 trade union members (8% of the adult male workforce) were eligible for unemployment benefits, 580,000 were eligible for sickness benefits, and 429,000 were eligible for old age (superannuation) benefits. By 1908, 1,474,000 workers (12% of the male workforce, 66% of union members) were eligible for unemployment benefits, and 729,000 were eligible for sickness benefits.[45] The relatively small number of union members eligible for sickness benefits was due largely to their being provided by friendly societies, and the fact that many union members were members of friendly societies.

Table 3.9 (column 3) presents data on insurance benefits paid out by trade unions for selected years from 1870 to 1913. Before 1900 union expenditures were small, and concentrated among a few unions of skilled workers. In 1886, 62% of spending was done by four unions with 115,800 members – the Amalgamated Engineers, the Iron and Steel Shipbuilders, the Ironfounders, and the Amalgamated Carpenters and Joiners. The number of unions offering insurance benefits expanded in the 1890s; still, as late as 1908, seven large unions accounted for 51% of total expenditures.[46] Spending on unemployment benefits typically exceeded spending on every other type of benefit, and in cyclical downturns, such as 1886 or 1908, unemployment benefits accounted for most of union benefit expenditures.

The benefits paid by friendly societies and trade unions to sick or unemployed members grew over time, but at a slower rate than wages, so that the ratio of benefits to wages fell from 1870 to 1914. The average weekly sickness benefit paid by friendly societies increased from 10s. in the 1870s

---

[44] Beveridge (1909, 227), the Webbs (1897), and other contemporaries maintained that trade unions were better able than friendly societies, or for that matter, the government, to determine whether applicants for unemployment benefits were in fact eligible for benefits, and whether benefit recipients were actively searching for work.

[45] Data for 1892 are from the Board of Trade's *Seventh Annual Report on Trade Unions* (1893, 5). Data for 1908 are from the Board of Trade's *Report on Trade Unions in 1908–10* (1912, xxxv). Data on the size of the adult male workforce and total union membership in 1892 and 1908 are from Bain and Price (1980, 37).

[46] These unions were the Amalgamated Engineers, the Amalgamated Carpenters and Joiners, the Operative Bricklayers, the Iron and Steel Shipbuilders, the Friendly Society of Ironfounders, the Durham Miners, and the Amalgamated Cotton Spinners. Their combined membership was 434,000. Three unions – the Engineers, Shipbuilders, and Carpenters – accounted for 36% of spending. Expenditure data for 1908 are from Board of Trade, *Report on Trade Unions in 1908–10* (1912, 80–113).

to 12s. by 1900, and remained at that level until 1914.[47] The typical trade union sickness or unemployment benefit was 9s.–10s. per week in 1892. Benefits increased little if at all in the next two decades; in 1908 the median union sickness or unemployment benefit was 9.25s.–10s. per week.[48] The median wage for manual workers was 31.5s. per week in 1914; the upper quartile of workers averaged 39.3s. (Bowley 1937, 46). Thus, the average friendly society benefit replaced about a third of lost wages in 1914, while the typical union benefit replaced somewhat less. Benefit payments were enough to feed a moderate sized family in 1900, but not high enough to also cover rent, fuel, clothing, and sundries.[49] Benefits were supplemented "by the earnings of wife and children, by private saving, by assistance from fellow-workmen and neighbours, by running into debt, by pawning and in other ways," but they served "as a nucleus," and kept their recipients from having to apply for public assistance (Beveridge 1909, 225). Some workers obtained additional sickness insurance by joining more than one friendly society, or by belonging to both a friendly society and a trade union paying sickness benefits.[50]

The combined expenditures of friendly societies and trade unions increased from £2.2 million in 1870 to £4.0 million in 1886 and £9.1 million in 1908 (see Table 3.9). In 1870 spending by friendly societies and trade unions was less than one-half of poor relief expenditures; in 1886 it was 94% of poor relief expenditures, and in 1908 40% greater than poor relief expenditures. In real terms, the expenditures of friendly societies and trade unions in 1908 were 4.5 times greater than in 1870. Meanwhile, the real value of working-class savings deposits, another form of insurance, increased nearly 4.4 times from 1870 to 1908.

The data in Tables 3.6–3.9 show that workers in 1908 were far better able cope with financial insecurity than their grandfathers or great-grandfathers had been; the Victorian self-help movement was a resounding success. And

---

[47] The estimates of average sickness benefits are from Riley (1997, 280–1). Riley states that some societies paid as much as 15s. per week, and Johnson (1985, 61) reckons that the average benefit might have been as high as 14s. in the decade before 1914.

[48] Union benefit levels in 1892 are from *Royal Commission on Labour:, Rules of Associations of Employers and of Employed*, Parliamentary Papers (1892, vol. XXXVI). Benefit levels in 1908 are from Board of Trade, *Report on Trade Unions in 1908–10* (1912, xxxv).

[49] Rowntree (1901, 110) estimated that a minimum necessary food expenditures for a family consisting of husband, wife, and two children was 10.5s. per week in 1899. Minimum expenditures on rent, fuel, clothing, and sundries was 8.33s. Minimum weekly food expenditures for a family with three children was 12.75s.

[50] Rowntree (1901, 356–8) surveyed 400 men with sickness insurance through either a trade union or a friendly society, and found that 185 (46%) belonged to more than one friendly society or to a union and one or more friendly societies. William Allen, the secretary of the Amalgamated Society of Engineers, commented in 1867 that a "great many" members of the union "join other benefit societies . . . in order to have a sufficient amount during illness" (quoted in Boyer 1988, 330).

yet, in the decade before the First World War, Parliament adopted several pieces of social welfare legislation collectively known as the Liberal welfare reforms, which created government programs to provide benefits that large numbers of workers already obtained privately through friendly societies and trade unions. The two major pieces of legislation were the 1908 Old Age Pension Act, and the 1911 National Insurance Act, which established compulsory sickness and unemployment insurance.

IV. THE LIBERAL WELFARE REFORMS AND THE RETURN OF PUBLIC ASSISTANCE

However willing the working classes may be to remain in passive opposition merely to the existing social system, they will not continue to bear, they cannot, the awful uncertainties of their lives. Minimum standards of wages and comfort, insurance in some effective form or other against sickness, unemployment, old age – these are the questions and the only questions by which parties are going to live in the future. (Winston Churchill, letter to editor of the Westminster Review, 1907)[51]

The Liberal welfare reforms represented a major reversal in British social policy after seven decades of increasing stinginess. What led to Parliament's acceptance of social spending and its apparent rejection of the ideology of self-help? The timing of the Liberal welfare reforms can be explained largely by three factors: the increased middle-class knowledge of workers' economic insecurity; the slowdown in economic growth, especially in income growth for low-skilled workers; and the increased political voice of the working class.

Beginning in the 1880s, the British public became increasingly aware that there were gaps in the public–private safety net. The poverty studies by Booth (1888; 1892b) and Rowntree (1901) revealed large numbers of underemployed, sick, and old people living in poverty. They had little or no savings, were not members of friendly societies or trade unions, and did not apply for poor relief, either out of shame or fear of the workhouse.[52] Moreover most of those living in poverty were poor because of economic circumstances rather than personal failure, as many earlier reformers had argued. Booth (1892b, vol. 1, 146–9) concluded that nearly two-thirds of the poor were in poverty because of low wages or lack of work, and only one-seventh were poor because of "questions of habit" – idleness, thriftlessness, or drunkenness. Rowntree (1901, 120) found that 57% of those living in "primary poverty" were poor because of low wages or lack of work, and

---

[51] The quote can be found in Hay (1978, 72).

[52] Booth (1892b, vol. 2, 2–21) estimated that in the late 1880s 8.4% of London's population was very poor and 22.3% was poor, and Rowntree (1901, 111–12) estimated that 9.9% of the population of York was living in "primary" poverty in 1899. In York, 3,451 persons, 4.5% of the population, received poor relief in 1900, less than half of the 7,230 persons estimated to be living in primary poverty (Rowntree 1901, 112, 365–7).

another 21% were poor because of the death, illness, or old age of the household's chief wage earner. He went on to argue that a large share of the working class found themselves in poverty at some point in their lives. In fact, a typical laborer would expect to be in poverty at some point in childhood; in early middle age, when he had three or more children too young to work; and in old age, when he could no longer work (Rowntree 1901, 136–8).

Elderly pauperism rates remained alarmingly high. In 1891–2 nearly 30% of those aged 65 and older received poor relief (Booth 1894). The elderly pauperism rate remained constant from 1892 to 1900 and then declined to 1903, before returning in 1906 to a level slightly above that of 1892 (Boyer and Schmidle 2009). Given the stigma attached to applying for poor relief, it is probable that, on the eve of the adoption of the Old Age Pension Act, one-third or more of those aged 65 and older lived in poverty. The continued high level of pauperism led Booth, Joseph Chamberlain, and leaders of the British labor movement to argue that a large share of the working class could not afford to save for old age (Macnicol 1998; Thane 2000).[53]

Public awareness of unemployment as a "chronic social problem" increased in the late 1880s. The change in public perceptions was influenced by increased agitation by the unemployed, spurred on by socialist groups such as the Social Democratic Federation, which starting in the mid-1880s organized protest marches at times of high unemployment. With each subsequent cyclical downturn (1893–5, 1904–5, 1908–9) unemployment became more of a political issue (Harris 1972). The Royal Poor Law Commission of 1906–09 devoted much attention to unemployment relief, as did the Webbs (1909) in their Minority Report. Most contemporaries were impressed by the trade union unemployment insurance schemes, but in 1908 only 12% of manual workers were eligible for unemployment benefits (Boyer 2004).

One reason for the mounting concerns about unemployment and old-age poverty was the fact that real incomes increased at a much slower rate after 1891 than in previous decades. Real full-time wages of manual workers increased by just 13.6% from 1891–2 to 1911–12 after increasing by 37.9% from 1871–2 to 1891–2 (Feinstein 1995, 264–5).[54] Moreover, there was an upward trend in unemployment; the industrial unemployment rate averaged 6.1% from 1870 to 1891, and 7.2% from 1892 to 1908 (Boyer and Hatton 2002, 662). The pressure on living standards was most severe

---

[53] The Select Committee on Aged Deserving Poor (1899) concluded that large numbers of aged poor people, "whose conduct and whose whole career has been blameless, industrious, and deserving, find themselves from no fault of their own ... with nothing but the workhouse or inadequate out-door relief, as the refuge for their declining years." See *Report from the Select Committee on Aged Deserving Poor*, Parliamentary Papers (1899), Vol. VIII, p. iv.

[54] Even this meager growth was not shared by all sectors. Real wages in agriculture increased by 5.5% from 1891–2 to 1911–12, and in the building trades by only 2.1% (Feinstein 1995, 260–1). Bowley (1937, 30) estimated that real wages of manual workers increased by only 5.4% from 1891–2 to 1911–12.

among low-skilled workers, whose employment opportunities deteriorated both absolutely and relative to those of skilled workers.[55] The increase in unemployment, combined with the slow growth in wage rates for the low-skilled, suggests that those who were most likely to turn to the Poor Law for assistance suffered at best a stagnation of income from 1892 to 1908.

While self-help worked well for those who could save or join friendly societies or trade unions, it remained largely outside the sphere of the bottom third of the income distribution. In 1911, just half of adult males were members of friendly societies or trade unions that offered sickness benefits, and fewer were eligible for old-age benefits. Most working-class households had savings accounts by 1911, but the balances in those accounts were typically quite small. In 1913, 78% of all Post Office Savings Bank accounts had balances of £25 or less (Johnson 1985, 101). The average balance in these accounts was £4.4, which was the equivalent of less than 2.5 weeks' pay for a machinist or a skilled worker in the building trades, and less than four weeks' pay for a police constable or a bricklayer's laborer.[56]

The fact that a significant share of working-class households had little savings and were not members of friendly societies frustrated many middle-class observers, who criticized workers for their "thoughtlessness," "self-indulgence," or "ignorance."[57] However, the low wages of unskilled workers made saving difficult. The average *full-time* earnings of adult male unskilled laborers in 1906 was 21.7s. per week.[58] Rowntree (1901, 110) estimated that in York the minimum necessary expenditure for a family of five (six) in 1899 was 21.67s. (26s.); while Bowley and Burnett-Hurst (1915, 82, 129, 169) estimated that for Reading, Northampton, and Warrington in 1912–13 the required expenditure of a family with three school-aged children was 24.58s.[59] These data suggest that many low-skilled workers had incomes that precluded them from saving much or joining friendly societies.[60]

---

55 See Boyer and Hatton (2002, 659–60). The able-bodied male indoor pauperism rate, a good proxy for unemployment among the bottom decile of the income distribution, increased sharply in London and northern England in the 1890s and the first decade of the 20th century (MacKinnon 1986, 306–7).

56 Wage data for 1912 are from the *Fifteenth Abstract of Labour Statistics* (1912, 52–63).

57 See, for example, the quotes of middle-class observers in Johnson (1985, 217–19).

58 Earnings data are from contemporary Board of Trade earnings reports, summarized in Routh (1980, 112–13).

59 A family consisting of a man, woman, and two children (one aged 5–14, and one under 5), paying 5s. rent, had a minimum necessary weekly expenditure of 21s. (Bowley and Burnett-Hurst 1915, 82). Bowley (1913, 685) estimated that, for Reading in 1912, the minimum necessary weekly expenditure of a family consisting of a husband, wife, and three school-age children, paying rent of 5s., was 24.83s.

60 For young adults, emigration represented another possible response to economic insecurity. Emigration rates from Britain were 50.4 per thousand mean population in the 1870s, 70.2 per thousand in the 1880s, 43.8 per thousand in the 1890s, and 65.3 per thousand in

There were, then, many economic and humanitarian reasons to adopt government social welfare programs and increase social spending at the turn of the century. However, these reasons had existed for several decades without leading to a government response. Indeed, workers' economic insecurity had been greater in 1840 and 1870 than it was in 1908. Public knowledge of the economic plight of low-skilled workers increased in the 1880s and 1890s, but their plight was not unknown to politicians and middle-class reformers earlier. To explain the timing of the Liberal welfare reforms, it is necessary to add a political dimension to the story.

The Role of Political Voice

Lindert (2004, Chapter 4) has argued convincingly that it is not possible to understand the fall and rise of British social welfare spending from 1834 to 1914 without including political voice. During this period, the franchise was extended three times; in 1832, 1867, and 1884. The Great Reform Act of 1832 gave the vote to the middle class, and increased the size of the electorate by nearly 65% (Acemoglu and Robinson 2006, 3). While the landed aristocracy had been sympathetic to poor relief, the newly enfranchised, many of whom were petty capitalists and shopkeepers, were far less enthusiastic. The extension of the franchise to "self-employed males" in 1832 may help account for the sharp decline in real per capita relief spending from 1834 to 1840 and its stagnation for several decades thereafter (Lindert 2004, 71–3, 80–3).

The Second Reform Act of 1867 – Disraeli's "leap in the dark" – granted the vote to all household heads living in boroughs (including a substantial share of urban working-class males), and increased the electorate by 85%.[61] And in 1884 the Third Reform Act extended the franchise to household heads living in the counties, increasing the electorate by a further 88%. The 1884 Act gave most agricultural laborers and coal miners the vote. In 1885,

---

the first decade of the 20th century (Hatton and Williamson 1998, 10). The majority of emigrants were young unskilled or semiskilled workers. Once they were settled in their new homes, many of these emigrants sent remittances back to family members in Britain. Magee and Thompson (2006, 553–4) estimate that from 1875 to 1913, £200 to £270 million (in 1913 £s) were remitted back to the UK. Some unknown share of these remittances went to relatives or friends who were unable to work due to unemployment, sickness, or old age. Indeed it is likely that, for some households, the emigration of a son or daughter with the expectation of remittances in time of need was part of a household strategy for dealing with economic insecurity.

[61] The electorate of the United Kingdom increased from 1,350,000 in 1865 to 2,485,000 in 1868 (Mitchell 1988, 795). The number of voters in English and Welsh boroughs increased by 138% as a result of the Act. In 1871, 44.7% of adult males were on the electoral registers in the boroughs, as compared to 19.7% in 1861 (Hoppen 1998, 253). Lindert (2004, 72) estimates that the share of United Kingdom adult men who had the right to vote increased from 18.0% in 1866 to 31.4% in 1868.

the electorate totaled 5.7 million, or 63% of the adult male population.[62] The Redistribution of Seats Act of 1885 increased the representation of northern cities and created single-member constituencies in both boroughs and counties. Some of the new urban constituencies were "overwhelmingly middle-class or working-class," which encouraged "the development of a class-based electoral system." The Acts of 1884 and 1885 thus produced "a 'mass' electorate . . . in which the traditional parties who ignored the wishes of manual workers would do so at their peril" (Searle 1992, 49–50).

The Liberal Party seemed to most contemporaries to be the logical home of the newly enfranchised workers. However, in the two decades after 1884 the party did not go out of its way to appeal to working-class voters, and it paid a heavy price at the polls. The general elections of 1886, 1895, and 1900 were "resounding Liberal defeats" (Searle 1992, 51). The Conservatives also outpolled the Liberals in the 1892 election, but the Liberals were able to form a minority government with the support of 81 Irish Nationalist MPs. Dissatisfaction with the two major parties by a portion of the working class led in 1893 to the founding of the Independent Labour Party (ILP), which catered directly to working-class interests. In 1900, the ILP merged with other Socialist groups to form the Labour Party, which won two seats in that year's general election.

The 1906 election was a landslide victory for the Liberals, who gained a 143-seat majority over the Conservatives.[63] The election also saw a five-fold increase in the number of votes cast for Labour, and an increase in the number of Labour MPs from 2 to 29 (Craig 1989, 18). The Liberals had not campaigned for the adoption of social welfare policies, as had the Labour Party. Its 1906 election manifesto stated that underfed schoolchildren, the aged poor, and the unemployed had been neglected by Parliament. The manifesto ended with an appeal to workers: "you have it in your power to see that Parliament carries out your wishes" (Dale 2000, 10–11).

The rise of Labour worried the Liberal leadership. In 1908, with the Liberals' popularity declining as a result of rising unemployment, Campbell-Bannerman resigned as Prime Minister and was replaced by Herbert Asquith, who appointed Winston Churchill to the Presidency of the Board of Trade and made David Lloyd George Chancellor of the Exchequer. With these changes, "the tempo of reform dramatically quickened" (Searle 2004, 366). Churchill, Lloyd George, and other "New Liberals" strongly supported social welfare programs on national efficiency, humanitarian, and political grounds. They believed that the adoption of old age pensions and national sickness and unemployment insurance would appeal to working-class voters

---

[62] The United Kingdom electorate increased by nearly 2.7 million from 1880 to 1885 (Mitchell 1988, 795).

[63] The Liberals won 399 seats in Parliament, compared to 156 for the Conservatives and Liberal Unionists. The total number of seats was 670.

and therefore slow the growth of the Labour Party. In October 1906, Lloyd George stated that, if the Liberal Parliament would do something "to remove the national degradation of slums and widespread poverty and destitution" and would provide "an honourable sustenance for deserving old age," then "the Independent Labour party will call in vain upon the working men of Britain to desert Liberalism that is so gallantly fighting to rid the land of the wrongs that have oppressed those who labour in it" (Lloyd George 1910, 36–9). In a letter to his brother in 1908, he wrote that the Old Age Pension Act before Parliament would appeal "straight to the people" and thus "help to stop the electoral rot" (George 1958, 220). Churchill agreed. He wrote to the Prime Minister in December 1908 that a program of national sickness and unemployment insurance "would not only benefit the state but fortify the party" (Churchill 1969, 862–4).

Under the leadership of Lloyd George and Churchill, the Old Age Pension Act was adopted in 1908 and the National Insurance Act (which established compulsory sickness and unemployment insurance) in 1911. These Acts significantly extended the government safety net, and reduced economic insecurity for workers and their families. The number of pension recipients turned out to be far greater than the government had anticipated. In March 1909, 393,700 persons, or 37% of those aged 70 and over, received a pension; and in March 1911, after the Poor Law disqualification was abolished, the number of pension recipients increased to 613,873.[64] Government spending on old age pensions totaled £5.2 million in 1910, and £8.3 million in 1913 (see Table 3.9, column 6). The ratio of spending by friendly societies and trade unions to government social welfare spending fell from 1.4 in 1908 to 0.7 in 1913.[65]

The Liberal welfare reforms did not, however, have the political effects that Lloyd George and Churchill had hoped to achieve. While old age pensions, which were non-contributory, were "immensely popular" with the working class, national insurance, which was contributory and required deductions from workers' wages, was far less popular, at least in the short run.[66] Rising class tensions after 1910 also hurt the Liberal Party's popularity with the working class. During the "Great Labour Unrest" of 1910–14 there were 4,658 industrial disputes, involving the loss of nearly 92.3 million working days. Aggregate trade union membership increased by 67%

---

[64] Data on the number of pension recipients are from the Board of Trade, *Seventeenth Abstract of Labour Statistics* (1915, 184).

[65] I am defining government social welfare spending to equal poor relief spending plus spending on old age pensions. I have not been able to determine the total governmental spending on sickness and unemployment benefits in 1913. Adding these to government social welfare spending would reduce the ratio for 1913 below 0.7.

[66] Roberts (1990, 84) relates that old people spending their pension allowance at his family's shop in Salford "would bless the name of Lloyd George as if he were a saint from heaven."

during these years, from 2.48 million in 1909 to 4.15 million in 1914.[67] The industrial unrest and growth in union membership increased the militancy of the Labour Party (Searle 1992, 112–20). There was "a growing feeling in the country that the Liberal Party was no longer the party of the working classes, but that in some perceived if indefinable way the Labour Party was" (McKibbin (1974, 70–1). While the First World War postponed the rise of Labour, in the general election of 1918 the Labour party polled nearly 2.25 million votes, just 540,000 fewer than the Liberals. In 1924, by which time Churchill had returned to the Conservative Party, Labour outpolled the Liberals by over 2.5 million votes. The Liberals won only 40 seats in the 1924 general election, and effectively were finished as a major party.

In sum, the adoption of the Liberal welfare reforms was due in large measure to the extension of the franchise in 1867 and 1884 and the subsequent rise of the Labour Party. The new social transfer programs represented, at least in part, an attempt by the Liberal Party to win votes by appealing to recently enfranchised working-class voters. Unfortunately for the Liberals, the reforms did not in fact "stop the electoral rot." Most working-class voters believed their interests would be better served by a working-class party than by a middle-class party catering to the working-class (Searle 1992, 68–76).

The Liberal welfare reforms marked the beginning of an era of increasing social transfer spending in Britain. The 1918 Representation of the People Act extended the franchise to nearly all males aged 21 and over and to most women over 30, and increased the electorate by 175%. In 1928 the voting age for women was reduced to 21. The 1920s saw a rapid growth in social spending. The Unemployment Insurance Act of 1920 extended compulsory unemployment insurance to virtually all workers except the self-employed and those in agriculture or domestic service. The generosity and maximum duration of benefits were raised at various points during the decade. The 1925 Widows', Orphans' and Old Age Contributory Pensions Act provided insured workers and their wives with a weekly pension after age 65; the act also established benefits for widows and children under age 14. Housing Acts of 1919, 1923, and 1924 provided subsidies for the construction of low-cost housing. Overall, social transfer spending increased from 1.0% of GDP in 1900 to 2.24% of GDP in 1930 (Lindert 2004, 12–13).

V. CONCLUSION

Insecurity of income was a reality of working-class life throughout the nineteenth century, but the strategies for dealing with it underwent a major shift from 1830 to 1900. During the first third of the nineteenth century, workers relied heavily on the Poor Law. The Poor Law Amendment Act of 1834,

---

[67] Data on industrial disputes are from Mitchell (1988, 142–4). Data on union membership are from Bain and Price (1980, 37).

however, reduced the appeal of poor relief and led to an increase in private saving and friendly societies. This shift toward self-help was accelerated by the Crusade Against Outrelief of the 1870s and by the sharp increase in real wages in the second half of the century. By the beginning of the twentieth century, the ideology of self-help was well entrenched in working-class culture. Still, up to a third of working-class households had incomes that were too low to enable them to join friendly societies.

The history of government social welfare spending from 1800 to 1913 was not a "unilinear progression in collective benevolence" from poor relief to national insurance (Titmuss 1958, 34). The role played by the Poor Law in assisting the needy was greater in the period 1795 to 1834 than at any time during Queen Victoria's reign. The prototype for the Liberal welfare reforms cannot be found in the Victorian Poor Law – there is no support for a "Whig theory of welfare" (Rose 1981, 52).

Engerman and Sokoloff (2005, 908) contend that changing the composition of the electorate can fundamentally affect "the types of policies adopted by the elected representatives," and Lindert (2004) has shown that in order to understand the fall and subsequent rise in social spending from 1834 to 1913 it is necessary to take into account changes in the British electorate. The extension of the franchise in 1832 to lower middle class males – who were more interested in keeping their tax rates low than they were in assisting the poor, most of whom they believed to be "undeserving" – helped lead to the decline in social spending in early Victorian Britain. However, the granting of the vote to urban and then rural household heads in 1867 and 1884 gave political voice to a large share of the working class and led to the formation of the Labour Party in the 1890s. The welfare reforms of 1906–11 were, in part, an attempt to win working-class support. While they were unsuccessful at slowing the growth of the Labour Party, the Liberal welfare reforms significantly reduced workers' financial insecurity, and paved the way for the rise of the welfare state in the 1940s.

References

Official Publication

Great Britain, Board of Trade. 1887. *Statistical Tables and Report on Trade Unions.* London: HMSO.

Great Britain, Board of Trade. 1893. *Seventh Annual Report on Trade Unions.* London: HMSO.

Great Britain, Board of Trade. 1900. *Sixth Abstract of Labour Statistics of the United Kingdom.* London: HMSO.

Great Britain, Board of Trade. 1907. *Eleventh Abstract of Labour Statistics of the United Kingdom, 1905–06.* London: HMSO.

Great Britain, Board of Trade. 1910. *Earnings and Hours of Labour of Workpeople of the United Kingdom. III. – Building and Woodworking Trades in 1906.* London: HMSO.

Great Britain, Board of Trade. 1912. *Fifteenth Abstract of Labour Statistics of the United Kingdom*. London: HMSO.

Great Britain, Board of Trade. 1912. *Report on Trade Unions in 1908–10*. London: HMSO.

Great Britain, Board of Trade. 1915. *Seventeenth Abstract of Labour Statistics of the United Kingdom*. London: HMSO.

Great Britain, Parliamentary Papers. 1837–38, XXVIII. *Fourth Annual Report of the Poor Law Commissioners for England and Wales*.

Great Britain, Parliamentary Papers. 1874, XXIII. *Fourth Report of the Royal Commission Friendly and Benefit Building Societies*.

Great Britain, Parliamentary Papers. 1892, XXXVI. *Royal Commission on Labour: Rules of Associations of Employers and of Employed*.

Great Britain, Parliamentary Papers. 1893–4. *Royal Commission on Labour: Minutes of Evidence*.

Great Britain, Parliamentary Papers. 1895, XIV. *Report of the Royal Commission on the Aged Poor*.

Great Britain, Parliamentary Papers. 1899, VIII. *Report from the Select Committee on Aged Deserving Poor*.

Great Britain, Parliamentary Papers. 1905, LXXXIV. *British and Foreign Trade and Industrial Conditions*.

Great Britain, Parliamentary Papers. 1910, XLIX. *Minutes of Evidence . . . of Witnesses further relating to the subject of Unemployment* (Appendix volume IX of the Royal Commission on the Poor Laws and Relief of Distress).

Great Britain, Parliamentary Papers. 1910, LIII. *Statistics relating to England and Wales* (Appendix volume XXV of the Royal Commission on the Poor Laws and Relief of Distress).

Other References

Acemoglu, Daron and James A. Robinson. 2006. *Economic Origins of Dictatorship and Democracy*. Cambridge: Cambridge University Press.

Bain, George S. and Robert Price. 1980. *Profiles of Union Growth: A Comparative Statistical Portrait of Eight Countries*. Oxford: Basil Blackwell.

Baxter, R. Dudley. 1868. *National Income. The United Kingdom*. London: Macmillan.

Bell, Lady Florence. 1907. *At the Works: A Study of a Manufacturing Town*. London: Edward Arnold.

Beveridge, William H. 1909. *Unemployment: A Problem of Industry*. London: Longmans.

Beveridge, William H. 1948. *Voluntary Action: A Report on Methods of Social Advance*. London: Macmillan.

Blaug, Mark. 1964. "The Poor Law Report Reexamined." *Journal of Economic History* 24: 229–45.

Boot, H. M. 1990. "Unemployment and Poor Law Relief in Manchester, 1845–50." *Social History* 15: 217–28.

Booth, Charles. 1888. "Condition and Occupations of the People of East London and Hackney, 1887." *Journal of the Royal Statistical Society* 51: 276–339.

Booth, Charles. 1892a. "The Inaugural Address of Charles Booth, Esq., President of the Royal Statistical Society. Session 1892–93. Delivered 15th November, 1892." *Journal of the Royal Statistical Society* 55: 521–57.

Booth, Charles. 1892b. *Life and Labour of the People in London.* 2 Volumes. London: Macmillan.

Booth, Charles. 1894. *The Aged Poor in England and Wales.* London: Macmillan.

Booth, Charles. 1899. "Poor Law Statistics as Used in Connection with the Old Age Pension Question." *Economic Journal* 9: 212–23.

Bowley, A. L. 1913. "Working-Class Households in Reading." *Journal of the Royal Statistical Society* 76: 672–701.

Bowley, A. L. 1937. *Wages and Income in the United Kingdom since 1860.* Cambridge: Cambridge University Press.

Bowley, A. L. and A. R. Burnett-Hurst. 1915. *Livelihood and poverty: A study in the economic conditions of working-class households in Northampton, Warrington, Stanley and Reading.* London: G. Bell & Sons.

Boyer, George R. 1988. "What Did Unions Do in Nineteenth Century Britain?" *Journal of Economic History* 48: 319–32.

Boyer, George R. 1990. *An Economic History of the English Poor Law, 1750–1850.* Cambridge: Cambridge University Press.

Boyer, George R. 2002. "English Poor Laws." In Robert Whaples, ed., *EH.Net Encyclopedia.*

Boyer, George R. 2004. "The Evolution of Unemployment Relief in Great Britain." *Journal of Interdisciplinary History* 34: 393–433.

Boyer, George R. and Timothy J. Hatton. 2002. "New Estimates of British Unemployment, 1870–1913." *Journal of Economic History* 62: 643–75.

Boyer, George R. and Timothy Schmidle. 2009. "Poverty among the Elderly in Late Victorian England." *Economic History Review*, forthcoming.

Churchill, Randolph S. 1969. *Winston S. Churchill. Companion Volume II, Part 2 1907–1911. Young Statesman.* Boston: Houghton Mifflin.

Craig, F. W. S. 1989. *British Electoral Facts 1832–1987.* Aldershot, UK: Parliamentary Research Services.

Dale, Iain. 2000. *Labour Party General Election Manifestos, 1900–1997.* London: Routledge.

Dearle, Norman B. 1908. *Problems of Unemployment in the London Building Trades.* London: J. M. Dent.

Digby, Anne. 1975. "The Labour Market and the Continuity of Social Policy after 1834: The Case of the Eastern Counties." *Economic History Review* 28: 69–83.

Engerman, Stanley. 1994. "Reflections on 'The Standard of Living Debate': New Arguments and New Evidence." In John A. James, J. and Mark Thomas, eds., *Capitalism in Context.* Chicago: University of Chicago Press, pp. 50–79.

Engerman, Stanley. 1997. "The Standard of Living Debate in International Perspective: Measures and Indicators." In Richard H. Steckel and Roderick Floud, eds., *Health and Welfare during Industrialization.* Chicago: University of Chicago Press, pp. 17–45.

Engerman, Stanley and Claudia Goldin. 1994. "Seasonality in Nineteenth-Century Labor Markets." In Thomas Weiss and Donald Schaefer, eds., *American Economic Development in Historical Perspective.* Stanford: Stanford University Press, pp. 99–126.

Engerman, Stanley and Kenneth L. Sokoloff. 2005. "The Evolution of Suffrage Institutions in the New World." *Journal of Economic History* 65: 891–921.

Feinstein, C. H. 1972. *National income, expenditure and output of the United Kingdom, 1855–1965.* Cambridge: Cambridge University Press.

Feinstein, C. H. 1995. "Changes in Nominal Wages, the Cost of Living and Real Wages in the United Kingdom over Two Centuries, 1780–1990." In Peter Scholliers and Vera Zamagni, eds., *Labour's Reward: Real wages and economic change in 19th- and 20th-century Europe.* Aldershot, UK: Edward Elgar, pp. 3–36.

Feinstein, C. H. 1998. "Pessimism Perpetuated, Real Wages and the Standard of Living in Britain during and after the Industrial Revolution." *Journal of Economic History* 58: 625–58.

Fishlow, Albert. 1961. "The Trustee Savings Banks, 1817–1861." *Journal of Economic History* 21: 26–40.

Floud, Roderick. 1997. *The People and the British Economy 1830–1914.* Oxford: Oxford University Press.

Gazeley, Ian. 2003. *Living Standards and Poverty in Britain, 1900–1960.* Basingstoke, UK: Palgrave Macmillan.

George, William. 1958. *My Brother and I.* London: Eyre and Spottiswoode.

Gilbert, Bentley B. 1966. *The Evolution of National Insurance in Great Britain: the Origins of the Welfare State.* London: Joseph.

Gosden, P. H. J. H. 1961. *The friendly societies in England, 1815–1875.* Manchester: Manchester University Press.

Gosden, P. H. J. H. 1973. *Self-Help: Voluntary Associations in the 19th Century.* London: B. T. Batsford.

Gorsky, Martin. 1998. "The Growth and Distribution of English Friendly Societies in the Early Nineteenth Century." *Economic History Review* 51: 489–511.

Harris, José. 1972. *Unemployment and Politics 1886–1914.* Oxford: Clarendon Press.

Hartwell, R. M. and Stanley Engerman. 1975. "Models of Immiseration: The Theoretical Basis of Pessimism." In A. J. Taylor, ed., *The Standard of Living in Britain in the Industrial Revolution.* London: Methuen, pp. 189–213.

Hatton, Timothy J. and Jeffrey G. Williamson. 1998. *The Age of Mass Migration.* Oxford: Oxford University Press.

Hay, J. R. 1978. *The Development of the British Welfare State, 1880–1975.* London: Edward Arnold.

Hobsbawm, Eric. 1975. *The Age of Capital, 1848–1875.* London: Weidenfeld and Nicolson.

Hopkins, Eric. 1995. *Working-class Self-help in Nineteenth Century England: Responses to Industrialization.* New York: St. Martin's Press.

Hoppen, K. Theodore. 1998. *The Mid-Victorian Generation 1846–1886.* Oxford: Clarendon Press.

Humphreys, Robert. 1995. *Sin, Organized Charity and the Poor Law in Victorian England.* New York: St. Martin's Press.

Hunt, E. H. 1981. *British Labour History, 1815–1914.* London: Weidenfeld and Nicolson.

Johnson, Paul. 1985. *Saving and Spending: The Working-Class Economy in Britain 1870–1939.* Oxford: Clarendon Press.

Johnson, Paul. 1993. "Small Debts and Economic Distress in England and Wales, 1857–1913." *Economic History Review* 46: 65–87.

Jones, Gareth Stedman. 1971. *Outcast London: A Study in the Relationship between Classes in Victorian Society.* Oxford: Clarendon Press.

Keyssar, Alexander. 1986. *Out of Work: The First Century of Unemployment in Massachusetts.* Cambridge: Cambridge University Press.

King, Steven. 2000. *Poverty and Welfare in England, 1700–1850: A Regional Perspective.* Manchester: Manchester University Press.

King, Steven and Alannah Tomkins. 2003. "Conclusion." In Steven King and Alannah Tomkins, eds., *The Poor in England, 1700–1850: An Economy of Makeshifts.* Manchester: Manchester University Press, pp. 258–79.

Lee, C. H. 1979. *British Regional Employment Statistics, 1841–1971.* Cambridge: Cambridge University Press.

Lees, Lynn Hollen. 1998. *The Solidarities of Strangers: The English Poor Laws and the People, 1700–1948.* Cambridge: Cambridge University Press.

Lindert, Peter H. 1994. "The Rise of Social Spending, 1880–1930." *Explorations in Economic History* 31: 1–37.

Lindert, Peter H. 1998. "Poor Relief before the Welfare State: Britain versus the Continent, 1780–1880." *European Review of Economic History* 2: 101–40.

Lindert, Peter H. 2004. *Growing Public, Social Spending and Economic Growth Since the Eighteenth Century. Volume 1, The Story.* Cambridge: Cambridge University Press.

Lindert, Peter H. and Jeffrey G. Williamson. 1983. "English Workers' Living Standards during the Industrial Revolution: A New Look." *Economic History Review* 36: 1–25.

Lloyd George, David. 1910. *Better Times: Speeches by the Right Hon. D. Lloyd George.* London: Hodder and Stoughton.

MacKinnon, Mary. 1986. "Poor Law Policy, Unemployment, and Pauperism." *Explorations in Economic History* 23: 299–336.

MacKinnon, Mary. 1987. "English Poor Law Policy and the Crusade against Outrelief." *Journal of Economic History* 47: 603–25.

Macnicol, John. 1998. *The Politics of Retirement in Britain, 1878–1948.* Cambridge: Cambridge University Press.

Magee, Gary B. and Andrew S. Thompson. 2006. "'Lines of Credit, Debts of Obligation': Migrant Remittances to Britain, c. 1875–1913." *Economic History Review* 59: 539–77.

McKibbin, Ross. 1974. *The Evolution of the Labour Party 1910–1924.* Oxford: Oxford University Press.

Mitchell, Brian R. 1988. *British Historical Statistics.* Cambridge: Cambridge University Press.

Money, L. G. Chiozza. 1912. *Insurance versus Poverty.* London: Methuen.

Neave, David. 1996. "Friendly Societies in Great Britain." In Marcel van der Linden, ed., *Social Security Mutualism: The Comparative History of Mutual Benefit Societies.* Bern: Peter Lang, pp. 41–64.

Neison, Francis G. P. 1877. "Some Statistics of the Affiliated Orders of Friendly Societies (Odd Fellows and Foresters)." *Journal of the Statistical Society of London* 40: 42–89.

Pember Reeves, Maud. 1913. *Round About a Pound a Week*. London: G. Bell & Sons.

Perkin, Harold. 1969. *The Origins of Modern English Society, 1780–1880*. London: Routledge & Kegan Paul.

Pollard, Sidney. 1954. "Wages and Earnings in the Sheffield Trades, 1851–1914." *Yorkshire Bulletin of Economic and Social Research* 6: 49–64.

Popplewell, Frank. 1912. "The Gas Industry." In Sidney Webb and Arnold Freeman, eds., *Seasonal Trades*. London: Constable & Co., pp. 148–209.

Porter, J. H. 1970. "Wage Bargaining under Conciliation Agreements, 1860–1914." *Economic History Review* 23: 466–75.

Poyntz, Juliet Stuart. 1912. "Introduction: Seasonal Trades." In Sidney Webb and Arnold Freeman, eds., *Seasonal Trades*. London: Constable & Co., pp. 1–69.

Preston, Samuel H., Nathan Keyfitz, and Robert Schoen. 1972. *Causes of Death: Life Tables for National Populations*. New York: Academic Press.

Quadagno, Jill. 1982. *Aging in Early Industrial Society: Work, Family, and Social Policy in Nineteenth-Century England*. New York: Academic Press.

Riley, James C. 1997. *Sick, Not Dead: The Health of British Workingmen during the Mortality Decline*. Baltimore: Johns Hopkins University Press.

Roberts, Robert. 1990. *The Classic Slum: Salford Life in the First Quarter of the Century*. London: Penguin Books.

Rose, Michael E. 1965. The Administration of Poor Relief in the West Riding of Yorkshire c. 1820–1855. D. Phil. Thesis, Oxford University.

Rose, Michael E. 1970. "The New Poor Law in an Industrial Area." In R. M. Hartwell, ed., *The Industrial Revolution*. Oxford: Oxford University Press, pp. 121–43.

Rose, Michael E. 1971. *The English Poor Law 1780–1930*. Newton Abbot: David & Charles.

Rose, Michael E. 1981. "The Crisis of Poor Relief in England, 1860–1890." In W. J. Mommsen, ed., *The Emergence of the Welfare State in Britain and Germany, 1850–1950*. London: Croom Helm.

Rostow, W. W. 1948. *British Economy of the Nineteenth Century*. Oxford: Clarendon Press.

Routh, Guy. 1980. *Occupation and Pay in Great Britain, 1906–79*. London: Macmillan.

Rowntree, B. S. 1901. *Poverty: A Study of Town Life*. London: Macmillan.

Searle, G. R. 1992. *The Liberal Party: Triumph and Disintegration, 1886–1929*. New York: St. Martin's Press.

Searle, G. R. 2004. *A New England?: Peace and War 1886–1918*. Oxford: Clarendon Press.

Smiles, Samuel. 1866 [2002]. *Self-Help: With Illustrations of Character, Conduct, and Perseverance*. Oxford: Oxford University Press.

Sokoloff, Kenneth L. and David Dollar. 1997. "Agricultural Seasonality and the Organization of Manufacturing in Early Industrial Economies: The Contrast between England and the United States." *Journal of Economic History* 57: 288–321.

Southall, Humphrey R. 1986. "Regional Unemployment Patterns among Skilled Engineers in Britain, 1851–1914." *Journal of Historical Geography* 12: 268–86.

Southall, Humphrey R. 1988. "The Origins of the Depressed Areas: Unemployment, Growth, and Regional Economic Structure in Britain before 1914." *Economic History Review* 41: 236–58.

Southall, Humphrey R. 1998. "The Economics of Mutuality: An analysis of trade union welfare systems in 19th century Britain." Unpublished manuscript.

Supple, Barry. 1974. "Legislation and Virtue: An Essay on Working Class Self-Help and the State in the Early Nineteenth Century." In Neil McKendrick, ed., *Historical Perspectives, Studies in English Thought and Society*. London: Europa, pp. 211–54.

Thane, Pat. 2000. *Old Age in English History: Past Experiences, Present Issues*. Oxford: Oxford University Press.

Titmus, Richard M. 1958. *Essays on 'The Welfare State'*. London: George Allen and Unwin.

Treble, John G. 1987. "Sliding Scales and Conciliation Boards: Risk-Sharing in the Late 19th Century British Coal Industry." *Oxford Economic Papers* 39: 679–98.

Tressell, Robert. 1955 [2005]. *The Ragged Trousered Philanthropists*. Oxford: Oxford University Press.

Webb, Augustus D. 1912. "The Building Trade." In Sidney Webb and Arnold Freeman, eds., *Seasonal Trades*. London: Constable & Co., pp. 312–93.

Webb, Sidney and Beatrice Webb. 1897. *Industrial Democracy*. London: Longmans, Green.

Webb, Sidney and Beatrice Webb. 1909. *The Minority Report of the Poor Law Commission. Part II: The Public Organization of the Labour Market*. London: Longmans, Green & Co.

Wilkinson, J. Frome. 1891. *Mutual Thrift*. London: Methuen.

Williams, Karel. 1981. *From Pauperism to Poverty*. London: Routledge & Kegan Paul.

Wood, George H. 1901. "Stationary Wage-Rates." *Economic Journal* 11: 151–56.

PART II

INSTITUTIONS AND SCHOOLING

4

The Evolution of Schooling in the Americas, 1800–1925

Stanley L. Engerman, Elisa V. Mariscal,
and Kenneth L. Sokoloff

The importance of institutions in economic growth has come to be more fully appreciated in recent years, and schools are widely acknowledged as among the most fundamental of such institutions. Levels of schooling and literacy have been related theoretically as well as empirically to labor productivity, technological change, and rates of commercial and political participation. It is well understood, moreover, that in addition to promoting growth, education institutions can have a powerful influence on the distribution of their benefits through providing avenues for individuals to realize upward mobility.[1] Despite these reasons why the substantial differences in the prevalence of schooling and literacy across countries may have been important contributors to disparities in their patterns of economic growth, we lack a basic understanding of how these differences first emerged and evolved over time.

---

[1] For discussion of the importance of institutions generally in growth, see North (1981). For seminal discussions of the importance of schooling and literacy, see Schultz (1963) and Easterlin (1981). For recent studies similar in spirit to our own, in terms of trying to understand what accounts for the variation in the establishment of public schools and other public goods, see Goldin (1998); Goldin and Katz (1997a, 1997b, and 2008); Alesina, Baqir, and Easterly (1999) and Go and Lindert (2007).

We would like to express deep appreciation for the help of our research assistants Patricia Juarez, Luis Zegarra, and Leah Brooks. We have also benefited from discussions with Stephen Haber, Daron Acemoglu, Sam Bowles, Gregory Clark, Gerardo della Paolera, David Dollar, David Eltis, Claudia Goldin, Aurora Gomez, Karla Hoff, Estelle James, Lawrence Katz, Zorina Khan, Elizabeth King, Naomi Lamoreaux, Frank Lewis, Peter Lindert, Nora Lustig, Douglass North, James Robinson, Jean-Laurent Rosenthal, Mary Shirley, Federico Sturzenegger, William Summerhill, Alan Taylor, Mariano Tommasi, Miguel Urquiola, John Wallis, and participants in seminars at the NBER and an All-UC Conference in Economic History held at UC Davis. We gratefully acknowledge financial support from the National Science Foundation, as well as from the Academic Senate and International Studies and Overseas Programs at the University of California at Los Angeles.

The New World is ideal for studying investment in schooling and literacy, because many of the societies arising out of European colonization were sufficiently prosperous by the early nineteenth century to support the broad establishment of institutions of primary education.[2] Only a relatively small number, however, made such investments on a scale sufficient to serve the general population before the twentieth century. At a general level, such contrasts in institutional development across the Americas have often been attributed to differences in wealth, national heritage, culture, or religion, but systematic comparative studies are rare.[3] Even those that have been conducted confine their focus to cross-sectional variation in the contemporary world and neglect how the institutions developed over the long run.

One striking feature of the development of education institutions in the Americas is the major investment in primary education made by the United States and Canada early in their histories. Virtually from the time of initial settlement, residents in mainland North America above the Rio Grande seem generally to have been convinced of the value of providing their children with a basic education, including the ability to read and write; and they established schools to accomplish that goal. In colonial New England, schooling was frequently organized at the village or town level, and funded through a variety of sources: charity, lotteries, sales of public lands, and license fees for dogs, taverns, marriages, traders in slaves, as well as the so-called "rate bill" – whereby all but designated paupers would be charged when they had children enrolled. Instruction by family members, neighbors, or private tutors often filled in where formal schools were not convenient or available. The United States had probably the most literate population in the world by the beginning of the nineteenth century, but the "common school movement," getting under way in the 1820s, put the country on a new path of investment in education institutions. Between 1821 and 1871 nearly every northern state enacted a law strongly encouraging or requiring localities to establish "free schools," open to all children and supported by general taxes, although various localities had previously introduced the practice.[4] Although the movement made slower progress in the South, schooling had spread sufficiently by the middle of the nineteenth century that more than 40 percent of the school-age population in the United States overall was enrolled, and nearly 90 percent of white adults were literate. In early-nineteenth-century Canada schools were also common, and even though this northernmost English colony lagged behind the United

---

[2] Engerman and Sokoloff (1997 and 2002). Literacy refers to the ability to read and/or write at an adequate level. This, of course, means that standards may vary over time and place.

[3] For a comparative approach to the study of the rise of social spending in OECD countries, see Lindert (1994), and for a detailed study of Latin America, see Ramirez and Salazar (2008).

[4] See Goldin and Katz (2008, 139–146), particulary Table 4.1.

States by several decades in establishing tax-supported primary schools with universal access, its literacy rates were nearly as high.

The rest of the hemisphere trailed far behind the United States and Canada in education and literacy. Although municipal and state (or provincial) governments were virtually everywhere granted the authority to establish schools and to levy taxes to mobilize resources on their behalf, few were effective at doing so, except in these two northern countries. Public schools were thus exceedingly rare elsewhere in the Americas, and parents who sought primary education for their children had to rely largely on private classes until late in the nineteenth century, when some national governments began to promote the expansion of public education. For example, despite enormous wealth, the British colonies in the Caribbean basin were very slow to organize schooling institutions that would serve broad segments of the population. It was not until emancipation, when the British Colonial Office took a direct interest in the promotion of schooling, perhaps inspired by the movements to increase support for public schools in Britain itself, that significant steps were taken in this direction. Even Argentina and Uruguay, the most progressive of the Latin American countries, were more than 75 years behind the United States and Canada in providing wide access to primary schooling and attaining high levels of literacy. Most of Latin America was unable to achieve these standards until well into the twentieth century, if then.

This relative backwardness in the organization of institutions of primary education could well have had a significant impact on the long-run development of these other nations of the Americas, and thus the question of what accounts for this pattern is especially intriguing. Differences in the resources available to invest in schooling, as reflected in say per capita income, is perhaps the first possibility that comes to mind in explaining why the rest of the hemisphere lagged behind the United States and Canada; however these countries do not appear to have been much advantaged in that dimension at the time they began to move ahead in the promotion of education. Religion is another potentially significant factor, and some have suggested that societies in which Catholics predominated may have been slow to invest in public schools, either because the Church valued education, at least for ordinary people, less than their Protestant counterparts, or because the Church stifled individual or community initiatives to organize private or public schools. Although plausible and consistent with the greater prominence of Catholicism in Latin America, this view has to contend with the relatively high levels of schooling and literacy in French Canada, as well as the modest levels among the British (and largely Protestant) colonies in the Caribbean basin.

A third possibility is that differences in ethnicity or national heritage played an important role in determining which societies made major investments in schooling early in the process of development and which did not.

This sort of explanation encompasses arguments that Native Americans did not consider the establishment of schools an attractive use of resources because of the association of schooling with western ways of thinking, or that populations with English backgrounds had a greater appreciation for education than those of Spanish descent. Yet another possibility is that the long tradition of centralized structures of government in Latin America countries may have impeded the organization of schools on a widespread basis. For example, local or provincial governments may have been more constrained in carrying out such initiatives in Spanish America than elsewhere, even though they had similar legal authority.

Another hypothesis is that the long-standing greater degree of inequality in Latin America, as compared to the United States or Canada, played a role in explaining the differential record in establishing educational institutions. Several mechanisms could have led extreme levels of inequality to depress investments in schooling institutions. First, in a setting where private schooling predominated, or where parents paid school user fees, greater wealth or income inequality would generally reduce the fraction of the school-age population enrolled. Second, greater inequality may also have exacerbated the collective action problems associated with the establishment and funding of universal public schools, because the distribution of benefits across the population would be quite different from the incidence of taxes and other costs, or because population heterogeneity made it more difficult for communities to reach consensus on public projects. Given that early public schooling systems were almost universally organized and managed at the local level, these problems may have been especially relevant. Where the wealthy enjoyed disproportionate political power, elites could procure schooling for their own children, and resist being taxed to underwrite or subsidize services to others.[5] Extreme inequality in wealth or income might also lead to low levels of schooling on a national basis if it were associated with substantial disparities across communities or geographic areas. As long as schools had to be supported by local resources, poor districts might not have been able to sustain an extensive system of primary education. Only the populations of wealthy districts, presumably small in number, would then have easy access to schooling.

Our original motivation for undertaking this comparative examination was an interest in whether and how the extreme differences across countries in the extent of inequality in wealth, human capital, and political power that emerged early in their histories might have influenced the evolution of education institutions, and thus their paths of development over time. Indeed, this concern with the impact and persistence of the extreme inequality

---

[5] Acemoglu and Robinson (2000) argue that the increase in the equality of political power associated with the extension of the franchise led to increased funding for public schools in a number of European countries.

characterizing much of the New World is largely responsible for the organization of the paper. In the next two sections, we survey the record of schooling and literacy in the Americas, highlighting salient patterns and discussing the general consistency of the history with some of the explanations for divergence that have been suggested. In the fourth section we systematically examine the evidence, and find that, although investment in schooling is strongly and positively correlated with per capita income over time and across countries, much variation remains to be explained. Moreover, the extent of inequality in political power, as reflected in the proportion of the population who can vote, does seem to be associated with lower literacy and schooling rates. Although the comparison between the experiences of the United States and Canada with those of other countries in the hemisphere serves as our reference point, we are also concerned with the variation within the latter group. Argentina, Uruguay, Cuba, Costa Rica, Chile, and Barbados may have lagged behind the United States and Canada, but they made earlier and greater progress at educating their populations than did their neighbors. Other explanations for the variation across the Americas in levels of investment in education may ultimately prove as powerful as ones derived from differences in the degree of inequality, but this comparative examination should nevertheless help improve our understanding of the differential paths of development observed in the New World. Whatever tended to reduce or delay investments in schooling institutions fostered inequality in the distribution of human capital, and likely retarded long run economic growth.

II

It was not long after the Europeans established permanent settlements on the northern part of the North American mainland that they began to organize schools. Foremost among them were primary schools for local children that communities administered and supported. Massachusetts is frequently celebrated as the leader, but other colonies in New England conceded little in their enthusiasm for basic and widespread education.[6] Indeed, all of the region's states had made some provision for public education by 1800, generally requiring towns beyond a certain size to support a primary or grammar school. Despite resistance to the levying of school taxes slowing the responses to these government initiatives, New Englanders already enjoyed relatively broad access to primary education and had attained high rates of literacy through a combination of local public schools, private institutions, and home instruction. Elsewhere in the United States, schooling was not so widespread. Private schools generally predominated in the Middle Atlantic and the South. Until the early 1800s, few governments in these regions, aside

---

[6] The classic source on the early history of schooling is Cubberley (1920).

from New York, went beyond requiring public schooling to be provided to the children of paupers. Access to schools was especially limited in the South, even among the white population.

A major breakthrough in the expansion of schooling occurred during the second quarter of the nineteenth century with a series of political battles, known as the "common school movement," for tax-supported, locally controlled "free" schools, that took place throughout the country. Such schools were to be open to all, supported primarily through local taxes (though often receiving some aid from state governments), and managed by local authorities (with state-appointed officers typically providing some oversight to the multitude of local school systems that operated within the respective states). The movement is usually dated as beginning about 1821 and ending about 1871, by which time virtually every northern state had passed and implemented laws to encourage townships or counties to establish common schools.

This fifty year period was marked by intense political struggles in state after state, with especially strong support for free schools coming from urban dwellers, members of labor organizations, and residents of western states – reflecting the general drive for democratization that occurred during the Jacksonian era. Opposition is said to have come from religious and private-school interests as well as from the wealthier classes who might have expected to bear a disproportionate increase in taxes.[7] Entirely free schools emerged only gradually, however, as the progression of laws and township policies chipped away incrementally at the traditional use of permanent endowments, licensing fees, lotteries, and "rate bills" (tuition or user fees) to finance the schools, and replaced them with general taxes. Resistance to raising rates or levying new taxes was always a factor to be overcome, and state governments often tied inducements like financial aid for schools to decisions by districts to agree to tax themselves. Some northern states continued to rely on a combination of taxes and "rate-bills" to fund their schools as late as 1871 (New Jersey). Although some southern states passed legislation allowing for free schools as early as the 1830s, there was limited progress in establishing them until after the Civil War.[8]

Historians of education typically highlight the fact that the common school movement was one of a number of campaigns for democratization included in various social and economic policies that coincided with, or followed shortly after, widespread extension of the suffrage.[9] Until early in the nineteenth century and despite the sentiments popularly attributed to the Founding Fathers, voting in the United States was largely a privilege reserved for white men with significant amounts of property. By 1815, only

---

[7] See Cubberley (1920), as well as the discussion in Soltow and Stevens (1981).
[8] Cubberley (1920).
[9] Again, see Cubberley (1920).

four of the original thirteen states (and seven overall) had adopted universal white male suffrage, but as the movement to do away with political inequality gained strength, they were joined by the rest of the country as virtually all new entrants to the Union extended voting privileges to all white men, and older states revised their laws. The shift to full white manhood suffrage was largely complete by the late 1840s.[10] Overall, the timing of the movements for extending the suffrage as well as for common schools is consistent with the view that increasing equality in political influence helped promote increased investments in public schooling, and correspondingly greater access to primary education. That the southern states were generally the laggards in both broadening the electorate and starting common schools, while New England and the western states were leaders in both, likewise provides support for this view. Since doing away with property restrictions on the franchise enhanced the political voice of the groups that would benefit most from the establishment of tax-supported free schools, and the most important single source of tax revenue for local and state governments were property taxes, it should not be surprising if greater equality in political influence led to the institutional changes that contributed to greater equality in the distribution of human capital.

Although both the French and English areas of Canada had relatively few schools and low levels of literacy in 1800, as compared to their neighbor to the south, this northern-most country in the hemisphere was another leader in extending institutions of primary education to the general population. By the end of the nineteenth century, Canada ranked second in the world, only behind the United States, in terms of literacy and the fraction of its school-aged population actually enrolled. Despite being influenced by political developments in both Britain and France, there was a pronounced impact on Canada arising from extensive economic contacts with the northeastern part of the United States. Whatever the source, Canadian concern with the establishment of a broad system of public schools began increasing at the beginning of the nineteenth century. The organization, management, and financing of education were carried out primarily at the district level, but some supervision and financial aid was provided by provincial governments. The second quarter of the nineteenth century was a period when Canada's school systems expanded and there was growing support from public resources, as was happening in the United States. Tax-supported free primary schools, however, were not fully realized on a widespread basis until the third quarter of the nineteenth century.[11] Under the Union Act

---

[10] For discussions of the series of reforms involving both the extension of the franchise and the conduct of voting more generally, see Porter (1918), Albright (1942), Kleppner (1982), and Flora (1983).

[11] Compulsory education legislation followed over the 1870s (Ontario (1871), British Columbia (1873), and Manitoba (1876)), but Quebec did not pass such legislation until

of 1841 and the British North America Act of 1867, allowance was made for separate secular and religious schools, both of which would be state-financed for those provinces that wanted them.[12] Although Canada was clearly behind the United States in both schooling and literacy for most of the nineteenth century, she managed to virtually close the gap by 1895 in terms of the ratio of students in school to the population aged 5 to 19 (0.60 to 0.62 respectively). In both countries the progress of the movement for tax-supported public schools coincided generally in time with, or followed soon after, extensions of the franchise.[13]

Many elements seem to have contributed to the early spread of tax-supported primary schools in the United States and Canada. First, these societies may have been more inclined to invest in public education because of the religious views that were more prevalent in English colonies. Proponents of the idea that religious faith was an important, if not critical, factor typically cite the example of seventeenth-century New England, where the organization of primary schools was often rationalized as necessary for ensuring that all members of the population were able to read the Bible. Although the role of religion is undeniable, the force of the argument can be exaggerated. Not only did New England account for only a small share of the U.S. population at the end of the eighteenth century, but even there rates of adult illiteracy were substantial, if markedly lower than in other areas of the country. That all regions of the United States and Canada compared favorably in literacy to England, Europe more generally, and to the British colonies in the Caribbean, would seem to cast doubt on the notion that their high rates of primary schooling were due solely to either English heritage or religion. It is worth noting how the supporters of public schooling during the common school movement stressed the economic and civic importance of education, rather than the religious. Schooling would help equip men for self-governance and participation in a democracy, and provide an avenue for self-improvement and upward mobility.[14]

1943. For detailed histories of schools in Canada, see Phillips (1957) and Wilson, Stamp, and Audet (1970). For a useful study of economic growth in nineteenth-century Canada, see Lewis and Urquhart (1999).

[12] Most important here was Quebec, which maintained, in addition to a secular school system, separate Catholic and Protestant schools.

[13] For a discussion of the process involved in the extension of the franchise, and its effects in Western Europe, see Acemoglu and Robinson (2000).

[14] Common schools served girls (despite their lacking the vote) as well as boys, and estimates of literacy from the late 1700s through the 1850s suggest that although the expansion of common schools benefited all, they helped females close a gender gap. See Soltow and Stevens (1981) for more discussion of the temporal and regional patterns of literacy in the United States, and how well they conform to various hypotheses about why that country and Canada should be so distinctive. See also Kaestle (1983) for a discussion of the ethnic and religious debates in northern schooling in the antebellum United States.

Another potential explanation for why the United States and Canada were well ahead of their hemispheric neighbors in making commitments to public schooling is that they could better afford the cost. The United States, and to a lesser extent Canada, were beginning to industrialize and to pull ahead of most of their neighbors in the Americas in terms of per capita income by the time they embraced the common school movement during the mid-nineteenth century, although the high wage effects of industrialization may have meant a shift for children from schooling to employment.[15] Certainly their levels of material resources were a contributing factor. However, although they were no doubt aided by their prosperity, it is important to remember that the United States and Canada had begun to distinguish themselves in their propensity to invest in schooling long before they enjoyed a marked advantage in per capita income. Moreover, a number of New World economies continued to surpass or at least rival their northern neighbors in this gauge of economic performance well into the nineteenth century, and it is clear that the great majority commanded sufficient resources to establish institutions offering broad access to primary education throughout the period.

A related idea is that the greater support for public education institutions in the United States and Canada was due not to differences in their capacity to pay as gauged by per capita income, but rather to differences in their ability or willingness to mobilize tax revenue for that purpose. This way of framing the problem highlights issues of government or administrative structure as well as of political economy. Although the societies of the Americas evolved diverse governmental structures, it is striking that during the early nineteenth century virtually all of them (in their laws or constitutions) explicitly gave local or provincial governments responsibility for operating public schools and granted them authority to levy taxes. That all throughout the Americas local and provincial governments apparently had the power to levy taxes to support public schools leads to the question of why some were so much more inclined to take effective advantage of this capacity. We have been especially concerned with the possibility that such differences across countries, if not jurisdictions, may have had something to do with differences in income inequality or ethnic homogeneity.[16] The logic is based on the observation that the well-to-do can always obtain schooling for their children through the private market, but that public investment in schooling systems, or broad access to schooling, generally involves some transfers between those who bear a disproportionate share of the costs and

---

[15] Engerman and Sokoloff (1997).

[16] For a discussion of this idea in another context, see Goldin and Katz (1997b, 2008). For a detailed account of how inequality, and especially political inequality, played a role in restricting the access of blacks to schooling and other public goods in the postbellum South, see Kousser (1974) and Higgs (1977).

those who realize a disproportionate share of the benefits. In the nineteenth-century U.S., for example, it was typical for local governments – the main providers of public schools' funds – to raise the overwhelming share of their revenue through property taxes. As a result, where there was relative equality or population homogeneity, as in the United States and Canada (compared to elsewhere in the Americas), one would expect a relatively even sharing of costs and benefits and less severe collective action problems, thus resulting in a greater likelihood of a community taxing itself to finance universal primary schools. However, where inequality was more extreme, and especially where the wealthier segments of the population had disproportionate political influence, one would expect a lower propensity of communities to tax themselves to support investment in public goods. Support for this notion of the significance of political equality comes from the coincidence in time between the common school movement of the 1820s and 1830s in the United States and the broadening of the franchise during that same era, and from similar associations between suffrage reform and the passage of measures to support public schools in both Canada, England, and elsewhere in Europe.[17]

Whatever the reasons for it, the United States and Canada benefited from their greater investments in public schooling, as evidenced by how far ahead of their neighbors in the Americas they were in attaining literacy throughout the 1800s and well into the 1900s (see Table 4.1). By 1870, more than 80 percent of the population aged 10 or above in both the United States and Canada were literate, more than triple the proportions in Argentina, Chile, Costa Rica, and Cuba, and four times the proportions in Brazil and Mexico. These stark contrasts were partly due to high literacy in the United States and Canada, but much of the explanation seems to be in the poor performance of the other societies in the Americas. Even during the era of European colonization – when their levels of per capita income were comparable – these societies clearly trailed the colonies, that were to become the United States and Canada, in developing institutions of primary education and in literacy. Moreover, even those that were more successful at realizing economic growth in the late nineteenth and early twentieth centuries, such as Argentina, were much slower to establish systems of public schooling that reached broad segments of their populations. Even the non-white population in the United States had literacy rates comparable to, or higher than, those for the entire population in Argentina at 1870, 1890, and 1910.

Overall, the United States and Canada were the only societies in the Americas to attain high levels of literacy by the middle of the nineteenth

---

[17] Also consistent with this view is the cross-sectional correspondence across states between leadership in broadening the franchise and leadership in the establishment of universal common schools. For discussions of the connection between extensions of suffrage and public schooling in many countries and contexts, see Cubberley, *History of Education*.

TABLE 4.1. *Literacy Rates in the Americas, 1850–1950*

	Year	Ages	Rate
Argentina	1869	6+	23.80%
	1895	6+	45.6
	1900	10+	52
	1925	10+	73
Barbados	1946	10+	92.7
Bolivia	1900	10+	17
Brazil	1872	7+	15.8
	1890	7+	14.8
	1900	7+	25.6
	1920	10+	30
	1939	10+	57
British Honduras	1911	10+	59.6
(Belize)	1931	10+	71.8
Chile	1865	7+	18
	1875	7+	25.7
	1885	7+	30.3
	1900	10+	43
	1925	10+	66
	1945	10+	76
Colombia	1918	15+	32
	1938	15+	56
	1951	15+	62
Costa Rica	1892	7+	23.6
	1900	10+	33
	1925	10+	64
Cuba	1861	7+	23.8(38.5, 5.3)*
	1899	10+	40.5
	1925	10+	67
	1946	10+	80.0
Guatemala	1893	7+	11.3
	1925	10+	15
	1945	10+	20
Honduras	1887	7+	15.2
	1925	10+	29
Jamaica	1871	5+	16.3
	1891	5+	32
	1911	5+	47.2
	1943	5+	67.9
	1943	10+	76.1
Mexico	1900	10+	22.2
	1925	10+	36
	1946	10+	48.4

(continued)

TABLE 4.1 *(continued)*

	Year	Ages	Rate
Paraguay	1886	7+	19.3
	1900	10+	30
Peru	1925	10+	38
Puerto Rico	1860	7+	11.8(19.8, 3.1)*
Uruguay	1900	10+	54
	1925	10+	70
Venezuela	1925	10+	34
Canada	1861	20+	82.5
Eng-majority counties	1861	20+	93
Fr-majority counties	1861	20+	81.2
United States			
No. Whites	1860	20+	96.9
So. Whites	1860	20+	56.4
All	1870	10+	80.0(88.5, 21.1)*
	1890	10+	86.7(92.3, 43.2)*
	1910	10+	92.3(95.0, 69.5)*

* The figures for Whites and Non-Whites are reported respectively within parentheses.
Sources: For the countries in South America, Central America, and the Caribbean, see Carlos Newland (1991; 1994); Aline Helg (1987); George W. Roberts (1957); John A. Britton (1994); West Indian Census, *General Report on the Census of Population 9th April, 1946.* Kingston: Government Printing Office, 1950. For the United States, see U.S. Bureau of the Census (2005, II, Table BC 793–797). For Canada, see Marc Egnal (1996, 81).

century. In contrast, not until late in the 1800s were two other sets of New World societies able to raise literacy rates much above the relatively modest level of 30 percent. The first of these groups were a number of British colonies in the Caribbean basin, where investments in public schools date back to the British emancipation of slaves in 1834, when grants were made to each colony for the education of blacks. These grants ended in 1845, after which each colony was responsible for its own educational policies and expenditures. Only Barbados seems to have maintained, if not increased, this early support for primary schools, with costs being covered by a mixture of local taxes, charity, school fees, and private aid generally provided to both religious as well as secular schools. The British Colonial Office continued to support the expansion of public schooling, however, and their advocacy may have been responsible for the general upturn in school enrollments and literacy that got under way throughout the British Caribbean during the last several decades of the century.[18] Barbados appears to have been the major success story, with estimated literacy rates placing it among the

[18] Compulsory schooling laws did begin to be introduced, first in British Guyana in 1876, with St. Lucia and the Leeward Islands following in 1889 and 1890, respectively, but they were rather ineffectively enforced.

more developed nations of the world. In other colonies, like Belize and Jamaica, however, improvements were steady but slower, with the most striking increases in literacy occurring after 1891.[19]

The other group of New World societies that began to realize substantial increases in literacy and major extensions of public schooling during the late 1800s was a subset of former Spanish colonies. Argentina and Uruguay were the clear leaders among them (although still far behind the United States and Canada), with more than half their populations (10 years and older) literate by 1900. Chile and Cuba trailed somewhat behind, with roughly 40 percent literacy, and Costa Rica further behind still, at 33 percent. These five countries, which varied considerably in many important respects, had attained literacy rates greater than 66 percent by 1925. In contrast, a broad range of other Latin American countries, including Mexico, Brazil, Venezuela, Peru, Colombia, Bolivia, Guatemala, and Honduras, were not able to move much beyond 30 percent literacy until after 1925.

III

Although virtually all New World economies enjoyed high levels of per capita income by the standards of the period, the United States and Canada had pulled far ahead of their Latin American neighbors in the establishment of schools and literacy attainment by the beginning of the nineteenth century. This dramatic contrast with the North is perhaps the most salient feature of Latin America's overall record in the development of education institutions, but it should not be allowed to obscure the important differences across countries within the region (see Tables 4.1 and 4.2). There was little public provision of primary education anywhere in Latin America until late in the nineteenth century, but literacy rose quickly in those countries that took the lead in promoting schooling. By 1900, Argentina, Chile, Cuba, and Uruguay had literacy rates of over 40 percent, followed by Costa Rica with 33 percent. These figures are quite low relative to those of the United States and Canada, but much higher than those of the two largest Latin American nations, Mexico and Brazil, which had rates of only 22 and 25 percent respectively. Moreover, countries like Bolivia, Guatemala, and Honduras fell even further behind, with literacy rates ranging from 11 to 17 percent. Since all these countries had similar government structures (federations), and national heritages (Spanish or Portuguese), the issue of the sources of these large differences seems both intriguing and relevant to understanding the conditions that were conducive to early investment in primary schools.

---

[19] Rates of literacy for blacks were generally lower in most of the British colonies in the Caribbean than in the United States but were comparable to or above those of most countries in South and Central America.

TABLE 4.2. *Literacy Rates in Selected Cities*

Place	Year	Male	Female	Total	Country Literacy Rate
Boston, MA	1850			91.1	5.1(*)
New York City, NY	1850			93.6	93.9(*)
Philadelphia, PA	1850			93.2	93.1(*)
Santiago, Chile	1854	52.4	43.3	47.1	13.3
Buenos Aires	1855	56.0	48.0	52.0	23.8 (1869)
San Juan, P.R. (W)	1860	67.4	79.4	71.8	19.8
San Juan, P.R. (C)	1860	22.5	15.4	18.2	3.1
San Juan, Puerto Rico	1860	52.3	43.0	47.9	11.8
Havana (W)	1861	58.4	55.6	57.5	38.5
Havana (C)	1861	8.2	6.7	7.4	5.3
Havana, Cuba	1861	45.9	34.1	41.3	23.8
San Jose, Costa Rica	1864	57.0	23.0	40.2	23.6 (1892)
Buenos Aires	1869	55.0	47.0	52.2	23.8
Kingston, Jamaica	1871			40.4	16.3
Santiago, Chile	1875	37.0	33.3	34.4	25.7
Sao Paulo, Brazil	1882			42.0	15.3 (c.1882)
Kingston, Jamaica	1891			59.2	32.0
Buenos Aires	1895	75.0	64.0	71.8	45.6

Note 1: (*) Literacy level is for the state, not the country, i.e. Massachusetts, New York, Pennsylvania. Also, literacy rates correspond to population over the age of 20.

Note 2: W = white, C = colored population.

Source: Carlos Newland (1991); Leslie Bethell (1984, vols. 4 & 5); George W. Roberts (1957, 78); *Seventh Census of the United States: 1850, 1853.*

The local governments established under Spanish colonial rule reflected the corporate quality of Latin American society, characterized by a hierarchical structure where only *vecinos* (neighbors) were considered citizens.[20] Such sharp distinctions in social class endured after independence, and *vecinos* continued to dominate the political order throughout the nineteenth century by way of political systems based on indirect elections and restrictions on voting that included some combination of income and wealth, as well as literacy requirements. With extreme inequality in the distributions of income and political power, it is perhaps not surprising that in Latin America local governments often failed to organize schools that were tax-supported and open to all. In Latin America national governments often had to intervene directly in promoting education institutions before substantial progress was

---

[20] See the discussion of *vecinos, vecindad* privileges, and the structure of the *cabildo* (government of any settlement that included both the executive and judicial branches) in Bayle (1952). See also Pietschmann (1996). For schooling patterns in the early settlement of Spanish America, see Haring (1947). For a useful bibliography of the history of education in Latin America, see Sociedad y Educación (1995).

made. This pattern stands in stark contrast with the experience in the United States and Canada, where local and state governments were the pioneers in establishing such schools.[21]

The greater importance of national government policy in Latin America, and some of the conditions that influenced the timing for national government involvement, are illustrated by the experiences which we discuss below of the following selected cases: Argentina, Chile, Colombia, Costa Rica, Cuba, Guatemala, Mexico, and Peru. Several patterns stand out. First, across countries, or across regions within countries, the polities that had greater equality or population homogeneity generally led in establishing broad access to primary schooling and in attaining higher literacy. Urban areas are an example of such polities, and were more able or inclined to make such investments. Second, within a country, the timing of the major expansions of public schools seems to have been more closely associated with economic booms or with campaigns to attract immigrants from outside the polity than with political turmoil or civil strife (Cuba stands out as an exception). Third, although it was not uncommon for some isolated cities or provinces to undertake significant investment in public schooling, the country as a whole would make substantial progress only when national governments chose, or were able, to get involved in promoting this goal. In Latin America, federalism, with its greater potential for competition between states or provinces in the provision of public services to attract migrants, was not enough to ensure higher investments in education.

Argentina

Though initially constrained by the 1853 constitution assigning provincial governments the responsibility for primary schooling, during the 1860s the national government began to play an active role in promoting mass education. These efforts were led by President Domingo Sarmiento and others who saw the United States and Canada as models for development.[22] Their conviction that the provincial governments were not expanding access to schools seems borne out by the low rates of literacy in the country especially among the native born and those living outside of Buenos Aires (see Table 4.5). The first major intervention came in 1881, with the granting of authority

[21] Those skeptical of the contrast being so stark might question how well groups such as Native Americans and blacks were served by schools in the United States or Canada. However, as is indicated in Table 4.1, the literacy rates for U.S. blacks in the late nineteenth and early twentieth centuries were as high, if not higher, than those for the entire population of Argentina. Since the immigrants to Argentina were significantly more literate than the native born, this implies that blacks born and schooled in the United States had higher literacy than those born and schooled in Argentina.

[22] Our brief overview of the development of schooling in Argentina draws on Maltoni (1988); Misuriello (1993); República Argentina (1910); and Recchini de Lattes and Lattes (1969).

for schools in the federal district of Buenos Aires and national territories to the National Council of Education.[23] Education policy outside these federal districts continued to be made by local and provincial authorities, but the national government assumed the right to intervene where elementary school systems proved to be inadequate or resources for education were scarce. This opening to federal involvement was soon followed by an 1884 law calling for free primary schools, compulsory attendance for all children between the ages of 6 and 14, limits on the distance that a student would have to travel to attend, and the establishment of one school for every 1,500 inhabitants. These standards were not uniformly adhered to, however, and in 1904 the Lainez Law undercut local authority further by giving the federal government the power to establish primary schools anywhere in the country in order to raise school standards. This extension of the powers of the central government led to a sharp rise in federal funds over the next few decades.

These efforts to expand primary schooling in time produced impressive advances in educational attainment; the literacy rate rose from 22.1 percent in 1869 to 65 percent in 1914. Progress was far from even across geographic areas, however. The more prosperous regions, large cities such as Buenos Aires, and areas with greater numbers of foreign born had higher attendance rates and much higher literacy, a pattern that was typical of New World societies other than the United States and Canada (see Table 4.5).

Part of this gap between the urban and the rural was undoubtedly due to the amount of resources invested in schooling. Federal funds were largely restricted to the capital city and other federal territories, while poor provinces were less able to raise the funds to establish and operate a high quality primary school system. Between 1874 and 1896, virtually all regions in Argentina substantially boosted their per capita expenditures on primary schooling. Nevertheless, the province of Buenos Aires, which included the capital city as well as the most productive farmlands in the country, pulled far ahead as it increased per capita spending by nearly 300 percent, a significant increase compared to the national average which rose by roughly 140 percent (see Table 4.4).

Tables 4.4 and 4.5 present literacy rates by province and country of birth, and allow for a closer examination of the relationships between literacy, expenditures on primary schools, and geographic location. Among the features that stand out are first, a general cross-sectional correspondence between increases in the literacy rates of native born, and growing expenditures on primary schooling, at least through 1896 – which is the last year for which we have information on provincial governments' expenditures before

---

[23] It is notable that when the responsibility for the Federal District was transferred to the national government, the municipal government of Buenos Aires was explicitly required to increase its expenditures on education.

TABLE 4.3. *Students as a Percentage of Population in Selected Latin American Countries*

Countries	Population (c. 1895)	Students (c. 1895)	Students as a Percentage of Total Population (c. 1895)
Costa Rica	243,205	21,829	8.98%
Uruguay	800,000	67,878	8.48
Argentina	4,086,492	268,401	6.57
Paraguay	329,645	18,944	5.75
Mexico	11,395,712	543,977	4.77
Guatemala	1,460,017	65,322	4.47
Venezuela	2,323,527	100,026	4.30
Nicaragua	282,845	11,914	4.21
Ecuador	1,271,861	52,830	4.15
El Salvador	777,895	29,427	3.78
Chile	3,267,441	95,456	2.92
Peru	2,700,945	53,276	1.97
Colombia	3,878,600	73,200	1.89
Brazil	14,002,335	207,973	1.49
Bolivia	2,300,000	24,244	1.05

Source: *Resúmenes Estadísticos: Años 1883–1910, Demografía.* Oficina Nacional de Estadística, República de Costa Rica (1912). This is a Costa Rican document, with no sources and discussion provided. The level of schooling, the length of the school year, nor the mix of private vs. public schools is provided. The document does provide, however, unusual information that is somewhat consistent with other data, although not perfectly correlated with literacy.

federal aid became more substantial and widely disbursed. Thereafter a trend toward regional convergence followed. Table 4.4 shows that the more prosperous regions and large cities had higher per capita expenditures; the notable outlier being Buenos Aires, consistent with, if not proof of, our view. It is notable that the rich agricultural provinces of the Littoral and Andina regions were clearly ahead of the provinces of the Central and Norteña regions in support of primary schooling. Turning to Table 4.5, we see that the figures on the literacy of the native born indicate dramatic improvement within a few decades around the turn of the twentieth century – paralleling the major increase in public support for primary schooling. Finally, the foreign born, mainly from Spain and Italy, had much higher literacy rates than did the native born, although the disparity declined over the late nineteenth and early twentieth centuries as public schooling in Argentina expanded.[24]

[24] It is interesting to note that the differential between the foreign and native born appears to have been due virtually exclusively to the sharp contrasts in literacy among the respective groups of adults. This is yet another indication that literacy rates were rising rapidly over cohorts born in Argentina during this period.

TABLE 4.4. *Provincial Government Expenditures on Primary Education in Argentina, on a Per Capita Basis*

Provinces	Per Capita Annual Expenditures (Nominal Pesos)	
	1874	1896
Buenos Aires	0.30	1.16
Santa Fé	0.47	0.67
Entre Ríos	0.12	0.50
Corrientes	0.56	0.48
LITTORAL	0.37	0.56
Córdoba	0.09	0.29
San Luis	0.29	0.42
Santiago del Estero	0.06	0.24
CENTRAL	0.11	0.29
Mendoza	0.71	0.72
San Juán	0.55	0.78
La Rioja	0.10	0.34
Catamarca	0.14	0.48
ANDINA	0.38	0.60
Tucumán	0.50	0.49
Salta	0.18	0.38
Jujuy	0.07	0.38
NORTEÑA	0.36	0.46
TOTAL	0.28	0.68

Note: 1896 data were converted into pesos fuertes ($1 peso = $0.35 peso fuerte), to make figures comparable. Per capita figures obtained by dividing provincial budgets for education for the years 1874, 1896 by census figures for the population for 1869 and 1895.
Source: Juan Carlos Vedoya (1973, 89).

Although the foreign born in Buenos Aires were more literate than those elsewhere in Argentina, regional variation in literacy was much less among the foreign born than among natives.

Overall, the late-nineteenth- and early-twentieth-century surge in investment in public schooling is consistent with the idea that such expenditures were at least partially driven by income; the Argentine economy boomed during these decades, and its economic growth made more resources available and, at the same time, raised both the private and social rates of return to education. The increasing prosperity of Argentina also encouraged many policymakers, such as Sarmiento, to conceive of the United States and Canada as offering the country realistic models for development. Immigration, which grew rapidly over these decades, also seems to have had a positive impact on literacy. Not only were the foreign-born relatively more literate than the native population and more demanding of public services such as

TABLE 4.5. *Literacy Rates for Argentina by Province and Country of Birth: 1895, 1909, and 1914*

Province (Year)	Foreign Born			Natives		
	1895 (All Ages)	1909* (6–14)	1914 (All Ages)	1895 (All Ages)	1909* (6–14)	1914 (All Ages)
Capital	68%	71%	74%	53%	78%	65%
Martin García Island	n.a.	100	71	n.a.	61	72
LITTORAL: EAST						
Buenos Aires	60	57	64	37	60	50
Santa Fé	60	52	63	30	59	46
Entre Ríos	57	52	64	27	50	42
Corrientes	41	52	55	18	45	33
CENTRAL						
Córdoba	58	51	67	27	51	43
San Luis	70	58	74	27	49	46
Santiago del Estero	71	52	63	11	33	26
ANDINA: WEST						
Mendoza	53	45	54	31	49	42
San Juán	56	52	51	32	54	42
La Rioja	65	48	63	22	39	39
Catamarca	68	59	69	21	40	39
NORTEÑA						
Tucumán	64	56	56	19	50	38
Salta	41	55	53	18	64	36
Jujuy	25	42	24	17	43	30
TERRITORIES						
North						
Misiones	20	38	38	17	45	34
Formosa	31	44	39	20	50	33
Chaco	51	52	56	15	50	35
Los Andes	n.a.	8	47	n.a.	28	26
Center						
La Pampa	61	44	67	18	41	34
West						
Neuquén	23	47	42	8	39	22
South						
Río Negro	44	46	54	20	43	28
Chubut	77	63	67	28	56	36
Santa Cruz	73	n.a.	77	26	n.a.	45
Tierra del Fuego	84	67	78	39	61	54
TOTAL	55	57	59	25	56	40

Note 1: The 1909 figure for the total is a weighted average.

Note 2: Los Andes existed transitorily between the years 1900 and 1943. Its surface was then divided between the provinces of Catamarca and Jujuy. We therefore classify it among the northern territories.

Sources: For years 1895 and 1914 *Resúmen de la República.* República de Argentina. The numbers represent the literate foreign (native) population divided by the total foreign (native) population. For the year 1909. *Censo General de Educación (1909)* República de Argentina, Buenos Aires (1910). The number represents the literate foreign (native) population divided by the foreign (native) population between the ages of 6 and 14.

schools, but the Argentine government was concerned with attracting these more discriminating European immigrants. The provision of public primary education served both as a means of encouraging immigration and of helping immigrants assimilate.[25]

It is hard to think of the expansion of the public schools in Argentina as part of a general movement for democratization. Major electoral reforms did not precede the first big push at establishing more and better-funded public schools as they did in the United States and Europe. The 1853 Constitution had not included restrictions on the right to vote based on income, wealth, or literacy; though a venue for political expression by the poor and illiterate was constrained by the absence of a secret ballot and the limited number of polling places that characterized elections until the Sáenz Peña Law of 1912.[26] Indeed, partly due to a puzzling lack of desire by the foreign born to apply for citizenship and obtain the right to vote, the fraction of the population who voted remained very low until the reforms of 1912.[27] Although the impetus of the late-nineteenth century movement to expand public schools was not related to any wave of democratization, the extent of economic and political equality in Argentina may help to understand why the country was one of the leaders in extending access to schooling in Latin America, but lagged the United States and Canada. Compared to other Latin American nations in the late nineteenth century, Argentina (and Uruguay) had relatively scarce labor and a homogenous population – conditions that in principle made it easier for Argentina to work out collective action problems associated with financing public primary schools. Indeed the possibility of attracting immigrants through investments in public schools provided incentives for political and economic elites to support such policies. On the other hand, the country was in other dimensions much less equal than its peers in the northern hemisphere, and thus would be expected to have lagged in public school investment.

Chile

Schooling institutions in early-nineteenth-century Chile resembled those in most of the other former Spanish colonies in the Americas that had recently

---

[25] Evidence that suggests the conscious socializing element that education had for the national government is a 1920 law that established that the primary educational system should create state schools without ethnic or religious discrimination.

[26] For an excellent discussion of who held the right to vote, the conduct of elections, and who actually voted, see Alonso (1993 and 1996). Among her findings are that in Buenos Aires, both the proportion of the population who voted and the relative probability of illiterate individuals voting were extremely low.

[27] As evident in Series C 181–194 in U.S. Bureau of the Census (1975), the rate of naturalization was also low in the United States at the turn of the twentieth century (between 60 and 70 percent for males over age 21). However, the rate in the United States appears to have been much higher than in Argentina.

gained independence. Despite expressions of support for education in the Constitution of 1833, schools of any sort – public or private – were few in number and served a very small fraction of the population. Most of the limited funding for public institutions came from municipal governments, and what came from the national government was predominantly directed to the University of Chile, which was founded in 1842, or to other schools above the primary level. Literacy rates were quite low, especially among the native born in Chile. For example, in 1854 the rate of literacy was 13.3 percent for the country as a whole, but 46.3 percent for the foreign-born.[28]

Expanding primary schooling began to receive higher priority around mid-century. Between 1845 and 1860, the share of the national budget's allocation to education rose from 11 percent to 31 percent.[29] As in Argentina, however, the real surge in public school expenditures appears to have begun with an economic boom, related to exports of nitrates and other mineral products, which took place during the second half of the nineteenth century and coincided with a wave of immigration. In 1860, a law was enacted committing the state to free primary schooling. At the same time, it was acknowledged that municipal governments might be unable to provide adequate funds, and so an enhanced role for the national government was recognized in establishing, financing, and operating schools. Although the rhetoric may have been inclusive, the growth in national government expenditures on schooling seems to have been associated with greater regional disparities in schooling and literacy. Literacy among the entire population rose from 28.9 percent in 1885 to 40.0 percent in 1907, but even in 1907, the literate were heavily concentrated either in large cities or in provinces that benefitted from revenues derived from the export of nitrates. Among the first group were the cities of Santiago and Valparaíso with literacy rates of 50.6 and 53.6 percent respectively; in the second group were the provinces of Tacna, Tarapaca, and Antofagasta with rates of 47.7, 57.0 and 56.6, respectively.

Striking about the Chilean experience is its ability to attain relatively high levels of education and literacy when compared with the rest of Latin America, despite a substantial share of its population being of Native American descent. For example, in 1925, Chile's literacy rate of 66.0 percent was similar to Cuba's 67 percent, and rivaled Argentina's and Uruguay's, which stood at 73 and 70 percent, respectively. By Latin American standards, Chile's accomplishment in supporting education may seem a bit puzzling. While systematic estimates of income or wealth equality are not available for the period, laws governing who could vote, the fraction of the population that did vote in elections, and evidence of the low literacy rate among the native born are consistent with the judgment of historians of Chile that

---

[28] Newland (1991).
[29] Even then, only about two-thirds of primary and secondary students were enrolled in public schools. See Yeager (1991). See also Brahm, Cariola, and Silva (1971).

there was rather marked political and economic inequality.[30] Such inequality would normally be expected to hamper the development of a public school system and, in so doing, keep literacy rates low. That expectation is realized but only to the extent that Chile did not do well by the standards of its more prosperous neighbors in North America, countries with greater political and income equality and more homogeneous populations.

The real issue though is why Chile had one of the best records of Latin American societies in promoting primary education and attaining high rates of literacy. There are several factors that may have played a role. First, Chile – like Argentina – was competing with other countries to attract immigrants from Europe who were better educated and valued schooling more than the native born. Under such circumstances, it should not be surprising that the national government would have supported public schools, especially in the larger cities and mining centers where foreign immigrants were most likely to settle. A second factor is that by the second half of the nineteenth century, Chile had among the most urban populations in Latin America. Many observers attribute this development to the growth of the mining sector, and the stimulus it provided to the expansion of urban industries. Given that private and social returns to schooling and literacy are generally higher in urban than in rural jobs, greater urbanization should have encouraged more investment in education. Finally, the boom in nitrates and other mineral products generated revenue that could be invested in the public school system.

As was true of other Latin American countries, economic booms, whether at the regional or national level, often triggered a resource-based increase in public schools funding. In contrast, governments that had to rely more on direct taxes levied on voters seem to have faced greater resistance to public investment in education. Whatever the precise role of these explanatory factors, in Chile, as elsewhere in Latin America, the initial shift toward a policy of promoting schooling institutions appears not to have been induced by a wave of democratization.

Colombia and Peru

These two often-compared Andean nations both have large Native-American populations and great topographic diversity. Nonetheless, they

---

[30] The 1833 constitution established income and property requirements that could easily be met by artisans, salaried workers, miners, petty merchants, and public employees. It deliberately lowered even those thresholds in 1840 to enfranchise 60,000 national guard troops. There was, however, a rather binding literacy requirement, although veterans of the wars of independence were exempted from both the literacy and income tests. In 1874, the income and wealth tests were dropped, as was the literacy requirement in 1878, but the latter was restored in 1885. Overall, political power may not have been as unequally distributed in Chile as in most of Latin American, but perhaps more unequally distributed than in Argentina, Costa Rica, and Uruguay.

are generally regarded as having followed divergent paths of political development, and it is perhaps surprising then to find that in 1925 their average literacy rates were quite similar at the national level, and both experienced similar variation in literacy rates within each country.

Both countries explicitly recognized the importance of schooling and education in their early constitutions and laws. By the 1820s, the government of Francisco de Paula Santander began to promote the establishment of primary schools in Colombia.[31] The government used the Lancasterian system of mutual instruction to overcome the scarcity of qualified teachers. Through the 1830s, Santander's program was remarkably successful in increasing the number of schools and students, but national support for schools slackened by the end of his presidency. The federal government renewed a role in supporting schools by the late 1860s, when it enacted a tax on property to finance public education. It also assumed responsibility for creating a school to train teachers, as well as developing public libraries. The financing and operation of schools was left largely to state or municipal governments.

Few polities appear to have had the resources and political will to make major investments in public schooling. One exception is the state of Antioquia, which stands out most in promoting education. Distinguished at first by a relatively sparse population, the increased production of gold and the introduction of coffee during the mid-nineteenth century substantially increased its income and led to policies directly aimed at attracting migrants from other parts of the country. Throughout this period, the state and municipal governments in Antioquia were mostly controlled by Conservative governments who wished to encourage this internal migration, and their support of public schools as well as the liberal land policies they pursued were certainly consistent with this goal.[32] The neighboring "frontier" states of Caldas and Valle Del Cauca were similar in many ways to Antioquia and they too remained far ahead of the country in literacy and schooling enrollment rates into the twentieth century. Both their prosperity and their relative equality was associated with a scarcity of labor, high rates of land ownership, and the prevalence of small and medium-sized farms, which contributed to their relatively strong educational outcomes. The only, and intriguing, exception to this pattern is San Andres y Providencia, which had the highest literacy rate in Colombia in 1918. This small, isolated island in the Caribbean had originally been colonized by the Puritans in the early seventeenth century, but was taken over by the Spanish soon after.

Thus, in Colombia, even with a decentralized and federalist approach to education, only a small number of states had made substantial investments

---

[31] See Helg (1987) and Safford (1976).

[32] For a discussion of land policies, see Palacios (1980) and LeGrand (1986). For evidence of the rapid expansion of schooling in Antioquia, see Departamento Administrativo Nacional de Estadistica (1981, 120–21).

in public schooling by the early twentieth century. Most other states lagged far behind, with the result that around 1920 the national literacy rate of 32 percent was roughly half that of Argentina, Uruguay, or Chile. In 1925, Peru had a literacy rate of 38 percent, and, as was the case of Colombia, it exhibited extreme inter-regional variation in schooling and literacy. In 1876, when the national literacy rate was 18.9 percent, literacy rates in the major cities of Lima, Ica, and Callao were between 44 and 68 percent. Such inequality persisted into the twentieth century.[33]

The high literacy of the more urbanized coastal cities and provinces was likely due to the fact that the national government played a minor role promoting public schools throughout the nineteenth century. Although the right to an education was generally recognized in the various Peruvian constitutions, actual efforts to promote public schooling were sporadic, ineffective, and largely confined to establishing advisory bodies or commissions. Since there was not a sustained commitment of funds, the financial burden fell almost exclusively on municipal governments. The resources and organizational capacity to meet those challenges were centered in cities, not in the highlands and the jungle provinces, where the Native Americans were predominant. Of course, the higher rates of schooling and literacy in the large cities related also to the fact that many more urban residents had the means to obtain private schooling for their children. Still, in 1876, roughly 60 percent of the 215 primary schools in Lima were public schools.[34] It was not until the twentieth century during the presidencies of Jose Pardo and Augusto Leguia that the national government began to contribute significant and ongoing resources to the support of public schools, and to devote attention to racial and regional disparities.

Costa Rica and Guatemala

Costa Rica has long been recognized as the Latin American society with perhaps the least inequality, its distinctiveness a result of factor endowments: a high land to labor ratio and a relatively homogenous population. Early in its history, a small indigenous population, the lack of precious minerals, and its mountainous terrain led to an economy dominated by small farmers.[35] In this respect, Costa Rica was perhaps more like the United States and Canada than any other Latin American economy.

Costa Rica was also like the United States and Canada in the important role played by local governments in education. After independence, the

---

[33] This pattern mirrors that in 1940, when the national rate was 40.4 percent, and the figures for Lima, Ica, and Callao were 82.1, 72.1, and 91.2 percent, respectively.

[34] For the figures on Lima, provincial rates of literacy, and more detail on the history of schooling in Peru, see Basadre (1961); Fernandez and Rosales (1990); Diaz (1974); and Paulston (1971).

[35] See, for example, Booth (1988) and Woodward (1976).

country maintained *ayuntamientos* (city councils), which had been originally set up by Spain's Cádiz Constitution between 1812 and 1814, as a basic governmental structure with many powers and responsibilities that included the provision and control of schooling.[36] Indeed, the central role of the municipalities in running the schools was bolstered during the 1820s as the national government instituted a series of measures that helped municipal governments raise revenue for education.[37] The 1869 Constitution made primary education obligatory for both sexes and tuition-free, and explicitly left municipalities in charge of the schools and all other expenses associated with operating them. At the same time, the federal government extended its rights to inspect and oversee the schools, and the Treasury assumed the responsibility for paying teachers' salaries.[38] Perhaps the key changes, not wholly unlike those introduced in parts of the United States, came in 1885 and 1886, with two laws, the Fundamental Law of Public Instruction and the General Law of Common Education, that set the basis for reform "from the bottom up." While ultimate control was reserved for the national executive, primary education was to be administered by local authorities, and all citizens of a district were required to pay for public schools' infrastructure.[39]

The increase in national government funds assigned to primary education in the 1885 and 1886 laws reflected an interest in and support of public schooling in Costa Rica unlike that of any other Latin American country

[36] See Sibaja (1995) for a discussion of the responsibilities and powers granted to the councils. During the conflicts for control of the newly independent states in Central America that went on between Guatemala and León (in Nicaragua), these councils assumed many of the functions that are now typical of a national state, such as defense, and until 1823 they decided to rotate the seat of government every three months between the four principal cities: Cartago, San José, Alajuela, and Heredia. It is therefore not surprising that after the newly independent nation of Costa Rica was established, the government chose to honor the authority of the *ayuntamientos*.

[37] Fischel (1987). Local taxes included taxes on butchering cattle (the largest source of revenue), fines (including those charged for not attending school), money from the commutation of a sentence, taxes for the sale of tobacco and liquor, donations and contributions, vacant inheritances, and taxes on heads of family.

[38] Primary schools were a high priority, and the assistance of the Treasury appears to have been motivated by a recognition of the severe fiscal problems faced by local governments.

[39] This duty became an obligation when the resources collected were insufficient. In addition, the laws increased the federal budget allocated to education, and the national government began buying school supplies in bulk and selling them to the local boards of education at a discount. In August 1888, Congress approved a federal loan for education of $300,000 (pesos) at 9 percent interest. Although the districts that benefited most from this loan were those that had enough revenue to cover the interest payments, localities with lower revenues were entitled under the law to receive government aid if they could not raise sufficient funds by taxing their own constituents. One important reason for the success of these reforms was that the Minister of Public Instruction, Mauro Fernández, was also the Minister of Finance at this time; which made the coordination of the educational reforms and the reforms concerning local public finances easier to implement.

FIGURE 4.1. Ratio of Federal Expenditures on Education to Total Ordinary Expenses: Costa Rica, 1869–1930.
Source: Fischel (1987, 239–41).

(see Figure 4.1). Costa Ricans attributed particular significance to primary education, which was seen as the basis for a democracy, and were quite unusual in the degree to which they made it a priority. During the 1881 economic crisis, when the price of coffee fell and a fiscal crisis ensued, subsidies from the federal government to the school system were suspended for secondary and higher education (including normal schools), but not for primary education.[40] The priority given to primary schools stands in stark contrast with other Latin American nations. In 1875 Chile, for example, while substantial resources were assigned for education, primary schools received roughly equivalent amounts as secondary, and higher education institutions, in spite of the fact that many more students attended primary school. This unequal per capita spending in the different levels of education can also be seen in 1900 Mexico, as government spending for every secondary and higher education student was estimated to be 105 pesos and 126 respectively, while per capita funding for primary students was only 0.20 pesos.

Guatemala, a close neighbor of Costa Rica, makes for an interesting contrast. Despite its proximity and similar reliance on coffee exports,

[40] Fischel (1987).

Guatemala, if not the rest of Central America generally, has always been distinguished from Costa Rica by a relative abundance of labor (due largely to an initial and continuing dense population of Native Americans), and a much larger scale of agricultural production. That Guatemala was characterized early by extreme inequality and low per capita income partially helps account for an abysmal record at investing in primary education. For the first half century after independence, the operation of schools was overwhelmingly left to the Church. By 1867, a report to the Guatemalan Congress noted that government spending (at any level) on education was minuscule, and that the ratio of students enrolled to total population was among the lowest in Latin America, just 0.6 percent. Although government funding of schools increased during the 1870s when coffee exports boomed and the Liberal governments displaced the Conservatives in power, enrollments were not enough to have a big impact on literacy. In 1925, the literacy rate for those aged 10 and over was just 15 percent, far below Costa Rica's 64 percent level. During the twentieth century, Guatemala continued to lag its hemispheric neighbors. In 1950, it, along with Nicaragua, Honduras, and Bolivia, ranked near the bottom in both school enrollment rates and literacy for the continents as a whole.

Cuba

Despite enjoying one of the highest levels of per capita income in all the Americas, well into the nineteenth century, Cuba was much slower than the United States and Canada in extending its system of public schooling and achieving high rates of literacy. During the eighteenth and early nineteenth centuries, public authorities paid more attention to higher education than to primary schooling, as they did in other parts of Latin America. Primary schooling was almost exclusively private and obtained through religious congregations, payment of fees, or the rather isolated efforts of various private organizations. But during the 1830s, interest in public education began to grow, and in 1842 the first Law on Public Instruction was enacted. Public schools were to be supported by municipal governments and managed locally, but a central colony-wide office for inspection and coordination as well as a school to train teachers were set up. These actions spurred the formation of both primary and secondary public schools. Still, by 1860, just 60 percent of the country's 464 schools were public. Overall literacy was as high in Cuba as anywhere in Latin America, but at 23.8 percent, much less than in the United States or Canada.[41]

---

[41] See the extensive discussion of the early development of schooling in Cuban Economic Research Project (1965, ch. 2). The estimate of the rate of literacy in 1899 presented there (44.6 percent) is slightly higher than the estimate we have reported in Table 4.1, apparently because it includes those who attended school but did not report an ability to read.

The War of 1868, which Cubans fought unsuccessfully to obtain their independence from Spain, was a catalyst for change. Within a few years of regaining control, Spain embarked on a series of reforms, including a royal decree and a second Law of Public Instruction that authorized a major expansion of public school system education at both the primary and secondary levels. Municipalities were obliged to cover the costs of primary and secondary public schools, which were free to all children from low-income families. The change in policy did yield some results: between 1861 and 1899, many new schools were opened, enrollments increased, and the literacy rate rose to 40.5 percent. In addition, the gap between blacks and whites narrowed considerably. On the other hand, the gains were less than in other parts of Latin America, such as Argentina, Uruguay, and Chile, which had advanced even more rapidly and, by 1900, had higher rates of literacy than Cuba. Once independence was achieved, the United States began to provide extensive assistance to build up the educational institutions of the new nation. By 1925, Cuba was again near the forefront of Latin American countries in literacy, and roughly maintained that position through 1950. Argentina and Uruguay were the only peers to consistently surpass Cuba in this dimension.

Mexico

In Mexico, schooling was regarded as important from the very beginning of Spanish rule, as the Catholic Church used schools to convert the indigenous population. By the end of the eighteenth century the Bourbon dynasty set up a system to encourage the expansion of schooling by giving *cabildos* (town councils) control over all matters relating to primary education. The 1812 Cádiz Constitution established a General Directorate to oversee all educational matters in the colonies, and instructed the colonial government to build primary schools where children would be taught to "read, write and count, and catechism." After independence, the 1824 Constitution sought to preserve local authority in issues related to schooling, and recognized the right of the new federal entities to organize their education according to their specific needs.[42]

In principle, local governments had the right to control schools, but the climate of uncertainty created by 10 years of civil war, following Iturbide's rule

---

[42] Annino (1996). Even though most of the articles in the Cádiz Constitution were not implemented as law, due to the wars of independence (1810–21), it began a process of decentralization by creating more *cabildos*. These town councils were used as a political instrument aimed at weakening insurgency, but in fact gave towns greater local autonomy and reinforced insurgency from the periphery to the center. Schooling was obviously an important issue, and attracted frequent comment. It was declared "necessary for all citizens" in the provisional constitution of 1814, and in addition to the 1824 constitution, the 1833 constitution declared schooling obligatory for men and women, children and adults. Also see Solana, Reyes, and Martínez (1981).

in the 1820s, together with almost 50 years of persistent deadlock between conservative and liberal governments, complicated the task of expanding the public school system. Progress was slow, and it was not until the late 1860s that laws of public instruction incorporating a legal outline were enacted.

Significant investment in public schools began under the presidency of Porfirio Diaz.[43] In contrast to the Costa Rican experience, Mexico moved to centralize education, as a reorganization took place at the national level.[44] The laws of 1867 and 1869 suppressed religious education, and set out conditions relating to the number of schools, study plans, and calendars that were meant to apply throughout the country. However, because of Mexico's federal structure the laws were implemented only in the Federal District or capital city (DF) and the federal territories (Baja California, Quintana Roo, and Tepic). Conflicts soon arose over the perceived erosion of state and municipal authority in educational matters, with Congress supporting more local control and opposing the executive. From 1896 onward, the Diaz government had to implement all legislation relating to education by presidential decree. This strategy of bypassing Congress continued long after the Porfiriato.[45]

With the 1888 Federal Law of Primary Instruction, the federal government began the process of establishing a network of tuition-free primary schools. At least partially motivated by the desire to maintain some authority in education policy, many state governments soon passed similar laws supporting municipal schools, which had received little or no support. By the 1920s schools were run by a system of parallel bureaucracies – one associated with the state government and the other with the federal.[46] Thus, it was the federal government that initiated the expansion of the public school system, although both federal and state governments gradually took over the responsibility for education.[47]

---

[43] The period of the Porfiriato starts in 1876 when Porfirio Díaz assumes the presidency for the first time; it ends in 1910 with the Mexican Revolution.

[44] Our brief overview of the experience in Mexico draws on Escobar Alvarez (1987); Hernández Chávez (1996); Pani (1918); and Rivera Borbón (1970).

[45] A key example was what happened with the Law of Public Instruction of 1888, which created a unified federally directed primary school system. The result was a de facto congressional veto, which was essentially overturned when the Minister of Public Instruction called two national education congresses and got them to agree on a uniform national system. See Vaughan (1982).

[46] The 1920s also marked the creation of the Ministry of Education (1921) and the launching of the first national campaigns to implant literacy nationwide (called cultural missions) by the two most prominent secretaries of education in Mexican history: José Vasconcelos (1921–24) and Moises Sáenz (1928). These campaigns coincided with the largest increase in the federal budget for education at that time, 15 percent of the total federal budget for the year 1923, which then fell to its pre-Revolutionary level of 7–9 percent by 1930.

[47] Vaughan (1982). State expenditures on schooling went from 10.52 percent in 1878 to 23.08 in 1910, becoming the largest item in states' budgets. Combined expenditures in education

During the Porfiriato, when the federal government began pursuing an active educational policy, the gap between the expenditures of the federal government and those of the states widened. By 1910 6.92 pesos per person were being spent in the DF and federal territories, and just 0.36 pesos per person were spent by the state governments (see Table 4.6). The difference reflected the federal government's area of authority in educational matters, as well as the limited support of public schools by most states. However, the generally more prosperous states of northern Mexico were an exception. Coahuila, Sonora, Nuevo León, Tamaulipas, and Chihuahua had among the highest educational expenditures and literacy rates in the country (see Table 4.6). In some of these areas public schools with broad access were established early in the nineteenth century, not unlike what happened in the United States and Canada.

The cities and towns of northern Mexico had relatively homogeneous populations of largely European descent, who had isolated or exterminated the indigenous groups of the region. The result tended toward communities with relative equality in income and created and reinforced the power of local governments. The city of Chihuahua, for example, founded in 1709, opened its first primary public school in 1786 when its population was 18,288, and in 1797 efforts were begun to develop a system of public schools in every large town in the state of Chihuahua. By 1808 there were public primary schools in five different localities.[48] The centralization of political power that took place in the late nineteenth century and the center's control of resources left many localities and states without the funds to set their own priorities. It is likely that some of the more progressive states, like those in the north, may have actually had their school systems deteriorate because of a redistribution of resources across states, or toward the center, by federal taxation.

Although Mexico is a rather extreme case of the centralized administration of education, it resembles Argentina and Chile – if not quite Costa Rica and Colombia – in the leadership role played by the national government in primary schooling. This approach, which was characteristic of Latin America, raises the question of why national governments were more important than state or local governments, in those societies in the Americas where public schooling came late.[49] One possible answer is that in localities with greater inequality or population heterogeneity, elites, who would have borne a greater than proportionate share of the costs and received a less than proportionate share of the benefits, used their disproportionate political influence to limit the mobilization and disbursement of funds for

---

for both the federal and state governments during the Porfiriato increased at an impressive pace: $26,767,224 in 1878, and $126,177,950 in 1910 – a rise of more than 370 percent.

[48] Alboites (1994). See also De la Peña (1948) and Ahumada (1896).

[49] Another interesting question is how schooling systems managed and funded by national governments differ from those managed and funded by local governments.

TABLE 4.6. *Combined State and Municipal Revenue and Primary School Expenditures (in Pesos Per Capita), Mexico During the* Porfiriato

State	Combined State and Municipal Revenue		% Increase in Per Capita Revenue	Expenditures in Primary Education		% Increase in Primary School Expenditures
	1888	1907	1888–1907	1874	1907	1874–1907
North West						
Baja California*						
Baja California Sur*						
Nayarit*						
Sinaloa	4.44	4.65	4.73%	0.31	0.60	93.55%
Sonora	3.67	6.56	78.75	0.38	0.98	157.89
North						
Chihuahua	2.96	6.98	135.81	0.02	0.98	4800
Coahuila	3.47	6.66	91.93	0.25	1.12	348
Durango	1.15	2.47	114.78	0.10	0.53	430
Zacatecas	2.62	2.87	9.54	0.08	0.52	550
North East						
Nuevo León	1.40	3.31	136.43	0.36	0.68	88.89
Tamaulipas	1.34	5.66	322.39	0.07	0.77	1000
Central West						
Aguascalientes	1.40	4.24	202.86	0.11	0.38	245.45
Guanajuato	1.74	2.01	15.52	0.24	0.19	−20.83
Jalisco	1.09	2.53	132.11	0.05	0.34	580
Querétaro	1.49	2.45	64.43	0.09	0.18	100
San Luis Potosí	2.63	2.53	−3.80	0.17	0.28	64.71
Gulf						
Tabasco	3.26	5.35	64.11	0.25	0.52	108
Veracruz	4.82	4.05	−15.98	0.19	0.46	142.11
Central South						
Distrito Federal*						
Hidalgo	2.10	2.80	33.33	0.18	0.39	116.67
México	1.24	2.93	136.29	0.24	0.31	29.17
Morelos	3.20	4.04	26.25	0.27	0.51	88.89
Puebla	2.15	3.64	69.30	0.20	0.30	50
Tlaxcala	1.12	2.09	86.61	0.16	0.35	118.75
South						
Chiapas	0.66	2.43	268.18	0.03	0.23	666.67
Colima	2.25	4.45	97.78	0.21	0.61	190.48
Guerrero	1.58	1.25	−20.89	0.22	0.18	−18.18
Michoacán	1.16	1.56	34.48	0.07	0.12	71.43
Oaxaca	0.77	1.59	106.49	0.09	0.24	166.67

(continued)

TABLE 4.6 *(continued)*

State	Combined State and Municipal Revenue		% Increase in Per Capita Revenue	Expenditures in Primary Education		% Increase in Primary School Expenditures
	1888	1907	1888–1907	1874	1907	1874–1907
South East						
Campeche	3.16	7.24	129.11	0.18	1.00	455.56
Quintana Roo*						
Yucatán	2.35	11.51	389.79	0.17	0.80	370.59
TOTAL	38.17	68.69		3.12	7.39	
AVERAGE	2.01	3.62	95.58	0.16	0.39	185.58

Note 1: The federal government funded only states marked with an asterisk.
Note 2: The federal government spent \$1.37 per inhabitant on education in 1878, and \$6.92 in 1910.
Note 3: The regional division for Mexico is based on Angel Bassols's (UNAM, Department of Economics) economic classification of states, based on the physical characteristics of the region.
Source: Mary Kay Vaughan (1982).

public schools. In such cases, the federal government needed to step in to solve the collective action problem or compel a redistribution of resources. Another possibility is that the national government was best positioned to appreciate the positive externalities associated with the expansion of public schooling, whether through increased immigration or the effects of having a better educated citizenry.

The experience of these eight countries illustrates that the pattern common to the northern part of North America, where early on localities or states mobilized resources to establish widely accessible primary schools, was rare in Latin America. Moreover, those relatively few areas where there was early public support, such as large cities, or certain regions (parts of northern Mexico, the highlands of Colombia, and Costa Rica), either had large middle classes, or were regions that resembled the United States and Canada in being labor scarce and having relatively homogeneous populations.[50] Our findings seem consistent with the idea that the degree of population homogeneity and equality in economic and political circumstances may be the key to understanding differences in educational investment. From this perspective, it is not surprising that the highly stratified societies of Latin America

[50] Northern Mexico and Costa Rica are both, along with Argentina and Uruguay, noted for having relatively small proportions of Native Americans in their populations as compared to other parts of Latin America. To say that the population of northern Mexico was homogenous may not be strictly accurate. Although precise figures are not available, it seems likely that there were many Native Americans living in isolated rural areas. The towns and more densely settled districts, however, had relatively homogeneous populations of European descent.

TABLE 4.7. *Laws Governing the Franchise and the Extent of Voting in Selected American Countries, 1840–1940*

		Lack of Secrecy in Balloting	Wealth Requirement	Literacy Requirement	Proportion of the Entire Population Voting
1840–80					
Chile	1869	N	Y	Y	1.60%
	1878	N	N	N[a]	–
Costa Rica	1890	Y	Y	Y	–
Ecuador	1848	Y	Y	Y	0.0
	1856	Y	Y	Y	0.1
Mexico	1840	Y	Y	Y	–
Peru	1875	Y	Y	Y	–
Uruguay	1840	Y	Y	Y	–
	1880	Y	Y	Y	–
Venezuela	1840	Y	Y	Y	–
	1880	Y	Y	Y	–
Canada	1867	Y	Y	N	7.7
	1878	N	Y	N	12.9
United States	1850[b]	N	N	N	12.9
	1880	N	N	N	18.3
1881–1920					
Argentina	1896	Y	Y	Y	1.8%[c]
	1916	N	N	N	9.0
Brazil	1894	Y	Y	Y	2.2
	1914	Y	Y	Y	2.4
Chile	1881	N	N	N	3.1
	1920	N	N	Y	4.4
Colombia	1918[d]	N	N	N	6.9
Costa Rica	1912	Y	Y	Y	–
	1919	Y	N	N	10.6
Ecuador	1888	N	Y	Y	2.8
	1894	N	N	Y	3.3
Mexico	1920	N	N	N	8.6
Peru	1920	Y	Y	Y	–
Uruguay	1900	Y	Y	Y	–
	1920	N	N	N	13.8
Venezuela	1920	Y	Y	Y	–
Canada	1911	N	N	N	18.1
	1917	N	N	N	20.5
United States	1900	N	N	Y[e]	18.4
	1920	N	N	Y	25.1

(continued)

TABLE 4.7 *(continued)*

		Lack of Secrecy in Balloting	Wealth Requirement	Literacy Requirement	Proportion of the Entire Population Voting
1921–40					
Argentina	1928	N	N	N	12.8%
	1937	N	N	N	15.0
Bolivia	1951	?	Y	Y	4.1
Brazil	1930	Y	Y	Y	5.7
Colombia	1930	N	N	N	11.1
	1938	N	N	N	5.9
Chile	1920	N	N	Y	4.4
	1931	N	N	Y	6.5
	1938	N	N	Y	9.4
Costa Rica	1940	N	N	N	17.6
Ecuador	1940	N	N	Y	3.3
Mexico	1940	N	N	N	11.8
Peru	1940	N	N	Y	18.5
Uruguay	1938	N	N	N	19.7
Venezuela	1940	N	Y	Y	–
Canada	1941	N	N	N	41.1
United States	1940	N	N	Y	37.8

[a] After eliminating wealth and education requirements in 1878, Chile instituted a literacy requirement in 1885, which seems to have been responsible for a sharp decline in the proportion of the population who were registered to vote.

[b] Three states, Connecticut, Louisiana, and New Jersey, still maintained wealth requirements at 1840, but eliminated them soon afterwards. All states except for Illinois and Virginia had implemented the secret ballot by the end of the 1840s.

[c] This figure is for the city of Buenos Aires, and likely overstates the proportion who voted at the national level.

[d] The information on restrictions refers to national laws. The 1863 Constitution empowered provincial state governments to regulate electoral affairs. Afterwards, elections became restricted (in terms of the franchise for adult males) and indirect in some states. It was not until 1948 that a national law established universal adult male suffrage throughout the country. This pattern was followed in other Latin American countries, as it was in the United States and Canada to a lesser extent.

[e] Eighteen states, 7 southern and 11 non-southern, introduced literacy requirements between 1890 and 1926. These restrictions were directed primarily at Blacks and immigrants.

lagged far behind the United States and Canada in establishing schooling institutions and attaining high rates of literacy.

We have emphasized two closely related reasons why population homogeneity might favor successful completion of collective action projects like the establishment of universal schools. First, citizens with similar values, endowments, and behavior should find it easier to agree on whether and how to carry out such an enterprise. Second, unequal distribution of benefits and costs of a project will increase the probability that a group might attempt to block the project, particularly where this group enjoys disproportionate political power. This type of situation is seen throughout Latin America in the restrictions on the conduct of elections – who had the right to vote and whether ballots were secret or public. Income (or wealth) and literacy requirements for suffrage were common, but it was mainly the latter, combined with low literacy, that limited the population who could participate politically as citizens. Thus, the inequality in the distributions of income, political power, and human capital that arose out of the conditions of colonial settlements tended to persist over time – perpetuated at first by the institutions of imperial Spain and then by those that evolved (or failed to evolve) in the newly formed states after independence.

IV

Our argument that the extent of inequality affected the social spending decision to invest on public education seems reasonable and consistent with the evidence on the Americas, but one would like to subject the proposition to more systematic tests. There are, however, several hurdles to overcome. First, estimates of income and wealth inequality in the nineteenth century are available for only a few countries. Second, identifying the line of causation is difficult because schooling, especially public schooling, affects the degree of inequality in each of the various dimensions we focus on: wealth/income, human capital, and political power. In this case, discerning what is exogenous and what is endogenous is not transparent.

The equality of political power illustrates this problem. Throughout the nineteenth century, citizenship and the right to vote were both linked to literacy in most of the Americas. Nearly all Latin American countries maintained, with minor exceptions, both literacy and wealth requirements for the franchise up to the early twentieth century (see Table 4.7). In addition, Latin American countries conditioned citizenship to literacy. In Venezuela citizens had to have the capacity to read and write; Cuba and Puerto Rico, which followed the Cádiz Constitution of 1812, required their citizens to be literate by the year 1830; Peru went back and forth, first stating in its 1823 Constitution that literacy should be a binding condition for citizenship by the year 1840, while a new constitution in 1826 made it a binding condition immediately; in Mexico, although each state decided on the date when literacy would become a binding requirement for citizenship, most states set the dates between 1836 and 1850.[51] As evident from both

---

[51] Tanck de Estrada (1979, 17). The literacy requirements may have been especially binding because schools typically taught individuals to write after they had learned to read, and many of the definitions of citizenship in the newly independent Latin American countries made reading and writing separate requirements; an individual had to read and to write in

Tables 4.7 and 4.8, the proportions of the population voting in Latin American elections varied markedly across countries and were generally low, especially in those countries with low literacy rates. The result was that in countries with low literacy rates the obstacles to mobilizing support for public schools were all the more formidable because those who had the right to vote were most likely those who would have paid most of the taxes for operating new schools, while reaping fewer of the benefits. Thus inequality in human capital and political power were self-reinforcing.

A test of the hypothesis that inequality in political power delayed the establishment of a broad-based system of public schooling is to compare schooling levels with the extent of the franchise. Summary information about the policies governing who had the right to vote in the Americas is reported in Table 4.7. Until the early twentieth century, the right to vote was generally restricted to adult males, but the United States and Canada were the clear leaders in doing away with limits based on wealth and literacy, and a much higher fraction of their populations voted than anywhere else in the New World. In terms of voting rights, the United States and Canada were about a half-century ahead of even the most democratic countries of Latin America, namely Uruguay, Argentina, and Costa Rica. Up to 1940, the proportion voting in the United States and Canada was three times higher than in Mexico, up to ten times higher than in countries such as Brazil and Bolivia, and 50 to 100 percent higher than in the most progressive countries of Latin America.

This empirical association between education and voting rights is consistent with our hypothesis, but there might be alternative interpretations for this finding. The low proportions voting in countries with low literacy may be a consequence of the fact that such societies tended to have literacy requirements. But this begs the questions of why it was that countries with low literacy rates were more likely to maintain the literacy requirements, or why countries that dropped such restrictions were more likely to establish public schools. The empirical association, it might be argued, was largely due to the legacy of British institutions; but there are reasons to be skeptical of this view as well. Not only does it fail to explain the variation in schooling within Latin America, it also ignores the fact that few of the many British colonies in the Americas came close to matching the records of the United States and Canada.

order to obtain full citizenship rights. The literacy restrictions seem generally to have been enforced, albeit with some exceptions. In Chile, a voting registry was created from the very beginning and political parties sought to enroll most of their supporters in this registry, one logical choice of supporters for the ruling parties was the National Guard. In order to enfranchise the National Guard, the government had to lower income restrictions and lower literacy requirements (a person was required to read and write their name), and by doing so it enfranchised most of the population. See Valenzuela (1996).

TABLE 4.8. *International Comparisons of Laws Relating to Suffrage and the Extent of Voting*

	Year When Secret Ballot Attained	Year When Women Gain the Vote	Year of Universal Equal Suffrage	Proportion of Population Voting
Austria	1907	1919	1907	7.9%
Belgium	1877	1948	1919	22.0
Denmark	1901	1918	1918	16.5
Finland	1907	1907	1907	4.6
France	1831	1945	1848	28.4
Germany	1848	1919	1872	22.4
Italy	1861	1946	1919	6.8
Netherlands	1849	1922	1918	12.0
Norway	1885	1909	1921	19.5
Sweden	1866	1921	1921	7.1
Switzerland	1872	1971	1848	22.3
United Kingdom	1872	1918	1948	16.2
Canada	1874	1917	1898[a]	17.9
United States	1849[b]	1920	1870[c]	18.4
Argentina	1912	1947	?	1.8[d]
Bolivia	?	?	1956	–
Brazil	1932	1932	1988	3.0
Chile	1833	1949	1970	4.2
Costa Rica	1925	1949	1913	–
Ecuador	1861	1929	1978	3.3
El Salvador	1950	1939	1950	–
Guatemala	1946[e]	1946	1965	–
Peru	1931	1955	1979	–
Uruguay	1918	1932	1918	–
Venezuela	1946	1945	1946[f]	–

[a] By 1898, all but two Canadian provinces had instituted universal equal suffrage for males.
[b] By the end of the 1840s, all states except for Illinois and Virginia had adopted the secret ballot.
[c] Eighteen states, 7 southern and 11 non-southern, introduced literacy requirements between 1890 and 1926. These restrictions were directed primarily at Blacks and immigrants.
[d] This figure is for the city of Buenos Aires, and likely overestimates the national figure.
[e] Illiterate males do not obtain the secret ballot until 1956; females do not obtain it until 1965.
[f] The 1858 Constitution declared universal direct male suffrage, but this provision was dropped in later constitutions. All restrictions on universal adult suffrage were ended in 1946, with the exception of different age restrictions for literate persons and illiterates.

The extension of suffrage in the United States and Canada, and its relationship to the establishment of tax-supported primary schools, help establish a path of causation. Although not excluding the possibility of other factors influencing social decisions to expand public schooling, they show that at least in some of the countries in the Americas a change in the extent of political inequality acted as a salient stimulus for investment in education. The achievement of universal white male suffrage in the United States was the product of a long series of hard-fought political battles over the first decades of the nineteenth century – not due to a commitment on the part of those who drafted the Constitution. Historians of education have judged it no coincidence that this movement triumphed in the 1820s in the United States at the same time that the movement for "common schools" got started. Other prominent occurrences of extension of suffrage being implemented just before major expansions of schooling include the passage in England of the landmark Elementary Education law of 1870 (and a series of further laws through 1891 expanding access to primary schools) not long after the Second Reform Act of 1867.[52]

By providing an even broader international perspective, Table 4.8 highlights how slow most of the New World societies, despite being nominal democracies, were to extend the franchise. The great majority of European nations, as well as the United States and Canada, introduced secrecy in balloting and universal adult male suffrage long before the countries in Latin America and the Caribbean, and the proportions of the population voting in the former were always higher, often four to five times those in the latter. Although many factors may have contributed to the relatively low vote percentages in Latin America and the Caribbean, political decisions to maintain wealth and literacy requirements appear to have been of central importance.

In order to examine the empirical association between the extent of suffrage (a proxy for the degree of equality in political power) and investment in schooling institutions more directly, we bring together information on student enrollment with the fraction of the population who cast votes for a wide range of countries in the Americas and Europe (see Table 4.9). Several features are immediately apparent. First, the United States and Canada stand out early as having the highest proportions of children attending school in the world – 62 and 60 percent, respectively, in 1895. The only other nations that came close were France, Germany, and Switzerland (the only three of the countries in Europe that attained universal equal male suffrage in the nineteenth century) with 56, 54, and 53 percent, respectively. Notably, Britain lagged behind its neighbors despite having higher per capita income. The United States and Canada were also distinguished at 1895 as having, with the exception of Belgium, the highest fractions of their populations voting.

The Latin American countries generally lagged their North American neighbors and Europe both in schooling participation and the extension of

---

[52] Cubberley (1920, 641–44).

TABLE 4.9. *Ratio of Students in School to Population Ages 5–19 and the Proportion of the Population Voting for Selected Countries, 1895–1945*

	c. 1895	c. 1920	c. 1945
Argentina			
Schooling ratios[a]	0.21	0.41	0.51
Suffrage[b]	1.8%	10.9%	15.0%
Bolivia			
Schooling ratios	0.14	–	0.18
Suffrage	–	–	–
Brazil			
Schooling ratios	0.08	0.10	0.18
Suffrage	2.2%	4.0%	5.7%
Chile			
Schooling ratios	0.16	0.34	0.43
Suffrage	4.2%	4.4%	9.4%
Colombia			
Schooling ratios	–	0.18	0.18
Suffrage	–	6.9%	11.1%
Costa Rica			
Schooling ratios	0.25	0.22	0.29
Suffrage	–	10.6%	17.6%
Cuba			
Schooling ratios	–	0.31	0.31
Suffrage	–	–	–
Mexico			
Schooling ratios	0.13	0.17	0.22
Suffrage	5.4%	8.6%	11.8%
Peru			
Schooling ratios	–	–	0.31
Suffrage	–	–	–
Uruguay			
Schooling ratios	0.13	0.34	–
Suffrage	–	13.8%	–
Canada			
Schooling ratios	0.60	0.65	0.64
Suffrage	17.9%	20.5%	41.1%
United States			
Schooling ratios	0.62	0.68	0.76
Suffrage	18.4%	25.1%	37.8%
Austria			
Schooling ratios	0.45	0.52	0.58
Suffrage	7.9%	46.1%	46.9%
Belgium			
Schooling ratios	0.42	0.46	0.53
Suffrage	20.1%	26.3%	28.9%
Denmark			
Schooling ratios	0.49	0.49	0.50
Suffrage	9.9%	30.3%	50.8%

(continued)

TABLE 4.9 *(continued)*

	c. 1895	c. 1920	c. 1945
Finland			
Schooling ratios	0.12	0.29	0.53
Suffrage	4.6%	27.3%	44.3%
France			
Schooling ratios	0.56	0.43	0.60
Suffrage	19.4%	21.0%	49.3%
Germany			
Schooling ratios	0.54	0.53	0.55
Suffrage	14.6%	45.6%	48.8%
Ireland			
Schooling ratios	0.32	0.54	0.53
Suffrage	–	21.9%	41.1%
Italy			
Schooling ratios	0.27	0.36	0.47
Suffrage	4.1%	16.2%	52.5%
Netherlands			
Schooling ratios	0.44	0.45	0.56
Suffrage	5.1%	20.5%	49.5%
Norway			
Schooling ratios	0.48	0.50	0.52
Suffrage	7.9%	32.1%	47.5%
Portugal			
Schooling ratios	0.14	0.17	0.26
Suffrage	–	–	–
Spain			
Schooling ratios	–	0.27	0.34
Suffrage	–	–	–
Sweden			
Schooling ratios	0.50	0.42	0.45
Suffrage	2.8%	11.2%	46.4%
Switzerland			
Schooling ratios	0.53	0.54	0.49
Suffrage	11.8%	19.2%	20.5%
United Kingdom			
Schooling ratios	0.45	0.51	0.66
Suffrage	9.8%	30.4%	49.9%

[a] Schooling ratios were calculated by dividing the total number of students (regardless of age) by the population between the ages 5–19. When groups of population were different from this range (5–19) we assumed that there was the same number of people in each age group, and weighed the population figures so as to make them comparable. An example of this was Bolivia.
[b] Suffrage is used here to represent the proportion of the population that votes in each country.
Sources: For the schooling data: B. R. Mitchell, *International Historical Statistics: The Americas 1750–1988*, and *International Historical Statistics: Europe 1750–1988*.
For the data on suffrage: Peter Flora et al. (1983, vol. 1); and Dieter Nohlan, ed. *Enciclopedia Electoral Latinamericana y del Caribe*.

the franchise. In South and Central America, Argentina had the highest proportion attending school in 1895, but at 0.21 this was barely a third of the levels prevailing in the United States and Canada. Given the especially small proportion of the Argentinean population voting in 1895, 1.8 percent, it seems inaccurate to attribute the country's relatively high schooling ratio to factors related to the franchise. At the same time, it might be noted that Argentina was the one Latin American nation to have done away with both wealth and literacy restrictions. Also, the greater preference of immigrants for education may have played a role.[53] By 1920, both Argentina and Uruguay had introduced the secret ballot and made other reforms, and both the schooling ratios and the proportions of voting soared. By 1920, they had the highest proportions voting as well as the highest schooling ratios – with the exception of Chile nosing out Uruguay for second place – in Latin America.

Between 1895 and 1945, nearly all the European countries, as well as the United States and Canada, further extended the franchise, both through broadening male suffrage and giving women the right to vote. The United States, Canada, France, Germany, and Belgium, which already had achieved high schooling participation and had high voting percentages by 1895, achieved only modest increases in their schooling ratios through 1945, even though a greater percentage of their population was now voting. Those that began in 1895 with rather low schooling ratios and proportions voting, such as Finland, Ireland, Italy, and the Netherlands, experienced both a great expansion of suffrage as well as substantial increases in the fraction of the school-aged population in school. Portugal and Spain, which had monarchies with no significant voting rights, had the lowest schooling ratios in Europe throughout the entire period. Only three of the Scandinavian countries, Sweden, Norway, and Denmark, deviated significantly from the general pattern. Despite restrictions on the franchise and low proportions voting, they had high schooling ratios in 1895.

Schooling ratios and the proportions voting rose over time throughout Latin America, but they remained consistently low by general international standards. By 1945 Argentina, Uruguay, and Chile did, however, approach the schooling ratios in some European democracies, notably Italy, Sweden, and Switzerland.[54] From a broad international perspective, the empirical association between the extent of the franchise and schooling participation is clear, but it holds as well, though in a weaker form, within Latin America.

---

[53] Although even qualified immigrants were reluctant (mysteriously so to the many scholars who have studied the phenomenon) to change their citizenship to obtain the right to vote, their children would be doing so within a generation.

[54] The other exception to this generalization is the European monarchies (Portugal and Spain), who fell comfortably within the Latin American distribution in schooling ratios.

TABLE 4.10. *Schooling and Suffrage, 1895–1945*

	Coefficient	t-statistic
constant	−1.09	−6.02
Suffrage	0.496	5.37
Year 1920	−0.087	−2.97
Year 1945	−0.132	−3.77
Log (per capita income)	0.189	7.92
Number of Observations	56	
Adjusted R²	0.72	

Note: The schooling ratio is the dependent variable. Data on per capita income from Madison (1995).

These comparative statistics are informative, but a multivariate analysis with controls for variation across countries and over time in per capita income would improve our understanding of the systematic patterns in the data. Table 4.10 presents a pooled cross-section (from the data for 1895, 1920, and 1945) regression with the ratio of students in school to the school-age population as the dependent variable. The schooling ratio is positively and significantly related to per capita income. Although one cannot feasibly distinguish between alternative paths of causation from these regressions alone, the results indicate that inequality in political power, as reflected in the proportion of the population who voted, was significantly related to the fraction of the population provided with schooling. The coefficient on the variable representing the proportion of the population voting is positive and large. It is, moreover, of an analytically important magnitude as well as statistically significant. Overall, it is quite impressive that suffrage is significantly related to the schooling ratio, even after controlling for year and per capita income. One implication is that the regional differences in schooling can be fully "accounted for" by differences in per capita income and our measure of inequality in political influence.

V

In earlier work we highlighted the potential relevance of differences across societies in the degree of inequality in wealth, human capital, and political power in accounting for differential paths of development in the Americas, and argued that the roots of these disparities lay in differences in the initial factor endowments of the respective colonies. We argued that the extent of inequality exerted significant influence on the way in which economic institutions evolved over time. Where inequality was relatively low, the institutions that tended to develop extended opportunity to the general population, promoting growth by stimulating broad participation in commercial activities, increasing productivity, and preserving relative equality in the society at large. Where inequality was relatively high, institutions favored the elite groups, maintained inequality, and reduced the prospects for sustained economic growth.

Here we have examined the development of primary schools and the increase in literacy in the Americas. Not only were the United States and Canada well ahead of their neighbors in establishing institutions of public primary education open to all, but even among the other countries in the New World, those societies that were more equal organized public schools earlier, and attained higher levels of literacy. The cross-sectional patterns are not the only features of the record that are consistent with the proposition that equality and education are related. In both the United States and Canada, political decisions to expand public schools closely followed the extension of suffrage. Moreover, the observation that in many Latin American societies the goal of increasing schooling rates was often frustrated by collective action problems at the local or state/provincial levels, especially where there was great inequality and populations were heterogeneous, and that progress typically required the intervention of national governments, also lend support to our view.

Although our account focuses on the importance of inequality in explaining how education institutions such as universal primary schooling and high literacy rates evolved in the Americas, other factors, both systematic and idiosyncratic, also played significant roles. Foremost among them was income, or the availability of resources to invest in schooling institutions. Although many of the societies in the Americas were sufficiently prosperous during the nineteenth century to bear the costs of providing the broad population with a primary education, few did. Those that did tended to be more equal and homogeneous, but they also had higher per capita incomes. Moreover, economic booms often triggered public authorities to increase investments in schooling. Another contribution to the expansion of public education was immigration. In Argentina, Chile, and the highlands of Colombia, the desire to attract immigrants encouraged investments in public schooling and raised literacy. Immigrants to Latin America tended to place a higher value on education and were generally more literate than the native born. Another issue of importance in Latin America was the relationship between the national government and local and state authorities. In contrast to the experience in the United States and Canada, national governments were almost always the central force behind the establishment of public schools in Latin America countries. They were better positioned to overcome the collective action problems that made it difficult for local and even provincial governments to raise sufficient revenue on their own. But even when the national governments provided resources to promote public schooling, they had to resolve difficulties in coordination that arose from the demarcation of legal authority. Both the form and the severity of these problems varied across countries, and influenced the timing and effectiveness of national government intervention in education policy.[55]

Overall, the evidence is consistent with the hypothesis that the extent of inequality and population heterogeneity had a major impact on the evolution of educational institutions in the New World. The relative inequality characteristic of Latin America, in contrast with the United States and Canada, helps account for why universal schooling and high literacy came much later and may also explain why extreme inequality in Latin America has persisted to the present day. Our hypothesis remains speculative and clearly requires further study, but we hope that this attempt to examine how the paths of various New World economies diverged will stimulate more work on the interplay between factor endowments, inequality, institutions, and economic growth – in this context and in general.

References

Acemoglu, Daron and Robinson, James A. 2000. "When Did the West Extend the Franchise? Growth, Inequality and Democracy in Historical Perspective." *Quarterly Journal of Economics* 115 (November): 1167–99.

Alesina, Alberto, Reza Baqir, and William Easterly. 1999. "Public Goods and Ethnic Divisions." *Quarterly Journal of Economics* 114 (November): 1243–84.

Ahumada, Miguel. 1896. *Memoria de la Administración Pública del Estado de Chihuahua.* Chihuahua: Impresa del Gobierno en Palacio.

Alboites, Luis. 1994. *Breve Historia de Chihuahua.* Mexico: Colegio de Mexico, and Fondo de Cultura Económica (FCE).

Albright, Spencer D. 1942. *The American Ballot.* Washington, DC: American Council on Public Affairs.

Alonso, Paula. 1993. "Politics and Elections in Buenos Aires, 1890–1898: The Performance of the Radical Party." *Journal of Latin American Studies* 25 (October): 464–87.

Alonso, Paula. 1996. "Voting in Buenos Aires before 1912." In Eduardo Posada-Carbó, ed. *Elections before democracy: the history of elections in Europe and Latin America.* New York: St. Martin's Press.

Annino, Antonio. 1996. "The Ballot, Land and Sovereignty: Cadiz and the Origins of Mexican Local Government, 1812–1820." In Eduardo Posada-Carbó, ed. *Elections before democracy: the history of elections in Europe and Latin America.* New York: St. Martin's Press.

---

[55] Perhaps another factor in accounting for the variation across economies is what might be called the British colony effect. Although it seems unlikely that the early investments in public schooling by the United States and Canada can be attributed solely to their British heritage, the rapid increase in schooling throughout the British colonies in the Caribbean basin in the late-nineteenth century may well have been related to the activities of the British Colonial Office during that period. As is indicated in Table 4.9, schooling ratios in the United States and Canada were generally much higher (on the order of 30 percent through 1920) than in Britain. For a discussion of the role of differential factor endowments on political and economic factors, see Engerman and Sokoloff (2002; 2005).

Arce Gurza, Francisco. 1981. "En Busca de una Educación Revolucionaria: 1924–1934." In Josefina Zoraida Vazquez et al., eds. *Ensayos sobre historia de la educación en México*. Mexico, D.F.: Colegio de Mexico.

Barquin, Manuel. 1986. "La Reforma Electoral de 1986–87 en México: Retrospectiva y Análisis." In *Sistemas Electorales y Representación Política en Latinoamérica*, Fundación Friederich Ebert Madrid: Instituto de Cooperación Iberoamericana.

Basadre, Jorge. 1961. *Historia de la Republica del Peru*. Vol. I-X. Lima: Editorial Cultura Antartica S.A.

Bayle, Constantino. 1952. *Los Cabildos Seculares en la America Española*. Madrid: Sapientia.

Bazant, Milada. 1982. "La República Restaurada y el Profiriato." In Francisco Arce Gurza et al., eds. *Historia de las Profesiones en México*. Mexico, D.F.: Colegio de Mexico.

Beck, J. Murray. 1968. *Pendulum of Power: Canada's Federal Elections*. Scarborough: Prentice-Hall.

Bethell, Leslie, ed. 1984. *The Cambridge History of Latin America*, 5 vols. Cambridge, UK: Cambridge University Press.

Booth, John A. 1988. "Costa Rica: The Roots of Democratic Stability." In Larry Diamond, Juan J. Linz, and Seymour Martin Lipset, eds. *Democracy in Developing Countries*. Boulder: L. Rienner.

Brahm, Luis A., Cariola, Patricio S.J., and Silva, Juan José. 1971. *Educación Particular en Chile: Antecedentes y Dilemas*. Santiago de Chile: Centro de Investigación y Docencia Económica (CIDE).

Britton, John A., ed. 1994. *Molding the Hearts and Minds: Education, Communications, and Social Change in Latin America*. Wilmington, DE: Scholarly Resources.

Bulmer-Thomas, Victor. 1994. *The Economic History of Latin America since Independence*. New York: Cambridge University Press.

Campos, Harriet Fernando. 1960. *Desarrollo Educacional 1810–1960*. Santiago de Chile: Editorial Universitaria.

Cantón, Darío. 1973. *Elecciones y partidos políticos en la Argentina; historia, interpretación y balance: 1910–1966*, First ed. Buenos Aires: Siglo Veintiuno Argentina Editores.

Castillo, Tito Cabezas. 1997. "Sistema Electoral y sus Consecuencias Políticas: Caso Ecuatoriano." In Carlota Jakisch, ed., *Sistemas Electorales y sus Consecuencias Políticas*. Buenos Aires: Centro Interdisciplinario de Estudios sobre el Desarrollo Latinoamericano.

Censo de Educación. 1909. Vols. 1–3. Buenos Aires: República Argentina.

Cuban Economic Research Project. 1965. *A Study on Cuba: The Colonial and Republican Periods*. Miami: University of Miami Press.

Cubberly, Ellwood P. 1920. *The History of Education*. Boston: Houghton Mifflin.

De la Peña, Moises T. 1948. *Chihuahua Económico. Tomos I, II, III*. Mexico: Patrocinado por el Ing. Fernando Foglio Miramontes Gobernador Constitucional del Estado de Chihuahua.

Departamento Administrativo Nacional deEstadistica. 1981. *Panorama Estadistico de Antioquia, Siglos XIX y XX*. Bogotá: Dane.

Diaz, Alida. 1974. *El Censo del 1876 en el Peru*. Lima: Seminario de Historia Rural Andina.

Dominion Bureau of Statistics. 1926. *Illiteracy and School Attendance in Canada*. Ottawa: F.A. Acland.

Easterlin, Richard A. 1981. "Why Isn't the Whole World Developed?" *Journal of Economic History* 51 (March): 1–19.

Egnal, Marc. 1996. *Divergent Paths: How Culture and Institutions Have Shaped North American Growth*. New York: Oxford University Press.

Engerman, Stanley L. and Sokoloff, Kenneth L. 1997. "Factor Endowments, Institutions, and Differential Paths of Growth Among New World Economies: A View from Economic Historians of the United States." In Stephen Haber, ed., *How Latin America Fell Behind*. Stanford: Stanford University Press.

Engerman, Stanley L. and Sokoloff, Kenneth L. 2002. "Factor Endowments, Inequality, and Paths of Development Among New World Economics." *Economia* 3 (Fall): 41–109.

Engerman, Stanley L. and Sokoloff, Kenneth L. 2005 "The Evolution of Suffrage Institutions in the New World." *Journal of Economic History* 65 (December): 891–921.

Escobar Alvarez, Miguel Angel. c.1987. *La instrucción pública en México desde 1910 hasta 1917; los adminstrativos de Porfirio Díaz, León de la Barra, Francisco I. Madero, Victoriano Huerta y del gobierno preconstitucionalista*. Madrid: OEA.

Fernández, Hernan and Rosales, Jorge. 1990. *Educacion, una Mirada hacia adentro: analfabetismo, repitencia y desercion*. Lima: Instituto de Pedagogia Popular.

Fernández Rojas, José. 1933. *El Proceso de la Educación Pública en México*. Saltillo Mexico: Impresora de Coahuila.

Fischel, Astrid. 1987. *Concenso y Represión: una interpretación socio-política de la educación costarricense*. San José Costa Rica: Editorial Costa Rica.

Fischel, Astrid. 1992. *El uso ingenioso de la ideología en Costa Rica*. San José Costa Rica: Universidad Esatal a Distancia.

Flora, Peter et al. 1983. *State, Economy and Society in Western Europe: 1815–1975*, Vol. 1. Chicago: St. James Press.

Franco, Rolando. 1985. *Democracia "a la uruguaya": análisis electoral, 1925–1985*, Second ed. Montevideo: El Libro Libre.

Go, Sun and Lindert, Peter. 2007. "The Curious Dawn of American Public Schools." Unpublished.

Goldin, Claudia and Katz, Lawrence F. 1997a. "Human and Social Capital: The Rise of Secondary Schooling in America, 1910 to 1940." Manuscript, Harvard University.

Goldin, Claudia and Katz, Lawrence F. 1997b. "Why the United States Led in Education: Lessons from Secondary School Expansion, 1910 to 1940." National Bureau of Economic Research Working Paper 6144 (August).

Goldin, Claudia. 1998. "Egalitarianism and the Returns to Education During the Great Transformation of American Education." Manuscript. Harvard University and National Bureau of Economic Research.

Goldin, Claudia and Katz, Lawrence F. 2008. *The Race Between Education and Technology*. Cambridge, MA: Harvard University Press.

Gonzalez Casanova, Pablo. 1965. *La Democracia en Mexico*, First edition. Mexico: Ediciones Era.

Haring, C.H. 1947. *The Spanish Empire in America*. New York: Oxford University Press.

Helg, Aline. 1987. *La Educación en Colombia, 1918–1957: una historia social, económica y política*. Bogotá Colombia: Fondo Editorial CEREC.

Hernández Chávez, Alicia. 1996. "Las tensiones internas del federalismo mexicano." In Alicia Hernández Chávez, ed. *Hacia un nuevo federalismo?* Mexico: Fondo de Cultura Económica (FCE).

Higgs, Robert. 1977. *Competition and Coercion: Blacks in the American Economy, 1865–1914*. Cambridge: Cambridge University Press.

Instituto Nacional deEstadística Geografía e Informática. 1994. *Estadísticas Históricas De Mexico*. Vols. 1 and 2. Aguascalientes Mexico.

Kaestle, Carl F. 1983. *Pillars of the Republic: Common Schools and American Society*. New York: Hill and Wang.

Kleppner, Paul. 1982. *Who Voted? The Dynamics of Electoral Turnout, 1870–1980*. New York: Praeger.

Kousser, Morgan J. 1974. *The Shaping of Southern Politics: Suffrage Restrictions and the Establishment of the One-Party South 1880–1910*. New Haven: Yale University Press.

Labarca Hubertson, Amanda. 1939. *Historia de la enseñanza en Chile*. Santiago de Chile: Imprenta Universitaria.

LeGrand, Catherine. 1986. *Frontier Expansion and Peasant Protest in Colombia, 1850–1936*. Albuquerque: University of New Mexico Press.

Lewis, Frank D. and Urquhart, M.C. 1999. "Growth of the Standard of Living in a Pioneer Economy: Upper Canada, 1821 to 1851." *William and Mary Quarterly* 56 (January): 151–81.

Lindert, Peter H. 1994. "The Rise of Social Spending." *Explorations in Economic History* 31 (January): 1–37.

Maddison, Angus. 1991. *Dynamic Forces in Capitalist Development: A long-run comparative view*. New York: Oxford University Press.

Maddison, Angus. 1994. "Explaining the Economic Performance of Nations, 1820–1989." In William J. Baumol, Richard R. Nelson, and Edward N. Wolff, eds. *Convergence of Productivity: Cross-National Studies and Historical Evidence*. New York: Oxford University Press.

Maddison, Angus. 1995. *Monitoring the World Economy, 1820–1992*. Paris: OECD.

Maltoni, Marta. 1988. *Educación y Reformas constitucionales, 1819–1987*. Buenos Aires: Librería "El Ateneo" Editorial.

Martínez Jiménez, Alejandro. 1988. "La Educación Elemental en el Profiriato" *Historia Mexicana* 22, no. 4: 514–52.

Misuriello, Vincenzo. 1993. *Política de la Inmigración en la Argentina: 1853–1970*. Tucumán: Ediciones del Gabinete Secretaría de Post-Grado de la Universidad Nacional de Tucumán.

Mitchell, B.R. 1992. *International Historical Statistics: Europe 1750–1988*. New York: Stockton Press.

Mitchell, B.R. 1993. *International Historical Statistics: The Americas 1750–1988*. New York: Stockton Press.

Mulhall, M.G. and Mulhall, E.T. 1885. *Handbooks of the River Plate*. London: Trubner.

Newland, Carlos. 1991. "La Educación Elemental en Hispanoamérica: Desde la Independencia hasta la Centralización de los Sistemas Educativos Nacionales." *Hispanic American Historical Review* 71 (May): 335–364.

Newland, Carlos. 1994. "The Estado Docente and its expansion: Spanish America elementary education, 1900–1950." *Journal of Latin American Studies* 26 (May): 449–67.

Nohlan, Dieter, ed. 1993. *Enciclopedia Electoral Latinoamericana y del Caribe*. San José Costa Rica: Instituto Interamericano de Derechos Humanos.

North, Douglass. 1981. *Structure and Change in Economic History*. New York: Norton.

Oficina Nacional deEstadística. 1912. *Resúmenes Estadísticos: Años 1883–1910*. Demografia. San José Costa Rica: Imprenta Nacional.

Ortuste, Gonzalo Rojas and Oblitas, Moira Zuazo. 1997. "Análisis Del Sistema Electoral y sus Consecuencias Políticas en el Marco de la Reforma Estatal: el Caso de Bolivia." In Carlota Jakisch, ed., *Sistemas Electorales y sus Consecuencias Políticas*. Buenos Aires: Centro Interdisciplinario de Estudios sobre el Desarrollo Latinoamericano.

Pani, Alberto J. 1918. *Una Encuesta Sobre Educación Popular*. Mexico: Departamento de Aprovisionamientos Generales.

Palacios, Marco. 1980. *Coffee in Colombia, 1850–1970: An Economic, Social and Political History*. Cambridge: Cambridge University Press.

Paulston, Rolland. 1971. *Society, Schools and Progress in Peru*. Oxford: Pergamon Press.

Phillips, Charles E. 1957. *The Development of Education in Canada*. Toronto: W.J. Gage.

Pietschmann, Horst. 1996. *Las reformas borbónicas y el sistema de intendencias en Nueva España: un estudio político administrativo*. Mexico: Fondo de Cultura Económica (FCE).

Porter, Kirk H. 1918. *A History of Suffrage in the United States*. Chicago: University of Chicago Press.

Qualter, Terence H. 1970. *The Election Process in Canada*. Toronto: McGraw-Hill.

Ramirez, Maria Teresa, and Salazar, Irene. 2008. "The Emergence of Education in the Republic of Colombia in the 19th Century: Where Did We Go Wrong?" Unpublished.

Recchini de Lattes, Zulma, and Lattes, Alfredo. 1969. *Migraciones en la Argentina*. Buenos Aires: Instituto Torcuato di Tella.

República Argentina. 1910. *Censo General de Educación, 1909*. Volumes 1–3. Buenos Aires: Talleres de Publicación de la Oficina Meteorológica Argentina.

República de Colombia Registraduría Nacional del Estado Civil. 1988. *Historia electoral colombiana*. Bogotá: La Registraduría.

Resúmen de la República, Buenos Aires: República Argentina.

Rivera Borbón, Carlos. 1970. *El Gasto del Gobierno Federal Mexicano a través de la Secretaria de Educación Pública*. México.

Roberts, George W. 1957. *The Population of Jamaica*. Cambridge: Cambridge University Press.

Safford, Frank. 1976. *The Ideal of the Practical, Colombia's Struggle to Form a Technical Elite.* Austin: University of Texas Press.

Schultz, Theodore W. 1963. *The Economic Value of Education.* New York: Columbia University Press.

Sibaja, Luis Fernando. 1995. "Ayuntamientos y Estado en los Primeros Años de Vida Independiente de Costa Rica (1821–1835)." In *Actas del III Congreso de Academias Iberoamericanas de la Historia: El Municipio en Iberoamérica (Cabildos e Instituciones Locales).* Montevideo Uruguay: Instituto Histórico y Geográfico del Uruguay.

Sociedad y Educación; Ensayos sobre Historia de la educación en América Latina. 1995. First edition. Santafé de Bogotá: Univeridad Pedagógica Nacional Bogotá.

Solana Fernando, Reyes, Raúl Cardiel, and Martínez, Raúl Bolaños, coordinators. 1981. *Historia de la educación pública en México.* Mexico: Fondo de Cultura Economica.

Soltow, Lee and Stevens, Edward. 1981. *The Rise of Literacy and the Common School in the United States.* Chicago: University of Chicago Press.

Staples, Anne. 1981. "Panorama Educativo al Comienzo de la Vida Independiente." In Josefina Zoraida Vazquez et al., eds., *Ensayos sobre historia de la educación en México.* Mexico: Colegio de Mexico.

Tanck de Estrada Dorothy. 1979. "Las Cortes de Cádiz y el desarrollo de la educación en México." *Historia Mexicana* 29, no. 1: 3–34.

Tena Ramírez, Felipe. 1964. *Leyes Fundamentales de México 1808–1964*, Second ed. Mexico: Editorial Porrúa.

Urquhart, M.C., ed. 1965. *Historical Statistics of Canada.* Cambridge: Cambridge University Press.

U.S. Bureau of the Census. 1853. *Seventh Census of the United States: 1850.* Washington, DC: Government Printing Office.

U.S. Bureau of the Census. 1967. *Education of the American Population*, by John K. Folger and Charles B. Nam (1960 Census Monograph). Washington, DC: Government Printing Office.

U.S. Bureau of the Census. 1975. *Historical Statistics of the United States: Colonial Times to 1970.* Washington, DC: Government Printing Office.

U.S. Department of the Interior. 1898. *Annual Reports of the Department of the Interior. Report of the Commissioner of Education.* Washington, DC: Government Printing Office.

Valenzuela, J. Samuel. 1996. "Building Aspects of Democracy before Democracy: Electoral Practices in Nineteenth Century Chile." In Eduardo Posada-Carbó, ed. *Elections before democracy: the history of elections in Europe and Latin America.* New York: St. Martin's Press.

Vaughan, Mary Kay. 1982. *The State, Education, and Social Class in Mexico, 1880–1928.* DeKalb Illinois: Northern Illinois University Press.

Vaughan, Mary Kay. 1990. "Primary Education and Literacy in Nineteenth-Century: Research Trends, 1968–1988." *Latin American Historical Research Review* 25, no. 1: 31–66.

Vedoya, Juan Carlos. 1973. *Cómo fue la enseñanza popular en la Argentina.* Buenos Aires: Plus Ultra.

Ward, Norman. 1950. *The Canadian House of Commons: Representation.* Toronto: University of Toronto Press.

West Indian Census. 1950. *General Report on the Census of Population 9th. April, 1946.* Kingston Jamaica: Government Printing Office.

Wilcox, M. and Rines, G. 1917. *Encyclopaedia of Latin America.* New York: Encyclopedia Americana.

Wilson, J. Donald, Stamp, Robert M., and Audet, Louis-Philippe. 1970. *Canadian Education: A History.* Scarborough: Prentice-Hall of Canada.

Woodward, Ralph Lee Jr. 1976. *Central America: A Nation Divided.* New York: Oxford University Press.

Yeager, Gertrude M. 1991. "Elite Education in Nineteenth-Century Chile." *Hispanic American Historical Review* 71(February): 73–105.

5

Why the United States Led in Education: Lessons from Secondary School Expansion, 1910 to 1940

Claudia Goldin and Lawrence F. Katz

In the first several decades of the twentieth century, the United States pulled far ahead of all other countries in the education of its youth. It underwent what was then and now termed the "high school movement," a feat most other western nations would achieve some 30 to 50 years later. We address how the "second transformation" of American education occurred and what aspects of the society, economy, and political structure enabled the United States to lead the world in education for much of the twentieth century.[1]

From 1910 to 1940, America underwent a spectacular educational transformation. Just 9 percent of 18-year olds had high school diplomas in 1910, but more than 50 percent did by 1940 (see Figure 5.1). The transformation was even more rapid in many non-southern states and cities. Secondary-school enrollment and graduation rates, in most northern and western states, increased so rapidly that by the mid-1930s rates were as high as they would be by 1960. The high school movement set the United States far ahead of all other nations in its human capital stock.[2]

Earlier in its history, the United States had also taken a commanding position in education. During the mid-nineteenth century, America surpassed

---

[1] The first transformation was the achievement of widespread public primary education accomplished in the mid-nineteenth century. The third transformation, still in motion, is the rise of higher education that swiftly increased after World War II. By "education" we mean years of formal schooling rather than the content of schooling and training.

[2] Canada underwent a similar, but slower, increase in secondary schools at the same time. See Urquhart and Buckley (1965).

This paper is a revised version of our presentation at a Rochester Conference in honor of Stanley Engerman, which in turn was a revised version of NBER Working Paper no. 6144. We acknowledge research support from the Spencer Foundation (Major Grant no. 200200007) and the National Science Foundation (Grant no. SBR199515216). We thank the many research assistants who assisted with cross-country data and those who assembled the state- and city-level secondary school data. Robert Whaples generously provided some of the 1910 and 1920 city data. Frank Lewis provided helpful comments on the conference paper. A fuller version of the ideas in this paper can be found in Chapters 5 and 6 of Goldin and Katz (2008).

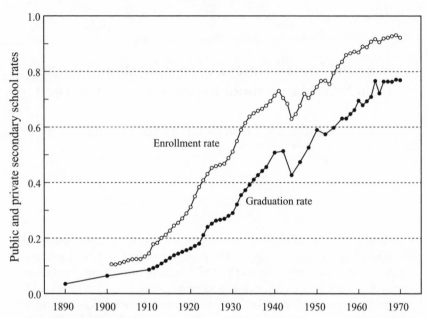

FIGURE 5.1. Secondary School Enrollment and Graduation Rates: Entire United States, 1890 to 1970. *Notes:* Enrollment figures are divided by the number of 14- to 17-year olds; graduation figures are divided by the number of 17-year-olds. The data include both males and females in public and private schools (excluding preparatory departments in colleges and universities). Year given is end of school year. *Sources:* U.S. Department of Education (1993) and Goldin's calculations for graduation rate data from 1910 to 1930.

the impressive enrollment levels achieved in Germany and took the lead in primary (grammar, elementary, or common) school education (Easterlin 1981). But by the turn of the twentieth century, various European countries had narrowed their educational gap with the United States (Lindert 2004). As the high school movement took root in America, however, the wide educational lead of the United States reappeared and was expanded considerably to mid-century.

Educational differences between youths in the United States and those in many European countries would not again be reduced for some time and in many cases have been narrowed only recently. Differences in formal schooling rates for older youths (15 to 19 years old) between various European countries and the United States were substantial in the mid-1950s.[3] As can be seen in Figure 5.2, the U.S. secondary school enrollment rate for older

---

[3] We use enrollment by age rather than by type of school because of the lack of comparability across educational institutions. Secondary schooling began at age 14 in some countries but at age 11 in others.

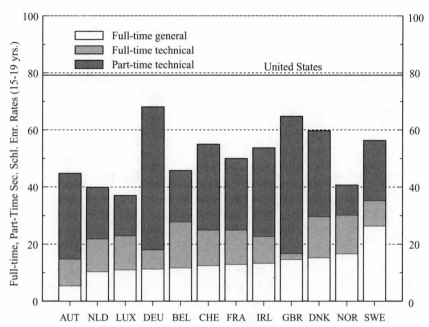

FIGURE 5.2. Secondary School Enrollment Rates for European Nations and the United States, c. 1955. *Notes:* The data refer to the number of youths in public and private upper and lower secondary schools (of the types listed) ranging from those who turned 15 years old during the school year to those who turned 19 years old during that year. Thus, the age group under consideration is approximately all 15- to 18-year-olds, plus one-half of 14- and 19-year-olds. No youths in elementary schools or colleges and universities are included even if they were in the included ages. The procedure ensures consistency but implicitly favors countries, such as the Nordic nations, that have late starting ages and penalizes those, such as France and the United States, that have earlier starting ages. The computation for the United States assumes 100 percent enrollment for the 14-year-olds and then adds all enrolled in ninth through twelfth grades and divides by the age group given above. All data are for c. 1955. We have included only those countries for which we have data for all three educational types. Abbreviations are: Austria (AUT), Netherlands (NLD), Luxemburg (LUX), Germany (DEU), Belgium (BEL), Switzerland (CHE), France (FRA), Ireland (IRL), Great Britain (GBR), Denmark (DNK), Norway (NOR), and Sweden (SWE). The countries are arrayed in increasing order of their full-time general schooling rate, given by the bottom portion of the histogram bar. *Sources:* European nations: Dewhurst et al. (1961). The Dewhurst et al. data for England and Wales, France, Germany (including the Saar and West Berlin), and Sweden have been checked against the original administrative records and small errors have been corrected. United States: U.S. Department of Education (1993), tables 1 and 9.

youths in 1955 was just below 80 percent. No European country, however, had a full-time general schooling rate for youths in this age bracket exceeding 25 percent.

These substantial differences in full-time formal schooling are only slightly reduced by including youths enrolled in full-time technical programs (the two bottom portions of the histogram bar). With this addition, no European country had a general and technical full-time enrollment rate exceeding 40 percent. To make the point even more extreme, the wide U.S. lead in education remains even after including those in part-time technical programs (the entire histogram bar). The relative stock of educated workers, therefore, was considerably greater in the United States than in most European countries until the 1970s and even to the 1980s.[4]

We examine the expansion of U.S. secondary schooling by exploiting the wide variation in education, income, wealth, and economic and demographic structure across states and cities from 1910 to 1940. In 1928 – the approximate mid-point of the period – the ratio of the secondary school graduation rate at the top decile to that at the bottom decile of states was about three, as was the ratio for income per capita.[5] These are large differences and span those found across many of the other countries of the developed world over the same period. The range of schooling rates, incomes, urbanization, demographic composition, and industrial development found in the United States over this period is similar to that found across a wide group of countries.[6] Thus, an analysis of the determinants of differences in secondary schooling across U.S. states and cities may shed light on the reasons the United States moved to the forefront of educational attainment in the first half of the twentieth century. The various factors that account for the variation in schooling rates across U.S. states and cities appear also to have been important in explaining differences between Europe and the United States (and Canada) and possibly in addition within Europe.[7]

The areas of the United States that led in secondary school education, we will show, had higher taxable wealth per capita, greater per capita income,

---

[4] This point does not necessarily follow from the previous statements on educational flows since the educational stock (meaning average years of school) of Americans was often diluted by the arrival of lower-educated immigrants. But because the level of education of the native-born population was so high, compared with that in Great Britain, for example, the dilution effect does not overturn the statement that the educational stock of the American workforce was greater than that in European countries.

[5] These are the numbers for the ratio of the state at the ninetieth percentile to that at the tenth percentile. The ratio of the highest to the lowest state was 4.6 for the 1928 graduation rate and about 4 for income per capita in 1929.

[6] Although we have assembled schooling rates by age for a large number of European nations in 1955, we cannot do so for various years in the first half of the twentieth century.

[7] See Engerman, Mariscal, and Sokoloff (2009) on factors similar to those we identify, which help explain differences within the Western Hemisphere, such as wealth distribution, income and wealth level, bureaucratic decentralization, rapid growth in income, and the need to attract immigrants.

higher proportions of their population that were older, and a tighter distribution of wealth and income.[8] As well, a lower proportion of their total employment was in manufacturing and a lower share was foreign born and Catholic. Homogeneity of economic and social condition and the social stability of community fostered the extension of education to the secondary school level, given a modicum of income or wealth.

Also of importance was the state's prior commitment to publicly funded colleges because the existence of inexpensive and universally available higher education increased the return to high school graduation. The state university system, moreover, took an active interest in both the quality and quantity of secondary school students for they were their potential clients. More school districts per youth also appear to have mattered.

Some of the explanatory variables that we find to be significant are consistent with a simple model of educational investment by families. Where the opportunity cost of schooling was high and family income or wealth was low, education, not surprisingly, lagged. But because education is most often a publicly supplied private good, an individual choice framework by itself is insufficient. A framework of public choice is also needed. The importance of small districts, with homogenous tastes for education and a narrow distribution of income or wealth, comes into focus in the public choice framework.

In order to extend education to the secondary level, schools had to be built and teachers had to be hired. These actions were not based simply on the aggregation of individual family choices concerning whether or not to allow children to attend school. Rather the decision was whether a school district, township, county, or state would tax *everyone* regardless whether they had children who would attend the school. Areas with greater homogeneity of economic condition, higher levels of wealth, and more community stability were the earliest to extend education to the secondary level and experienced the greatest expansion during the initial years of the high school movement.

We begin with a brief description of the high school movement in the United States and then assess what factors explain differences in secondary schooling rates across states and cities during the period of the high school movement.

I. THE HIGH SCHOOL MOVEMENT IN THE UNITED STATES: 1910 TO 1940

By the first decade of the twentieth century the vast majority of American youth outside the South attended school until they were 14 years old, and

---

[8] One might have expected a *lower*, not higher, proportion older in the population in areas that led in secondary school education. Today, in contrast to the past, citizens without children do *not* generally support educational expenses as much as they support those for pensions and healthcare.

those in the northern and western states, as in some European countries, had attained nearly universal "common schooling" of at least six years. America was poised for a transition from the elementary and common schools to the secondary level.[9]

Starting around the 1890s the demand for educated workers to staff ordinary white-collar jobs began to soar. People even in rural areas spoke of having a high school education as a means of succeeding in the business community and parents across diverse communities saw secondary education as the premier ticket to their children's prosperity. By the 1910s families across America were calling for the expansion of high schools.[10] America was still largely a rural nation and parents recognized that education would enhance economic mobility in part by fostering geographic mobility.

Publicly supported high schools existed in the nation's larger cities beginning in the 1820s and private academies dotted the smaller towns by the mid-nineteenth century. The high school movement does not signify the beginning of secondary schools in America. Instead, the movement marks an enormous expansion in the number and geographic reach of high schools, the spread of a more uniform curriculum, and a replacement of many private high schools with public ones.[11]

The first public high school in the United States was established in Boston in 1821 and most of the larger coastal cities of the East founded public high schools soon after. Smaller cities were not without post-elementary educational institutions as private academies mushroomed in the mid-nineteenth century. Some academies were college preparatory schools but most were secondary schools indistinguishable from their public counterparts, except that academies charged fees. Some academies taught vocational skills such as bookkeeping, mechanical drawing, and navigation, which all drew on academic courses, although most academies taught standard subjects as well.

---

[9] Of all native-born white men 40 to 49 years old in 1940, 27 percent had not completed eighth grade, and of those born outside the South 19 percent had not. Just 7 percent of this latter group had not completed 6 years. Those who were 40 to 49 years old in 1940 would have been about 14 years old from 1905 to 1914. *Source:* 1940 PUMS 1/100 sample.

[10] World War I did much to solidify these notions. According to the Iowa Commissioner of Education, "Those who have a high school education have risen in rank [during World War I]. The business world is also more and more demanding young men and women of high school training" (Iowa Department of Public Instruction 1916–1918, 45). Most of the reports of educational commissioners in the more progressive states speak to this point, but these documents might be considered suspect since state bureaucracies had interests in propagandizing. The aspirations of ordinary Americans can also be gleaned from the literature of the day. Theodore Dreiser, O. Henry, Sinclair Lewis, Sherwood Anderson, Willa Cather, and John Dos Passos all wrote of the high school educated. In Dreiser, O. Henry, Lewis, Cather, and Anderson a high school education gave their characters the ability to leave rural America. For all these writers high school was associated with respectability and success. It also signified, as in Sinclair Lewis's feminist novels, potential independence for women.

[11] See Reese (1995) on the early history of secondary schools in the United States.

The aggregate enrollment in academies is difficult to establish given the quality of the surviving records.[12] We do know, however, that the number of academies declined sharply with the arrival of publicly funded high schools. We also know that enrollments in academies were considerably below those of the public secondary schools that replaced them. So even though public secondary schools displaced many private schools, the high school movement led to an enormous net increase in enrollment.

What had changed in the United States in the late nineteenth century to increase the demand for education beyond the primary years? We have shown elsewhere that the premium to ordinary white-collar employment in the immediate pre–World War I period was high and that it probably had been equally high throughout the latter part of the nineteenth century (Goldin 1999; Goldin and Katz 1995; 2001). The increased scale of firms, the rise of large retail establishments, and the emergence of various segments of the service sector increased the demand for white-collar workers.

Using individual-level data for 1914, we also demonstrate that the return to a high school education was substantial. It was high even within a host of blue-collar occupations and even within farming.[13] That is, the return to education did not accrue only to those who were enabled to shift from manual occupations to white-collar ones. Rather, the high return also existed *within* blue-collar and white-collar jobs. Other work of ours has shown that the newer and technologically innovative industries of the early twentieth century employed a far larger fraction of high school graduates in their blue-collar labor forces than did other industries of the day (Goldin and Katz 1998).

Although secondary schools were present in almost all large U.S. cities and in many smaller towns before 1900, the curriculum was not yet standardized. Secondary schools in large cities often had close connections with local universities or colleges and trained students to pass their entrance exams. Almost half of all high school graduates in 1910 expressed an intention to continue their studies in a four-year college or another form of higher education (e.g., in teaching or normal schools, library schools, and nursing

---

[12] The social statistics portions of the 1850, 1860, and 1870 U.S. population censuses collected information on public and private schools. These data have often been cited as evidence on the large number of students who attended academies. But the data often include the lower elementary grades as well and are, in consequence, unusable for many parts of the nation particularly the South.

[13] Direct evidence from individual-level data on earnings and education from the Iowa State Census of 1915 yields a return to a year of high school in Iowa of 11 percent for males and 10 percent for females (these returns are higher for young adults). These estimates are from log annual earnings regressions that include, among other variables, a quartic in potential experience, foreign-born status, years in the United States, and race. Note that these estimated returns do not include the potential for additional returns from migrating out of Iowa to areas with higher income for the more educated. See Goldin and Katz (2000).

schools). The fraction that actually entered some degree-granting institution was probably around 35 to 40 percent. Both percentages declined considerably by the mid-1930s as high school enrollments soared (Goldin 1998, Table 5.2).[14] The modern high school that we now know – with its diverse curriculum, vocational courses, tracking, electives, 45-minute periods – was invented in America during the first decades of the twentieth century (see Krug 1964; 1972). The junior high school also originated in this era – in 1909 to be precise – as a means to keep 14-year-olds in school for an additional year by offering vocational training and a diploma.[15] Americans devised the secondary school for the masses to train youth "for life" and not just "for college."

Figure 5.1 shows the extraordinary rise in secondary schooling for the entire United States from 1910 to 1940. But this graph does not reveal the differing patterns across regions. The 1940 U.S. population census – the first to include information on educational attainment – could be used to address the issue. But its schooling data for older cohorts are somewhat suspect and have been shown to substantially overstate the numbers claiming to have graduated from secondary school.[16] To produce state figures and to check the reliability of the national series we have used, instead, the contemporaneous reports of state and federal departments of education to construct the number of students enrolled and graduated. The data were assembled as part of a study of education in the twentieth century (Goldin 1994; 1998).

[14] The 35 to 40 percent figure can be derived in two independent ways. One uses the reports of high school principals concerning what graduating seniors claimed they would do after graduation. In 1910, 35 percent of all public and private high school graduates (not including those in the preparatory divisions of colleges and universities) claimed they would continue to college, whereas 50 percent said they would continue with some form of higher education. Another source for the statistic comes from taking the total number of secondary school graduates in 1910 (156,000 for public and private) and dividing it by the number of entrants to degree-granting institutions of higher learning, which we estimate to have been 60,975. There were 174,213 students in collegiate programs (excluding graduate and professional students but probably including those in teachers' colleges). We use our estimate that 35 percent were in their first year. See U.S. Bureau of Education, *Biennials* 1928–1930, p. 338.

Ravitch (2000), citing an article by Edward Krug, is critical of estimates regarding the fraction of high school graduates who continued to college, asserting that the numbers are inflated because data on entering undergraduates are too high. Our calculations are consistent with reasonable college figures and are also consistent with Krug's own estimates.

[15] The first junior high school appeared in 1909 in two college towns: Berkeley, CA and Columbus, OH. By 1923, 47 percent of cities (with populations exceeding 10,000 in 1910) outside the South had at least one junior high school and 70 percent did by 1927 (based on U.S. Bureau of Education, *Biennials*, various years).

[16] For evidence concerning why the 1940 federal population census contains suspect data overstating the educational attainment of older cohorts, see Goldin (1998). Only two states, prior to 1940, had censuses that inquired of educational attainment (Iowa in 1915 and 1925; South Dakota in 1915). Various U.S. federal population censuses inquired as to the attendance of individuals in school at any time during the preceding year. We use these data in the city-level analysis, but the statewide levels for this variable do not appear reasonable, especially for the South.

The schooling data include all students in grades nine through twelve in public and private secondary schools, as well as those in the preparatory departments of colleges and universities.[17] For the state-level data we have two measures: enrollments and number of graduates.[18] Each measure is transformed into a rate by dividing by the relevant demographic group.[19] To conserve space, we present information only on graduation rates; the trends and regional differences in enrollment are similar. We first summarize considerable information by presenting time series of the graduation rates aggregated by census divisions (Figure 5.3) and the data for 1928 in map form by states (Figure 5.4).

As can be seen in Figure 5.3A, the increase in the graduation rate in parts of the North and West was so steep that even as early as the 1930s many states had achieved rates equal to those of the 1950s. The national data in Figure 5.1 give the misleading impression that the increase in graduation rates was more continuous and extended into the 1960s. Because the South lagged far behind the North, the data for the entire country show a more continual increase.

The states of the South were not the only laggards. The Mid-Atlantic was the non-southern region with the lowest graduation rates before 1940. Its three states had a more industrial economy than the other regions included in Figure 5.3A and lagging states in other regions were also those that were more industrial (e.g., Michigan). With the onset of the Great Depression and with the passage of National Industry Recovery Act codes (1933 to 1935) making youth employment in manufacturing illegal, teenagers in the industrial states flocked to high school, closing wide educational differentials among the states outside the South.

The South, as can be seen in Figure 5.3B, had graduation rates that were initially the lowest in the nation and remained low even during the period of the high school movement. But after the 1940s secondary schooling expanded rapidly. By the 1960s the South had narrowed, although not yet closed, the gap with other regions such as the East North Central (included

---

[17] The data include those in two-, three-, or four-year public and private high schools, in the final year of junior high, and in the preparatory departments of colleges and universities. They do not generally include students attending common schools beyond eight years, although in some states they may. Students in the preparatory departments of colleges and universities have been omitted from all other series we know of despite the fact that they accounted for about one-third of all private-school students in the 1910s.

[18] Attendance data cannot be easily obtained for all states and all years in our sample. For the states we have been able to find, the average daily attendance is generally more than 80 percent of enrollment. We have average daily attendance data in our city-level sample. There is no apparent reason for an overstatement of enrollment since the states provided little to localities. Graduation data, however, are generally cleaner in the sense that the concept is less ambiguous than is enrollment. States, then as today, set their own requirements for graduation.

[19] We divide by 17-year-olds for the graduation rate, and by 14- to 17-year-olds for the enrollment rate.

Panel A: Four Regions of the North and West

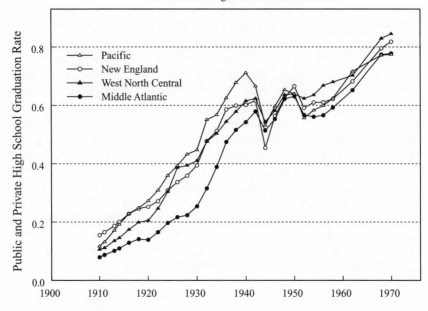

Panel B: Two regions of the South and the East North Central for comparison

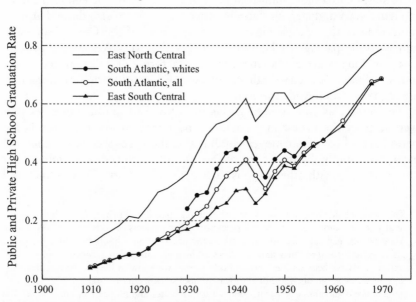

FIGURE 5.3. Public and Private High School Graduation Rates, 1910 to 1970. Panel A: Four Regions of the North and West, Panel B: Two regions of the South and the East North Central for comparison. *Notes:* Includes both males and females in public and private schools (including preparatory departments of colleges and universities). Graduates are divided by the approximate number of 17-year-olds in the state. Constant growth rate interpolations of population data are made between census years. *Sources:* State-level high school graduation data set from various sources; see Goldin (1994; 1998).

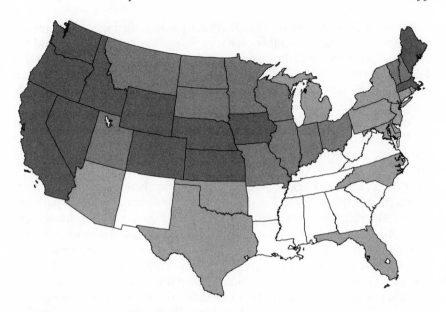

Shading	Graduation Rate Ranges
	11.8 < 18.4%
	18.4 < 31.5%
	31.5 < 38.8%
	38.8 < 55.6%

FIGURE 5.4. Public and Private High School Graduation Rates by State, 1928. *Notes:* The public and private graduation rate is the number of graduates from all public and private secondary schools, including preparatory divisions of colleges and universities, divided by the number of 17-year-olds in the state. Constant growth rate interpolations of population data were made between census years. Shading divides states into four approximately equal groups. *Source:* Goldin (1998).

in Figure 5.3B for comparison). The low graduation rates in the South before the 1950s, moreover, were not due solely to the abysmally low education levels of the African-American population. The white population also had far lower rates, as can be seen in the comparison with whites in the South Atlantic.

Several other features in the underlying data are also worth mentioning. Although the disaggregated data for the states begin with 1910, by necessity, estimates for the entire nation reveal that change was slow during the preceding four decades. That is, the level in 1910 was not much higher than it was in 1870.[20] The 1910 to 1940 segment in Figure 5.3, therefore, can be thought of as the rapidly rising portion of a diffusion or logistic function.[21]

---

[20] See U.S. Department of Education (1993, table 19).

[21] It is an odd logistical function, however, because it later rises again. High school graduation rates increased in much of the nation after 1960.

Another point is that World War II cut deeply into the high school graduation (and enrollment) numbers for regions such as New England and the Pacific largely because of the relatively high wages of young workers, not just because of the draft.[22] Finally, young women went to and graduated from secondary schools at higher rates than did young men, with the possible exception of the 1930s when the rates were almost on par.

At the start of the high school movement in 1910, New England was at the forefront of secondary education, as it had been in elementary education during the nineteenth century. Several states in the mid-section of the country, the West North Central in particular, also had substantial schooling rates. By 1928 New England had been eclipsed by these states and by others across the North and West. The group appears to form an "educational belt" across America, as can be seen in the map of Figure 5.4. Enrollment and graduation rates in California, Indiana, Iowa, Kansas, Nebraska, Oregon, Washington, the Mountain states, and parts of New England were far higher than they were in Michigan, New Jersey, New York, Pennsylvania, Wisconsin, and, of course, the South. Although there was considerable catch-up by 1938 between the leaders and the more industrial states, the rankings of the states in 1928 and 1938 are similar. We will use data from 1910, 1928, and 1938 in state-level regressions to understand the correlates of the high school graduation rate.

Comparisons across states over time are facilitated by consulting Table 5.1, which gives summary statistics for the graduation rate from 1910 to 1938. Both the unweighted and weighted standard deviations of state graduation rates suggest widening dispersion.[23] Table 5.1 reveals growing gaps in high school education across the nation during the period of the high school movement. Within the non-South, however, the Great Depression produced a narrowing in high school graduation rates (see the weighted results), as the industrial states of the North narrowed the gap between them and the states of the West and Plains.

By 1940 high schools in all regions, except the South, were fairly complete in their geographic coverage. Given their absence in all but the larger cities in 1910, this was a spectacular, but expensive, achievement. Most estimates show that the direct cost of educating a high school student was twice that of an elementary-school pupil (Goldin 1998). Thus an area that moved from

---

[22] One indication that many high school males left school to take the relatively well-paying unskilled jobs in the wartime economy is that young women did as well.

[23] The coefficient of variation of the state's graduation rate, in contrast, shows convergence across states. But there is good reason to prefer the standard deviation. Because the log of income, according to substantial evidence, is approximately linear in years of schooling, the standard deviation of education in years (alternatively, as here, the standard deviation in high school graduation rates) is a sensible proxy for the standard deviation in (log) permanent income. This measure is, therefore, a reasonable one for the impact of education on income inequality.

TABLE 5.1. *High School Graduation Rates, Summary Statistics by State*

	Unweighted			Weighted		
	Mean	Standard Deviation	Coefficient of Variation	Mean	Standard Deviation	Coefficient of Variation
			48 States			
1910	0.088	0.049	0.557	0.086	0.043	0.500
1920	0.180	0.085	0.472	0.162	0.069	0.426
1928	0.300	0.117	0.390	0.270	0.100	0.370
1938	0.504	0.145	0.289	0.482	0.130	0.270
			32 Non-southern States			
1910	0.112	0.043	0.384	0.111	0.033	0.297
1920	0.223	0.069	0.309	0.199	0.056	0.281
1928	0.361	0.093	0.258	0.321	0.086	0.268
1938	0.581	0.097	0.167	0.559	0.075	0.134

Notes and Sources: State-level high-school graduation data from various sources; see Goldin (1994; 1998). Weighted data use the number of 17-year olds in the state. The coefficient of variation is the (standard deviation/mean).

universal elementary education (8 years of school) to universal secondary education (12 years of school) doubled its educational tax bill.

An important feature of the story we will soon tell is that the areas to which high schools spread most rapidly were among the more sparsely settled. In 1925 the average farm in Iowa had 160 acres and that in Nebraska, 330 acres (U.S. Department of Commerce 1926). Although Iowa and Nebraska were farm country, they were also two of the leading states in the high school movement. Given that 50 percent of Americans were still living in rural areas in 1920, the timing of the high school movement may not be surprising given the obvious importance of the internal combustion engine (school buses, cars) and improved roads to the education of rural populations.

The modern U.S. public high school was a quintessential American innovation: generally free, open to all who completed eighth grade, gender neutral in admission, secular, fiscally controlled by local governments, and a guarantor of acceptance to a state college for its graduates, in most states. Nowhere else in the world was that the case when the U.S. high school movement was in its early stages, even though similar economic incentives in the form of wage differentials were present in parts of Europe (Phelps Brown 1977; Piketty 2003).[24]

---

[24] North America, not just the United States, was the distinctive part of the world. Canadian secondary school (public and private) enrollment rates by province are similar to, though far lower than, those in the states just south of the border. In 1941, for example, the

II. EXPLAINING DIFFERENCES IN HIGH SCHOOL PARTICIPATION RATES ACROSS THE UNITED STATES

To understand the wide differences in high school attendance and graduation rates across states we investigate the determinants of secondary school
rates at the beginning of their steep ascent. We first examine (public and private) graduation rates at the dawn of the high school movement in 1910. We
next explore the transformation in education from 1910 to 1928. Finally,
we explore the changes that took place from the eve of the Great Depression
(1928) to just before World War II (1938). A city-level data set affords a
wider range of variables but requires the use of a slightly different measure
of the schooling rate.[25] The motivation for all the estimations is a standard
model of human capital investment in which the educational return, opportunity cost, and capital constraints affect private decisions. A public-choice
framework is then layered on that model.

The simplest form of the investment decision is a two-period model in
which a representative individual can either work or attend high school in
period 1. If he works, he earns w_1. Attending high school, the alternative,
entails a direct cost C and an opportunity cost w_1. The individual in period 2
earns $w_2 \geq w_1$ with no high school and $E_2 > w_2$ with high school. The
decision to attend high school, under lifetime income maximization and
given discount rate r, hinges on whether the discounted benefits exceed the
first period costs (all measured relative to the second period wage):

$$\frac{(E_2/w_2) - 1}{1 + r} > \frac{C + w_1}{w_2}.$$

Expressed in terms of the rate of return calculation, the issue is whether
the returns are greater than the discount rate:

$$\frac{E_2 - w_2}{C + w_1} > 1 + r.$$

Thus the schooling decision is negatively related to the opportunity
cost of schooling (w_1), the direct cost (C), and the discount rate (r), and

---

contemporaneous secondary school enrollment rate for Ontario was 40.3 percent; that for
the Mid-Atlantic was 83.6 percent. The rate for British Columbia was 55.3, whereas for the
Pacific states it was 92.0 percent. The Maritimes and Quebec look more like the American
South in this comparison. See Urquhart and Buckley (1965).

[25] Rather than using administrative data for the contemporaneous schooling data, we must use
U.S. population census data on whether youths, at particular ages, attended school during
the year. The administrative data cannot be easily used because youths from outside city
boundaries attended school in the city and thus we have no reliable denominator for some
of the smaller cities. Although the enrollment data given in the population census provide an
inflated measure of the high school enrollment rate for rural youth in this period, they seem
more consistent with administrative secondary school enrollment data for urban youth in
large cities.

positively affected by the high school wage premium, $(E_2 - w_2)/w_2$ or E_2/w_2.[26]

This simple formulation of the educational investment decision does not, however, speak to the public nature of most schooling. Public support for secondary school was rarely justified on the basis of the creation of a literate citizenry, the same way that primary school was in the nineteenth century. Public funding was, rather, rationalized on the grounds of capital-market imperfections. Communities were groups of families at different stages of their lifecycle, and publicly funded education was an intergenerational loan, a means of consumption smoothing.[27]

Families (or clans) are not identical, however, and the essence of the public-goods problem is the characterization of the majority-voting equilibrium. Rather than having all adult family or clan members earn w_2, in the absence of high school, a distribution of w_2 can exist. The problem, then, is finding a majority-voting equilibrium with respect to both public education and the size of the (income) tax to fund it. Under many reasonable scenarios, the greater the variance of w_2, given its mean, the less support there will be for public secondary education and the lower the probability that public secondary schooling will be approved by voters.[28]

Thus the level of income or wealth and the distribution of each should have been important determinants of public high school education. The extent to which individuals consider themselves members of the same community is another element of the public choice framework. Greater social cohesion, intergenerational propinquity, and community stability should all have increased the support for publicly funded education.[29]

We postulate a reduced-form equation for the high school enrollment (or graduation) rate (HS) in a jurisdiction that includes the following elements:

$$\text{HS} = f[(C + w_1)/w_2, (E_2/w_2), r, \bar{Y}, \sigma_Y, X],$$

---

[26] Individual high school enrollment decisions are also likely to depend positively on family wealth endowments both through an income effect on the consumption demand for schooling and the easing of capital market constraints (i.e., increased wealth effectively lowers r). Note that we express the wage premium relative to the second period wage because the absolute difference is less meaningful.

[27] Becker and Murphy (1988) make a similar point. They go one step further and suggest that the intergenerational loan was paid back in the form of social security. We, on the other hand, are conceptualizing the intergenerational loan as being shifted within the community from one group of grandparents to the next.

[28] See Epple and Romano (1996), who analyze the level of support, and Fernandez and Rogerson (1995), who investigate the existence of public education.

[29] Alesina, Baqir, and Easterly (1999) show in a majority-voting model that an increase in the polarization of preferences concerning spending on public goods (formally an increase in the median distance from the median) reduces the amount of public goods provision. They find, using a cross-section of U.S. cities c. 1990, a negative relationship between spending on "productive" public goods (schooling, roads, and libraries) and the city's degree of ethnic fragmentation.

where $\bar{Y}$ and σ_Y measure the mean and dispersion of income (or wealth), and X is a vector of variables relating to the stability, cohesion, and intergenerational propinquity of the community. Other terms are defined as before.

State-level Regressions

In the empirical analysis at the state level we analyze the correlates of the public and private high school graduation rates in 1910 and 1928 and of changes in the graduation rate from 1910 to 1928 and 1928 to 1938. The variables approximate the key determinants of family-level education decisions and those factors relevant in a public choice framework.

All youth are assumed to face the national market for white-collar employment conditional on receiving a high school degree. In fact, the earnings of white-collar workers were far more similar across the United States in the 1909 to 1919 period than were the earnings of production workers.[30] Thus, we do not include a variable for the earnings of white-collar workers (E_2). We do, however, include variables to account for the opportunity cost of schooling (w_1) and the (locally determined) blue-collar earnings of adults without high school education (w_2). Since employment opportunities for older youth in this period were likely to be found in manufacturing, we approximate the opportunity cost of high school education by both the fraction of the work force in manufacturing and the manufacturing wage.

Various measures of income and wealth (state income per capita, taxable wealth per capita, and agricultural income per agricultural worker) proxy the household capital constraints and the consumption demand for education. The return to high school was probably greater where publicly supported colleges were available and we therefore include, in the change regression for 1910 to 1928, a variable for the public university enrollment rate in the base year.

The decision by the municipality to build and staff high schools is more complicated. The frameworks we have cited emphasize the distribution of wealth, the stability of community, and social distance or propinquity. The social stability of communities can be inferred, in part, from the proportion elderly in the state. Social distance or propinquity might be proxied by variables relating to the fraction foreign born or Catholic.[31]

---

[30] The coefficient of variation of city-level mean clerk wages is smaller than that for production workers in a sample of 227 non-southern cities in 1919. Similar patterns are apparent in 1909 and 1914. See Goldin and Katz (1995) for a description of the data, which come from the U.S. census of manufactures.

[31] We have also divided non-Catholics into two other groups: non-hierarchical religions that encourage the reading of the Bible by the laity (e.g., Lutherans, New England Protestants) and non-hierarchical ones that did not (e.g., most evangelical religions). Only the percentage Catholic is of statistical and economic significance. Race is another important factor in U.S. educational history. But given the large percentage of blacks living in the South during the

The distribution of income or wealth is a difficult variable to obtain for the period in question. An estimate of automobile registrations per capita is a good substitute for more obvious, but unavailable, measures. Automobile registrations per capita may seem an odd variable given the nearly ubiquitous ownership of cars today, but in the 1920s automobile ownership required a much higher relative level of income or wealth. Consider two income distributions each having the same mean but different variance and for which the cutoff point for automobile ownership is somewhere below the mean. The narrower distribution will have a higher fraction of car owners among the population. Thus under certain conditions, and given the mean of income (or wealth), the variable "automobile registrations per capita" is a good proxy for the variance of income (or wealth). The number of automobile registrations per capita, therefore, is an indication of the share of voters likely to be wealthy enough to favor financing an expensive public good, such as a high school.

With just 48 states in each year we must be judicious in our inclusion of variables. A further constraint is that many of the variables are highly correlated. The fractions of the population that are urban, foreign born, and Catholic are all strongly collinear, and each of these variables is also collinear with the fraction of workers employed in manufacturing. Similarly, per capita wealth, income, agricultural income, and automobile registrations are all collinear. We use a subset of each of these groups in the regressions. Where only one of the many variables mentioned is included, the results are robust to the inclusion of the others.[32]

The number of districts per youth was mentioned in the discussion of the provision of local public goods as being potentially important. Numerous, small, fiscally independent districts can foster secondary school expansion in its early phase. The cross-state correlation of school districts per youth in 1932 and the high school graduation rate in 1928 is 0.56. This significant positive relationship between the density of school districts and the high graduation rate is reflected in high school graduation regressions that control for population density or the urban share of the population and the relationship is also maintained for states outside the South. But the number of school districts per youth is closely related to wealth, automobile registrations per capita, and agricultural income per farm worker. Therefore the variable is not statistically significant in regressions that include these variables.

The estimations are admittedly of the reduced-form variety, but they are as a group suggestive of the forces that both encouraged and impeded secondary-school education. Table 5.2 summarizes the main results. The first three columns report regressions where the dependent variable is in

1910 to 1940 period, there is little systematic relationship between percentage non-white and graduation rates once measures of income and wealth and a South dummy are included in the state-level regressions.

[32] In constructing Table 5.2, we chose variables from these groups to illustrate the role of each.

TABLE 5.2. *Explaining Total (Public and Private) Secondary-School Graduation Rates Across States*

	(1) Levels	(2) Levels	(3) Levels	(4) Differences	(5) Differences	(6) Differences	(7) Means (s.d.)	(8) Means (s.d.)
	1910	1928	1928	1928–1910	1938–1928	1938–1928	1910	1928
Log per capita taxable wealth, 1912 or 1922, × 10^{-1}	0.236 (0.0901)	0.852 (0.368)		0.857 (0.260)	1.25 (0.345)		7.471 (0.451)	7.926 (0.386)
% ≥ $65 years, 1910 or 1930	2.13 (0.260)	1.423 (0.788)	1.846 (0.774)	−1.749 (0.737)	−0.527 (0.866)		0.0414 (0.0143)	0.0547 (0.0142)
% of labor force in manufacturing, 1910 or 1930	−0.0673 (0.0335)	−0.144 (0.0972)	0.989 (0.481)	−0.0495 (0.0947)	0.126 (0.0934)	0.203 (0.0723)	0.248 (0.124)	0.255 (0.103)
% Catholic, 1910 or 1926	−0.0913 (0.0305)	−0.377 (0.0867)	−0.274 (0.0849)	−0.265 (0.0900)	0.0595 (0.0841)		0.150 (0.121)	0.151 (0.123)
South	−0.0449 (0.00932)	−0.0935 (0.0272)	−0.131 (0.0294)	−0.0735 (0.0267)	0.0375 (0.0306)			
New England	0.0444 (0.0121)	0.100 (0.0310)		0.0811 (0.0333)				
Middle Atlantic			−0.0635 (0.0338)		0.0620 (0.0188)			
Males in public colleges /17-year-olds, 1910				1.09 (0.384)			0.0316 (0.243)	
Wage in manufacturing, 1929, × 10^{-1}			0.0241 (0.00974)					1191 (254)
Wage × % in manufacturing, × 10^{-1}			−0.0827 (0.0375)					
Auto registrations per capita, 1930, × 10^{-2}		0.0568 (0.0230)	0.0449 (0.0218)					0.224 (0.648)
Log agricultural income per agricultural worker, 1920						0.0985 (0.0174)		

Change % unemployment, 1930 to 1940, × 10^{-1}						0.0900
						(0.0306)
Constant	−0.136	−0.468	−0.0962	−0.324	−0.814	−0.541
	(0.0709)	(0.273)	(0.115)	(0.199)	(0.276)	(0.104)
R^2	0.895	0.874	0.864	0.758	0.679	0.708
Root MSE	0.172	0.0451	0.0476	0.0474	0.0400	0.0368
Mean (unweighted) of dependent variable	0.0882	0.291	0.291	0.212	0.204	0.204

Notes: Standard errors are in parentheses; ordinary least squares regressions, unweighted except for the 1928 to 1938 change regressions (cols. 5, 6). Weight for state i is $(S_{i,28} \cdot S_{i,38})/(S_{i,28} + S_{i,38})$ where $S_{i,t}$ = share of state i 17-year olds in U.S. total in year t. Weighting does not affect results in cols. (1) to (4). The 1928 to 1938 regressions are weighted due to two outliers (DE and NV). Number of observations is 48 in all columns; DC is excluded. AZ and NM were territories until 1912 but are included with the 1910 states.

Dependent variable:
Total (public and private) graduation rate by state: Goldin (1998); the number of graduates divided by the number of 17-year-olds in the state.

Independent variables:
Variables listed as percent (%) are entered as fractions. Note that in the change equations of columns (4), (5), and (6) the explanatory variables are those at the beginning of the period and reflect starting conditions.

Per capita taxable wealth, 1912 or 1922: Taxable wealth/population, U.S. Department of Commerce (1926), *Statistical Abstract*.

% ≥$65 years, 1910 or 1930: U.S. Bureau of the Census (1975), series A 195–209.

% in manufacturing, 1910 or 1930: U.S. Bureau of the Census (1932a, 1912).

% Catholic, 1910 or 1926: U.S. Department of Commerce (1930), *Religious Bodies: 1926*, Vol. I, table 29. The 1910 numbers are extrapolated from those for 1906 and 1916. All are expressed per state resident.

South: South includes the census divisions South Atlantic, East South Central, and West South Central.

New England: census division New England.

Middle Atlantic: census division Middle Atlantic.

Males in public colleges/17-year-olds, 1910: U.S. Bureau of Education (1910), table 31, p. 850. Military academies receiving public support are excluded. The denominator contains both males and females.

Wage in manufacturing, 1929: Kuznets et al. (1960), table A 3.5, p. 129.

Auto registrations per capita, 1930: U.S. Department of Commerce (1940), *Statistical Abstract*, table 467.

Agricultural income per agricultural worker, 1920 (mean = $943): Kuznets et al. (1960), table A4.3, p. 187. The variable is agricultural service income per agricultural worker.

% unemployment, 1930 (mean = 5.74%), 1940 (mean = 8.83%): U.S. Bureau of Commerce, *Statistical Abstract*, (1932a) table 341, (1948) table 203. Unemployment for 1930 refers to April 1930 and is the sum of Class A (non-layoff) and Class B (layoff).

Sources: For complete notes regarding the sources see Goldin and Katz (1997), from which this table is derived.

levels for 1910 (col. 1) and 1928 (cols. 2, 3). In the next three columns (cols. 4, 5, 6) the dependent variable is in first differences.[33] The last two columns report the means of the variables for 1910 (col. 7) and 1928 (col. 8).

The association between the key factors of our framework and high school graduation rates at the start of the high school movement in 1910 is summarized in col. (1). Per capita wealth (in 1912), the proportion older than 64 years (in 1910), the percentage of the labor force in manufacturing (in 1910), the percentage Catholic (in 1910), and dummy variables for the South and New England are strong predictors of high school graduation and together they account for almost 90 percent of the cross-state variation.

Wealth per capita (or state income per capita, or agricultural income per capita), not surprisingly, is positively related to the high school graduation rate and the impact is reasonably large – a shift from the 25th percentile to the 75th percentile increases the graduation rate by about 1.5 percentage points in 1910 (or by 16 percent of the mean). Having more manufacturing, on the other hand, was a drag on education; moving from the 25th to the 75th percentile reduces the graduation rate by 1 percentage point in 1910 (or by 12 percent of the mean). The larger the proportion older than 64 years, the higher is the graduation rate. This strikingly strong positive relationship at the dawn of the high school movement between high school graduation rates and the fraction of older persons in the population (a raw correlation of 0.79) is illustrated in Figure 5.5A. We attribute the effect to the stability of community and not to differential fertility or immigration, for neither of those variables reduces the positive impact.

Our finding that educational attainment is positively related to the fraction of older persons in the state, and thus to the persistence of population, is the reverse of the conclusion from several studies using current data (e.g., Poterba 1997). There is good reason for the difference. Older citizens today are highly mobile as a group. A large fraction live far away from their community of origin and as a political unit they appear to have far less interest in the use of public resources to enhance education than did those early in the twentieth century who continued to reside in their communities.[34]

---

[33] The estimates in cols. (1) to (4) are unweighted, but these results are not very sensitive to weighting by state population. Cols. (5) and (6) are weighted by the population of 17-year olds in each state because unweighted estimates of models to explain the change in graduation rates from 1928 to 1938 are greatly influenced by two extreme outliers (DE and NV). Thus we present the more robust, weighted estimates.

[34] Today's elderly can, and do, escape the higher taxation that comes with more and better quality education. In the period we are examining, the elderly generally did not, or could not, move from places with more expensive educational public goods. Grandparents who lived in towns and villages at the turn of this century often boarded their grandchildren who lived on farms to enable them to attend high school. This interpretation is consistent with the findings in Hoxby (1998) concerning the impact of the elderly on expenditures across the twentieth century.

In col. (2) of Table 5.2 we examine the determinants of high school graduation rates in 1928 and find results similar to those for 1910, when converted into elasticities. But for 1928 we can include variables that we cannot for 1910 and they add substantially to the story. The most interesting of the new variables is automobile registrations per capita (in 1930).

Automobile registrations per capita exhibits a strong positive relationship to the high school graduation rate, even when a direct measure of per capita wealth is included. The specification in col. (2) implies that increasing auto registrations per capita from the 25th percentile to the 75th percentile increases the graduation rate by 5 percentage points (or by 17 percent of the mean level in 1928).[35] Automobile registrations per capita is a key explanatory variable and speaks to the importance of a more equal distribution of wealth, given its mean, in the provision of education as a public good.[36] The states with the most automobile registrations per capita in 1930 – California, Iowa, Kansas, Nebraska, and Nevada – were all at the high end of the educational distribution in 1928 (see Figure 5.5B).[37]

Also of interest are manufacturing as a share of employment, the manufacturing wage, and their interaction as shown in Table 5.2, col. (3). The 1910 results show that a large manufacturing sector was a potent deterrent to high school graduation. For the 1928 regression we can add the manufacturing wage and the interaction between it and the size of the manufacturing sector. Having a greater percentage of the labor force in manufacturing, given the manufacturing wage, was a drag on education, as we found in the 1910 analysis. But in the 1928 analysis we can see that the relationship holds only when the wage is high enough, in this case above the mean. Similarly, a higher manufacturing wage was not an impediment to education until the percentage of the labor force in manufacturing exceeded its mean. The lowest graduation rates outside the South were found in the industrial states with relatively high manufacturing wages such as New Jersey, New York, and Pennsylvania. The opportunity cost of education in these states was high and the availability of manufacturing jobs was substantial enough to deter education.

We have also estimated a state fixed-effects model (not shown) that pools data from 1910, 1920, and 1930. We find results similar to the levels

[35] If (log) per capita wealth were omitted from col. (2), the role of automobiles per capita would greatly increase. A shift from the state at the 25th percentile to that at the 75th percentile would increase the graduation rate by 8 percentage points or by 27 percent of the mean graduation rate in 1928.

[36] The strong positive impact of automobile registrations per capita on graduation rates is robust to the inclusion of controls for population density, percentage urban, and access to improved roads.

[37] Lindert (1994; 1996), in two cross-country studies of the twentieth century, finds that greater equality fosters more social spending (e.g., transfer programs) and that a greater percentage of Catholics lowers it.

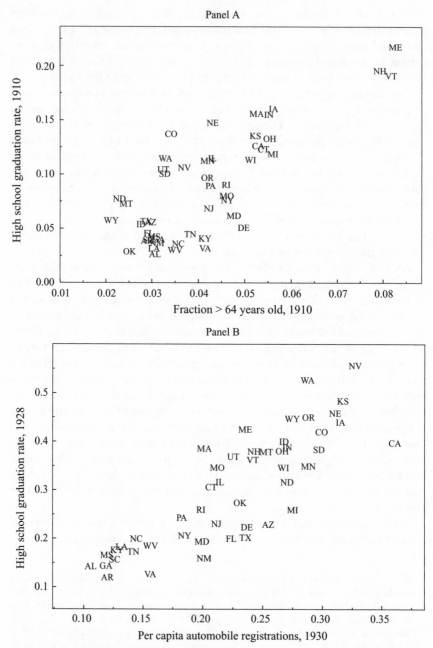

FIGURE 5.5. High School Graduation Rates and State Characteristics: 1910 to 1930. *Notes and Sources:* See Table 5.2.

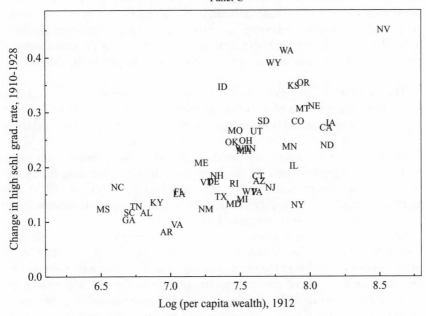

Panel C

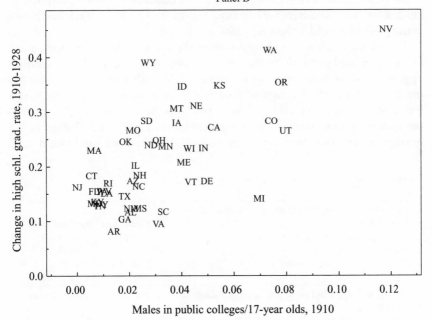

Panel D

FIGURE 5.5 (*continued*)

regressions in cols. (1), (2), and (3).[38] Auto registrations per capita and the percentage older than 64 years remain strongly and positively related to the state graduation rate. Percentage Catholic and the manufacturing employment share variables have coefficients similar to those in the cross-section regressions but are not as precisely estimated due to persistent differences by state.

The first difference regression for 1910 to 1928, given in col. (4), reinforces the interpretation of many of the variables that featured in the levels regression – with one addition and one exception. The independent variables for the difference regressions capture the *initial* conditions in a state. More wealth in 1910, for example, hastened the growth of high schools from 1910 to 1928 and a greater share of the labor force in manufacturing (in 1910) slowed it. The positive relationship between (log) per capita wealth at the start of the high school movement and the expansion of high schools from 1910 to 1928 can be seen in Figure 5.5C.

We add to the levels results (see col. 4) the fraction of youth in the state who attended public colleges and universities in 1910, which is a predetermined variable in the difference regression and has a strong positive effect on the high school graduation rate. It appears that the returns to high school were higher in states with large publicly funded institutions of higher education (see also Figure 5.5D), although we cannot entirely rule out an explanation based on differences in tastes for education. The only variable to change signs in the difference regression compared with the levels regression is the percentage older than 64 years.

Lastly, we analyze the change during the 1930s. The estimation in col. (5) is configured similarly to that in col. (4) for the 1910s and 1920s. Much appears to have been altered by the 1930s. Wealth remains an important determinant, but the fraction of the labor force in manufacturing no longer has a strong negative effect. The sparse specification in col. (6) focuses on factors unique to the Great Depression and adds the change in the unemployment rate from 1930 to 1940.[39] High school graduation rates

---

[38] The fixed-effects regression for 1910, 1920, and 1930 is:

Dependent variable: *Public and private graduation rate* Independent variables:	Coefficient	Standard error
Auto registrations per capita × 10	0.0765	(0.0126)
Fraction ≥65 *years*	3.093	(0.980)
Share of labor force in manufacturing	−0.0994	(0.163)
Fraction Catholic	−0.196	(0.0257)

Notes: Includes a full set of state and year dummies. Number of observations = 144; $R^2 = 0.959$.
Sources: See Table 5.2

[39] Agricultural income (natural log of) per agricultural worker in 1920 is used here instead of the (log) wealth variable. The results are virtually unchanged if (log) wealth in 1922 is used.

during the Great Depression increased the most in states that underwent the largest increases in unemployment, given the level of income, and they also increased the most for the leading manufacturing states. The 1930s produced greater educational homogeneity among non-southern states, as was seen previously in Table 5.1, by eliminating jobs that had once employed teenagers. Ironically, the Great Depression may have spurred educational attainment in industrial America.

We have not yet mentioned state legal constraints, such as compulsory education and child labor laws, the expansions of which during the Progressive Era are considered by many to have been crucial in extending education into the teenage years. These laws were highly complex. The maximum age of compulsory education was often not the binding constraint. Rather, youths in most states were excused from school if they were employed and met age and education requirements.[40]

Recent work on whether these laws spurred the high school movement has concluded that compulsory education laws were by themselves ineffective in increasing years of schooling, but when combined with child labor laws they had a positive, albeit modest, effect.[41] A prior literature had argued similarly that compulsory education laws were passed in states that already had extensive school attendance.[42] The econometric evidence to date leads us to conclude that, although the laws had some impact on the education of teenagers, their influence on high school *graduation* was small.[43]

Less attention has been paid to another set of state laws that enabled early high school expansion. A somewhat forgotten group of laws, often labeled "free tuition" legislation, appear to have been instrumental in the early expansion of high schools in the more sparsely settled states of the Midwest and West. These laws mandated that school districts that did not maintain their own secondary schools pay the tuition of resident youths

[40] In 1917, for example, although 30 states had a maximum age of compulsory school of 16 years, all but four granted labor permits at or before age 14 and the remaining four granted them at age 15. The education required for a labor permit was nowhere more than 8 years and was exactly 8 years in just five states. In 1928 the maximum age of compulsory schooling had increased to 18 in five states and to 17 in another five states. But labor permits were still issued to those under 16 years of age in all but two states and the education required for a labor permit was nowhere greater than 8 years. The laws, therefore, do not appear to have effectively constrained youths to remain in high school, let alone mandated graduation from high school. See Keesecker (1929); U.S. Bureau of Education, *Biennials* 1916–1918.

[41] See Lleras-Muney (2002), who uses the 1960 U.S. population census to estimate the impact of the laws on the educational attainment of individuals who were 14 years old at some year from 1915 to 1939.

[42] See, for example, Edwards (1978); Landes and Solmon (1972); Margo and Finegan (1996); and Schmidt (1996). Margo and Finegan, using the 1900 census, find some impact of compulsory education laws on the schooling of 14-year-olds, but only when combined with child-labor legislation.

[43] See, as well, Acemoglu and Angrist (2000) and Goldin and Katz (2003).

to attend school in neighboring districts that did. Prior to the adoption of these laws, parents had to pay tuition to these schools. Many western states adopted free tuition laws of various types from 1907 to the 1920s, some of which applied to all districts in the state whereas others constrained only the districts of counties that approved the laws (e.g., Nebraska in 1907 and Iowa in 1913 were both statewide; California in 1915 was at the county level).[44]

City-level Regressions

At the start of the high school movement in 1910, Americans were still a predominantly rural people. Half lived in places that were either unincorporated or had fewer than 1,000 persons. Just one-third lived in cities of more than 25,000. The remaining sixth lived in small cities and villages. Young people who lived in towns and villages had the highest school rates in both 1910 and 1920. Somewhat lower were the school rates of youth in the open country and in small cities, and lower still were those of youth residing in cities with populations exceeding 25,000. Lowest of all were the school rates of youth in the largest cities.[45]

---

[44] An interesting question is why voters in districts that already had high schools cared that other districts in their state did not. There are various possibilities. One is ideological. Another is that town and village high schools were crowded with youth from the "open country" who boarded with relatives to avoid tuition payments. Yet another is that districts that imposed higher taxes to support their schools wanted to prevent their older residents from escaping higher rates by moving across districts. This possibility seems less likely. By 1925 virtually all non-southern states had a form of "free tuition" legislation (Hood 1925).

[45] We use the 1910 and 1920 PUMS to construct estimates of the school attendance rates of 16 and 17-year-olds. School attendance is defined here to include only those who attended school and who were *not* also employed for pay or by their families. The restriction eliminates many who went to school for brief periods or who did not attend day schools. We find the following for areas outside the South:

Percentage of 16- and 17-year-olds attending school, non-South U.S.		
	1910	1920
Rural [unincorporated or <1,000]	37.7%	38.7%
Town [1,000 <10,000]	40.5	43.9
Small city [10,000 <25,000]	36.9	35.1
All large cities [>25,000]	26.1	31.7
Medium cities [25,000 <100,000]	31.5	35.9
Larger cities [>100,000]	24.0	30.1

The 1910 sample contains 9,607 observations and that for 1920 has 11,955. A similar pattern is apparent, but modestly attenuated, in a linear probability model of full-time enrollment (enrolled but not employed) with controls for census division and dummy variables for race, sex, foreign-born status, parents' foreign-born status, and father's occupational group. See Goldin and Katz (1999) for a more detailed analysis of this issue.

Cities provide another laboratory to study the transition to mass secondary school. Our data contain a wider group of variables than that for the states, and the number of observations is almost five times as large. Our data set contains the 289 cities with populations exceeding 10,000 in 1910.[46] As in the state-level analysis, a simple human-capital model motivates the selection of variables and the estimation is, once again, of a reduced-form nature. The dependent variable, which is from the U.S. population census, differs from the one we used in the state-level analysis and refers to the attendance of youth (15 to 17, or 16 to 17 years old) in any school. Thus the dependent variable does not include attendance in secondary schools alone and could include sporadic attendance in various types of schools. Even though these data generally overstate the actual rate of school attendance among youths, they provide reasonable measures of differences across cities.[47]

The city-level regressions (Table 5.3) contain results that are similar in many respects to those at the state level. Manufacturing, measured by the fraction of production workers in the population, has a strong negative effect on school-going, and the importance of particular industries (e.g., textiles, clothing) known to have hired the less skilled and child workers adds to the effect. The variable indicating the percentage child workers in manufacturing in 1910 speaks to the effect of certain industries on the opportunity cost of youth, the capital constraints of parents, and possible myopia regarding education common in certain industrial settings.

The fraction foreign born for 1910, and Catholic for the other two years, are strongly and negatively related to attendance.[48] Because the dependent

---

[46] The main constraints on sample size for the various regressions are as follows: 226 cities have data on schooling for 1910, 229 have wealth data for 1925, and 259 have data on school density in 1933.

[47] The U.S. federal population census in 1910, 1920, and 1930 asked whether an individual had attended school at least one day during the preceding year. Attendance could have been at a night, correspondence, industrial, music, commercial, private, parochial, or regular-day school, among others. Another measure is available for our group of cities. It is similar to our state-level measure and gives average daily attendance in the school district, which was almost always the entire city. The problem with this variable is that families living outside the city, in areas without a high school, often went to the schools in the city (tuition was sometimes paid by the student's school district or parents). To convert the attendance data into a rate, the city's population of 14- to 17-year-olds must be used, but the population will, on occasion, omit some who went to the school. Over time, we can observe large changes in the rates of some cities, possibly reflecting the opening of high schools in neighboring communities and thus the reduction in attendance in the city. Empirical findings concerning the correlates of city high school attendance rates and city characteristics are quite similar for both the census enrollment rate measure and the city average daily attendance rate measure for the sub-sample of cities with reasonable average daily attendance data.

[48] Following Alesina, Baqir, and Easterly (1999), we have explored the relationship between city enrollment rates and ethnic fragmentation (measured by 1 minus the Herfindahl index of ethnic group population shares) in 1920 using a decomposition of each city's population into 14 ethnic groups based on race and parents' birthplaces. Ethnic fragmentation is strongly

TABLE 5.3. *Explaining School Attendance of 15-, 16-, and 17-Year-Olds across Cities: 1910, 1920, and 1930*

	1910 (15 to 17-Year-Olds)		1920 (16 to 17-Year-Olds)		1930 (16 to 17-Year-Olds)	
% production workers, in year	−0.642	(0.0806)	−0.340	(0.0690)	−0.380	(0.110)
% child in mfg., 1910 or 1920[a]	−2.07	(0.262)	−0.493	(0.277)	−0.738	(0.438)
Log city population in year × 10⁻¹	−0.174	(0.0512)	−0.141	(0.0597)	0.0215	(0.0814)
% foreign born in year	−0.189	(0.0582)	0.0359	(0.0763)	0.287	(0.109)
% non-white in year	−0.0126	(0.0707)	0.0718	(0.0772)	−0.556	(0.144)
% Catholic, 1926			−0.147	(0.0419)	−0.188	(0.0511)
Log per capita wealth, 1925 or 1930			0.0498	(0.0150)	0.0649	(0.0220)
Population density in year × 10⁻²			−0.256	(0.0911)	−0.579	(0.128)
School density, 1923 or 1933			70.6	(31.6)	118.2	(36.9)
Vocational school density, 1933					218.8	(87.7)
% managers in mfg., 1920			0.628	(0.139)		
% textiles & clothing in mfg., 1920			−0.0998	(0.0515)		
% chemicals in mfg., 1920			−0.722	(0.363)		
% white collar in labor force, 1930					0.805	(0.176)
% bldg. trades in labor force, 1930					−0.852	(0.355)
Dummies for census divisions	yes		yes		yes	
Constant	0.897	(0.0599)	0.377	(0.119)	0.305	(0.160)
R^2	0.636		0.667		0.664	
Root MSE	0.0659		0.0677		0.0847	
Mean of dependent variable	0.442		0.407		0.623	
Number of observations	225		261		235	

[a] The 1910 and 1920 estimations use the 1910 values; the 1930 estimation uses the 1920 values.

Notes: Standard errors are in parentheses. Ordinary least squares estimation used with no weighting (weighting by population does not affect the results). Cities include all with more than 10,000 persons in 1910. The few cities that merged with another or divided into two were kept as one unit, either merged or separated, throughout the sample period.

Dependent variable: Percentage of 16- (or 15-) to 17-year-olds who attended any school during some time in the year preceding the census: U.S. Bureau of the Census (1912; 1923a; 1932a).

Independent variables: All variables are from the U.S. Bureau of the Census, census of population or manufactures for the relevant years, except where noted. Unless specified as the census of manufactures, the source is the population census in the relevant year. Population censuses are U.S. Bureau of the Census (1912; 1923a; 1932a); censuses of manufactures are U.S. Bureau of the Census (1913; 1923b; 1933).

% *production workers, in year*: production workers in manufacturing as a percentage of the city population. Production worker data are from the census of manufactures.

% *child in mfg., 1910 or 1920*: child workers in manufacturing as a percentage of all production workers in manufacturing in the city. Production worker and child worker data are from the census of manufactures for 1909, and 1919.

Log city pop. in year: log of the city population in either 1910, 1920, or 1930.

% *foreign born in year*: percentage of city population that is foreign born in 1910, 1920, or 1930.

% *non-white in year*: percentage of the city population that is non-white in 1910, 1920, or 1930.

% *Catholic in year*: percentage of the city population (average of 1920 and 1930) who are members of the Roman Catholic Church in 1926. U.S. Department of Commerce (1930).

Log wealth, 1925 or 1930: log of the estimated true value of per capita wealth of the city. U.S. Bureau of the Census (1927; 1932b). The 1920 estimation uses the 1925 per capita wealth value and the 1930 value × (mean 1920 value/1930 value = 0.8823) for cities not listing one in 1925.

Population density in year: population in year divided by the area (in acres) of city. Area data are mainly from U.S. Bureau of the Census (1932b).

School density: number of secondary schools in 1923 (or 1933) divided by the area (in acres) of the city in 1925 or 1930. Number of secondary schools = number of high schools + (0.3) · number of junior high schools. U.S. Bureau of Education, *Biennial Surveys* (various years).

Vocational school density: number of vocational high schools in 1933 divided by the area (in acres) of the city in 1930. U.S. Bureau of Education, *Biennial Surveys* (various years).

% *managers in manufacturing*: percentage of all manufacturing workers who are managers; obtained from Robert Whaples.

% *textiles & clothing in mfg.*: percentage of all manufacturing workers employed in the textiles and clothing industries; obtained from Robert Whaples.

% *chemical in mfg.*: percentage of all manufacturing workers employed in the chemicals industry; obtained from Robert Whaples.

% *white collar in labor force*: professional, clerical, trade, public service workers/all in labor force in city.

% *bldg. trades in labor force*: workers in the building trades/all in labor force in city.

Sources: For complete references to the sources, see Goldin and Katz (1997). We have not listed all the source references in this paper. The current sample includes southern cities, which were excluded from our previous paper.

variable includes all schools, parochial as well as public, the effect cannot be due to the use of private schools by Catholics and some ethnic groups.

The role of race is complicated. In 1910 and 1920 the fraction of youth attending school was similar by race in southern cities, where the majority of blacks lived. But the quality of education for blacks in the South was considerably lower than for whites and it is likely that the fraction attending school by age greatly overstates the grades eventually attained.[49] By 1930 many non-southern cities had substantial black populations and the large effect of race in the 1930 regression derives primarily from the impact of blacks on non-southern school attendance rates.[50]

Population density, reflecting the greater poverty of the denser cities, is negatively related to school attendance whereas wealth per capita is positively related. High school density, a variable we cannot construct at the state level, has a strong positive effect, showing the importance of proximity to schools, even in cities.[51] The average city in 1930 had 7,000 acres and three secondary schools. If a city doubled its secondary schools, it would increase attendance by 5 percentage points. Interestingly, the 1930 regression suggests a much larger response of attendance rates to an additional vocational, rather than regular, high school.

III. IMPLICATIONS FOR CROSS-COUNTRY DIFFERENCES AND FOR ECONOMIC GROWTH

Secondary schooling spread rapidly in the United States from 1910 to 1940. When the United States entered World War II, the median 18-year old was a high school graduate and secondary schooling had become part of mass education. The same was not true of Europe, not even of its economically leading nations.

What factors can explain the extraordinary spread of secondary education in the United States? Can they also help us understand why Europe lagged? In other words: why did the United States lead in secondary school education?

Schooling differences within the United States suggest the importance of the level as well as the distribution of wealth, and the level as well as the

---

and negatively correlated with enrollment rates for 16- to 17-year-olds in northern cities in 1920. But it is also highly correlated with the fraction foreign born and Catholic and is insignificant when either is included in the enrollment model.

[49] In a previous draft of this paper (Goldin and Katz 1997), we omitted southern cities for these reasons. The results with and without southern cities are similar overall.

[50] Many southern urban school districts did not report to the federal government in the 1930s and the reasons for their apparent noncompliance were not recorded in the *Biennials*. Of the 36 cities that drop from the sample between 1920 and 1930, 30 must be excluded due to missing information on school density. Of those, 28 are in the South.

[51] We cannot construct the variable at the state level because some states, often those with low schooling rates, included elementary schools as giving high school instruction.

composition of manufacturing employment. They hint to the importance of cultural and religious homogeneity among people, and stability of community. And they suggest that state expenditures on public colleges and universities created a powerful incentive for youths to graduate from high school. We do not know, however, what stronger state or national control relative to the local governments would have achieved, for educational funding was mainly at the local level in the period under consideration.[52] In 1925, for example, localities raised 84 percent of the revenue for primary and secondary education; states, counties, and the federal government together funded just 16 percent (U.S. Department of Education *Biennials* 1924–1926). We find that the number of school districts is positively correlated with educational outcomes, although the relationship is not robust to the inclusion of certain other factors.

Thus many of the features of America that made it an egalitarian haven in the first part of the nineteenth century allowed it to expand its system of education in the twentieth, even after economic inequality had greatly increased. In the 1910s when inequality of non-agricultural income was probably at one of its heights for the century, local governments began to fund an expensive transition that would soon lead to nearly universal secondary school education.[53]

The aristocratic features of Europe that led many to abandon it for America, on the other hand, hindered the spread of secondary education. In England and Wales, education beyond grammar school was, until 1944, either privately provided and funded or only partially funded by the government. Secondary schooling was, most often, preparatory training for university, but higher education was not publicly funded. Students in Germany, France, and Great Britain were tracked before their teenage years and only some were allowed to go on to secondary school and then university.

Although the U.S. economy had become quite unequal by the early twentieth century, several factors encouraged publicly funded secondary school education. One was local provision. The poor were distinct regionally (southern incomes were half those nationally in 1920) and they were also distinct within regions (the foreign-born, particularly from the newer sending countries, were far more urbanized than were native-born whites). Thus the average school district, with the exception of those in large urban areas, contained a relatively homogeneous citizenry. In most European countries, on the other hand, where decision-making was at the national, state, or provincial level, the broader distribution of income and wealth militated against publicly funded secondary school education. Inequality of material

---

[52] In most southern states, counties controlled tax rates and per student allotments. Thus, the region that provides the exception to the rule concerning the large numbers of fiscally independent districts had far lower schooling rates. But the roles of race, income, and the rural economy figure in as well.

[53] On economic inequality in the twentieth century see Goldin and Katz (2001).

condition appears to have perpetuated Old World institutions that, for some time, reinforced the existing distribution. As in various models of educational finance, this appears to be a classic case of the "ends against the middle" (Epple and Romano 1996; Fernandez and Rogerson 1995).

But there is another factor, far harder to identify, that in the early twentieth century set U.S. education apart from that in Europe. America had a stronger tradition of egalitarian institutions and impulses emphasizing equality of opportunity, and these survived the rise in economic inequality. Among these institutions were the public colleges and universities of the Midwest and West, and they were a contrast not just to the elite institutions of Europe but also to their counterparts in the northeastern states, such as New York, Connecticut, and Massachusetts.

But what did the high school movement signify for economic growth within the United States and between America and Europe? A large literature links economic growth to a more educated population either because educated people are more productive or because education indirectly increases growth through a variety of routes (Barro 1997). Our state-level data allow a suggestive, although not conclusive, exploration of the relationship.

Per capita income converged markedly across the states, particularly after the 1930s (Barro and Sala-I-Martin 1991). Convergence forces were so powerful that they appear to leave little else to account for differences in per capita income growth. Yet, in a convergence equation framework for the 1929 to 1947 period, the public high school enrollment rate in 1928 has a significant, positive, and strong effect on the growth of income, whereas the proportion urban or manufacturing has a negative effect. In the 1920s, the per capita incomes of high-education states grew faster, given initial levels.[54]

---

[54] The estimates are robust to weighting and to the inclusion of other measures of initial education such as the graduation rate, public or total. We admit, though, that any of the strong explanatory variables for education (such as automobile registrations per capita) are also equally good predictors of the residual variance in the convergence equation. A representative convergence regression follows. The relationship, although weaker, remains for the longer 1929 to 1959 period.

Dependent variable:
Log(income per capita, 1947/income per capita, 1929); weighted mean = 0.660

Independent variables:	Coefficient	Standard error
Log (per capita income, 1929)	−0.357	(0.0710)
Public enrollment rate, 1928	0.317	(0.0819)
Percent urban, 1930	−0.219	(0.126)
Constant	2.96	(0.377)

Notes: Number of observations 48; R^2 =.912. Regression is weighted by the state's adult population in 1930.

Sources: *Public enrollment rate, 1928*: Goldin (1994; 1998); *Per capita income 1929, 1947*: U.S. Department of Commerce (1984); *Percent urban, 1930*: U.S. Bureau of the Census (1975).

We do not yet have an answer to a related question of larger significance, whether the substantial differences between education in the United States and in Europe are part of what differentiated the interwar and post-World War II growth experiences of these economies.

The increase in secondary school education is the largest component of the increase in the educational stock of Americans over the twentieth century.[55] It was high school and not college that dominated the rapid expansion of educational attainment before the 1970s. Many of the "super-education" states of the high school movement era (e.g., Iowa) have continued to be among the top educational performers today, with the regrettable exception of California.

Why the United States has fallen behind many countries in the quality of its secondary-school education may be rooted, ironically, in some of the characteristics that are considered to have been virtuous earlier in the twentieth century. These characteristics include small, numerous, and fiscally independent districts; public funding and provision; an absence of uniform standards for advancement; and an open, forgiving, and second-chance system. These virtues once led to the expansion of high schools but have increasingly come under attack for a variety of reasons.[56]

References

Acemoglu, Daron, and Joshua Angrist. 2000. "How Large Are Human Capital Externalities? Evidence from Compulsory Schooling Laws." *NBER Macroeconomics Annual 2000* 15: 9–59.

Alesina, Alberto, Reza Baqir, and William Easterly. 1999. "Public Goods and Ethnic Divisions." *Quarterly Journal of Economics* 114 (November): 1243–84.

Barro, Robert J. 1997. *Determinants of Economic Growth: A Cross-Country Empirical Study*. Cambridge, MA: MIT Press.

Barro, Robert J., and Xavier Sala-I-Martin. 1991. "Convergence across States and Regions," *Brookings Papers on Economic Activity*, vol. I. Washington, DC: The Brookings Institution: 107–82.

Becker, Gary S., and Kevin M. Murphy. 1988. "The Family and the State." *Journal of Law and Economics* 31 (January): 1–18.

DeLong, J. Bradford, Claudia Goldin, and Lawrence F. Katz. 2003. "Sustaining U.S. Economic Growth." In H. Aaron, J. Lindsay, and P. Nivola, eds., *Agenda for the Nation*. Washington, DC: Brookings Institution Press.

[55] DeLong, Goldin, and Katz (2003), using data from the 1940 to 1990 U.S. population censuses and the 1999–2000 Current Population Surveys, find that mean educational attainment of U.S. natives (adjusted to age 30) increased by 6.75 years from the birth cohort of 1880 (7.07 years) to the birth cohort of 1970 (13.82 years). This increase of 6.75 years of schooling, for those who were young adults from the beginning of the twentieth century to nearly its end, is made up of 1.4 years of elementary school (grades 1 to 8), 3.13 years of secondary school (grades 9 to 12), and 2.22 years of higher education.

[56] See Goldin (2001) and the discussion in Goldin and Katz (2008, ch. 9).

Dewhurst, J. Frederic, John O. Coppock, P. Lamartine Yates, and Associates. 1961. *Europe's Needs and Resources: Trends and Prospects in Eighteen Countries.* New York: Twentieth Century Fund.

Easterlin, Richard. 1981. "Why Isn't the Whole World Developed?" *Journal of Economic History* 51 (March): 1–19.

Edwards, Linda Nasif. 1978. "An Empirical Analysis of Compulsory Schooling Legislation, 1940 to 1960." *Journal of Law and Economics* 21 (April): 203–22.

Engerman, Stanley L., Elisa V. Mariscal, and Kenneth L. Sokoloff. 2009. "The Evolution of Schooling in the Americas, 1800–1925." In David Eltis, Frank Lewis, and Kenneth Sokoloff, eds., *Human Capital and Institutions: A Long-Run View.* Cambridge: Cambridge University Press.

Epple, Dennis, and Richard E. Romano. 1996. "Ends Against the Middle: Determining Public Service Provision When There Are Private Alternatives." *Journal of Public Economics* 62 (November): 297–326.

Fernandez, Raquel, and Richard Rogerson. 1995. "On the Political Economy of Education Subsidies." *Review of Economic Studies* 62 (April): 249–62.

Goldin, Claudia. 1994. "Appendix to: How America Graduated From High School: An Exploratory Study, 1910 to 1960." NBER-Historical Series Working Paper no. 57 (June).

Goldin, Claudia. 1998. "America's Graduation from High School: The Evolution and Spread of Secondary Schools in the Twentieth Century." *Journal of Economic History* 58 (June): 345–74.

Goldin, Claudia. 1999. "Egalitarianism and the Returns to Education during the Great Transformation of American Education." *Journal of Political Economy* 107 (December): S65–S94.

Goldin, Claudia. 2001. "The Human Capital Century and American Leadership: Virtues of the Past." *Journal of Economic History* 61 (June): 263–92.

Goldin, Claudia, and Lawrence F. Katz. 1995. "The Decline of Noncompeting Groups: Changes in the Premium to Education, 1890 to 1940." NBER Working Paper no. 5202 (August).

Goldin, Claudia, and Lawrence F. Katz. 1997. "Why the United States Led in Education: Lessons from Secondary School Expansion, 1910 to 1940." NBER Working Paper no. 6144 (August).

Goldin, Claudia, and Lawrence F. Katz. 1998. "The Origins of Technology-Skill Complementarity." *Quarterly Journal of Economics* 113 (June): 693–732.

Goldin, Claudia, and Lawrence F. Katz. 1999. "Human Capital and Social Capital: The Rise of Secondary Schooling in America, 1910 to 1940." *Journal of Interdisciplinary History* 29 (Spring): 683–723.

Goldin, Claudia, and Lawrence F. Katz. 2000. "Education and Income in the Early Twentieth Century: Evidence from the Prairies." *Journal of Economic History* 60 (September): 782–818.

Goldin, Claudia, and Lawrence F. Katz. 2001. "Decreasing (and Then Increasing) Inequality in America: A Tale of Two Half Centuries." In F. Welch, ed., *The Causes and Consequences of Increasing Income Inequality.* Chicago IL: University of Chicago Press.

Goldin, Claudia, and Lawrence F. Katz. 2003. "Mass Secondary Schooling and the State: The Role of State Compulsion in the High School Movement." NBER Working Paper no. 10075 (November).

Goldin, Claudia, and Lawrence F. Katz. 2008. *The Race between Education and Technology*. Cambridge MA: Harvard University Press.

Hood, William R. 1925. *Legal Provisions for Rural High Schools*. U.S. Bureau of Education, Bulletin No. 40. Washington, DC: G.P.O.

Hoxby, Caroline M. 1998. "How Much Does School Spending Depend on Family Income? The Historical Origins of the Current School Finance Dilemma." *American Economic Review, Papers and Proceedings* 88 (May): 309–14.

Iowa Department of Public Instruction. 1916–1918. *Iowa School Report*. Des Moines IA.

Keesecker, Ward W. 1929. *Laws Relating to Compulsory Education*, U.S. Bureau of Education Bulletin No. 20. Washington, DC: G.P.O.

Krug, Edward A. 1964. *The Shaping of the American High School: 1880–1920*. Madison WI: University of Wisconsin Press.

Krug, Edward A. 1972. *The Shaping of the American High School*: Volume 2, 1920–1941. Madison, WI: University of Wisconsin Press.

Kuznets, Simon, Ann Ratner Miller, and Richard A. Easterlin. 1960. *Population Redistribution and Economic Growth: United States, 1870–1950*. Vol. II. *Analyses of Economic Change*. Philadelphia PA: The American Philosophical Society.

Landes, William, and Lewis Solmon. 1972. "Compulsory Schooling Legislation: An Economic Analysis of Law and Social Change in the Nineteenth Century." *Journal of Economic History* 32 (March): 45–91.

Lindert, Peter. 1994. "The Rise of Social Spending: 1880–1930." *Explorations in Economic History* 31 (January): 1–37.

Lindert, Peter. 1996. "What Limits Social Spending?" *Explorations in Economic History* 33 (January): 1–34.

Lindert, Peter. 2004. *Growing Public: Social Spending and Economic Growth since the Eighteenth Century*. Cambridge: Cambridge University Press.

Lleras-Muney, Adriana. 2002. "Were Compulsory Attendance and Child Labor Laws Effective? An Analysis from 1915 to 1939." *Journal of Law and Economics* 45 (October): 401–435.

Margo, Robert A., and T. Aldrich Finegan. 1996. "Compulsory Schooling Legislation and School Attendance in Turn-of-the-Century America: A 'Natural Experiment' Approach." *Economic Letters* 53 (October): 103–10.

Phelps Brown, E. H. 1977. *The Inequality of Pay*. Oxford: Oxford University Press.

Piketty, Thomas. 2003. "Income Inequality in France, 1901–1998." *Journal of Political Economy* 111 (October): 1004–42.

Poterba, James. 1997. "Demographic Structure and the Political Economy of Public Education." *Journal of Policy Analysis and Management* 16 (Winter): 48–66.

Ravitch, Dianne. 2000. *Left Back: A Century of Failed School Reforms*. New York: Simon and Schuster.

Reese, William J. 1995. *The Origins of the American High School*. New Haven CT: Yale University Press.

Schmidt, Stefanie. 1996. "Compulsory Education Laws and the Growth of American High School Attendance, 1914–1934: Evidence from the 1940 Census and a Case Study of New York State." Paper presented at the Cliometrics conference, Nashville TN, May 1996.

U.S. Bureau of the Census. 1912. *Thirteenth Census of the United States: 1910. Population*. Washington, DC: G.P.O.

U.S. Bureau of the Census. 1913. *Census of Manufactures, 1909.* Washington, DC: G.P.O.

U.S. Bureau of the Census. 1923a. *Fourteenth Census of the United States: 1920. Population.* Washington, DC: G.P.O.

U.S. Bureau of the Census. 1923b. *Census of Manufactures, 1919.* Washington, DC: G.P.O.

U.S. Bureau of the Census. 1927. *Financial Statistics of Cities, 1925.* Washington, DC: G.P.O.

U.S. Bureau of the Census. 1932a. *Fifteenth Census of the United States: 1930. Population.* Vol. III. Washington, DC: G.P.O.

U.S. Bureau of the Census. 1932b. *Financial Statistics of Cities, 1930.* Washington, DC: G.P.O.

U.S. Bureau of the Census. 1933. *Census of Manufactures, 1929.* Washington, DC: G.P.O.

U.S. Bureau of the Census. 1975. *Historical Statistics of the United States: Colonial Times to 1970.* Washington, DC: G.P.O.

U.S. Bureau of Education. [various years]. *Biennial Reports of the Commissioner of Education [year].* Washington, DC: G.P.O. Note: These volumes are called *Biennials* in the text and notes.

U.S. Department of Commerce. [various years]. *Statistical Abstract of the United States, [year].* Washington, DC: G.P.O.

U.S. Department of Commerce. 1930. *Religious Bodies: 1926.* Volume I: *Summary and Detailed Tables.* Washington, DC: G.P.O.

U.S. Department of Commerce. 1984. *State Personal Income by State: Estimates for 1929–1982.* Washington, DC: G.P.O.

U.S. Department of Education. 1993. *120 Years of American Education: A Statistical Portrait.* Washington, DC: G.P.O.

Urquhart, M. C., and K. A. H. Buckley. 1965. *Historical Statistics of Canada.* Cambridge: Cambridge University Press.

6

The Production of Engineers in New York Colleges and Universities, 1800–1950: Some New Data

Michael Edelstein

The president of a Silicon Valley firm was asked by a possible merger partner how he would evaluate his company. The president replied, "a million dollars for each engineer."[1]

I. INTRODUCTION

In his classic work, *Modern Economic Growth: Rate Structure and Spread*, Simon Kuznets wrote that the modern economic era was characterized by the sustained increase in total product per capita and per worker. The increase was based on a fundamental historical innovation, "the extended application of science to problems of economic production" (Kuznets 1966, 9). By the mid-nineteenth century scientific knowledge was clearly being applied in the fastest growing regions of the globe, but characterizing the role of science in the first decades of sustained economic growth in the late eighteenth and very early nineteenth centuries is problematic.[2] Only a few of the new technologies that were invented and applied in Britain, Belgium, France, and the United States employed contemporary scientific knowledge. In these early decades, if there was a link to science, most frequently it was in the

---

[1] Related to my colleague Elizabeth Field-Hendrey by the president of the targeted firm.

[2] See, for example, Landes (1969, Chs. 2–4); Rosenberg and Birdzell (1986, Ch. 5); Mokyr (1990, Ch. 5).

I would like to acknowledge the help of the archivists, librarians, and registrars at the seventeen colleges and universities in New York, the New York State Library, the New York State Archives, and the New York Public Library, Science and Business Branch. They are too numerous to acknowledge individually here but their generous help was essential for this project. This paper has benefited greatly from the Rochester Conference in honor of Stanley Engerman and seminars at Columbia, Northwestern, Virginia, Queen's University, and the Graduate School, CUNY. I would also like to thank Deidre McCloskey, Carmel U. Chiswick, Claudia Goldin, Gavin Wright, David Weiman, Simone Wegge, Diane Macunovich, and Richard Easterlin for their extensive comments. One and all are absolved from any errors.

use of a scientific experimental methodology when inventors and innovators tried new ideas and machines.

Yet, when many Western and Central European governments and manufacturing communities were confronted by the surging industrial economy of Great Britain in the first decades of the nineteenth century, it was widely believed that an important means of fortifying their economies was to inaugurate and strengthen institutions that supported applied science. One of the most important forms of this support was institutions of higher learning for formally training engineers and, to a lesser extent, for generating new scientific and technical knowledge. Across the Atlantic in these same decades, American transportation, mining, and manufacturing grew significantly and the United States also began to create such institutions.

Information on American professional engineers dates to the early nineteenth century when the profession first emerged in early republic. Yet *comprehensive annual data* enumerating the graduates from American engineering schools and the professional engineering work force do not exist before 1950 when the National Science Foundation took over systematic data collection on the nation's scientific, engineering, and technical personnel and the institutions that educated them. A. M. Wellington, the first historian of American engineering education, published annual data for about *half* the nation's engineering schools from their origins to the early 1890s.[3] In the 1920s and 1930s various professional engineering organizations funded large surveys of the U.S. profession but none had high response rates or can be treated as random samples. From 1870 onward the occupational surveys in the U.S. census provide decadal estimates of the number of employed professional engineers. Yet it is not until the 1940 census that detailed occupational categories were broken down by years of schooling. Indeed, when Dael Wolfle wrote his classic study on the nation's resources of specialized

---

[3] Wellington (1892–3). A. M. Wellington was an economist, engineer, educator, and journalist. His history was serialized in the weekly *Engineering News* in 40 articles from March 1892 to February 1993. The first articles discuss a comprehensive listing of the nation's stock of engineering schools in 1889, their founding dates, and the number of the degrees each awarded in 1889. The next block of articles offers detailed histories of the first engineering programs. Wellington was able to obtain annual graduation data for 52 schools from their origins to 1892. The remainder of the articles analyzes the evolution of engineering school curriculums. Wellington's data and school histories for the nineteenth century have had a long life. Their first major use was in Charles N. Mann's seminal *A Study of the Engineering Education*, commissioned by the Carnegie Foundation for the Advancement of Teaching and published in 1918. At the mid-twentieth century Blank and Stigler (1957) prefaced their study of post-WWII engineering demand and supply with a sketch of nineteenth century engineering, relying heavily on Wellington's data. Before the National Science Foundation began its collection and publication of annual data on engineering schools in the early 1950s, only the school-based studies done for the Society for the Promotion of Engineering Education in 1924 match Wellington's efforts to comprehend the scale and performance of American engineering education.

talent in 1954, his estimates of college degrees from 1900 onward combined backcasting from a 1947 *Time* magazine poll of graduates with decadal data from 1900 to 1950 on the distribution of faculty in 28 universities.[4]

Recent work attempting to explain the rapid economic growth rates of the United States in the late nineteenth and early twentieth century and the rise of the United States to world leadership in per capita income have focused on the period's intense technical change and its uniquely high rates of growth in secondary and tertiary education. On the matter of technical progress, David, Wright, and Nelson have linked the nation's comparative advantage in mineral resource intensive products with the innovative use of applied science in locating, extracting, and processing the nation's rich storehouse of ores and petroleum.[5] Rosenberg and Mowery have written insightfully on the early twentieth century links between American universities and the leaps in chemical technology.[6] Sokoloff and Lamoreaux have focused on the patenting process. Tracing the location and industry of inventors and patent holders, Sokoloff and Lamoreaux discovered a market for patented ideas, intermediated by patent attorneys, patent brokers, and others.[7] Underpinning these patterns of economic growth was the rapidly rising level of secondary and tertiary education across rural and urban America. It is difficult to imagine the speed of technological innovation and its diffusion in the absence of such mass higher literacy, numeracy, and familiarity with scientific knowledge.[8]

A study of the rise of formally educated engineers cuts across many of these areas of interest. College-educated mining, metallurgical, and chemical engineers were widely employed in the firms that made use of the nation's mineral resources.[9] College-educated mechanical, electrical, and civil engineers applied science to other sectors of the economy. While detailed information concerning the training of engineers who were involved with invention and obtained patents is still lacking, it is established that college-educated engineers increasingly participated in the patenting process and market by the turn of the twentieth century.[10] Finally, professional engineers were clearly an important product of the nation's rising secondary

---

[4] Wolfle (1954, Appendix B, esp. 289).

[5] Wright (1990); Nelson and Wright (1992); David and Wright (1997); Wright (1999).

[6] Mowery and Rosenberg (1989, 1998); Rosenberg (1998, 2000).

[7] Lamoreaux and Sokoloff (1999, 2001); Usselman (1999).

[8] Goldin (1998, 2001); Goldin and Katz (1999).

[9] See, e.g. Wright (1999).

[10] Examining successive birth cohorts of "great inventors" from 1739 to 1885, Khan and Sokoloff (2004, 397) found the proportion with some college education in engineering and natural science was 9.7% of those born 1820–1845; 32.4%, 1846–1865; and 60.5%, 1866–1885. See also Lamoreaux and Sokoloff (2001). Usselman (1999) notes the increasing role of college-educated engineers in railroad company research and invention, much of which was left unpatented.

and tertiary education sectors. Indeed, until business programs began to attract large numbers of undergraduates in the interwar period, engineering was one of the very few college majors that prepared students for business employment.

The new data presented here make it possible to describe *comprehensively* the rise of engineering education and the granting of engineering degrees, *annually*, from 1802 to 1950, in one state of the union, New York.[11] The new data will be compared with the number of other higher degrees issued in New York, both in the context of the state economy. This paper is part of a larger project focusing on the rise of the engineering profession and its relationship to modern economic growth in New England, the Middle Atlantic, and the East North Central regions, the industrial heartland of the nation in the years from 1800 to 1950.

II. THE U.S. ENGINEERING PROFESSION, 1800–1950

Sifting decadal census materials and other sources, Blank and Stigler documented the overall rise of the U.S. engineering and chemistry professions from 1870 to 1950 (see Table 6.1). Their estimates are somewhat quirky because the definition of a professional engineer changed from census to census, sometimes dramatically as in 1880. As Blank and Stigler note, census definitions likely changed because the technical knowledge that distinguished and defined the professional engineer vs. a machine operator, and graduate vs. non-graduate, increased and became more complex, sometimes radically so.

Yet the general direction of Blank and Stigler's professional engineering labor force estimates is clear. The engineering profession in the United States grew very rapidly from the late nineteenth to the mid-twentieth century. According to Table 6.1, in 1870 there were 7,094 professional engineers; by 1950 the profession had grown to 534,424. Relative to the labor force in mining, construction, manufacturing, transportation, and public utilities the engineering work force grew 11-fold, from 0.2% to 2.2% of the work force in these five sectors. The other occupation that most applied science to production in the five industries was the chemists. The increase in the number of chemists in the late nineteenth and early twentieth century was somewhat more rapid than that of engineers. Of course, the engineers and chemists were not the only occupations that required scientific knowledge

---

[11] Wellington estimated 721 engineering bachelor degrees were awarded in the United States in 1889 (Wellington March 26, 1892, 296). He noted that certain colleges were missing from his estimate and that some Bachelor of Science degrees that he included were probably not in engineering. According to Wellington, New York's engineering programs graduated 124 engineers in 1889, 17.2% of the U.S. total. Massachusetts programs were the second highest producers of engineering degrees with 105; Pennsylvania was third with 55.

TABLE 6.1. *The Growth of the Engineering and Chemical Professions, 1870–1950*

	Chemists	Engineers	Decadal % Growth Chemists	Decadal % Growth Engineers	Labor Force in Five Industrial Groups (000)	Engineers per 100,00 in Five Industry Labor Force
1870	774	7,094			(3,840)	(185)
1880	1,969	7,061	154.4	-0.5	(5,170)	(137)
1890	7,503	28,239	128.7	299.9	7,800	362
1900	8,847	43,239	96.5	53.1	10,450	414
1910	16,273	88,755	83.9	105.3	14,461	614
1920	32,921	136,121	102.4	53.4	18,075	753
1930	47,538	227,590	44.3	67.2	19,949	1,141
1940	60,005	277,872	26.2	22.1	20,399	1,362
1940(a)	56,825	291,465			20,399	1,429
1950(a)	75,747(b)	534,424(b)	33.3	83.4	24,418	2,189

Notes: (a) Chemists excluding metallurgists; engineers including metallurgists but excluding surveyors (who were 16,444 in 1940 and 26,229 in 1950). These data are based on the 1950 census in which definitions of chemists and engineers are slightly different from those used in the 1940 census. (b) These 1950 estimates do not include about 6,300 professors and instructors of chemistry and about 8,300 professors and instructors of engineering, who are not classified as "engineers, technical" in the published census. (c) The five industrial groups are mining, construction, manufacturing, transportation, and public utilities.

Sources: All except labor force in five industries, Blank and Stigler (1957, 5, 34). 1870–1880 labor force in five industries: gainful workers in five industries, Fabricant (1949, 42).

and training; agricultural scientists and technologists, veterinarians, dentists, and medical personnel also required and used scientific knowledge.

Most employed engineers before World War I did not hold an engineering degree. In 1870 perhaps 10% of the 7,094 employed engineers in the United States had earned a degree in engineering.[12] Yet, forty years later when the U.S. census reported 88,755 professional engineers employed, American schools of engineering had at that point awarded 38,372 engineering degrees.[13] While it is highly unlikely that all of these 38,372 engineering graduates were alive and practicing, the upward trend in the employment of formally trained engineers is unmistakable.

The 1940 Census was the first to measure the years of schooling associated with different occupations. The Census found that 57.0% of the nation's 291,465 engineers had four or more years of college. Interestingly, at the next Census when the national engineering work force had risen 84.4% over the decade to 534,424, a slightly lower 54.5% of engineers had four or more years of a college engineering education.[14] It seems likely that there was variation in the percentage of college-educated engineers across engineering specializations; electrical and chemical engineers were more likely degreed than those practicing civil, mining, and mechanical engineering, but until national counts of these specializations and their educational backgrounds are estimated, this hypothesis remains speculative.

Some proportion of practicing engineers studied in undergraduate engineering programs but did not obtain a degree. In both the 1940 and 1950 census, 17% of practicing engineers had done 1–3 years of college work. The absence of survey data on occupation and education before 1940

---

[12] Blank and Stigler (1957, 4–5). Blank and Stigler offer a conjecture of the proportion of formally educated engineers among employed engineers by contrasting an estimate of 866 degrees awarded before 1870 found in Mann (1918, 7) with their own reworking of census data, which estimated 7,094 practicing engineers in 1870. The latter estimate must be deemed a rough one because some of the earliest engineering graduates were dead by 1870, some had left the engineering profession, and there were international inflows and outflows. Since most of the engineering graduates were from the 1850s and 1860s, it is likely the departures from the profession, not deaths, dominated any gross outflow from the stock of practicing graduates. The percentage of practicing graduates in the employed profession was certainly less than the 12.2% calculated from the ratio of Stigler's accumulated graduates to the stock of practicing engineers.

[13] Across the nineteenth century, some 4,600 Americans matriculated to the German universities, of which a small proportion were engineering students (Thwing 1928, 42). Read (1941, 27–28) found 75 Americans graduated from the Freiburg School of Mines, 1819–1865, and 19 Americans graduated from the École des Mines, 1851–1890.

[14] Blank and Stigler (1957, 5, 74, 88). The published 1940 census did not count the non-graduate professional engineers who were less than 35 years old. The 1950 census revised the 1940 definition to include these younger non-graduate engineers and provided estimates for a 1940 count consistent with the 1950 definition. The percentages reported in the text use the 1950 definition. Blank and Stigler tables and appendices utilize special counts from the Bureau of Census provided to the Bureau of Labor Statistics. See also Folk (1970, 280).

prevents any accurate information on those with some college education in the late nineteenth and early twentieth centuries. Speculatively, one might note that the 1950 relative proportion of those with some college education and those who held a degree was 17% to 54.5%. If this ratio held in 1870 then roughly 3% of the engineers in 1870 had done some college work. Yet, this latter statement must be treated as a rough conjecture at best.

In sum, the overwhelming proportion of practicing engineers in the mid-nineteenth century learned their profession on the job, sometimes in formal apprenticeships. Yet, by the 1940 and 1950 censuses, a bit over 70% of practicing engineers had done some engineering college work, most having done the full undergraduate course of study. Clearly, engineers with formal training represent a significant and growing phenomenon in the profession from its origins to 1950.[15]

Beginning with the seminal works of Abramovitz (1956) and Solow (1957) in the early 1950s, economists have attempted to account for the sources of modern economic growth. Applying production theory Abramovitz and Solow separated the growth of output per worker into the growth of inputs per worker and a residual, called total factor productivity. Solow was inclined to treat the residual as the growth due to technological advances; Abramovitz was more circumspect, once calling it "a measure of our ignorance." Griliches, who spent most of his academic life trying to understand the role of research and development activities in the economy, believed the increased importance of the residual was the consequence of both better technologies and better organization. In any event in a recent survey of American macroeconomic growth across the nineteenth and twentieth centuries, Abramovitz and David (2000) reaffirmed the earlier Abramovitz and Solow evidence that as conventionally measured, the residual, not the growth of factor inputs per worker, accounts for most of the growth in product per worker in the twentieth century.

---

[15] The shift from on-the-job to formal training is a highly complicated topic (see Calvert (1967) on the shift in mechanical engineering). There is evidence that, to a significant degree, American engineers who earned a higher engineering degree were more likely to bring a larger stock of the latest scientific knowledge to bear on problems of construction, transportation, mining, and manufacturing. Furthermore, as new science became more essential for these sectors, formally trained engineers were in higher demand. The application of electricity and chemistry to manufacturing technologies and products in the late nineteenth century quickly led to the dominance of engineering graduates in electrical and chemical engineering. School-based civil engineering moved more firmly into academe in the early twentieth century when physics, chemistry, and mathematics began to provide more precise knowledge on such matters as load bearing, materials stress, etc., relevant to bridges and high rise urban structures. In sum, it is a plausible working hypothesis that following the course of university and college trained engineers, to an important degree, means tracking the value of formal science in the profession. Of course, with a firmer grasp of the circumstances and number of awarded engineering degrees, a better sense of the character and pattern of displacement will emerge. See Calvert (1967).

How can the training of engineers be included within the Abramovitz/ Solow framework? Typical growth accounting practice measures the labor input by hours of work, weighted by the average wages of age, gender, and education groupings, the implicit assumption being that a dollar's worth of labor is substitutable among groups. Whether this substitutability assumption is supported by U.S. data from the late nineteenth and early twentieth centuries has not been fully researched. Elizabeth Field-Hendrey's research on nineteenth century agricultural and industrial production functions would lead to skepticism (Field-Hendrey 1988; 1998). Her findings strongly suggest that labor was not substitutable across gender and condition of servitude. Thus, additive aggregation over gender and condition of servitude in nineteenth century production technologies would be incorrect; separate labor inputs by gender and condition of servitude are required. Carmel U. Chiswick's strong evidence on the substitutability and separability of physical capital, professional and non-professional labor in the twentieth century is closer to the issues raised in this paper (Chiswick 1979; 1985).[16] Her evidence, at a high level of aggregation of capital and labor inputs, suggests a high degree of substitutability. Yet, if engineers have key abilities – knowledge and experience – then a lower rate of substitutability is a plausible hypothesis. Thus, the issue becomes whether a scientifically trained engineer (apprenticed or degreed) can be easily substituted in the symphony of production.[17] Given the importance of applied science to the production of goods and services from the late nineteenth century onward, it is at least a plausible hypothesis that the labor that applied science to production was a separate factor of production.

Alternatively, one might simply ask *who* is the residual as conventionally measured. Or, as endogenous growth theorist Paul M. Romer (1994, 12) notes, "technical change comes from things people do." Counterfactually, how large would the growth of the residual in construction, manufacturing, transportation, and utilities be if there were no personnel who were formally or informally trained in science and its applications to production? Granted, efficiencies in organization were also crucial to the residual's growth. Indeed, much market, firm, and governmental innovation characterize the era of modern economic growth. Yet organizational innovation per se is not the distinguishing factor in the modern economic era. Innovative collective

---

[16] For evidence on labor–labor substitutability in the late twentieth century, see Hammermesh and Grant (1979).

[17] Can a poorly trained musician play Mozart? Yes, slowly and full of mistakes. Will people pay the musicians a living wage for such play, inclusive of a return to their training? Likely not. The evidence on the extent of practicing engineers without formal education is suggestive but not conclusive. Edison had no high school degree, yet he surrounded himself with highly educated research engineers and scientists. Largely self-educated in technical matters, he could have hired research personnel without degrees. It seems reasonable to hypothesize that hiring degreed personnel could both raise a firm's return and lower its risks.

(free and unfree) labor schemes, sophisticated divisions of labor, and sophisticated training regimes characterize pre-modern communities, organizations, and economies. But known evidence suggests that no organizational innovation in the pre-modern era was able to generate the sustained rates of per capita product growth seen after 1800.

This essay assumes that scientifically trained engineers either have a lower substitutability with other labor inputs and/or they are among the principal actors producing total factor productivity growth. On this basis it is a first step to count the number of bachelor's degrees awarded to engineers, classified by specialization and school. It is also useful to set the growth of this occupation in the context of the growth of other bachelor degrees and in the context of other industrial occupations. Finally, as engineering professionals also appeared in other advanced economies of the late nineteenth and early twentieth centuries, international comparison of New York State's production of college-educated engineers provides valuable information on the role of engineers in the state's pattern of economic growth.

III. EARLY HISTORY OF HIGHER EDUCATION IN ENGINEERING

The earliest schools and programs to teach applied science and certify their students with a higher degree appeared in the late eighteenth century in Austria, Germany, and France. The first engineering school was opened in Schemnitz, Hungary in 1763 on order from Empress Maria Theresa. Shortly after, in 1766, the Regent of Saxony funded the construction and operation of the more famous technical mining school at Freiberg. The first school devoted to civil engineering was the French school of bridges and roads, founded in 1775, largely attended by future military engineers. A new stage of educational development occurred when in 1794 France's revolutionary government founded the world's first university offering comprehensive scientific training. Its graduates were expected to be administrators in the nation's military, civil, and industrial sectors. From the start, however, the École Polytechnique's graduates were enthusiastically recruited into France's military and government administration, often in the planning and administration of military and civil government construction projects; few graduates of the Polytechnique were immediately employed in industry.[18] Somewhat in reaction to this bias, a group of private citizens founded the École Centrale in Paris in 1829 to train men for industrial technical leadership.[19] The German states were the first to copy the model of education at the École Polytechnique. They opened schools at Karlsruhe in Baden in 1825, Munich in 1827, Dresden in 1828, Stuttgart in 1829, Hannover in 1829, Berlin in 1831, Darmstadt in 1836, and Brunswick in 1845. About 30 years later

[18] Weiss (1982, 21–25); Artz (1966, 151–166, 230–253).
[19] Weiss (1982, 1–56, esp. 39–56).

these German polytechniques converted to *technische Hochschulen*. Their curriculum shifted toward applied science and their average entering student became an older teenager who was better prepared.

Strikingly, the founders of the Paris École Centrale and the German polytechniques in the 1820s and 1830s urged their case on the premise that a school of applied science was an effective means of countering the British lead in industrial affairs.[20] Public petitions, correspondence, and founding authorizations all testify to the desire of the founders and their funders, public and private, to provide technologists who would help them compete with Britain. Systematic study of science and technology, they argued, would narrow the gap.

The influence of these European developments was also felt in the United States, but there was nothing like the rapid proliferation of schools as occurred in the German states. The clearest connection between these European developments and what was happening in the United States was with the curriculum at the French schools and the first courses of study at the U.S. Military Academy at West Point, New York, founded in 1802, and at Rensselaer College in Troy, New York, founded in 1824. Both schools adopted versions of French engineering curriculums and both used French texts, as did the first German polytechniques. Along with the arts of military leadership, tactics, and weapons use, including the mathematics of trajectories, West Point trained its students in the construction of military fortresses, barracks, roads, and bridges and the practical chemistry of explosives. As is well known West Point graduates were among the professional civil engineers planning and managing construction of upstate New York's Erie Canal, the first important American canal. And, as is also well known, many American civil engineers who were engaged to construct other canals and the early railroads were trained on the job by the Erie Canal's master engineers. A. M. Wellington (1892–3) estimated that of the first 600 West Point cadets who graduated between 1802 and 1830, 74 went on to become practicing civil engineers in the private economy. By 1850, another 700 cadets had graduated, of whom 108 eventually entered the private sector as civil engineers.

Rensselaer College, privately founded in 1824, provided a scientific course of agricultural study for local farmers' sons. By the late 1820s it also offered courses in civil engineering, granting its first civil engineering degree in 1835

---

[20] One distinction between the polytechniques in France and Germany, on the one hand, and the École Central and the later German *technische Hochschulen*, on the other, was the use made of the graduates. Civil and mining engineering were most in demand by the governments of France and the German states in the first decades of the nineteenth century and the strongest focus of their polytechnique training. The later École Centrale and the evolved German *technische Hochschulen* taught civil and mechanical engineering and placed more of their graduates in private industry and mining: See Emmerson (1973, 77–90) and Weiss (1982, 85, 170).

and changing its name to Rensselaer Polytechnic Institute shortly afterwards. Toward the end of the 1840s courses of engineering were started at a number of the nation's older private colleges. In 1852 Union College in Schenectady, New York became the first of these colleges to award engineering degrees. Harvard's Lawrence Scientific School and Yale's Sheffield Scientific School both produced their first engineering graduates in 1853, and Dartmouth followed shortly after in 1855. At the end of the 1850s the University of Michigan, a state school founded in 1845, inaugurated an engineering course, awarding its first engineering degrees in 1860. The decade also saw the chartering of the Polytechnic College of Pennsylvania, which offered courses of study in civil engineering, mining engineering, mechanical engineering, chemistry, and architecture.[21]

Any momentum for additional engineering programs was halted by the early years of the Civil War. Yet the secession of the Southern states and the resulting realignment of political power in Washington have a good claim to creating a watershed in the history of U.S. engineering. For several decades the House and Senate had been besieged by resolutions, memorials, and reports urging federal government support for schools to teach the application of science to agriculture and industry. Just prior to the Civil War, Representative Morrill of Vermont sought Federal funding for state colleges to promote education in agriculture and the mechanical arts (Kandel 1917, 3–18). Representative Morrill's first bill was introduced in the House in 1857. Over strong opposition from state's rights advocates it passed the Senate in February 1859, only to be vetoed by President Buchanan.

Reintroduced in December 1861 the Morrill bill passed both Houses and was signed into law by President Lincoln on July 2, 1862, among the first significant legislative acts to reflect the absence of the South's delegates from Congress. The Morrill Land Grant Act offered each state 20,000 acres of federal public lands that could be sold to provide the financing for state colleges of higher learning. Training in agriculture and engineering was part of Morrill's original conception and that too was embodied in the legislation. Among the earliest schools to use land grant funds were the Massachusetts Institute of Technology (first engineering graduates in 1868), the University of Virginia (1869), and Cornell (1870).

In the 1870s and 1880s the largest number of new engineering programs was at land grant colleges. Wellington (1892–3) identified 92 working engineering schools of acceptable quality in 1889 and, of these, 54 were in public colleges and universities, awarding half the nation's engineering degrees. Four decades later in 1931 the Office of Education listed 144 U.S. schools

---

[21] Emmerson (1973, 153–56). The curriculum of the Polytechnic College of Pennsylvania was strongly influenced by the École Central and the Karlsruhe Polytechnische. Founded in 1853, the school disappeared in 1886 with the death of its sole director.

of engineering, of which 76 were public.[22] The proportions of private and public schools had changed very little. Yet by this point the land grant colleges had come to dominate engineering education. Public colleges and universities enrolled 62.3% of the 71,061 students in undergraduate engineering programs.[23]

While Wellington's data for the early 1890s and the several professional surveys of the 1920s and 1930s give some sense of national trends in the number and character of engineering schools and graduates, an economic history of the profession requires that we know more about the number and type of schools, the number and types of degrees, and their relation to other occupations based on training in colleges and universities. The students were making a costly investment that was expected to provide a long run stream of earnings. Engineering students were likely to have based their investment decisions on the employment opportunities available in local, regional, or even national labor markets. A first step in understanding this investment decision is to enumerate the realizations of that decision, the number of engineering degrees, the types of engineering degrees, their number relative to other human capital realizations, and their employment use.

IV. HIGHER DEGREES IN NEW YORK STATE, 1802–1950: DATA SOURCES

An examination of engineering bachelor's degrees in New York State is a useful starting point for research into the appearance and rapid growth of professional engineering in the United States. New York was among the first states to introduce modern transportation modes and where industry became significant.[24] As noted earlier, American higher learning in engineering began in New York State. And, importantly, no other prominent industrializing state collected comprehensive data on college and university degrees and enrollments.

The University of the State of New York was created by the state legislature on May 1, 1784, and was initially empowered to govern Columbia College, the state's only existing institution of higher education (Hough 1885, 5). By the 1790s the University of the State of New York had given up directly governing Columbia and taken on the task of certifying all degree-granting secondary and post-secondary educational institutions in the state. In 1795 Union College was the first new college so certified by the Regents.

---

[22] U.S. Department of Interior. Office of Education (1931, 10–13). It should be noted that these 1931 data cover only enrollments, not degrees.

[23] Average enrollments in public engineering programs were 50% larger than the average private school.

[24] New York was the leading state in manufacturing value-added from 1869–1949. The New York share of U.S. manufacturing value-added was: 1869, 19.6%; 1889, 19.8%; 1909, 17.9%; 1929, 15.7%; 1949, 12.6%. See Easterlin (1957, 694–95).

Any new degree programs at established institutions also required state cer-
tification. All secondary schools and colleges had to file annual reports that
included data on degrees granted, enrollments, and finances. Much of this
material was published in the annual reports of the Regents of the University
of the State of New York.[25] Fortunately many of the original college annual
filings are available in the New York State Archives in Albany.[26]

One drawback of the data published by the University of the State of
New York is that their engineering tabulation was restricted to self-identified
"schools" of engineering. Such schools were placed in the category, "engineering and technology." Some of these self-identified "schools" of engineering were within multi-disciplinary colleges and universities but some
constituted all or part of free standing polytechnic institutes. Some liberal
arts colleges that had a degree-granting engineering program did not have
their engineering degrees included in this "engineering and technology" category; their engineering degrees were counted among the degrees awarded in
the category, "arts and sciences." It is also the case that if the self-identified
schools of engineering offered non-engineering programs, such as chemistry or architecture, they were included in the total for "engineering and
technology."

In order to obtain a more accurate count of New York's engineering
graduates, a separate tabulation was made of the graduation records of the
seventeen engineering programs in New York founded between 1802 and
1950.[27] There were four principal sources for this separate annual count of
undergraduate engineering degrees. Some college registrars kept cumulative
records of the number and type of degrees annually awarded. Published annual college reports also proved useful. Another source were the annual com-
mencement programs or, in one case, college card files. Finally, use was made
of the original annual college filing with the University of the State of New
York. Importantly, for some of the self-identified "schools" of engineering it

---

[25] New York. Regents of the University of the State of New York (1886–1914); New York.
Department of Education (1915–1953). In 1885 the New York State Legislature published a
centenary history of the University of the State of New York authored by Franklin B. Hough.
Hough (1885) systematically examined the state's records every tenth year starting in 1793.
The first year he was able to provide data on enrollments and degrees awarded was 1823
(Hough 1885, 103–17). Since the USNY reports are unavailable for each year for the first
three quarters of the nineteenth century, it was decided to work with Hough's tabulations,
checking them against college records. The tables presenting USNY degree completions in
this essay continue Hough's count of every tenth year to 1953, with separate counts for
1940 and 1950 in order to examine the effects of World War II and the GI Bill. The annual
reports of the USNY were employed covering the years ending June 1893, 1903, 1913,
1923, 1933, 1940, 1943, 1950, and 1953. See New York, Regents of the University of the
State of New York (1886–1914); New York, Department of Education (1915–1953).

[26] New York, Education Department, Bureau of Statistical Services (1904–1953).

[27] A data appendix, available from the author, tabulates the number and type of undergraduate
engineering degree for New York's 17 colleges and polytechnics and their specific sources.

was possible to compare the published tabulations with independent counts from primary college sources. Differences in count were rare and very small, thus confirming that the University's "engineering and technology" count differed from the college sources for the reasons given above.

V. NEW YORK HIGHER DEGREES, 1823–1953

A century of New York State college and university degree completions is displayed in Tables 6.2–6.6. Table 6.2 summarizes the aggregate data. Notably, total degree awards either doubled or tripled every twenty years, 1853 to 1953. Of course, New York's population grew rapidly over this period so it is perhaps more important to mention that total degrees awarded per 100,000 of New York's population nearly doubled every twenty years, a bit slower than the total figure but still quite rapid. The most striking shift within the rapidly expanding total of degrees was the increase in the share of degrees awarded to women, rising from 1.8% in 1853 to a third of the degrees in 1923, jumping in the depression and WWII period but falling back in the post-WWII years to the earlier one-third level.

Growth was also quite rapid in the number of undergraduate engineering degrees awarded. Two estimates of undergraduate engineering awards are presented in Table 6.2. The first is based on the USNY censuses in the category of "engineering & technology." This estimate excludes some engineering degrees awarded by colleges without self-declared institutes or schools of engineering and technology. Furthermore, it includes an unknown number of non-engineering, technology degrees, most likely chemistry degrees. The second estimate is based on a college-level count that includes all first engineering degrees awarded in New York State at post-secondary educational institutions. The college-based estimate is a superior point estimate of purely engineering degrees, proving particularly useful in the years 1853 to 1893, when the USNY count grossly misses the engineering degrees granted by some of the state's liberal arts colleges. The college-based census shows engineering degrees growing four to five times every twenty years through 1913, but slowing to a doubling or so every twenty years thereafter. Clearly, engineering degrees were growing faster than all degrees through 1913, slower thereafter.

A deeper sense of the role of engineering human capital creation can be garnered by examining engineering awards relative to other types of degree awards. Table 6.3 presents the graduation data derived from the USNY counts, undergraduate and graduate, arranged by major; Tables 6.4 and 6.5 break down Table 6.3's totals for women and men, respectively.

Gender differences are quite striking. Women overwhelmingly acquired degrees in two specializations, arts and sciences, and education, continuing this pattern even as degrees awarded to women grew faster than men and as graduate degrees took hold after 1913 (Table 6.4). Total degrees awarded

TABLE 6.2. *New York State Higher Degrees, 1853–1953*

	Total Degrees	Total Degrees per 100,000	Female Degrees (%)	Total Undergraduate Engineering Degrees, USNY Est.	Total Undergraduate Engineering Degrees, College-based Est.	Total Engineering Undergraduate Degrees per 100,000, College-based Est.
1853	400	121	1.8	6	12	3.6
1863	636	158	5.0	12	14	3.5
1873	1,212	245	7.5	26	57	11.5
1883	1,673	313	5.0	53	74	13.8
1893	2,575	405	14.7	50	173	27.2
1903	3,982	512	27.5	377	355	45.6
1913	6,275	662	31.5	703	787	83.0
1923	10,570	961	33.2	732	772	70.2
1933	21,988	1,711	38.0	1,215	1,106	86.1
1940	26,596	1,973	44.0	1,565	1,389	103.0
1943	24,007	1,731	48.5	1,803	2,109	152.1
1950	58,249	3,928	27.8	5,988	5,741	387.1
1953	46,027	2,991	35.2	3,013	2,999	194.9

Sources: New York Degrees. See text. New York Population, 1853–1953, interpolated from 1850–1960 decadal census counts; see U.S. Bureau of the Census (1975, A195, 32).

TABLE 6.3. *New York State Higher Degrees, Total, by Specialization, 1823–1953*

	1823	1833	1843	1853	1863	1873	1883	1893	1903	1913	1923	1933	1940	1943	1950	1953
TOTAL UNGRD. DEG																
Architecture									13	30	40	86	57	68	194	129
Agriculture & Forestry									10	164	325	194	372	280	657	479
Arts & Sciences	104	121	151	156	301	450	526	921	1705	2215	3459	9033	11772	10941	25069	18415
Business									23	194	932	1088	1567	1593	4914	2886
Dental Hygiene															11	14
Dentistry						10	31	52	124	213	461	198	217	226		
Education					6			28	122	324	636	2163	1933	2255	4504	3895
Engineering & Technology					12	26	55	50	377	703	732	1215	1565	1803	5988	3013
Fine Arts							6	26	12	26	34	116	108	121	230	320
Home Economics											29	156	232	277	379	327
Indust. & Labor Relation															87	62
Journalism											49	55	27	4		
Law					66	240	217	419	534	586	1015	1186	984	491	1787	1971
Librarianship									3	17	17	186	280	182	90	18
Medicine	53	100	154	238	257	348	712	675	500	459	448	569	558	647		
Music & Performing Arts									5	1	8	17	141	119	328	363
Nursing														126	310	373
Optometry												33	47	35	96	40
Pharmacy							60	151	197	206	519	485	91	230	495	535
Podiatry											26	84	67	21	72	

194

	1	2	3	4	5	6	7	8	9	10	11	12	13	14	15	16
Theology							7	5	33	65	74	177	201	206	285	346
Veterinary Medicine																
TOTAL UNGRD. DEG	157	228	308	400	636	1081	1629	2400	3682	5231	8831	17064	20262	19662	45496	33186
Engineering, 1st. Deg.			2	12	14	57	74	173	355	787	772	1106	1389	2109	5741	2799
TOTAL GRD. DEG.																
Arts & Sciences, Total						40	44	175	291	719	998	2163	3047	2226	5966	6149
(A & S, PhDs only)										115	188	455	559	410	745	990
Business												192	181	80	738	829
Dentistry															215	244
Education									9	325	699	2359	2885	1860	3935	3440
Engineering & Technology											42	210	139	113	725	624
Journalism													60	47	70	62
Librarianship													22	19	138	143
Medicine															630	839
Optometry																83
Podiatry																63
Social Work															285	319
Veterinary Medicine															51	46
TOTAL GRD. DEG.						40	44	175	300	1044	1739	4924	6334	4345	12753	12841
TOTAL DEG. (U+G)	157	228	308	400	636	1121	1673	2575	3982	6275	10570	21988	26596	24007	58249	46027

TABLE 6.4. *New York State Higher Degrees, Female, by Specialization, 1853–1953*

FEMALE DEGREES	1843	1853	1863	1873	1883	1893	1903	1913	1923	1933	1940	1943	1950	1953
FEMALE UNGRD. DEG														
Architecture								2	6	5	8	5	12	19
Agriculture & Forestry								19	81	24	26	34	32	43
Arts & Sciences		7	32	75	84	290	936	1118	1684	4196	6262	6002	8080	7576
Business								1	77	116	188	247	319	207
Dental Hygiene													11	14
Dentistry							6	10	16		1	1		
Education						14	84	248	581	1160	1419	1846	2295	2712
Engineering & Technology								3	3	6	31	7	40	37
Fine Arts						18	7	17	26	82	77	100	102	135
Home Economics									29	117	190	225	285	321
Indust. & Labor Relation													5	9
Journalism									22	30	14			
Law							16	11	58	46	67	57	81	90
Librarianship							2	10	13	169	217	144	69	14
Medicine				9		38	22	14	40	33	42	39		
Music & Performing Arts							5	1	4	10	73	72	104	143

196

Nursing										3	126	310	368
Optometry											1	1	
Pharmacy					2	8	20	32	16	4	22	40	43
Podiatry								4	8	2	3		
Theology							1	1	29	13	44	33	61
Veterinary Medicine										4			
TOTAL FEMALE UNGRD. DEG	7	32	84	84	362	1086	1475	2677	6047	8641	8975	11819	11792
FEMALE GRD. DEG.													
Arts & Sciences, Total					17	6	258	389	794	1132	1218	1974	2138
Business									43	60	5	28	28
Dentistry												1	4
Education						4	242	444	1473	1838	1400	2016	1886
Engineering & Technology												12	8
Journalism										14	33	11	16
Librarianship										19	16	64	87
Medicine												87	57
Optometry													
Podiatry													1
Social Work												205	193
Veterinary Medicine												1	1
TOTAL FEMALE GRD. DEG.					17	10	500	833	2310	3063	2672	4399	4419
TOTAL FEMALE DEG.	7	32	84	84	379	1096	1975	3510	8357	11704	11647	16218	16211

TABLE 6.5 *New York State Higher Degrees, Male, by Specialization, 1843–1953*

MALE DEGREES	1843	1853	1863	1873	1883	1893	1903	1913	1923	1933	1940	1943	1950	1953
MALE UNGRD. DEG														
Architecture							13	28	34	81	49	63	182	110
Agriculture & Forestry							10	145	244	170	346	246	625	436
Arts & Sciences	151	149	269	375	442	631	769	1097	1775	4837	5510	4939	16989	10839
Business							23	193	855	972	1379	1346	4595	2679
Dental Hygiene														
Dentistry				10	31	52	118	203	445	198	216	225		
Education						14	38	76	55	1003	514	409	2209	1183
Engineering & Technology	3	6	12	26	55	50	377	700	729	1209	1534	1796	5948	2976
Fine Arts					6	8	5	9	8	34	31	21	128	185
Home Economics										39	42	52	94	6
Indust. & Labor Relation													82	53
Journalism									27	25	13	4		
Law			66	240	217	419	518	575	957	1140	917	434	1706	1881
Librarianship							1	7	4	17	63	38	21	4
Medicine	154	238	257	339	712	637	478	445	408	536	516	608		
Music & Performing Arts									4	7	68	47	224	220

Nursing														
Optometry														40
Pharmacy					60	149	189	186	487	469	87	208	455	492
Podiatry									22	76	65	18	72	
Theology							5		73	148	188	162	252	285
Veterinary Medicine				7			28	24	27	23	39	37		
TOTAL MALE UNGRD. DEG	308	393	604	997	1545	2038	2596	3756	6154	11017	11621	10687	33677	21394
MALE GRD. DEG.														
Arts & Sciences, Total				40	44	158	285	461	609	1369	1915	1008	3992	4011
Business							5			149	121	75	710	801
Dentistry								83					214	240
Education									255	886	1047	460	1919	1554
Engineering & Technology									42	210	139	113	713	616
Journalism											46	14	59	46
Librarianship											3	3	74	56
Medicine													543	782
Optometry														83
Podiatry														62
Social Work													80	126
Veterinary Medicine													50	45
TOTAL MALE GRD. DEG.				40	44	158	290	544	906	2614	3271	1673	8354	8422
TOTAL MALE DEG. (U+G)	308	393	604	1037	1589	2196	2886	4300	7060	13631	14892	12360	42031	29816

to men were spread more widely with large percentages in arts and sciences, law, medicine, and engineering, later joined by business from 1913 (Table 6.5). Notably, graduate degrees were relatively more important to women than men throughout this period.

Restricting attention to degrees roughly comparable to the undergraduate engineering degree in time and money invested, Table 6.6 displays the percentage of total *undergraduate* degrees for the dominant majors. With very rapid growth to 1913, as noted above, it is no surprise that the undergraduate share of engineering degrees rose strikingly to 15.0%. Thereafter it drops in the 1920s and again during the depressed 1930s. Recovering to 11–12% during WWII and the immediate post-WWII GI Bill era, it drops to 8.7% in 1953 as GIs became a decreasing presence in the state's undergraduate enrollments.

If entry into occupations and professions had been relatively free, the shifting percentage distributions of Table 6.6 would importantly reflect longer term economic forces of the supply and demand for various occupations. However, restrictive social mores, laws, and professional societies can claim an important role in the evolution of degrees granted. Gender obviously affected degree choice. Women form minuscule proportions of engineering, law, business, and the health professions during these years.

Apart from the gender division of labor, laws and professional societies also had profound effects on the number of majors. Historians of the American legal and medical professions have studied the increase in restrictive practices, often with legislative approval, in the early twentieth century (Numbers 1988). These New York data suggest more limited access started in the 1880s for medicine and the 1890s for the law. For example, by 1893 certified medical schools in New York were required to have a three-year course of study and ten years later this was increased to a four-year course. Interestingly, from 1913 to 1923 a time when the 1910 Flexner Report took hold in New York,[28] the percentage drop in the share of medical degrees was very close to the percentage rise in dentistry and pharmacy! (see Table 6.6).

In the same years, 1913–1923, almost percentage point for percentage point, engineering dropped (15.7% to 8.7%) as the new business degree took off (3.7% to 10.6%). It seems that these changes were linked to some extent. Until the appearance of business degrees in these years, engineering degrees were the only tertiary degree preparation in the state's colleges and

---

[28] When the famous muckraking report of Abraham Flexner on American medicine funded by the Carnegie Foundation appeared in 1910, New York had only recently begun to require at least one year of college of its medical students; by 1933 the requirement was two years. New York's medical school curriculum standards were also raised in the first decade of the twentieth century and after the Flexner report as well.

TABLE 6.6. *Dominant Majors, Undergraduate Degrees, 1853–1953*

	Arts & Sciences	Education	Law	Engineering College-Count	Business	Medicine	Dentistry	Pharmacy
				% of Total Undergraduate Degrees				
1853	39.0			3.0		59.5		
1863	47.3		10.4	2.2		40.4		
1873	41.6		22.2	5.3		32.2	0.9	
1883	32.3		13.3	4.5		43.7	1.9	3.7
1893	38.4	1.2	17.5	7.2		28.1	2.2	6.3
1903	46.3	3.3	14.5	9.6	0.6	13.6	3.4	5.4
1913	42.3	6.2	11.2	15.0	3.7	8.8	4.1	3.9
1923	39.2	7.2	11.5	8.7	10.6	5.1	5.2	5.9
1933	52.9	12.7	7.0	6.5	6.4	3.3	1.2	2.8
1940	58.1	9.5	4.9	6.9	7.7	2.8	1.1	0.4
1943	55.6	11.5	2.5	10.7	8.1	3.3	1.1	1.2
1950	55.1	9.9	3.9	12.6	10.8			1.1
1953	55.5	11.7	5.9	8.4	8.7			1.6

Note: After 1943, medical and dental degrees are counted in the graduate degree totals.

universities directly relevant for a business career. Of course, adult vocational courses provided some accounting and other preparation for business careers but a full specialized undergraduate course of study, other than engineering, did not exist. In this case, given the almost percentage point for percentage point substitution of business for engineering degrees, it appears that potential students who wanted to prepare for business positions other than engineering and production took the opportunity to drop the engineering course of study. On the other hand, there is some evidence that civil and mechanical engineering specializations had over-expanded in the 1910s, independent of the rise of business education, causing stagnant (mechanical) or falling (civil) degree awards in the 1920s. Importantly, apart from gender barriers, and unlike the health and law professions, there were few restrictions on the creation and expansion of engineering and business college and university degree programs, nor were there, for example, any professional qualifying examinations. A study of engineering salaries and unemployment rates would thus be both appropriate and necessary to begin to resolve the issues raised by this drop in engineering degrees.

VI. NEW YORK FIRST ENGINEERING DEGREES: SCHOOL AND SPECIALIZATIONS

Between 1802 and 1950, seventeen institutions of higher learning offered a first degree in engineering in New York. Table 6.7 presents the names of these seventeen institutions with their founding date and the date of their first engineering degree. The U.S. Military Academy, RPI, Cooper Union, Cornell, Clarkson, and the U.S. Merchant Marine Academy offered engineering degrees from their first years. Except for Cornell, all were envisioned primarily as schools of applied science. Most of the other institutions on this list were started as liberal arts colleges, a bachelor's in engineering being first offered some decades after their founding. The principal exceptions were the Polytechnic Institute of Brooklyn and the Pratt Institute. Brooklyn Polytechnic and Pratt began as schools offering vocational courses (e.g. drafting) with few if any science or mathematics prerequisites. Only later did these two schools decide to offer a higher degree with college-level science and mathematics in the first years of the curriculum.

In most cases the local business community was a catalyst for the founding of programs. The first engineering programs at RPI, Cooper Union, Syracuse, Clarkson, Brooklyn Polytechnic, Rochester, Alfred, and Pratt, all private institutions, were aided financially by local businessmen who wished to provide local firms a source of trained professionals. Sometimes the founding businessmen were seeking engineers for their own firms. Such was the case for T. S. Clarkson, founder of the Clarkson School of Technology, and L. C. Smith, the principal funder for the L. C. Smith School of Applied Science at Syracuse University. Ceramic firms in western New York urged

TABLE 6.7. *New York State Engineering Programs*

	Institutional Founding Year	Year of First Engineering Degree
U.S. Military Academy	1801	1802
Rensselaer College, later Rensselaer Polytechnic Institute	1824	1835
Union College	1795	1845
University of the City of New York, later New York University	1832	1857
Cooper Union	1859	1864
Columbia College	1754	1867
Cornell University	1865	1870
Manhattan College	1853	1894
Syracuse University	1870	1900
Clarkson School of Technology, later Clarkson University	1896	1900
Polytechnic Institute of Brooklyn	1854	1905
University of Rochester	1829	1914
Alfred University	1836	1918
City College of New York	1847	1921
Pratt Institute	1857	1938
U.S. Merchant Marine Academy	1942	1938
University of Buffalo, later State University of New York, Buffalo	1846	1947

Alfred to upgrade its ceramic programs and offer higher degrees in ceramic engineering. Rochester businessmen urged the University of Rochester to prepare engineers in optical engineering.

Columbia and Cornell had always sought students from a national pool and envisioned supplying a larger market. From the start students who enrolled in the Columbia School of Mines spent their summers working and studying in the Far West and many after graduation found their first jobs there. As New York's land grant institution, Cornell was expected to serve state-wide needs; its enrollments and its graduates' first jobs reflected this wider mandate.

The location of New York's engineering schools reveals two patterns. Clearly, New York City was an early and important center for engineering education. Located there in the mid-nineteenth century were Columbia, NYU, and Cooper Union, and then Manhattan, Brooklyn Polytechnic, CCNY, and Pratt after 1900. Brooklyn Polytechnic and Pratt were founded in the mid-nineteenth century but offered only vocational courses until the early twentieth century. Nearly all of the other engineering schools were founded along the axis of the Erie Canal, from RPI and Union in the east through Syracuse, Cornell, to Rochester, Alfred, and SUNY Buffalo in the west. Only Clarkson near the northern border with Canada sat off by itself. Construction of the Erie Canal (1817–1825) had a profound effect on upstate New York, first energizing agricultural production for longer distance export with attendant urbanization near the Canal and then in the mid-nineteenth century the beginnings of manufacturing growth. In his study of early American inventive activity Sokoloff (1988) found that the Canal and its attendant upstate economic development led fairly quickly to a jump in New York State patenting activity in both agriculture and manufacturing.

Rensselaer Polytechnic Institute was the dominant civilian New York school of engineering through the 1860s, displaced at first by Columbia's School of Mines, but then most strikingly by Cornell's civil and mechanical engineering programs (Tables 6.8 and 6.9). In the 1920s both Cornell and Columbia reduced the scale of their programs and the slack was taken up by the smaller programs in New York City and upstate New York. Columbia's decision to reduce its engineering program in the 1920s coincided with larger graduating classes from Pratt. In the 1930s, programs also expanded at CCNY, Cooper Union, and NYU. New York City's schools had produced roughly a third of the state's new engineering degrees from the 1870s to the 1920s but that share jumped to around 50% in the 1930s and 1940s.

Civil engineering was the dominant degree specialization through the 1880s, with mining engineers a sizable but much smaller specialization (Tables 6.10 and 6.11). The 1890s, 1900s, and 1910s saw civil engineering dropping to less than half the degrees awarded. Sizable numbers of mechanical and electrical engineering were first awarded in the 1890s, but curiously the share of electrical engineering dropped from 21.9% in the 1890s to 10.1% in the 1900s and 1910s, while mechanical engineering rose. Then, the electrical specialization jumped in the 1920s while mechanical engineering fell back a bit.

Since the use of electricity was increasing rapidly during the first two decades of the twentieth century the decline in electrical engineering degrees appears anomalous. At one level the explanation is simple: Cornell, the dominant electrical engineering school, stopped awarding a separate electrical engineering degree from 1904 to 1920. Instead, Cornell's electrical engineers received a mechanical engineering degree. Yet it is also the case that prior to 1920 applications of electrical power mainly involved a simple substitution of an electrical engine for a steam engine. Factories with multiple electrical engines and the introduction of new types of electrical equipment were a later development.

Chemical engineering degrees were first issued in the 1910s. In the 1920s the chemical, electrical, and mechanical specializations displaced civil engineering. Aeronautical engineering degrees appeared in the 1930s. They surged in the 1940s, in part, like marine engineering, heavily linked to the technical needs of World War II. Turning to the geographic distribution from the 1830s to the 1930s, upstate engineering schools produced more

TABLE 6.8. *New York State Engineering Bachelor Degrees Granted, By School, 1802–1953*

Years	1802–09	1810–19	1820–29	1830–39	1840–49	1850–59	1860–69	1870–79	1880–89	1890–99	1900–09	1910–19	1920–29	1930–39	1940–49	1950–53
Alfred											9	24	102	152	213	172
CCNY													126	1129	3164	2043
Clarkson											89	182	445	553	841	1066
Columbia							36	203	314	388	829	989	369	522	1227	643
Cooper Union							21	45	86	166	491	1019	966	1272	1090	484
Cornell								168	224	1127	2292	2707	2328	1735	2933	1231
Manhattan										20	57	121	160	351	581	823
NYU							13	54	43	50	183	365	597	1858	2720	1713
Polytechnic						4					104	413	752	866	1638	1824
Pratt														127	844	383
Rensselaer				61	80	83	157	240	257	241	436	814	1493	2132	3157	3216
SUNY Buffalo															225	655
Syracuse								9	12		286	506	454	619	865	1270
Union					8	37	72	78	91	76	154	345	427	293	267	264
Rochester												17	71	211	541	272
USMM														21	4285	600
USMA	52	179	355	430	433	397	465	515	504	609	913	1687	2247	3005	5556	2184
TOTAL, INCL. USMA	52	179	355	491	521	521	764	1312	1531	2677	5843	9189	10537	14846	30147	18843
TOTAL, EXCL. USMA				61	88	124	299	797	1027	2068	4930	7502	8290	11841	24591	16659

TABLE 6.9. *N.Y. Engineering Bachelor Degrees, by School and by Decade, % Distribution., excl. USMA, 1802–1953*

Years	1830–39	1840–49	1850–59	1860–69	1870–79	1880–89	1890–99	1900–09	1910–19	1920–29	1930–39	1940–49	1950–53
Alfred								0.2	0.3	1.2	1.3	0.9	1.0
CCNY										1.5	9.5	12.9	12.3
Clarkson								1.8	2.4	5.4	4.7	3.4	6.4
Columbia				12.0	25.5	30.6	18.8	16.8	13.2	4.5	4.4	5.0	3.9
Cooper Union				7.0	5.6	8.4	8.0	10.0	13.6	11.7	10.7	4.4	2.9
Cornell					21.1	21.8	54.5	46.5	36.1	28.1	14.7	11.9	7.4
Manhattan							1.0	1.2	1.6	1.9	3.0	2.4	4.9
NYU			3.2	4.3	6.8	4.2	2.4	3.7	4.9	7.2	15.7	11.1	10.3
Polytechnic								2.1	5.5	9.1	7.3	6.7	10.9
Pratt											1.1	3.4	2.3
Rensselaer	100.0	90.9	66.9	52.5	30.1	25.0	11.7	8.8	10.9	18.0	18.0	12.8	19.3
SUNY Buffalo												0.9	3.9
Syracuse					1.1	1.2		5.8	6.7	5.5	5.2	3.5	7.6
Union		9.1	29.8	24.1	9.8	8.9	3.7	3.1	4.6	5.2	2.5	1.1	1.6
Rochester									0.2	0.9	1.8	2.2	1.6
TOTAL (%)	100.0	100.0	100.0	100.0	100.0	100.0	100.0	100.0	100.0	100.0	100.0	100.0	100.0
TOTAL (#)	61	88	124	299	797	1027	2068	4930	7502	8290	11841	24591	16659

TABLE 6.10. N.Y. Engineering Bachelor Degrees, by Specialty and by Decade, excl. USMA, 1830–1953

Years	1830–39	1840–49	1850–59	1860–69	1870–79	1880–89	1890–99	1900–09	1910–19	1920–29	1930–39	1940–49	1950–53
Admin/Managerial										7	340	995	870
Aeronautical											205	1301	506
Ceramic								9	24	102	152	213	172
Chemical								15	291	720	1392	3126	1774
Civil	61	88	124	253	605	712	973	2001	3330	2446	3026	2760	2584
Electrical						43	585	592	787	2112	2731	4406	4393
Forestry								17					
Industrial									1	86	58	124	161
Marine											21	4285	600
Mechanical					39	63	406	1841	2463	2633	2891	5636	3995
Metallurgical					2	4	11	14	40	18	20	198	198
Mining				46	151	205	93	281	250	31			
Optical											23	81	23
Physics												14	85
Unspecified								160	316	135	982	1452	1298
TOTAL, EXCL. USMA	61	88	124	299	797	1027	2068	4930	7502	8290	11841	24591	16659

TABLE 6.11. *New York State Engineering Bachelor Degrees, by Specialty and by Decade, % Distribution., excl.USMA, 1830–1953*

Years	1830–39	1840–49	1850–59	1860–69	1870–79	1880–89	1890–99	1900–09	1910–19	1920–29	1930–39	1940–49	1950–53
Admin/Managerial										0.1	2.9	4.0	5.2
Aeronautical											1.7	5.3	3.0
Ceramic								0.2	0.3	1.2	1.3	0.9	1.0
Chemical								0.3	3.9	8.7	11.8	12.7	10.6
Civil	100.0	100.0	100.0	84.6	75.9	69.3	47.1	40.6	44.4	29.5	25.6	11.2	15.5
Electrical						4.2	28.3	12.0	10.5	25.5	23.1	17.9	26.4
Forestry								0.3					
Industrial									0.0	1.0	0.5	0.5	1.0
Marine											0.2	17.4	3.6
Mechanical					4.9	6.1	19.6	37.3	32.8	31.8	24.4	22.9	24.0
Metallurgical					0.3	0.4	0.5	0.3	0.5	0.2	0.2	0.8	1.2
Mining				15.4	18.9	20.0	4.5	5.7	3.3	0.4			
Optical											0.2	0.3	0.1
Physics												0.1	0.5
Unspecified								3.2	4.2	1.6	8.3	5.9	7.8
TOTAL, EXCL. USMM (%)	100.0	100.0	100.0	100.0	100.0	100.0	100.0	100.0	100.0	100.0	100.0	100.0	100.0
TOTAL, EXCL. USMM (#)	61	88	124	299	797	1027	2068	4930	7502	8290	11841	24591	16659

civil, electrical, and mechanical degrees than New York City from the 1830s to the 1930s (Table 6.12).[29] The dominance of Cornell in mechanical engineering is particularly notable. By the 1940s, however, New York City schools were dominant in all three specializations. Most of the engineering degrees in the 1940s were awarded after the war. It would thus appear that the soldiers who took advantage of the post-WWII GI Bill to fund an engineering education predominantly chose New York City. CCNY, Columbia, and Pratt expanded at striking rates in the immediate post-WWII years. In chemical engineering New York City generated more degrees than upstate New York. The proximity of New York City engineering schools to Northern New Jersey and its petrochemical complexes may have played a role in this pattern.

VIII. ENGINEERING GRADUATES IN THE NEW YORK LABOR FORCE

These tabulations of engineering degrees can contribute to the understanding of the role of graduate engineers in the New York labor force and economy. However, additional research is required on where the graduates found work. As a highly industrialized state, it is likely most of New York's graduates found work and career in New York. Yet, it is likely many took their advanced knowledge and experience elsewhere in the USA and some abroad. Furthermore, graduates from engineering schools in other states found work in New York, as did a small number of graduates from European engineering programs. Thus, with the gross flows of graduate engineers across New York's borders unknown with any precision, the net resident stock of engineers can be estimated only roughly. Casual examination of a limited set of alumni data suggests a larger share of RPI, Cornell, and Columbia graduates left the state than the graduates of the state's smaller programs, but clearly more research is warranted. Again, a substantial fraction of New York engineering graduates left the profession at some point in their work lives. Some moved to entrepreneurial and other business roles that utilized their engineering background. Others, however, took jobs outside of manufacturing, mining, and construction, that is, in the agricultural and service sectors.

Despite the data problems, it is still possible to develop rough estimates of the stock of graduate engineers in New York that allow some insight into their relation to the overall economy. Table 6.13 presents a crude measure of the stock of engineering graduates in New York along with international comparisons with France, Germany, and Sweden. The methodology

---

[29] Note that Columbia's records did not reveal the specialization of its engineering graduates from 1926 onward. Columbia's total degree production dropped in the 1920s and 1930s but recovered in the 1940s (see Table 6.9).

TABLE 6.12. Engineering Specialization, by School and Decade, 1835–1949

	1835–39	1840–49	1850–59	1860–69	1870–79	1880–89	1890–99	1900–09	1910–19	1920–29	1930–39	1940–49
Chemical Engineering												
CCNY								6		13	179	621
Columbia									145	101	276	299
Cooper Union										40		
NYU								7	65	123	153	294
Poly								1	21	75	115	334
Pratt											27	207
Clarkson								1	27	40	82	224
Cornell											45	359
RPI									28	252	334	493
Syracuse									5	57	106	149
Rochester										19	75	146
Civil Engineering												
CCNY								173	264	49	200	553
Columbia				21	63	105	156			26		
Cooper Union					45	86	166	480	734	300	338	146
Manhattan				13			20	57	121	155	335	286
NYU			4		54	43	50	139	223	121	434	306
Poly								38	227	175	229	220
Clarkson								38	67	114	131	99
Cornell					129	118	264	561	925	702	488	559
RPI	61	80	83	147	227	257	241	436	548	493	645	377
Syracuse				72	9	12		79	207	84	97	149
Rochester			37		78	91	76		14	227	129	65

Electrical Engineering

CCNY	1070	184	23	128	207	128	
Columbia	311	441	49	208	11		
Cooper Union			332			457	
Manhattan	260	11		85	50		
NYU	502	343	60				
Poly	451	281	233	47	34		43
Pratt	251	41			159		
Clarkson	206	155	154	135	131		
Cornell	471	326	455				
RPI	525	637	457	150			
Syracuse	140	148	151	34			
Union	202	164	198				
Rochester	17						

Mechanical Engineering

CCNY	920	106	34	162	148			
Columbia	334	217	42	77				
Cooper Union			294				63	
NYU	825	787	212	76	37			
Poly	503	241	269	80	15			
Pratt	386	59						
Clarkson	311	161	113	22	10			
Cornell	1014	622	1171	1782	1555	406		39
RPI	785	403	291	103				
Syracuse	261	182	155	144	76			
Rochester	297	113	52	17				

TABLE 6.13 *Estimates of the Stock of Engineering Graduates in New York State, France, Germany, and Sweden before World War I*

		Total Labor Force (millions)	Stock of Engineers	Eng. Stock/ L.F. p. 1000	L.F.Growth % p.a.	Eng. Stock Growth % p.a.	Eng/L.F. Growth % p.a.
			Panel A: New York State				
1860			249				
1870		1.491	508	0.3		7.4	
1880		1.885	1,162	0.6	2.4	8.6	6.1
1890		2.436	1,990	0.8	2.6	5.5	2.9
1900		2.977	3,612	1.2	2.1	6.1	2.9
1910		4.004	8,051	2	2.9	8.3	4.0
1920		4.503	13,196	2.9	1.2	5.1	5.3
1930		5.523	18,572	3.4	2.1	3.5	3.8
1940		5.677	26,092	4.6	0.3	3.5	1.4
1950		6.348	42,518	6.7	1.1	5.0	3.2
		Est. 5-Ind. L. F.	Panel B: International Comparisons				3.8
1880/84	France	5.584	17,000.0	3.0			
1880/84	Germany	6.690	26,600.0	4.0			
1880/84	Sweden	0.247	1,400.0	5.7			
1880/84	New York	1.188	1,262.2	1.1			
1910/14	France	7.648	40,600.0	5.3	1.1	2.9	1.9
1910/14	Germany	12.011	62,600.0	5.2	2.0	2.9	0.9
1910/14	Sweden	0.677	3,300.0	4.9	3.4	2.9	-0.5
1910/14	New York	1.582	8,448.4	5.3	1.0	6.5	5.5

Notes: (1) Ahlstrom (1982) estimates the stock of engineer graduates in France, Germany, and Sweden by cumulating the annual number of graduates, assuming a 40-year work life and death rate of 17 per thousand per year. The same methodology is used to estimate the New York stock. The New York stock excludes West Point and the marine engineering degrees for comparability. (2) The stock estimates for France, Germany, Sweden, and New York are approximate and, in general, overestimates. There is no adjustment for engineers who move to other occupations or the net movement of engineers across the relevant borders.

Sources: New York. Engineering degrees: Edelstein (2001). Total labor force: U.S. Bureau of the Census (1975, D26). Labor force in five industries (mining, construction, manufacturing, transportation, utilities): Easterlin (1957, 628). France, Germany, and Sweden. Engineering degrees: Ahlstrom (1982, 38). Total labor force and labor force in five industries: Mitchell (1975, Table C1, 155–162).

employed here is based on the approach and assumptions used by Ahlstrom (1982, 36–41) to his estimates of the stock of French, German, and Swedish graduates. Graduate engineers are assumed to have a 40-year work life and a death rate of 17 per 1000 during their active work life. There are no adjustments for movements across the New York's borders or for professional exits.

From 1860 to 1900, the stock of New York graduate engineers roughly tripled every 20 years and then from 1900 to 1950 approximately doubled every 20 years, anomalously slowing in the 1920s. This growth was considerably faster than New York's overall labor force. The number of engineers per 1000 of the total labor force rose rapidly from 0.3 in 1860 to 1.2 in 1900 and 6.7 in 1950; again slower growth in the 1920s stands out. These increases were almost certainly demand driven as New York State was one of the national economy's industrial leaders.

The number of engineers in New York compared with France, Germany, and Sweden also suggests a relatively strong and rising demand for these professional technologists in New York. Here, the measure of the intensity of engineer use is the *stock* of graduate engineers per 1000 in the labor force employed in mining, manufacturing, construction, transportation, and other utilities.

Relative to the European countries New York State had a significantly lower intensity of engineer employment in its industrial sectors as late as 1880.[30] By 1914, however, graduations from New York's engineering schools appear to have moved New York much closer to the European proportion. It is worth noting that while the European schools were heavily subsidized state institutions, Cornell was the only school in New York that was similarly supported during these decades.[31] Thus the graduation rate of most New York schools responded to the opportunities for their graduates, school ambitions, and the generosity of their private founders, not state funding.

VIII. CONCLUSION

From 1850 to 1950 New York was the leading industrial state in a nation that became the leading industrial nation in the world. The occupational distribution of the state shifted accordingly. New York's colleges and universities graduated engineers at very rapid rates throughout the period, strongly suggesting a highly elastic response of the state's higher education sector to

---

[30] Data on the total stock of professional engineers, graduate and non-graduate, do not currently exist for comparative purposes.

[31] City College of New York (CCNY) was a municipally supported school with free tuition but it began to produce engineers only after World War I; Buffalo, a state supported university, began graduating engineers in 1947. Interestingly, Cooper Union, a private engineering school, also did not charge its students tuition; their costs were covered by the school's large initial and growing endowment.

the demand for workers formally trained in science and the application of science to production. Furthermore, the twenty-fold increase in the intensity of engineer use makes it clear that engineers with their ability to apply science were a defining feature of New York's industrializing and growing economy.

Bibliography

Abramovitz, Moses. 1956. Resource and output trends in the United States since 1870. *American Economic Review* **46**: 5–23.

Abramovitz, Moses, and David, Paul A. 2000. American macroeconomic growth in the era of knowledge-based progress: the long-run perspective. In Engerman, Stanley F., and Gallman, Robert E. (eds.), *The Cambridge Economic History of the United States*. Volume III. *The Twentieth Century*. New York: Cambridge University Press, Chapter 1.

Ahlstrom, Goran. 1982. *Engineers and Industrial Growth: Higher Technical Education and the Engineering Profession during the 19th and Early 20th Centuries: France, Germany, Sweden and England*. London: Croom Helm.

Artz, Frederick B. 1966. *The Development of Technical Education in France, 1500–1850*. Cambridge, MA: MIT Press.

Blank, David M., and Stigler, George J. 1957. *The Demand and Supply of Scientific Personnel*. No. 62. General Series. New York: National Bureau of Economic Research.

Calvert, Monte A. 1967. *The Mechanical Engineer in America, 1830–1910. Professional Cultures in Conflict*. Baltimore: Johns Hopkins.

Chiswick, Carmel U. 1979. The growth of professional occupations in U.S. manufacturing: 1900–1973. *Research in Human Capital and Development* **1**: 191–217.

Chiswick, Carmel U. 1985. The elasticity of substitution revisited: the effects of secular changes in labor force structure. *Journal of Labor Economics* **3**: 490–507.

David, Paul A., and Wright, Gavin. 1997. Increasing returns and the genesis of American resource abundance. *Industrial and Corporate Change* **6**: 203–45.

Easterlin, Richard A. 1957. Estimates of manufacturing activity. In Kuznets, Simon and Thomas, Dorothy S., *Population Redistribution and Economic Growth: United States, 1870–1950*. Vol. I. Methodological Considerations and Reference Tables. Philadelphia PA: American Philosophical Society.

Edelstein, Michael. 2001. *Appendix A: Completed First Degrees in Engineering*, New York State, 1802–1953. Unpublished manuscript.

Emmerson, George S. 1973. *Engineering Education: A Social History*. Devon: David and Charles.

Fabricant, Solomon. 1949. The Changing Industrial Distribution of Gainful Workers: some comments on the American decennial statistics for 1820–1840. In Conference on Research in Income and Wealth, *Studies in Income and Wealth*, Vol. 11. New York: National Bureau of Economic Research, pp. 3–45.

Field(-Hendrey), Elizabeth. 1988. Free and slave labor on large and small farms: perfect substitutes or different inputs? *Review of Economics and Statistics* **70**: 654–659.

Field-Hendrey, Elizabeth. 1998. The role of gender in biased technical change: U.S. manufacturing, 1850–1919. *Journal of Economic History* **58**: 1090–1109.

Flexner, Abraham. 1910. *Medical Education in the United States and Canada: A Report to the Carnegie Foundation for the Advancement of Teaching*. Bulletin No. 4. New York: Carnegie Foundation for the Advancement of Teaching.

Folk, Hugh. 1970. *The Shortage of Scientists and Engineers*. Lexington, MA: D.C. Heath.

Goldin, Claudia. 1998. America's graduation from high school: the evolution and spread of secondary schooling in the twentieth century. *Journal of Economic History* 58: 345–74.

Goldin, Claudia. 2001. The human capital century and American leadership: virtues of the past. *Journal of Economic History* 61: 263–92.

Goldin, Claudia, and Katz, Lawrence F. 1999. The shaping of higher education: the formative years in the United States, 1890 to 1940. *Journal of Economic Perspectives* 13: 37–62.

Hammermesh, Daniel S., and Grant, J. 1979. Econometric studies of labor-labor substitution and their implications for policy. *Journal of Human Resources* 14: 518–42.

Hatch, Nathan O. (ed.) 1988. *The Professions in American History*. Notre Dame, IN: University of Notre Dame Press.

Hough, Franklin B. 1885. *Historical and Statistical Record of the University of the State of New York, During the Century from 1784 to 1884*. With an introductory sketch by David Murray. Albany, NY: Weed, Parsons, & Co.

Kandel, I. L. 1917. *Federal Aid for Vocational Education*. Bulletin No. 10. New York: Carnegie Foundation for the Advancement of Teaching.

Khan, B. Zorina, and Sokoloff, Kenneth L. 2004. Institutions and democratic invention in 19th-century America: evidence from the great inventors. *American Economic Review, Papers and Proceedings* 94: 395–401.

Kuznets, Simon. 1966. *Modern Economic Growth: Rate Structure and Spread*. New Haven, CT: Yale.

Lamoreaux, Naomi, and Sokoloff, Kenneth. 1999. Inventors, firms, and the market for technology in the late nineteenth and early twentieth centuries. In Lamoreaux, Naomi R., Raff, Daniel M. G., and Temin, Peter (eds.). *Learning by Doing in Markets, Firms, and Countries*. Chicago: University of Chicago Press, pp. 19–57.

Lamoreaux, Naomi, and Sokoloff, Kenneth. 2001. Market trade in patents and the rise of a class of specialized inventors in the 19th-century United States. *American Economic Review. Papers and Proceedings* 91: 39–44.

Landes, David S. 1969. *The Unbound Prometheus. Technological Change and the Industrial Development in Western Europe from 1750 to the Present*. New York: Cambridge University Press.

Mann, Charles Riborg. 1918. *A Study of Engineering Education*. Bulletin No. 11. Prepared for the Joint Committee on Engineering Education of the National Engineering Societies. New York: The Carnegie Foundation for the Advancement of Teaching.

Mitchell, B. R. 1975. *European Historical Statistics:1750–1970*. New York: Columbia University Press.

Mokyr, Joel. 1990. *Lever of Riches. Technological Creativity and Economic Progress*. New York: Oxford University Press.

Mowery, David, and Rosenberg, Nathan. 1989. *Technology and the Pursuit of Economic Growth*. Cambridge, UK: Cambridge University Press.

Mowery, David, and Rosenberg, Nathan. 1998. *Paths of Innovation. Technical Change in 20th Century America*. New York: Cambridge University Press.

Nelson, R. R., and Wright, G. 1992. The rise and fall of American technological leadership: the postwar era in historical perspective. *Journal of Economic Literature* 30: 1931–64.

New York. Education Department. 1915–1953. Annual Reports.

New York. Education Department. Bureau of Statistical Services. 1904–1953. Annual Financial and Statistical Reports of Universities, Colleges, and Junior Colleges. Albany, NY: New York State Archives,.

New York, Regents of the University of the State of New York. 1886–1914. *Annual Reports*.

Numbers, Ronald L. 1988. The fall and rise of the American medical profession. In Hatch, Nathan O. (ed.). *The Professions in American History*. Notre Dame, IN: University of Notre Dame Press, Chapter 3.

Read Jr., Thomas Thornton. *The Development of Mineral Industry Education in the United States*. New York: AIMM, 1941.

Romer, Paul M. 1994. The origins of endogenous growth. *Journal of Economic Perspectives* 8: 3–22.

Rosenberg, Nathan. 1998. Technological change in chemicals: the role of university-industry relations. In Arora, Ashish, Landau, Ralph, and Rosenberg, Nathan (eds.). 1998. *Chemicals and Long-Term Economic Growth. Insights from the Chemical Industry*. New York: John Wiley & Co., pp. 193–230.

Rosenberg, Nathan. 2000. *America's University/Industry Interfaces 1945–2000*. Unpublished manuscript. Department of Economics, Stanford University, January.

Rosenberg, Nathan, and Birdzell, L. E. 1986. *How the West Grew Rich. The Economic Transformation of the Industrial World*. New York: Basic Books.

Sokoloff, Kenneth I. 1988. Inventive activity in early industrial America: evidence from patent records, 1790–1846. *Journal of Economic History* 48: 813–850.

Solow, Robert M. 1957. Technical change and the aggregate production function. *Review of Economics and Statistics* 39: 312–320.

Thwing, Charles F. 1928. *The American and the German University*. New York: Macmillan.

United States. Bureau of the Census. 1943. Sixteenth Census of the United States: 1940. Population. *Comparative Occupational Statistics of the United States, 1870–1940*. Washington, DC: G.P.O.

United States. Bureau of the Census. 1950a. 1950 Census of the Population. Vol. II. *Characteristics of the Population*. Part 1. *United States Summary*. Washington, DC: G.P.O.

United States. Bureau of the Census. 1950b. 1950 Census of the Population. Vol. II. *Characteristics of the Population*. Part 32. *New York*. Washington, DC: G.P.O.

United States. Bureau of the Census. 1975. *Historical Statistics of the United States: Bicentennial Edition*. Washington, DC: G.P.O.

U.S. Department of Interior. Office of Education. Walton C. John. 1931. *A Study of Engineering Enrollments*. Mimeo.

Usselman, Steven W. 1999. Patents, engineering professionals, and the pipelines of innovation: the internalization of technical discovery by nineteenth-century

American railroads. In Lamoreaux, Naomi R., Raff, Daniel M. G., and Temin, Peter (eds.). *Learning by Doing in Markets, Firms, and Countries*. Chicago: University of Chicago Press, pp. 61–91.

Weiss, John Hubbel. 1982. *The Making of Technological Man. The Social Origins of French Engineering Education*. Cambridge, MA: MIT Press.

Wellington, Arthur Mellen. 1892–1893. The Engineering Schools of the United States. *Engineering News* 27: 277–8, 294–6, 318–9, 342–5, 371–3, 412–4, 433–4, 459–61, 514–6, 541–3, 589–90, 660–1; 28: 6, 28–9, 65–6, 87–9, 111–4, 139–40, 161–2, 186–7, 210–1, 231–3, 256, 268–9, 327–8, 354–5, 375–6, 401–2 414–7, 437–8, 471–2, 488–9, 518–19, 546–7, 595; 29: 29, 32–3, 66–8, 90–2, 101–2, 138–40.

Wolfle, Dael. 1954. *America's Resources of Specialized Talent. A Current Appraisal and a Look Ahead*. The Report of the Commission on Human Resources and Advanced Training. New York: Harper.

Wright, Gavin. 1990. The origins of American industrial success, 1879–1940. *American Economic Review* 80: 651–68.

Wright, Gavin. 1999. Can a nation learn? American technology as a network phenomenon. In Lamoreaux, Naomi R., Raff, Daniel M. G., and Temin, Peter (eds.). *Learning by Doing in Markets, Firms, and Countries*. Chicago: University of Chicago Press, pp. 295–326.

PART III

HUMAN CAPITAL OUTLIERS

7

Young Geniuses and Old Masters: The Life Cycles of Great Artists from Masaccio to Jasper Johns

David W. Galenson and Robert Jensen

THE PRODUCTIVITY OF PAINTERS

Artists occupy a distinctive place in our economic life. As the art historian Meyer Schapiro (1979: 224) observed, the works they produce are "perhaps the most costly man-made objects in the world." Supporting evidence abounds. Thus in the twelve months ending in July 2000, worldwide auction sales of works by Pablo Picasso totaled $232 million; this raised total auction sales of Picasso's work since 1988 to $1.5 billion (Barker 2000). And impressive as these numbers are, they vastly understate the wealth created by Picasso, for his most important works have long since been captured by museums, where they attract millions of viewers annually. It is not possible to estimate with any precision the market value of such landmark works as *Les Demoiselles d'Avignon*, the single most famous work owned by New York's Museum of Modern Art, or Madrid's *Guernica*, or the Picasso Museum's *Still Life with Chair Caning*. And although Picasso stands at the head of the line of modern painters, even among moderns he is hardly alone in having created work of enormous value, and it is likely that the wealth embodied in his work is modest compared to that of a number of old masters.

Curiously, economists have shown little interest in the extraordinary productivity of these workers: economists have devoted little attention to the determination of the market value of works of art, and even less to the process by which artists produce this value. The idea of making inexpensive materials the source of great wealth has long been a focus of popular interest, from the failed attempts of medieval alchemists to the sometimes successful efforts of contemporary Internet entrepreneurs, but for whatever reason modern economists have displayed little curiosity about how artists have turned simple canvas and paint into objects of great worth.

Artists themselves have occasionally offered answers to this question. A notable instance occurred in 1878, when in the course of a libel suit he had brought against a critic, James McNeill Whistler (1922: 5) was asked to justify the price of his work. When questioned by opposing counsel as to whether he really charged the purchaser of a painting the considerable sum of 200 guineas for the labor of just two days, Whistler replied "No, I ask it for the knowledge of a lifetime." In 1884, Vincent van Gogh (1958, Vol. 3: 399–400) suggested a different explanation, when he wrote to a fellow painter of his belief that "art is something greater and higher than our own adroitness or accomplishments or knowledge;... art is something which, although produced by human hands, is not created by these hands alone, but something which wells up from a deeper source in our souls."

Whether the value of great art stems from the accumulation of human capital, from divine intervention, or from some other source remains to be seen. Our work is intended as a step toward a systematic understanding of how some artists have created work of enormous value. Ours will doubtless not be the last word, for scientific study of this problem remains at an early stage, and as many art scholars are quick to insist, art history is a vastly complicated subject, full of idiosyncrasies and dark corners. Yet we believe that systematic comparative study of artists' methods and careers, an approach rarely used by art historians, can yield simple but powerful generalizations that can in fact explain many of these apparent idiosyncrasies and illuminate many of the previously dark corners.

ARTISTS AND AGE

Scholars of art have long been aware that most artists' work changes considerably over the course of their careers, and the literature of art history is replete with judgments of how the quality of artists' work has varied with age. Unfortunately, however, attempts at generalization have been rare: nearly all these judgments have been made about individual artists, and few scholars have even raised the question of whether there are typical life cycles for painters.

The most significant exception to this is probably art historians' attempts to describe what they have called artists' "Altersstil," or old-age style. The invention of the retrospective exhibition in the late nineteenth century prompted some art scholars to conjecture about artists' life cycles, and the most lasting consequence of this has been the hypothesis that some artists have shared certain stylistic characteristics in old age (Jensen 1994: 112, 303). Over the course of the past century, however, research on the relationship between age and artistic style has been desultory, and the results unimpressive. So for example art historian David Rosand (1987: 91), the organizer of a 1985 symposium titled "Old-Age Style," could observe that "While apparently a commonplace in art-historical thought, old-age style is hardly a concept that has been subjected to sustained serious examination, nor is it a phenomenon that has been adequately defined."

Even the meager research efforts art historians have devoted to old-age style appear to have been misguided. In part this is because attempts to identify the concept have been restricted to a small number of arbitrarily chosen artists. And a basic problem has been the assumption that aging artists should share some specific stylistic characteristics. This extremely restrictive assumption has virtually guaranteed that any attempt at generalization across artists separated widely in time and space would make little progress.

We believe that age – or more precisely experience – has had powerful common effects on artists' work, but that these effects have not involved stylistic similarities. We furthermore believe that there have been two very different life cycles for artists. These patterns appear to be related systematically both to the processes artists use in making their work and to artists' conceptions of the goals of their work. In this paper we will present a general hypothesis of artists' life cycles, and illustrate its application to the careers of some of the most celebrated painters in western history.

Before we can do this, however, it is necessary to consider the source of importance in art. This is because importance is the central criterion both for selecting artists to study – who are the most important artists? – and for assessing the impact of age on their work – what is an artist's most important work? Yet although defining importance in art might seem a daunting task, with any definition subject to nearly endless debate, this is actually not the case. The definition can in fact be provided quite readily, because there is a very broad consensus on this issue that has long been implicit in the critical literature of art history.

IMPORTANCE IN ART

Many misunderstandings of the history of art, by art scholars as well as those outside the discipline, result from a failure to recognize some key parallels between art and other intellectual activities. One basic similarity concerns importance. The source of importance for artists is no more nebulous or complex than for scholars: as in academic disciplines, the principal source of genuine importance in art is innovation. Important artists are innovators whose work changes the practices of their successors; important works of art are those which embody these innovations. Although many art historians object to what they fear to be the demythicizing effect of this simple formulation, some scholars have been willing to express these ideas directly. So for example in discussing the parallel in this respect between art and science, Meyer Schapiro (1979: 152) observed that a great artist is "a revolutionary spirit who remakes his art, disclosing ever new forms." Art historian George Kubler (1962: 33) similarly compared art to science: "Every important work of art can be regarded both as a historical event and as a hard-won solution to some problem."

Some scholars would reject this characterization of artists as problem-solvers: in their view science progresses, with new solutions surpassing old ones, but art does not, since new art does not supersede old art. Yet as Arthur Koestler (1964: 393–94) explained, this involves a misunderstanding of the evolution of art. Artists do solve problems, and their successors can use their discoveries without having to make them again. A valid distinction lies in the fact that unlike scientists, artists are free to choose whether to accept or reject the discoveries of their predecessors. But this does not change the fact that the earlier discoveries are available to them and consequently that "the achievements of art are indeed cumulative and irreversible, as those of science are."

Histories of art, like intellectual histories of academic disciplines, are properly concerned with identifying the most important artistic discoveries and tracing their impact on other artists. The procession of great artists is not the artificial or arbitrary construct of scholars, but the product of artists, whose work reveals which artists of their own, or earlier, generations have been most influential. The most important element in any historian's account is therefore not the historian's judgment of the artist's work on aesthetic or other grounds, but rather the historian's ability to discern the artist's influence on other artists, and to explain the causes and consequences of that influence. Populist protests notwithstanding, art history must be first a history of a canon of central figures of great artists, for their discoveries are the prime subject of the narrative of art history, and the relationships among those discoveries are the source of the coherence of that narrative. Just as artists must study the history of art in order to make their predecessors' innovations available to them, we must study the great artists of the past to be able to understand the uses later artists make of their innovations. Great artists therefore dominate the scholarship of art history for the same reason they dominate the collections of great museums. So Sir Alan Bowness (1989: 9–11), former director of the Tate Gallery, defines the purpose of the museum through reference to these "artists of genius," declaring that "the museum collection aspires to show a chronological sequence of the work of such artists, carrying forward an argument which forms the material of any history of modern art."

Yet although great artists must be the central focus of art history, in understanding their achievements it is important not to ignore another parallel between art and science. For contrary to the popular – and sometimes scholarly – view of great artists as isolated geniuses, artistic progress has been overwhelmingly a product of collective research and collaboration. Like scholars, artists learn from teachers, and they develop their craft together with others of their own generation. Great artists have been disproportionately likely to have worked with teachers who were themselves important artists, and to have spent the formative stages of their careers in collaborative relationships with other important artists their own age. Some great artists, like Monet and Picasso, arrived at their greatest discoveries while working closely with peers, but even in cases in which great artists produced their major work in isolation, these were often, as for Cézanne and van Gogh, the consequences of working out the implications of trains of research that had originated in earlier apprenticeships and collaborations.

A TYPOLOGY OF ARTISTIC INNOVATORS

The recognition that innovation is the principal source of artistic importance allows us to approach the issue of artists' life cycles from a new point of view. Rather than searching for some common style among aging artists, we can ask instead whether there has been a systematic association between age and innovation. Study of this question has led us to believe that there have been two distinct life cycles among important artists, each of which has been associated with a different type of innovation. We can consequently begin by describing these types. What distinguishes the innovations is not their importance, for as will be seen below both types are represented among the major innovations in the history of art. What distinguishes them instead is the method by which they are produced. One of these methods is based on induction and can be called aesthetically motivated experimentation, whereas the other is deductive, and can be called conceptual execution.

One way to define the key difference between the two methods is by modifying an analysis of the philosopher Richard Wollheim (1995: 396), who proposed that

> the production of an art object consists, first of all, in a phase that might be called . . . "work" *tout court*: that is to say, the putting of paint on canvas, the hacking of stone, the welding of metal elements. . . . But the second phase in artistic productivity consists in decision . . . : namely, the decision that the work has gone far enough.

To Wollheim's two stages we add another, which occurs prior to his two. This consists of any preparations the artist makes before starting to put paint on canvas. Making a painting then has three stages – planning, working, and stopping.

For the experimental artist, the planning of a painting is of little or no importance. The motif is often selected for convenience, as in many cases the artist simply returns to a subject he or she has used in the past. The experimental painter rarely makes detailed plans or sketches before beginning a particular painting. Once a painting is begun, the working stage is open-ended. The artist makes a series of decisions during this stage based on visual inspection of the developing painting, changing things when he isn't satisfied with the appearance of the work. The decision to stop is also based on visual inspection: the painter stops when he is satisfied with the work's appearance, or abandons it as a failed effort. The decision to stop is typically a difficult one, for lacking a specific goal, the artist often has trouble deciding whether he has achieved enough in any individual work. And the decision is generally provisional, so experimental artists often return to work on a painting they had earlier considered finished, even after long intervals.

In contrast, for the conceptual artist the most important decisions are made in planning a work. Before beginning, the artist either envisions the completed work, or specifies a set of procedures that will be used to produce it. Conceptual artists often make detailed preparatory drawings or studies. The working stage involves executing the plan, either by producing the preconceived image, or carrying out the prescribed procedures. The artist stops when he has achieved the preconceived image, or has fully carried out the process he planned.

The experimental artist's approach is inductive: the artist proceeds by trial and error, judging trials as successes or failures based on their appearance. He considers progress to be achieved gradually as the cumulative effect of a series of incremental successes. The conceptual artist's approach is deductive, as working methods are designed to achieve a discrete goal that is specified precisely in advance. Progress is attained in discrete steps, and works are judged as successes when they communicate the artist's ideas or emotions.

AGE AND ARTISTIC INNOVATION

The long periods of trial and error often required for experimental innovations mean that they tend to occur late in an artist's career. This tendency is reinforced by the fact that experimental innovations often depend on skills that are acquired slowly, involving the artist's craftsmanship in using materials. In contrast, conceptual innovations are arrived at suddenly, as the product of new ideas, and can occur at any age. Radical conceptual innovations are in fact most often made by young artists, who have not yet become accustomed to existing conventions and traditional methods, and are more likely to be able to perceive and appreciate extreme departures from these accepted ways of working.

CASE STUDIES

The value of our typology in explaining artists' life cycles can potentially be demonstrated in two very different ways. One is to test its prediction concerning the relationship between age and artistic innovation for large numbers of artists, using systematic econometric analysis. This process has been started elsewhere. A second approach is to examine the careers of individual artists, to see whether the life cycle that our typology predicts fits with the actual development of their art, and the timing of their major contributions. This is the method that will be used here.

The selection of the artists considered is dictated by their importance in the history of western art. They cannot simply be taken from any existing list of the most important western painters, because no such list has been created through systematic quantitative analysis. Although defining the canon of western art lies beyond the scope of this study, still it is possible to select artists who are obviously central to that canon. The nine artists we have chosen to consider are among a small group whose contributions have been so influential that it would effectively be impossible to exclude them from any coherent narrative of the development of western art.

Examining the careers of artists who have lived during the past two centuries presents fewer difficulties than for artists working earlier, because we know so much more about the lives and working methods of modern artists. Comparable information is much scarcer for the pre-modern era. It is for this reason that our selection of artists begins in Florence during the Italian Renaissance. It is only then that artists began to emerge from the artisan traditions of the Middle Ages to become known as individuals, recognized for specific contributions to an evolving body of new art. We are also fortunate to have a remarkably detailed account of Italian artists working between the early fourteenth century and the middle of the sixteenth century, written by the artist Giorgio Vasari, who was a friend and disciple of Michelangelo. First published in 1550, Vasari's *Lives of the Artists* is the first modern history of art. In addition to providing biographical information about scores of artists, Vasari's deep understanding of the development of art from the thirteenth century to his own day allowed him to identify the central innovations of the time, and to trace their influence.

MASACCIO (1401–1429?)

Masaccio (Maso di Ser Giovanni di Mone Cassai) was perhaps the first of the young geniuses who shaped the history of modern painting. Even though he died around the age of 28, Masaccio's innovations were widely recognized by his contemporaries and for generations after as founding achievements of the Italian Renaissance.

Masaccio's accomplishment was to blend three major elements into a radically new art. Two were borrowed from earlier innovators. The older of these was based on the discoveries of his great Florentine predecessor, Giotto, a century earlier, as Masaccio adopted the techniques Giotto had used to break away from the flat, static images of medieval art. Following Giotto, Masaccio used shading of light and dark, foreshortening of forms, and overlapping of figures to create an illusion of three-dimensionality. Masaccio then achieved even more convincing representations of depth by using the linear perspective developed by his friend Brunelleschi. Finally, to these borrowed techniques Masaccio added his own great innovation, by using a single, consistent source of light in his paintings. Later named "chiaroscuro," Masaccio's spotlight effect produced greater drama and visual excitement than the less highly focused illumination of Giotto.

In combination, Masaccio's blending of these elements achieved an unprecedented representational illusionism. Instead of the ideal or schematic images of medieval art, paintings could now be perceived as visual extensions of the viewer's own world. Masaccio's technique quickly spread: Vasari (1971: 131) observed that his frescoes in the Brancacci Chapel in the church of Santa Maria del Carmine in Florence, painted circa 1427, became a mecca for "all those who have endeavored to learn the art of painting... to grasp the precepts and rules demonstrated by Masaccio for the correct representation of figures."

Little is known about Masaccio's training, but his early artistic maturity is no doubt a consequence of the intensive apprenticeship system that Italian artists followed, from the medieval workshop tradition. Yet workshop practices also tended to discourage innovation. That Masaccio could contribute so much to the history of Renaissance art despite his very early death is a result of the conceptual nature of his contribution. His accomplishment was an extraordinary intellectual feat that gave painters a new vantage point that would dominate western art for five centuries, until another young genius would overthrow it with a new conceptual system.

MICHELANGELO (1475–1564)

Michelangelo Buonarroti might be assumed to have been a conceptual artist in view of the fact that he made his greatest contributions in media – sculpture, fresco painting, and architecture – not ordinarily conducive to experimentalism. All three generally involve careful planning, including preparatory drawings, and extensive teamwork, and all are inherently resistant to changes in program during the process of creation. Yet it is a measure of Michelangelo's artistry that he managed to impose on each of these media the sensibility of an experimental artist.

One of the distinctive features of Michelangelo's career was his consistent difficulty in bringing works to completion. Even the projects he did complete were often realized only under extreme pressure from his clients, as in his famous conflicts with Pope Julius II over the completion of the Sistine Chapel ceiling frescoes. Many other projects were either left unfinished or delivered in severely truncated form, such as the project to create a tomb for Julius, which exists only as a small fragment of Michelangelo's intended product. Among the parts of that project that have been preserved are the famous "bound slaves," which have long fascinated art lovers for the way in which their bodies appear to emerge out of the unfinished block of stone.

Art historians have often attributed Michelangelo's problems of concluding to his habit of taking on expensive, labor-intensive, and massively scaled projects. Instead, however, they appear to have stemmed primarily from the fact that in the process of executing commissioned works Michelangelo consistently extended their scope far beyond his patrons' expectations, or desires. In the case of the Sistine Chapel, for example, the Pope simply wanted Michelangelo to paint the forms of the twelve Apostles between the clerestory windows, and expected the ceiling to be finished quickly in a decorative pattern. What Julius got was instead an entire painted ceiling, such as had never been seen before, which illustrated key scenes from Genesis, and which was not completed until long after Julius had run out of patience.

Michelangelo's habit of revising his projects in the course of their execution was a consequence of his experimental approach. For the Sistine Chapel he radically changed the scale and style of the imagery as he worked on the ceiling. When he began, fearing that he lacked the requisite skill as a painter, Michelangelo enlisted numerous assistants to help him. But after having seen their preliminary drawings for the ceiling Michelangelo dismissed them all. Vasari tells us that Michelangelo even did without the usual apprentices who ground the paint pigments, preferring to perform every aspect of the project himself. When the ceiling was finally opened to public inspection it caused a sensation, but Michelangelo was still not satisfied. Vasari (1971: 252–53) reports that he wished to retouch the painting "in order to enrich and to heighten the visual impact," and that he was deterred only by the prospect of having to rebuild the elaborate scaffolding.

Michelangelo's old-age style has long been celebrated by art historians. Yet it was not the product of a radical break from his earlier art, but rather of steadily evolving techniques and ambitions. Michelangelo's early work shows that he shared in the High Renaissance love of classical art, joining such artists as Raphael and Leonardo in the search for a harmonious ideal in the perfection of form, gesture, and composition. Yet from the beginning Michelangelo was willing to subordinate physical verisimilitude, as evidenced in such things as correct bodily proportion, to the larger visual effect of his work, often achieved by the use of oversized, muscular figures, contorted in space. As he aged his dramatic distortions grew more extreme. Late in life, in his fresco of the Last Judgment in the Sistine Chapel, finished in 1541 at the age of 66, and the even more radical murals completed nine years later for the Vatican's Pauline Chapel, Michelangelo created extraordinarily complex compositions of interwoven figures, whose physical forms obeyed no laws other than Michelangelo's pictorial conception. By the end of his life Michelangelo's manner had become so idiosyncratic, and so far from the tastes of his own time, that despite his unmatched reputation as an artist his last paintings were virtually ignored until the twentieth century. Only modern tastes formed by the rise of expressionist painting have made these works more acceptable to audiences. Yet like his inability to consider his works finished, and the persistent need to revise his projects in progress, the continual, restless evolution of Michelangelo's art throughout his life are the hallmarks of an experimental artist.

RAPHAEL (1483–1520)

Raphael (Raffaello Santi) is paradigmatic of the young genius. Although his life was cut short at the age of just 37, he had completed his most famous painting, *The School of Athens*, in the Vatican, almost a decade earlier, at 28. Raphael's rich, harmonious colors, his idealized faces, and the essential clarity of form and composition of his pictures led many to consider Raphael the paragon of artistic perfection for more than four centuries. The newly founded art academies in the eighteenth century held Raphael's art to embody a set of clearly definable rules that could be taught to any student desiring good technique and beautiful painting. Through these art academies Raphael's art continued to exert influence on painting into the early twentieth century.

Raphael was admired by his contemporaries for the apparent ease with which he produced his paintings. He was credited with producing his paintings in a timely fashion, and with always satisfying his clients. Vasari implies that it was his efficiency as well as his art that made Raphael so popular with patrons.

Throughout his biography, Vasari depicts Raphael as an artist who easily and perfectly absorbed the styles of other artists. And indeed his earliest work so closely resembles in style that of his first teacher, Pietro Perugino, that Raphael's early paintings can barely be distinguished from his master's. Later Raphael was successively inspired by the work of Leonardo and Michelangelo. From Leonardo, Raphael learned the older artist's extraordinarily subtle chiaroscuro, his paintings' almost imperceptible gradations of form from dark to light. He also acquired from Leonardo the device of ordering his figure groups in a pyramidal structure, which gave their compositions an underlying stability and symmetry. Raphael, however, surpassed Leonardo in the compositional complexity of works like *The School of Athens*. This painting contains no less than fifty-two ancient Greek thinkers and scientists. Despite the large number of figures, and their wide variety in size, posture, and gesture, Raphael wove them into a visually interlocking group, so that the viewer perceives these philosophers as both individually attractive to the eye and intelligible and unified as a group (Janis Bell 1997: 85–113).

Raphael achieved these results through careful planning. His drawings were highly prized by collectors in his lifetime, and many have survived, providing a clear view of his working methods (Ames-Lewis 1986). Unlike earlier artists working in fresco, Raphael planned the placement of the figures in his compositions in advance. For *The School of Athens*, Raphael drew a full-scale preparatory cartoon that depicts the entire lower half of the painted composition (Oberhuber and Vitali 1972). The only significant difference between the cartoon for *The School of Athens* and the painting as it was executed was the addition of the architecture surrounding the figures, which Raphael built around them.

Whereas Vasari praised his friend Michelangelo as a solitary genius, he chose to denigrate Michelangelo's rival by portraying Raphael as the director of a large group of artists. There is an internal consistency to Vasari's account, however, that reveals Raphael's organizational genius and business acumen. For example, Vasari speaks of Raphael's enormous team of draftsmen, which he employed throughout Italy, and who, Vasari asserts (1971: 310), provided Raphael with "good designs which he could use in his work." Vasari notes that these artists often partially executed Raphael's paintings based on his initial designs. Vasari (1971: 306–07) even credits Raphael with inventing a new product line, of engraved reproductions of his own paintings. Engraving had been uncommon in Italy prior to Raphael; his initiative made the medium commonplace. Such engravings became an enormously important medium through which Italian Renaissance art spread its influence across Europe.

Raphael was a paragon of the conceptual artist. He achieved his greatest art work at an early age. His working methods were ruled by careful planning through the use of preparatory drawings and cartoons. His designs and instructions were so clear that Vasari suggests that even important parts of a painting could be left to assistants. He had the ability to change his style significantly in response to the work of other artists, conceptually reorganizing their influence into a distinctively new art whose influence would prove to be one of the greatest in the history of western painting.

TITIAN (C. 1485–1576)

During his unusually long life, Titian (Tiziano Vecellio) was one of the most sought-after artists in Europe. Courted by emperors, kings, princes, and popes, Titian reached a social prominence that no artist had achieved before. Titian's career anticipates the great court artists of the seventeenth century – painters such as Diego Velazquez, Peter Paul Rubens, Gianlorenzo Bernini, or Rubens' pupil Anthony van Dyck. Titian's example as a princely artist paralleled the influence his art exerted over painting for centuries after his death (Rosand 1982: 1–39).

Titian was an experimental artist. Although he was one of the most prolific painters of the sixteenth century, few of his drawings are known. Since the drawings of many contemporaries have survived in considerable numbers, this indicates that Titian rarely considered it necessary to plan his paintings in advance, which had been the norm of Italian workshop practice. A witness described Titian's manner of painting: "He used to sketch in his pictures with a great mass of colors, which served, as one might say, as a bed or a base for the compositions.... Having constructed these precious foundations he used to turn his pictures to the wall and leave them there without looking at them, sometimes for several months. When he wanted to apply his brush again he would examine them with the utmost rigor, as if they were his mortal enemies, to see if he could find any faults; and if he discovered anything that did not fully conform to his intentions he would treat his picture like a good surgeon would his patient. . . . [T]he final stage of his last retouching involved his moderating here and there the brightest highlights by rubbing them with his fingers, reducing the contrast . . . and harmonizing one tone with another" (Biadene 1990: 23–24).

Titian succeeded in combining what had previously been the two great independent stylistic tendencies of Renaissance painting, as his art joined the color and luminous surfaces of such Flemish artists as Jan van Eyck with Raphael's complex and harmonious compositions. As he matured, Titian went beyond High Renaissance conventions by creating new, dynamic spatial relationships, in which the figures in his paintings would not uniformly face a single position in front of the canvas, but would be arranged in groups to imply several distinct viewing positions. This produced the effect of giving spectators differing perceptions of a single work as they walked toward it, and pointed toward later developments in western painting in which artists increasingly aimed to make viewers active participants in the experience of seeing their work. Interestingly, X-ray analysis has revealed that Titian arrived at this innovation experimentally, reorienting the figures within a composition by a process of trial and error during the execution of individual works (Biadene 1990: 98).

Titian's manner changed greatly as he aged. Late in his life his paintings became more roughly worked and the surfaces of the canvases more thickly built up with paint. The visual clarity and precision of his early work gave way to a more atmospheric presentation, with features art historians have since categorized as "painterly," a style that emphasizes the worked surface of the painting, displaying rather than disguising the artist's touch. Vasari (1971: 458) described Titian's evolution, and suggested its source in the development of his experimental method: whereas "the early works are executed with incredible delicacy and diligence, and they may be viewed either at a distance or close at hand; . . . these last works are executed with bold, sweeping strokes, and in patches of color, with the result that they cannot be viewed from near by, but appear perfect at a distance. . . . [I]t is clear that Titian has retouched his pictures, going over them with his colors several times." In his late work Titian was considered to have pioneered a new approach to art, in which painting was no longer merely an imitation of the world, but an autonomous equivalent.

For three centuries Titian's name was identified with the art of color and the painterly performance. In contrast to the European academies, which came to espouse rigid absolute standards of aesthetic perfection enforced through a strict regimen for both artistic education and production, Titian's work presented an alternative model, of the individualistic artist who discovers his own method through the act of painting itself. This model of heightened autonomy became an inspiration to many later painters, just as Titian's glorious development in old age became a spur to art historians to ponder the sources of the old-age style. We can now recognize that both Titian's individualism and his brilliant late works are direct consequences of the experimental method by which he developed his signature style.

REMBRANDT (1606–1669)

Rembrandt van Rijn is one of the few artists whose name is nearly synonymous with art for those unfamiliar with the subject. His popular reputation may be traced to the fact that Rembrandt's art is fused with the popular perception of Rembrandt the artist. In the Rembrandt myth, the artist's genius compelled the painter to go against the tastes of his own time. As he aged, he fell into tragic isolation. We now know that Rembrandt was not isolated, that he had a school of imitators and admirers, and that for much of his life he was praised by his contemporaries as Holland's greatest painter. His famous loss of fortune during the second half of his life is now known to derive from his spending habits rather than from public neglect.

The artist's myth has its foundation in the way in which Rembrandt, especially through his self-portraits, seemed to place himself at the center of his art. Throughout all his work Rembrandt created the illusion of subjectivity for the people he painted, the sense that they possessed not merely an external appearance, but an interior self. His capacity to hint at the inner life of his subjects was unrivaled by any artist before him, and approached by few after. Complementing this psychological dimension of Rembrandt's art was his unprecedented realism, conveyed as much by his love of the quotidian as by his style of painting. He inspired many later generations of artists who followed the dictum that truth to nature is superior to imitating the traditions and conventions of past art.

Recent research has demonstrated convincingly that Rembrandt was an experimental painter. His draftsmanship is justifiably famed, but although hundreds of his drawings are known today, it is now recognized that few if any of these served as plans for later paintings (Alpers 1988: 15–16, 70–71). Like Titian, whom he admired and imitated, Rembrandt blocked out the schemes for his pictures directly onto the primed canvas, and X-rays of his paintings confirm that he made frequent and significant changes in his compositions as he worked on them. Some of his best known paintings appear to have remained undetermined even thematically until late in their production. His 1654 *Bathsheba*, for example, now in the Louvre, appears to have been initially simply a study of a female nude. The painting acquired its final designation only when, in what scholars generally agree to be the last element added to the picture, Rembrandt placed a letter in the woman's hand (van de Wetering 1998: 27–47).

Rembrandt's choice of subjects also reflects his experimental nature, as he frequently returned to familiar themes to create new variations. The most remarkable instance of this practice was one of his most striking innovations. He was the first western artist to paint himself more than a few times: his self-portraits, which number at least 40 paintings and more than 30 etchings produced over a period of forty years, constitute one of the earliest extended series of studies of a single subject in the history of art, and even today remain one of the most celebrated.

Rembrandt worked slowly and painstakingly, and had trouble parting with his works. As is often the case with experimental artists, he was notorious for his difficulties in completing commissions. In a famous incident, a commissioned work of his that was already hanging in the Amsterdam Town Hall was returned to Rembrandt's studio, where he resumed work on it. Substantially changed, the revised painting was never returned to its public position.

Rembrandt's contemporaries did favor his early work over that of his later years. But for subsequent generations Rembrandt's most significant work begins in the 1640s, when the artist was in his thirties, and gains in importance from then on. Both critical assessments are a consequence of Rembrandt's progressive departure from the dominant contemporary model of what constituted good craft in the art of painting. The most popular Dutch painters of the time produced works in what was known as a "smooth" style, marked by little or no surface texture and no visible evidence of the application of paint. As Rembrandt aged, the surfaces of his works became rougher and more uneven, departing more and more radically from the mirror-like surfaces of the smooth style. Yet is was precisely in this evolution that Rembrandt made one of his greatest innovations, for his construction of a surface marked by variation in both the roughness and the thickness of the paint, now believed to have been produced by the use of paints mixed to different viscosities, complemented his famous chiaroscuro in heightening the visual emphasis on the focal points of his works (van de Wetering 1997: 155–90). The gradual development of this innovation, which contemporaries called Rembrandt's "rough" style, reveals the experimental process of trial and error that lay behind its creation, and explains why it is Rembrandt's later works, which embody this innovation in its most extreme form, that are most celebrated today.

PAUL CÉZANNE (1839–1906)

When this investigation reaches the nineteenth century, important new sources of evidence often become available. One of these is artists' own descriptions of their methods and goals. Paul Cézanne's letters provide an eloquent account of his progress as an experimental innovator. So for example in September, 1906, just six weeks before his death, he wrote to his son:

I must tell you that as a painter I am becoming more clear-sighted before nature, but that with me the realization of my sensations is always painful. I cannot attain the intensity that is unfolded before my senses. I have not the magnificent richness of coloring that animates nature. Here on the bank of the river the motifs multiply, the same subject seen from a different angle offers subject for study of the most powerful interest and so varied that I think I could occupy myself for months without changing place, by turning now more to the right, now more to the left (Rewald 1995: 327).

In this short passage Cézanne describes nearly all of the basic characteristics of the experimental innovator, including his visual motivation, the elusiveness of his vague but ambitious goal, the slowness of his progress toward it, the incremental and serial nature of his enterprise, his view of his work as research, and his frustration.

The irony of Cézanne's frustration at this late date stems from the fact that in time not only would he come to be recognized as the most important painter of his era, but that it would be his latest works that would be judged his greatest contribution. This is witnessed by the market value of that work. For many modern painters, including Cézanne, enough of their paintings have been auctioned in recent decades to allow econometric estimation of age–price profiles, which express the value of their paintings as a function of the artist's age at the time of their execution (Galenson 2001: Chap. 2). Recent research has furthermore shown that the peaks of these age–price profiles generally correspond closely to the judgments of art experts as to when the artists produced their most important work (Galenson 2001: Appendixes 1–2). For Cézanne, Figure 7.1 shows a steep rise in value during the early decades, with a plateau in mid-career, followed by a final increase in the last decade of his life. With a painting from age 25 worth only one-seventh as much as one from 65, Figure 7.1 shows the relative unimportance of Cézanne's early, romantic works. The profile's first inflection point marks the beginning of Cézanne's artistic maturity. At 33, Cézanne moved to Pontoise, near Paris, where he spent the next few years learning the discoveries of Impressionism from Camille Pissarro, one of the movement's founders. Cézanne soon adopted several of the key innovations of the Impressionists, including the small brushstrokes, the bright palette, and the use of color instead of shading to achieve the illusion of depth.

Yet although he would ever thereafter share the Impressionists' devotion to painting nature, Cézanne rejected their goal of portraying the momentary effects of light and atmosphere. His apprenticeship to Pissarro allowed him to formulate his own goal, which would occupy the rest of his career, of making Impressionism more solid and timeless. His most radical achievements in this quest, which included his use of multiple viewpoints within a single picture and his trademark constructive brushstroke that simultaneously creates a two-dimensional surface pattern and tilts back into three-dimensional space, became seminal discoveries. These innovations appeared most clearly in his latest works, which influenced almost every significant artistic development of the next generation, including movements as diverse as the Cubists, who saw in Cézanne's brushstrokes a series of planes that

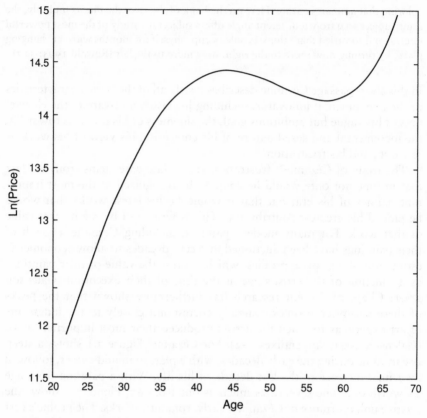

FIGURE 7.1. Age–Price Profile for Paul Cézanne.

could define three-dimensional space, and the Fauves, who seized instead on the surface pattern created by the colors of those brushstrokes.

Cézanne worked by trial and error. As a result, as critic Clive Bell (1982: 77) observed, for Cézanne "every picture was a means . . . something he was ready to discard as soon as it had served his purpose. He had no use for his own pictures. To him they were experiments. He tossed them into bushes, or left them in the open fields." His primary goal was not to create images, but to learn. A fellow painter who once worked with him reported that Cézanne "never ceased declaring that he was not making pictures, but that he was searching for a technique" (Rubin 1977: 37). As an experimental painter, Cézanne was acutely aware of the difficulty of reaching a definitive conclusion: near the end of his life he wrote to a younger painter that "I progress very slowly . . . and the progress needed is endless" (Rewald 1995: 302). But that he was in fact making progress is witnessed by the vast influence of his last works.

PABLO PICASSO (1881–1973)

In contrast to Cézanne, who told Maurice Denis "I seek in painting," the dominant artist of the next generation, Pablo Picasso, declared "I don't seek, I find" (Shiff 1984: 222). If there is little question that Cézanne was the most important experimental innovator in French modern painting, there is even less that Picasso was the most important conceptual innovator, and the greatest young genius in the history of modern art.

The ambitious young Spaniard arrived in Paris to settle in 1904. Recognizing that he would have to produce a major work to challenge Henri Matisse for the leadership of the city's advanced art world, late in 1906 Picasso began planning the largest painting he had ever attempted. For months he filled sketchbooks with preparatory drawings. Historian William Rubin (Rubin, Seckel, and Cousins 1994: 14, 119) has estimated that in all Picasso made between four and five hundred studies for the painting, "a quantity of preparatory work unique not only in Picasso's career, but without parallel, for a single picture, in the entire history of art." At the age of 25, Picasso thus deliberately set out to produce a masterpiece. Remarkably, he succeeded, as that work became the single most celebrated painting in the history of modern art.

Completed in 1907, *Les Demoiselles d'Avignon* combined influences as diverse as pre-Roman Iberian sculpture, African carvings, and the late style of Cézanne to announce the origins of Cubism, "perhaps the most important and certainly the most complete and radical artistic revolution since the Renaissance"(Golding 1988: xiii). From that point of departure, Picasso collaborated closely with Georges Braque to produce a series of innovations. Their goal was to represent the tangible nature of objects without the use of linear perspective, which they considered a mistaken convention, and without the Impressionists' use of color, which they believed revealed only a momentary reflection of light rather than a durable underlying reality. They based one of their most striking early developments on the late Cézanne's use of several vantage points in a single composition. Picasso and Braque extended this approach, as the faceting that gave rise to the (initially pejorative) name of Cubism allowed them to portray objects simultaneously from many viewpoints, showing features of the objects that an observer knows are present even when they are temporarily hidden from view. Another in the series of new developments occurred in 1912, when Picasso made the first collage, *Still Life with Chair Caning*. In this he broke with a basic tradition of western painting by attaching a material object to the surface of the work. In violating the two-dimensionality of the picture surface plane, and doing this with a discarded scrap of cloth, Picasso challenged the traditional aesthetic purity of painting as a fine art, and initiated a process in which the boundary between painting and other artistic media would increasingly be broken down.

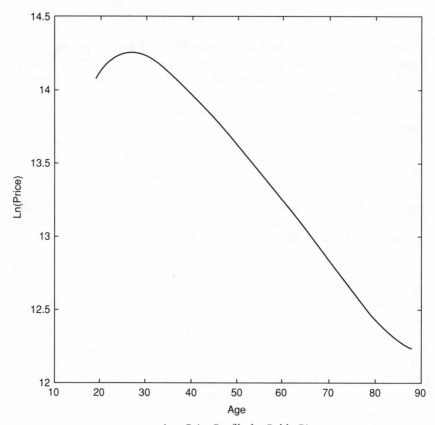

FIGURE 7.2. Age–Price Profile for Pablo Picasso.

Picasso would go on to paint for more than six decades after producing the *Demoiselles*. During his long and enormously productive career, he would become by far the most celebrated artist of the twentieth century. Yet he would never produce another painting as important as the *Demoiselles*, or create another body of work as significant as that he executed between 1907 and the outbreak of World War I, when Braque's service in the French army effectively ended the two artists' joint research in Cubism. Figure 7.2 shows that the value of Picasso's work peaked at age 26, the year he painted the *Demoiselles*, and declined steadily thereafter. That the greatest work of the greatest artist of the twentieth century was done at such an early age is a consequence of the conceptual nature of Picasso's approach. Thus as historian John Golding (1988:51) recognized,

the Cubism of Picasso and Braque was to be essentially conceptual. Even in the initial stages of the movement, when the painters still relied to a large extent on visual models, their paintings are not so much records of the sensory appearance of their subjects, as expressions in pictorial terms of their idea or knowledge of them. "I paint objects as I think them, not as I see them," Picasso said.

JACKSON POLLOCK (1912–1956)

Jackson Pollock was recognized as the leading member of the Abstract Expressionist movement even during his lifetime, and this perception has become stronger since his death in an automobile accident in 1956. Although the Abstract Expressionists were generally considered to be a group, by themselves as well as others, they did not share a common style. They were unified chiefly by their dissatisfaction with existing methods of painting, and by their desire to draw on the subconscious to create new forms of art. Many in the group also consciously wanted to depart from European art. Thus when an interviewer asked Pollock in 1943 whether he wanted to go abroad, he replied bluntly, "No. I don't see why the problems of modern painting can't be solved here as well as elsewhere" (Karmel 1999: 15).

The Abstract Expressionists shifted the center of the art world from Paris to New York. They attracted attention for their revolutionary working methods as well as for their dramatic new images. And it was Pollock who developed both the most celebrated technique and the most startling results. His signature drip method of applying paint, with the inevitable puddling and spattering that could not be completely controlled by the artist, was developed specifically in order to avoid preconception. In a frequently quoted statement, Pollock declared that

When I am *in* my painting, I'm not aware of what I'm doing. It is only after a sort of "get acquainted" period that I see what I have been about. I have no fears about making changes, destroying the image, etc., because the painting has a life of its own. I try to let it come through (Friedman 1995: 100).

For Pollock, producing a painting was a visual process. After a period of applying paint, he would study the work to see how he should continue. This required a considerable effort, because he worked on large canvases laid flat on the floor. His widow, Lee Krasner, recalled their procedure:

How well I remember when Pollock would want to study one of those big canvases up on the wall. He'd attach the top edge to a long piece of 2 × 4, and together we'd lift it up – do you know how much one of those big pictures with all that paint weighed? We'd take it to the wall, and lift it up ladders, and just nail the ends of the 2 × 4 – which stuck out – into the studio wall.

This process would be repeated a number of times, over a period of days or weeks, until Pollock felt the work was finished. Even then he often remained unsure, as Krasner recalled that "he'd have last-minute thoughts and doubts. He hated signing. There's something so final about a signature." And Krasner remembered that the extremity of the departure of Abstract

Expressionism often produced even deeper doubts: "in front of a very good painting... he asked me, 'Is this a painting?' Not is this a good painting, or a bad one, but a *painting*!" (Carmean and Rathbone 1978: 133–35, 37–38).

Abstract Expressionism departed from the goal of representing objects external to the artist, and made the work of art not only a representation of the artist's emotions, but a visible record of the process of its own creation. For centuries, a central objective of much of western art had been to make works that hid the evidence of the process by which the work was made. Since the mid-nineteenth century, one tendency of modern art had been to leave traces of the creative process in the finished work, in the form of visible brushstrokes, bare patches of canvases, and other devices. Abstract Expressionism carried this tendency further, by effectively making the process of creation the subject of the work, with the artist's gestures featured in the final product. And the Abstract Expressionists arrived at this result experimentally, with the work of each artist developing gradually over long periods.

Pollock made a number of specific innovations that proved influential. His technique of dripping paint on canvases laid on the floor offered a clear alternative to the traditional use of brushes and easels. His use of wall-sized canvases offered a new scale for paintings, and his all-over compositions, which had no central focal point of interest, offered new visual effects. Beyond these technical contributions, however, lay Pollock's conviction that "I paint it, I don't illustrate it," as his work inspired many artists to use paint and other materials not to create representations of objects or ideas, but instead as the record of gestures and motions.

Figure 7.3 shows that Pollock's work rose in value with age throughout most of the two decades of his career. During this time his work evolved by trial and error through a series of stages, from clumsy landscapes heavily influenced by Albert Pinkham Ryder and Pollock's teacher, Thomas Hart Benton, to Surrealist-inspired works derived from Joan Miró and Picasso, and then to the mature works in his signature style. There is a strong critical consensus that his greatest work was done during 1947–50, which is consistent with the peak his age–price profile reaches for paintings from 1950.

JASPER JOHNS (1930–)

Jasper Johns was a young genius in a generation of modern art dominated by them. During the late 1950s and '60s, Johns, Roy Lichtenstein (1923–97), Robert Rauschenberg (1925–), Andy Warhol (1928–87), Sol LeWitt (1928–), Frank Stella (1936–), and others created a series of new movements. In spite of their diversity, these movements shared a common basis in rejecting the methods of Abstract Expressionism and replacing them with conceptual approaches. Among the artists of that cohort, Johns is often

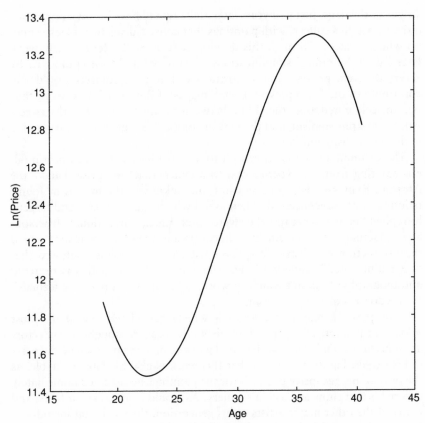

FIGURE 7.3. Age–Price Profile for Jackson Pollock.

considered to have been the key transitional figure in the shift from gesture painting to more mechanistic forms of art.

Johns entered the consciousness of the New York art world in dramatic fashion in January, 1958, when he had his first one-man show at the gallery of Leo Castelli. The show attracted great publicity; even before it opened. Thomas Hess, the editor of *Artnews*, had borrowed one of the paintings and placed it on the front of his January issue, putting Johns in the unique position of having his debut announced on the cover of a leading art magazine. The impact of the show stemmed from Johns' radical departure from gestural abstraction: although they used a painterly surface taken from Abstract Expressionism, the paintings in his show presented flat depictions of two-dimensional objects – targets, numerals, and flags. The influence of these images on young artists who were looking for alternatives to Abstract Expressionism was almost immediate. So for example Frank Stella, then a college senior, saw the show and was struck by Johns' repetitive use of the stripes of the flags. Just two years later Stella would have his own first show, also at Castelli's gallery, with paintings that consisted solely of black stripes on white surfaces. Through this development by Stella, Johns' early work later led to the radical simplifications of Minimal and Conceptual art. By a very different process, Johns' portrayals of everyday objects would also contribute to the flat representational images of Pop Art. Johns' work thus became celebrated as a crucial link between the dominant art of the 1950s, Abstract Expressionism, and the new art of the '60s and beyond, beginning with Minimalism and Pop.

The example of Johns' approach to art also helped to transform modern painting from an experimental to a conceptual enterprise. Unlike the Abstract Expressionists' journeys into the unknown, the images in Johns' paintings were preconceived: when asked why he painted flags and targets, he replied that it was because they were "preformed, conventional, depersonalized, factual, exterior elements." In contrast to the drama that surrounded the production of Abstract Expressionist paintings, Johns confessed that "often I'm bored" while working. And Johns' avowed goal was to avoid autobiography: "I didn't want my work to be an exposure of my feelings" (Varnedoe 1996: 112, 145, 199).

Now past the age of 70, Johns is widely considered one of the most important painters alive, and all of his work is eagerly sought by collectors and museums. But his most celebrated work remains that which he did early in his career. Figure 7.4 shows that this work is also his most valuable, as the peak of his age–price profile is for the paintings he executed immediately before his first show at Castelli's gallery. As would be the case for Stella and many of the other major artists of his generation, the work that introduced Johns to the art world was thus that which would remain his most significant. This is an obvious consequence of the conceptual nature of these artists' contributions, as the radical new ideas of the young geniuses of the late '50s and '60s replaced the expressive gestures of the Abstract Expressionists as the driving force of the modern art world.

QUANTIFYING ARTISTIC SUCCESS

Systematic evidence on the differing careers of the artists considered here can be drawn from textbooks of art history. Authors choose the illustrations in these books in order to show readers what they consider each artist's most important contribution, or contributions. Analyzing the illustrations in a number of textbooks can consequently offer a survey of art historians' opinions on when an artist produced his best work.

Table 7.1 clearly demonstrates the difference in the timing of the careers of the two types of innovators. Whereas the four conceptual innovators were all in their 20s in the single year of their careers that the 15 textbooks surveyed here deemed their most important, the five experimental innovators were

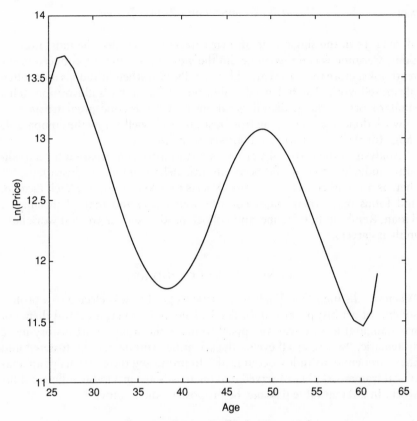

FIGURE 7.4. Age–Price Profile for Jasper Johns.

TABLE 7.1. *Survey of Illustrations in 15 Textbooks*

Artist	n	Artist's Age in Year of Median Illustration	Age in Single Year with Most Illustrations
Masaccio	35	26	24
Raphael	52	28	28
Picasso	88	31	26
Johns	13	26	25
Michelangelo	123	40	37
Titian	52	53	41, 53
Rembrandt	69	46	36
Cézanne	36	56	67
Pollock	17	38	38

Note: n is the total number of illustrations of each artist's work in the books surveyed.

Sources: Adams (1991); Britsch and Britsch (1984); Cleaver (1972); Cornell (1983); de la Croix and Richard G. Tansey (1975); Freeman (1998); Gebhardt (1998); Hartt (1989); Honour and Fleming (1999); Kemp (2000); Ruskin (1974); Spencer (1975); Stokstad (1995); Wilkins et al. (1997); Wood et al. (1989).

all over 35 in the single year of their careers that yielded the most illustrations. Cézanne was 67 when he did the work most often reproduced in the textbooks, more than 40 years older than Picasso when he did his most often illustrated work. The full age distributions of each artist's illustrations tell a similar story, as the median illustrations of the four conceptual artists were of work done at ages ranging from just 26 to 31, well below the comparable range for the five experimental artists, from 38 to 56.

Analysis of the textbooks provides quantitative confirmation for a qualitative judgment that would occasion little debate among art historians, for there is a broad consensus among experts that Masaccio, Raphael, Picasso, and Johns made their major contributions early, and that Michelangelo, Titian, Rembrandt, Cézanne, and Pollock produced their greatest work later in their careers.

CONCLUSION: BEYOND ART

When the distinguished English art critic Roger Fry was elected to a professorship of art history at Cambridge University in 1933, a central theme of his inaugural lecture was an appeal to make the study of art history more systematic, "where at all events the scientific attitude may be fostered and the sentimental attitude discouraged." In proposing the elements of an analytical framework, Fry observed that an artist's age inevitably influenced his work. In a remarkable passage, he proposed a dichotomy:

When we look at the late works of Titian or Rembrandt we cannot help feeling the pressure of a massive and rich experience which leaks out, as it were, through the ostensible image presented to us, whatever it may be. There are artists, and perhaps Titian and Rembrandt are good examples, who seem to require a very long period of activity before this unconscious element finds its way completely through into the work of art. In other cases, particularly in artists whose gift lies in a lyrical direction, the exaltation and passion of youth transmits itself directly into everything they touch, and then sometimes, when this flame dies down, their work becomes relatively cold and uninspired.

Fry (1962: 3, 14–15) acknowledged that these comments must appear "rather wildly speculative and hazardous" to his audience. Yet we believe that we have now devised a systematic approach that has led us to a typology much like the one Fry proposed. For in our view Titian and Rembrandt are prototypical examples of artists whose experimental approach to their work did result in an art that matured slowly, in contrast to such artists as Raphael and Picasso, whose conceptual approach led them to make their greatest contributions quickly and very early in life.

It is perhaps unsurprising that art historians have not responded more successfully to Fry's challenge to understand artists' life cycles, because in general art historians have largely ignored Fry's appeal for more systematic approaches to their subject. In view of the extraordinary productivity of artists, it is perhaps more remarkable that economists have not taken more interest in their careers. Yet economists' failure to consider the implications of this research has implications far greater than simply their inability to understand how and why some artists have made such large contributions to our society's wealth. For extensions of the research reported in the present study has demonstrated that the dichotomy presented here extends far beyond painters: thus it has been shown that poets, novelists, movie directors, sculptors, architects and song writers can also be divided into precocious conceptual innovators and mature experimental innovators (e.g. see Galenson 2006). Nor is this analysis relevant exclusively to the arts, for the same patterns can be found among academic economists and among entrepreneurs.

This research has demonstrated that human capital is not homogeneous. Experimental innovators improve their work over time, as they accumulate knowledge and experience, and their creative life cycles consequently correspond to conventional human capital analysis. Yet conceptual innovators make their most important contributions early, and for them the accumulation of experience seems to be the cause of the deterioration of their work, so their life cycles of creativity are very different from the normal human capital analysis. The quantitative dimensions of this phenomenon remain to be determined: perhaps there are not vast numbers of conceptual innovators in our world. Yet their impact may nonetheless be enormous, for their ranks include not only Pablo Picasso, James Joyce, and T. S. Eliot, but also Bill Gates, Sergey Brin, and Larry Page. Understanding the creativity of these innovators may help us not only to explain the source of their discoveries, but perhaps also to increase the productivity of some of the most important contributors to our economic life.

References

Adams, Laurie Schneider. 1991. *A History of Western Art*. New York: Harry N. Abrams.

Alpers, Svetlana. 1988. *Rembrandt's Enterprise*. Chicago: University of Chicago Press.

Ames-Lewis, Francis. 1986. *The Draftsman Raphael*. New Haven: Yale University Press.

Barker, Godfrey. 2000. "The Art Market's Two-Ton Gorilla." *Forbes* **166**, No. 16: 146.

Bell, Clive. 1982. "The Debt to Cézanne." In Francis Frascina and Charles Harrision, eds. *Modern Art and Modernism*. New York: Harper and Row.

Bell, Janis. 1997. "Color and Chiaroscuro." In Marcia Hall, ed. *Raphael's "School of Athens."* Cambridge: Cambridge University Press.

Biadene, Susanna, ed. 1990. *Titian: Prince of Painters*. Washington, DC: National Gallery of Art.

Bowness, Alan. 1989. *The Conditions of Success: How the Modern Artist Rises to Fame*. New York: Thames and Hudson.

Britsch, Ralph A. and Todd Britsch. 1984. *The Arts in Western Culture*. Englewood Cliffs, NJ: Prentice-Hall.

Carmean, E. A. and Eliza E. Rathbone. 1978. *American Art at Mid-Century: The Subjects of the Artist*. Washington DC: National Gallery of Art.

Cleaver, Dale G. 1972. *Art*, Second ed. New York: Harcourt Brace Jovanovich.

Cornell, Sara. 1983. *Art*. Englewood Cliffs, NJ: Prentice-Hall.

de la Croix, Horst and Richard G. Tansey. 1975. *Gardner's Art Through the Ages*, Sixth ed. New York: Harcourt Brace Jovanovich.

Freeman, Julian. 1998. *Art*. New York: Watson-Guptill Publications.

Friedman, B. H. 1995. *Jackson Pollock: Energy Made Visible*. New York: Da Capo Press.

Fry, Roger. 1962. *Last Lectures*. Boston: Beacon Press.

Galenson, David. 2001. *Painting outside the Lines*. Cambridge, MA: Harvard University Press.

Galenson, David. 2006. *Old Masters and Young Geniuses*. Princeton: Princeton University Press.

Gebhardt, Volker. 1998. *The History of Art*. New York: Barron's.

Golding, John. 1988. *Cubism*, Third ed. Cambridge, MA: Harvard University Press.

Hartt, Fredrick. 1989. *Art*, Third ed. Englewood Cliffs, NJ: Prentice-Hall.

Honour, Hugh and John Fleming. 1999. *The Visual Arts*, Fifth ed. New York: Harry N. Abrams.

Jensen, Robert 1994. *Marketing Modernism in Fin-de-Siècle Europe*. Princeton: Princeton University Press.

Karmel, Pepe, ed. 1999. *Jackson Pollock: Interviews, Articles, and Reviews*. New York: Museum of Modern Art.

Kemp, Martin, ed. 2000. *The Oxford History of Western Art*. Oxford: Oxford University Press.

Koestler, Arthur. 1964. *The Act of Creation*. New York: Macmillan.

Kubler, George. 1962. *The Shape of Time: Remarks on the History of Things*. New Haven: Yale University Press.

Oberhuber, Konrad and Lamberto Vitali. 1972. *Il cartone per la "Scuola d'Athene"*. Milan: Silvana Editoriale de'Arte.

Rewald, John, ed. 1995. *Paul Cézanne Letters*. New York: Da Capo Press.

Rosand, David. 1982. "Titian and the Critical Tradition." In David Rosand, ed. *Titian: His World and His Legacy*. New York: Columbia University Press.

Rosand, David. 1987. "Editor's Statement: Style and the Aging Artist." *Art Journal* 46: 91.

Rubin, William. 1977. *Cézanne: The Late Work*. New York: Museum of Modern Art.

Rubin, William, Hélène Seckel, and Judith Cousins. 1994. *Les Demoiselles d'Avignon*. New York: Museum of Modern Art.

Ruskin, Ariane. 1974. *History in Art*. New York: Franklin Watts.

Schapiro, Meyer. 1979. *Modern Art: 19th and 20th Centuries*. New York: George Braziller.

Shiff, Richard. 1984. *Cézanne and the End of Impressionism*. Chicago: University of Chicago Press.

Spencer, Harold 1975. *The Image Maker*. New York: Charles Scribner's Sons.

Stokstad, Marilyn. 1995. *Art History*. New York: Harry N. Abrams.

van Gogh, Vincent. 1958. *The Complete Letters of Vincent van Gogh*. London: Thames and Hudson, Vol. 3.

van de Wetering. 1998. *Rembrandt. The Painter at Work*. Amsterdam: Amsterdam University Press.

van de Wetering. 1998. "Rembrandt's Bathsheba: The Object and Its Transformations." In Ann Jensen Adams, ed. *Rembrandt's "Bathsheba Reading King David's Letter"*. Cambridge: Cambridge University Press.

Varnedoe, Kirk, ed. 1996. *Jasper Johns: Writings, Sketchbook Notes, Interviews*. New York: Museum of Modern Art.

Vasari, Giorgio. 1971. *The Lives of the Artists*. Harmondsworth: Penguin.

Whistler, James Albert McNeill. 1922. *The Gentle Art of Making Enemies*. New York: G.P. Putnam's Sons.

Wilkins, David G., Bernard Schultz, and Katheryn M. Linduff. 1997. *Art Present*. New York: Harry N. Abrams.

Wollheim, Richard. 1995. "Minimal Art." In Gregory Battock, ed. *Minimal Art: A Critical Anthology*. Berkeley: University of California Press.

Wood, Michael, Bruce Cole, and Adelheid Gealt. 1989. *Art of the Western World*. New York: Simon and Schuster.

8

An Elite Minority: Jews among the Richest 400 Americans

Peter Temin

Why are there so many rich Jews in America? This seems like an odd question to ask, but it arises in the context of studies of income mobility. The normal question in such studies is why one or another group does less well than anticipated. It is useful to ask as well why a group does better than might have been anticipated. That is the topic of this paper.

I begin by reviewing the evidence that brought this question to the fore. I then attempt to answer two questions. First, are Jews among the very rich because they were discriminated against in other activities? Second, are Jews among the very rich because of some aspect of minority behavior? I suggest that the answer is no to the first question and yes to the second. Along the way, I present a small probability model to show how classic minority behavior might have achieved the observed result. The assumptions needed for this demonstration are quite strong, implying other factors at work as well.

I

Forbes Magazine collects and publishes annually a list of the 400 richest people in the United States, as it has done since 1982. I examined the ethnic background of these rich people in the context of trying to explain why the CEOs of the *Fortune* 500 companies have remained male, white, and Protestant for a century or more (Temin 1999a; 1999b). The list of rich people was used as a control group in order to test for discrimination among the CEOs. Rich people are male, white, and non-Catholic, like the CEOs. But there are many more Jews among the richest people than among the top CEOs, and Jews are far more evident among the richest people than in

I thank the members of the Economics Seminar at the Hebrew University for suggesting this question, Ian Sigelow of MIT for research assistance, and Bronwyn Hall of UC-Berkeley and Nuffield College for help formulating and running the simulation models. All errors are mine alone.

TABLE 8.1. *Composition of the American Business Elite (Percent)*

	1900s	1990s
Women	o	o
African Americans	o	o
Asian Americans	o	o
Immigrants	10	5
Catholics	7	5–10
Jews	3	2–10

Source: Temin (1999a).

the American population as a whole. The data from this earlier inquiry are shown in Table 8.1. These observations give rise to this inquiry.

There have been Jews in the United States for almost as long as there were European immigrants of any sort. The proportion of the American population who are Jewish, however, has never risen very high. Jews make up 2.3 percent of the population of the United States (U.S. Census Bureau 2000). There is an extensive anecdotal literature on discrimination against Jews in America. Despite these accounts, there were Jews among the American business elite in 1900, and it is impossible to reject the hypothesis that the proportion of Jews among the business elite has not changed in a century (Temin 1999a). Jews in fact have been represented among the American business elite approximately in proportion to their presence in the population as a whole. Jews, however, are more educated than the population as a whole, and a smaller proportion of educated Jews than educated Protestants may be represented among the business elite. But even this more articulated hypothesis does not appear to be valid. The proportion of Jews in the *Fortune* 500 is larger than the proportion of Jews in the population, although not to the same degree as in the *Forbes* 400. Jews in the *Fortune* 500 may well be in proportion to the share of Jews among more educated Americans. It is hard to say that this is the result of discrimination.

In contrast to the small representation of Jews among the American business elite, they are represented heavily among the richest Americans. Over 20 percent of the richest 400, which includes slightly over 400 people due to the presence of families in the list, are Jewish. Jews are more present among the very rich than among the population as a whole by an order of magnitude! Over 15 percent of the richest 400 were Jewish in 1982, when *Forbes* first published this list. One-fifth is Jewish today. The proportion has risen in the past few decades, but the ratio of Jews in the richest 400 was far larger than their share of the population a quarter century ago, suggesting that the results for the recent past are typical of the late twentieth century as a whole.

The data were collected by examining the names and biographies of the richest 400. Biographies often do not include ethnicity or religion, and I therefore made the best estimate I could of Jewishness by looking at names, contributions to charities, membership in organizations, and other chance bits of information. When in doubt, I did not include a person among the Jews. As with all estimates of this sort, there must be some errors of attribution, although Lipset (1996) independently derived almost exactly the same number. I am confident that I have not over-counted the Jews among the very rich. If I have missed a few, then the point that they are numerous is even stronger. (For more details on methodology, see Temin 1999a.)

II

The first question is whether this phenomenon is due to discrimination. It clearly is not due to discrimination in all parts of the economy; I am trying to explain why there are so many rich Jews, not why there are so few. Instead, the argument is that Jews have become rich because they were discriminated against in large American corporations. They are more present among the very rich than among the business elite because they are discriminated against in the latter. There are two reasons to reject this reasoning. First, the current composition of the American business elite is not the result of current discrimination (Temin 1999b). Limited access to quality education – the result of past discrimination – may have reduced access to the business elite for some ethnic groups, but not for Jews. They have been present among the business elite in rough proportion to their presence in the population for the entire twentieth century.

Second, the structure of the argument is flawed. When a group is discriminated against in one area, its members are forced to go to another. But the second area must be less advantageous for this group than the first for the discrimination to matter. If the second area is better than the first, then members of the group would go there in the absence of discrimination. It is hard to argue from their presence there that they are the victims of discrimination elsewhere. In order to argue that Jews are rich because of discrimination in business, it is necessary to argue that it less desirable to be very rich than to be the CEO of a larger corporation.

This may be true. The sense of power one gets from heading a large organization may be better than the abstract command over resources that one gets from being rich. Membership among the business elite may get a Jew into clubs that are restricted so much that even great wealth would not promise entry. There may be other benefits as well. But none of these comparisons is compelling, and there is little evidence that any of them actually exist. Economic theory suggests that wealth is desirable, and we should be nervous about arguments that suggest the opposite.

I infer therefore that the large representation of Jews among the very rich is not the result of discrimination elsewhere in the economy. They are not in this group by default; they are there as a result of their economic achievements. The question is not why are Jews at a disadvantage here or elsewhere, but rather why are Jews able to operate so effectively in America.

A possible answer is that Jews are a small minority in America, and they exhibit behavior typical of minorities in other countries and at other times. This minority behavior provides at least part of the explanation for the over-representation of Jews among the richest 400 people in America.

There are many theories of minority behavior (Brezis and Temin 1999). The literature starts with Weber's famous essay on the Protestant ethic. He argued that it was the nature of Protestant thought that gave Protestants an advantage in industrial pursuits. Generations of scholars have disputed Weber's reasoning and the role of Protestants in economic development. The discussion has broadened to include the role of other minorities in economic affairs, sometimes spoken of as being "like Protestants." The similarity sometimes is taken to be the nature of their religious beliefs. Other authors emphasize the effect of being a minority, independent of beliefs. This is the line I wish to pursue here.

Minorities do well in conditions of asymmetric information. Consider the classic principal–agent problem. The principal is trying to induce certain behavior in the agent. The problem is that the agent's behavior is not fully observable even after the fact. The principal's problem is to define a contract that will induce a person acting as agent to act in the principal's interest despite the lack of monitoring. If the principal and agent belong to the same minority group, the monitoring problem may be less severe than if they are random members of the population. Typically information is shared more readily within a minority group than among random individuals, and this information can allow the principal and agent to formulate a better working arrangement, albeit seldom formalized in a written contract.

Greif (1994) argued that information sharing among the Maghribi traders in the Mediterranean approximately a millennium ago helps explain their success. These traders needed agents to transact business for them in distant places where it was impossible for the trader (the principal) to have current information. Greif demonstrated formally that the greater transmission of knowledge within the Meghribi group than among non-minority groups allowed the Maghribi traders to contract with agents on better terms. He traced the efficiency of the Maghribi traders to a very specific behavior trait. Within the Maghribi trading group, information about an agent who cheated his principal was circulated widely. Outside of this group, it was far harder to know if an agent presenting himself to a trader had cheated a previous trader in an earlier transaction.

This of course is classic minority behavior. Throughout the period before the Industrial Revolution, information about business transactions was costly to obtain. Merchants, financiers, and later producers of all sorts struggled to get commercial advantage through better information. And they did so often by exploiting family connections and the extended family connection of membership in a minority group. The five Rothschild brothers are only the most successful and well-known of these minority entrepreneurs.

Mathias (1999) argued that the scarcity of information was endemic in early modern Europe. What we call minority behavior, the "clannishness" of minorities who share information only among themselves, was pervasive in all business at this time. This behavior, he argued, was a rational response to conditions of costly information that gave related people, even those related only by being members of the same minority group, a commercial advantage. Minority groups were led to emphasize their separate identity and the relatedness of all their members. In some cases, they were able to lever their favorable control of information into success and enter the business elite.

Information is much cheaper in the industrial world. The daily press, telegraph, and now all sorts of electronic communication have sharply reduced the cost of information. But not all information has become cheap, and information that is expensive to obtain is still the key to success in some sectors of the economy. Principals still need to hire agents, and there are sectors in which it is still hard to write relatively complete contracts, despite the general cheapness of information. These sectors are those in which it is hard to monitor agent's effort and where success is the result of so many factors that it is hard to isolate the input of the agent. These conditions are more relevant to finance than to manufacturing. They apply more to industries like apparel and cosmetics in which fashion is dominant than in other industries. If the key to the relative success of Jews in America is due to this kind of classic minority behavior, we should expect to find that the Jews among the very rich disproportionately earned their money in sectors where information is costly and complete contracts are difficult to write.

Reder (2000) provides a vivid description of the environment in which successful Jews moved in Europe and America before the last half of the twentieth century. He does so by a careful analysis of statements by prominent economists of the day, principally – because he wrote so much – Keynes. Reder argues that there was a pervasive, albeit genteel anti-Semitism endemic among educated people before the Second World War. This did not preclude friendship and admiration of individual Jews, but it meant that any successful Jew had to endure continuing insults in the course of his or her professional and personal life, not of course directed at him or her personally. This context accentuated the natural tendency of a minority to deal with other members of his or her group. It eased in academic life only after the war as the boom in American university education created sufficient demand for Jewish faculty members that they could choose jobs where they did not have

TABLE 8.2. *The Richest 400 by Field, 1998*

Sector Number	Sector Definition	Percentage of Jews	Percentage in NY or CA
1	Apparel and Cosmetics	40	35
2	Banking and Finance	39	56
3	Food	22	22
4	Inheritance	9	35
5	Manufacturing and Mining	17	12
6	Media and Entertainment	25	35
7	Retail	24	12
8	Services	18	15
9	Technology	7	31
	TOTAL	21	32

to endure ethnic slurs. The process undoubtedly took place more slowly in the business world.

III

The importance of information transmission among the Jewish minority can be supported with data from the *Forbes* 400. It must be admitted that this support is suggestive rather than conclusive. If one can rank industries according to the costs of writing contracts between principals and agents, or group industries into those with higher and lower contracting costs, it should be possible to determine if Jews have been more prevalent in those industries with higher contracting costs.

The United States is a big country, and it is hard for minorities to maintain the coherence and relationships that are presumed in this model of behavior if they are spread across the country. If minority behavior is the key, then we should expect Jews who have prospered to be concentrated in a few locations as well as in a few areas of endeavor. The industries in which Jews have excelled consequently should be located in areas of relatively dense Jewish settlement. This reasoning therefore suggests two correlations. First, the richest Jews should be more concentrated than other rich Americans in sectors in which contracting is difficult. Second, the richest Jews are more likely to live in New York and California, states of densest Jewish settlement, than other rich Americans. These correlations can be evaluated from data compiled by *Forbes* and general observations about different industries.

Forbes lists the economic area from which the richest 400 receive their money. Inheritance is one category, which is less relevant for this inquiry than others. There are nine sectors, listed in Table 8.2. Also in that table are the proportion of Jews in the various sectors and the proportion in New

York or California. The overall share of Jews in *Forbes* 400 is 21 percent, so it is not surprising that many of the proportions are near twenty percent. Several are not, and they are of interest to us here. Jews are disproportionately represented in the first two sectors, Apparel and Cosmetics (1) and Banking and Finance (2). They are especially underrepresented in two sectors, Inheritance (4) and Technology (9). Surprisingly, they are not greatly over-represented in Media and Entertainment (6). I attempt to draw conclusions from these data, even though the assignment of people to sectors has more than a little uncertainty in it.

Consider first the sectors in which Jews are relatively few. Jews are less represented among people who have inherited great wealth than among those who have earned it in this generation. This suggests that the representation of Jews in the *Forbes* 400 is a post-war phenomenon. Before the Second World War, few Jews were able to accumulate great wealth. This is consistent with the conclusions of my previous paper in which I found that current discrimination was of small importance relative to past discrimination (Temin 1999b). Jews also are relatively few among those who have successfully introduced new technologies, chiefly electronic. This is consistent with the long history of Jews in the secular economy where they have been underrepresented in the development of technology, as distinct from contributing to science. Bairoch (1999) for example found that there were hardly any Jewish innovations during the British industrial revolution. The hypothesis that Jews were better able to prosper in new industries appears to be false.

The two industries in which Jews are found relatively frequently are those in which it is hard to evaluate the effect of an agent's actions in advance (Table 8.2, rows 1 and 2). Products in apparel and cosmetics are subject to the dictates of fashion, which can change rapidly and for no apparent reason. Consequently it is hard to know from an initial success if an agent like a buyer or designer is gifted or lucky. Activities in banking and finance of course are uncertain, particularly when great risks are involved. It is by taking great risks that investors become fabulously wealthy. The representation of Jews among the very rich therefore is consistent with the hypothesis that Jews are present where one can reduce uncertainty by dealing with members of the same minority group.

It also appears to be the case that Jews are particularly successful in traditional areas of Jewish economic activity. In the age of massive Jewish immigration to the United States before the First World War, half of the immigrants who had been gainfully employed in Russia were employed in the needle trades. This concentration of employment was typical of Jews in Russia, which in turn was determined in part by the exclusion of Jews from other activities (Kuznets 1975, 110).

The presence of Jews in banking and finance also is hardly new. Jews in Europe gravitated to urban occupations in the first Christian millennium, making use of their education which gave them a comparative advantage in crafts, trade, and banking (Botticini and Eckstein 2005). Later they were barred by law from owning land and engaging in many ordinary types of agricultural activity in many places; they gravitated toward cities and urban occupations. Finance was a traditional activity of Jews, because they were educated, outside the usury restrictions of the Church, and able to exploit the communication networks of minority communities. In the pre-industrial world, finance consisted largely of loans to sovereigns and the nobility.

Jews in America did not come from the great Jewish banking families of Europe, but they did focus on traditional activities, as Kuznets (1975) found that Russian Jews in America did later. Supple (1957) chronicled the progress of a group of Jewish immigrants from Germany who arrived in the United States in the 1840s, typically as young men in their twenties. Most of them came without financial resources of their own, and they went into some form of distribution, ranging from peddling to more stationary wholesaling and retailing. They prospered during the Civil War, settled in New York, and went into finance. Their enterprises grew with the buoyant economy of the Gilded Age, and there were many German–Jewish financial houses in New York by the end of the nineteenth century. August Belmont & Co., Goldman, Sachs & Co., Kuhn, Loeb & Co., Lehman Brothers, and J. & W. Seligman & Co. are among the best known of these investment bankers (Birmingham 1967).

Supple recounts their story and speculates about the difficult question I am concerned with here: "Why this particular group should have been as successful as it was in this particular field is not a question which permits of a satisfying answer. Clearly they were not concerned in a conspiracy to monopolize the money market. To some extent . . . the common background facilitated their dealing with each other and with some clients; but this was not a continuous process, and it could not explain their success in financial transactions involving non-Jews" (Supple 1957, 156–57).

We must applaud Supple's caution and judgment, but I think he underestimated the role of a common background. He considered the demand side of the financial transaction, but not the supply side. Most customers of the Jewish financiers were non-Jewish, if only because Jews were (and are) such a small minority in the United States. The advantage of membership in this minority group was the access to credit and the knowledge of how to arrange large blocks of funds. It is the problems of supplying finance in any case that have been the center of the literature on this topic.

Supple differentiated three increasingly exclusive paths through which these people created a tight community. First, they all came from Germany and revered German language, culture, and education. Second, they were Jewish and attended and supported the same synagogues in New York City. Third, they intermarried to create a very tight bond among them, almost an extended family. Supple created a complex genealogical chart that showed the resulting "interlocking structure, [in which] the fecund

Seligmans occupied an 'anchoring' position" (Supple 1957, 164). This diagram was reproduced in the popular book, *Our Crowd* (Birmingham 1967).

One example may illustrate this process. Goldman, Sachs was until recently the fabulously successful financial firm of our day, a century after the firm achieved prominence. Marcus Goldman, a former Philadelphia clothing merchant, started a commercial paper dealership in New York with his son-in-law, Samuel Sachs, in 1869. They discounted paper, that is, they provided credit, for diamond dealers and leather, dry-goods, and hardware merchants. The new firm prospered, helped by the large Jewish presence in the diamond trade and other distribution enterprises. It progressed into dealing with larger firms by exploiting the Jewish connections as well. It provided finance to Sears, Roebuck, headed by Julius Rosenwald – who was not only Jewish but a cousin of the Sachs family – and to the cigar-manufacturing business of Jacob Wertheim. These personal and business contacts continued over time, and when Goldman, Sachs moved into industrial underwriting in 1906, its first two flotations were for Sears, Roebuck and United Cigar Manufacturers. As Supple (1957, 173) commented, "Unknown in the underwriting world as Goldman, Sachs & Co. was, it is highly probable that only such personal relationships enabled it to convince the two clients of its ability to handle the business."

Having obtained the business, Goldman, Sachs needed to sell the new securities at a profit. It appealed for help to another Jewish firm headed by a personal friend of Marcus Goldman's son, Henry: Lehman Brothers. The two firms cooperated in 144 issues for 56 issuers in the next two decades before going their own ways in 1924. By that time Goldman, Sachs was established and moved into the general investment finance business. Both firms also hired important non-Jewish financiers at this time and moved into general American business practice both externally and internally.

This story illustrates the role of the Jewish community in the success of individual Jews. The community was very important in the early stages of business, when personal and business interests were intertwined. These contacts continued for many years and were important not only in the initial years of the business, but also at the time of expansion into a larger business environment. Over time, however, the role of the Jewish community decreased, and Goldman, Sachs moved into being a financial firm like other financial firms in New York. This story, although almost a century old, illustrates a process that appears to be effective in our generation.

It is a bit surprising that Jews are not more apparent in the media and entertainment field. There appears to be great uncertainty there as well as in the first two sectors, and much of the anecdotal literature about successful Jews focuses on Hollywood. Yet Jews are scarcely more frequent in this field than among the richest 400 as a whole. Perhaps the longer history of Jewish activity in the garment trades and finance also has been important in their success in those sectors.

One-third of the *Forbes* 400 live in either New York or California. These states are of course nice places to live, and it appears that the richest Jews do congregate together. It is hard to know if this is cause or effect of their wealth; one way in which the very rich spend their money is to live in these nice places. The only field in which the very rich are especially geographically concentrated is banking and finance. This is consistent with the hypothesis that the Jewish minority is concentrated in space as well as in economic activity. The absence of unusual geographical concentration in apparel and cosmetics, however, is not consistent with this hypothesis. I conclude that the data provide only suggestive support for the idea that the Jewish minority needs to be physically close together to exploit the information flows with the Jewish community.

IV

This has been an informal argument, and I now present a formal restatement in order to show how such a process of minority behavior can influence the economic life of a minority. This model of course does not prove that the Jewish community played the role attributed to it in the previous discussion. Instead, it shows a conceptually consistent way in which such a process could have happened. It strengthens the argument by exposing its theoretical structure.

I model getting very rich as a random process. This is not to say that the people actually in the *Forbes* 400 have been picked randomly from the population, but rather that the characteristics that helped them succeed are distributed randomly among the population. As I discussed in my earlier paper (Temin 1999b), this is not quite accurate. Education and family background clearly count in getting to the top of the economic heap. Even without any minority cohesion, Jews should have a better chance of getting to the top than random people because they are better educated. Since it is hard to quantify this effect, I ignore it in the formal model. I also ignore the sector concentration of the Jews in the *Forbes* 400, although I have argued that minority network behavior is particularly strong in these sectors. This makes the task of the model that much harder.

Let us approach this explanation by a series of very simple models that show the intuition involved. The first model is simply choosing balls from an urn with replacement.[1] I use choosing with replacement to keep the probability of choosing balls of different color the same over time, representing

---

[1] An "urn model" is a way to illustrate probabilities. Urn models without replacement are good for thinking about choosing teams from a population where you exhaust the candidates as you choose them. Urn models with replacement are useful when you want to keep probabilities the same except for changes introduced by assumption. In the first model, I assume that in every period, everyone has an equal chance of going from rags to riches. Subsequent models allow these probabilities to vary. Since the models generate probabilities, I simulated processes 50 times and graphed average paths.

the effect of external conditions. The urn contains 98 white balls and 2 black balls, representing the proportion of Jews in the United States. The chance of picking a black ball from this urn is two percent. If we regard choosing a ball as the success of an individual, as the chance that an individual rises to become a member of the *Forbes* 400, then this first model predicts that the proportion of Jews in the *Forbes* 400 would stay the same as their proportion of the population or two percent.

This of course is not what happened. The data in Table 8.2 which I have set out to explain show that the probability of being Jewish in the *Forbes* 400 is 20 percent, an order of magnitude larger than the share of Jews in the population. I therefore turn to a second model. This model shows the effect of minority group behavior as described earlier. This behavior can be termed a network effect, as Jews help each other, and more Jews among the rich provide more contacts to help a new Jewish aspirant. This network effect shows up in the model in the following way: each time a black ball is chosen, a white ball in the urn turns black. In other words, the success of one Jew encourages the success of other Jews. The model does not show the mechanisms involved, which were described in the narrative sections of this paper.

One can simulate the progress of Jews in this second model. For a while, there will be very few Jews among the richest 400, that is, very few black balls chosen. However, each time a black ball is chosen, the proportion of black balls in the urn increases by one. The probability of choosing a black ball increases over time as a result. In fact, after enough trials, all the balls in the urn will have turned black, and the model will predict that all the richest people will be Jews. This model has explained too much.

I therefore add an offsetting influence to generate a third model. This model adds an assimilation effect to the network effect of the second model. It idealizes the experience of Goldman, Sachs in the 1920s as it merged into the general community, both in its clientele and in its personnel. This model introduces assimilation in the simplest possible way. When the number of black balls gets over 20, then a black ball in the urn turns white. In plain words, when a fifth of very rich are Jews, they become indistinguishable from other rich people. They merge into the general community, and the network effects of the previous model atrophy.

This model tracks the previous model at first. Simulating picks from the urn reveals that few picks are black balls initially, but the proportion of black balls picked rises over time. The proportion of black balls picked does not rise without limit, however. Consider the choice when the urn contains 20 black balls and 80 white ones. With probability 4/5, the next ball chosen will be white. Nothing happens in the urn, and the composition of black and white balls does not change. The probability of choosing a white ball in the next round also does not change. With probability 1/5, the next ball chosen will be black. Since a black ball was chosen, then a white ball in

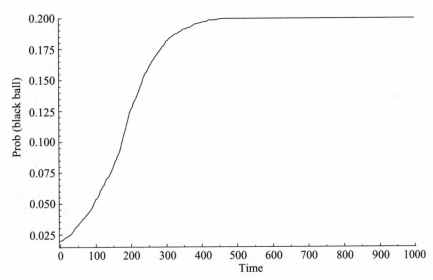

FIGURE 8.1. Drawing with replacement: Average of 50 Trials; Initial probability of black ball = .02; Ceiling probability = .25–25 [*P* of black ball].

the urn turns black. But since the proportion of black balls in the urn now exceeds 20, a black ball turns white. The two changes offset each other, and the composition of black and white balls does not change. The probability of choosing a white ball in the next round also does not change.

In other words, when the proportion of black balls in the urn reaches 20 percent, it stays there. The chance of Jews rising into the richest 400 rises to 20 percent in this model and then stays at that level. The data in Table 8.2 show an equilibrium level. This clearly is a very simple model, but it contains the elements needed to explain the observations in Table 8.2. It contains two offsetting effects, which take effect at different times. Networking among the minority community is most important when the community is new and the chance of success is slim. As the success of the minority group grows, so does its assimilation toward the dominant culture of its host country. As successful minority members assimilate, the network effect from belonging to the minority community decreases.

This third model is complex enough to provide some insight into the nature of the minority experience. Simulation of the model produces the predicted shape, but it takes almost 500 draws from the urn to reach that level. The average of 50 trials is shown in Figure 8.1; it has a drawn-out S shape, approximately linear for much of the rise. Each time the number of black balls rises, it increases the probability of finding another one, but this effect is small relative to the impact of adding another black ball. More complex models might have more realistic shapes, but this one shows that the hypothesized process takes a long time to create a rich minority.

(The simulated model is slightly more complex than the stated model to avoid a sharp corner at 20.)

If we think that each draw represents a generation, then there have only been at most a half-dozen generations since the days of the immigrant German–Jewish bankers. The time span since the first Jews appeared among the richest Americans cannot be much more than a century. There was not enough time for the model process to work itself out. In fact, there was hardly time for the process to get started. If this kind of behavior is to explain the data, modifications are needed. There are three kinds of changes that can make the model approach the historical experience more closely. I discuss them in turn.

First, we could say that the draws correspond to something more frequent than the march of generations. If people strike it rich every decade or even half-decade, then the model "runs" that much faster. Unfortunately, the draws would have to be made every month for the time scale of the model to fit the time scale of the phenomenon being explained. The problem with a monthly or even an annual draw is that the draws are supposed to be independent, that is, not related to previous draws. It is hard to think that the process of getting to the top of the income ladder is so much like a lottery that there is a new, independent draw each month or year. Running the model faster therefore loses in plausibility what it might gain in apparent fit to the data.

Second, we could argue that the draw comes not from the population as a whole, but from the educated population. We know that Jews value education, as they have done for two millennia. The growth of high schools in America, however, was fastest in areas without many Jews (Goldin and Katz 1999). To the extent that college was relevant, there also was discrimination in higher education in the early twentieth century (Rosovsky 1986). If the net effect was to make Jews twice as prevalent among high school graduates as they were in the population as a whole, this shortens the process of getting to the 20 percent limit by about 100 years. (This can be seen by starting the process in Figure 8.1 at .04 instead of .02, that is, counting draws only after .04 is reached.) In other words, the Jewish advantage in education would have to be very strong to make the process converge in a reasonable time.

Third, we could suggest that the network effect within the Jewish community was stronger than assumed in the models just described. When one Jew succeeded in getting rich, perhaps that opened the door to many other Jews. When one black ball is selected, more than one ball turns black. That clearly would speed up the process. It violates a bit of our sense of a network process as being the connection between individuals, but there is nothing contradictory in such an assumption. This modification models a process where a single successful Jew brings his or her whole extended family along with him or her. As in the previous suggestion, this one makes the model work better at the cost of making the assumptions harder to accept.

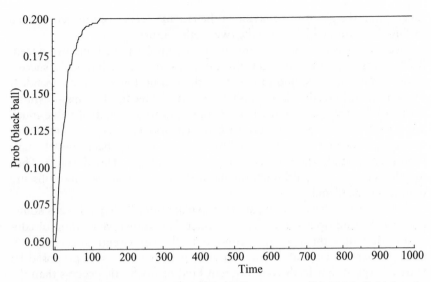

FIGURE 8.2. Drawing with replacement of 5 balls: Average of 50 Trials; Initial probability of black ball = .05; Ceiling probability = .25–25 [*P* of black ball].

A fourth model implements the last two suggestions. The probability of reaching the richest group is set initially at .05 to represent the presumed proportion of Jews among educated Americans. When a black ball is picked *five* balls turn black to show a strong networking effect. The same 20 percent limit due to assimilation is preserved. The results of 50 trials of this fourth model are shown in Figure 8.2.

It looks a lot better, although still not perfect. However, if we add the first adjustment to the two already in the model and assume annual draws, then the curve in Figure 8.2 fits the data rather well. The proportion of Jews rises close to 20 percent after a century and rises slowly in the quarter or half century after then. This is the result of assuming frequent chances to strike it rich, powerful effects of education, and a very powerful network effect in the Jewish community. The combination of these strong effects models the data in Table 8.2. It is a Procrustean bed, but I have made the model fit it.

The outcome of this discussion is the opposite of my expectation. I thought when I began this research that a very small preference for fellow minority members would be enough to generate large differences in fortunes in a simple model after only a few generations. This however is not true. Small preferences can generate large differences in these simple models, but only over a long time. Alternatively, large preferences can have large effects in a few generations. If this model of minority behavior is correct, then the evidence forces us to argue that Jews in business have a strong desire to deal with fellow Jews or were wildly successful in education. These simple models suggest that the clannish behavior of the late nineteenth century chronicled by Supple continued long into the twentieth century.

Of course, it is possible to formulate more complex models involving feedback processes that magnify the effect of any draw. In such models, success leads to more success, and draws from the urn no longer are independent of each other. In feedback models of this sort, the feedback loops substitute for repeated trials, and participation converges to an eventual value much faster than in the models described here. The models used here are simple contagion models that result in logistic curves; the feedback models have been used to study the evolution of academic careers (David 1994). They may be relevant here, although the nature of the feedback is more obscure than it is in academia.

Alternatively, there may be another explanation. Perhaps there is something in the tradition of Jews, such as their well-known veneration of education, that suits them for the economy of the late twentieth century. Or perhaps there is a social interaction among Jews of the sort proposed by Durlauf (1999) that leads to a different kind of stochastic process than the one I have hypothesized here. The models described here provide a starting point for the investigation of one or another of these ideas, but it is not clear at this stage how they should be modified.

IV

The conclusions of this small exploration are suggestive without being conclusive. There is some evidence that classic minority behavior has contributed to the success of Jews in post-war America. It also appears that the richest Jews are in sectors to which Jews were restricted by past discrimination. A formal probability model shows how the network and assimilation effects shown in the historical literature may have worked out. But the models explain the data only if strong effects are inserted into the models at the outset or if powerful feedback mechanisms are assumed. It must be admitted that the full reasons why Jews are far more numerous among the richest 400 people in America than among the population as a whole remain elusive.

References

Bairoch, Paul. 1999. The Jews, the English Industrial Revolution, Technological Innovation and the Sciences: From Absence to Predominance. In Elise Brezis and Peter Temin, eds. *Elites, Minorities, and Economic Growth.* Amsterdam: Elsevier, pp. 129–36.

Birmingham, Stephen. 1967. *'Our Crowd': the Great Jewish Families of New York.* New York: Harper and Row.

Botticini, Maristella, and Zvi Eckstein. 2005. Jewish Occupational Selection: Education, Restrictions or Minorities? *Journal of Economic History* 65: 1–26.

Brezis, Elise, and Peter Temin. 1999. Elites, Minorities and Economic Growth in an Interdisciplinary Perspective. In Elise Brezis and Peter Temin, eds. *Elites, Minorities, and Economic Growth*. Amsterdam: Elsevier, pp. 3–18.

David, Paul A. 1994. Positive Feedbacks and Research Productivity in Science: Reopening Another Black Box. In Ove Granstrand, ed. *The Economics of Technology*. Amsterdam: North Holland.

Durlauf, Seven N. 1999. The Memberships Theory of Inequality: Ideas and Implications. In Elise Brezis and Peter Temin, eds. *Elites, Minorities, and Economic Growth*. Amsterdam: Elsevier, pp. 161–77.

Goldin, Claudia, and Lawrence F. Katz. 1999. Human Capital and Social Capital: The Rise of Secondary Schooling in America, 1910–1940. *Journal of Interdisciplinary History* 29: 683–723.

Greif, Avner. 1994. Cultural Beliefs and the Organization of Society: A Historical and Theoretical Reflection on Collectivist and Individualist Societies. *Journal of Political Economy* 102: 912–50.

Kuznets, Simon. 1975. Immigration of Russian Jews to the United States: Background and Structure. *Perspectives in American History* 9: 35–124.

Lipset, Seymour Martin. 1996. *American Exceptionalism: A Double-Edged Sword*. New York: Norton.

Mathias, Peter. 1999. Minorities and Elites: How Do Minorities Become Elites? In Elise Brezis and Peter Temin, eds. *Elites, Minorities, and Economic Growth*. Amsterdam: Elsevier, pp. 115–28.

Reder, Melvin W. 2000. The Anti-Semitism of Some Eminent Economists. *History of Political Economy* 32: 833–56.

Rosovsky, Nitza. 1986. *The Jewish Experience at Harvard and Radcliffe*. Cambridge, MA: Harvard University Press.

Supple, Barry E. 1957. A Business Elite: German-Jewish Financiers in Nineteenth-Century New York. *Business History Review* 31: 143–78.

Temin, Peter. 1999a. The American Business Elite in Historical Perspective. In Elise Brezis and Peter Temin, eds. *Elites, Minorities, and Economic Growth*. Amsterdam: Elsevier, pp. 19–40.

Temin, Peter. 1999b. The Stability of the American Business Elite. *Industrial and Corporate Change* 8: 189–209.

U.S. Census Bureau. 2000. *Statistical Abstract of the United States, 1999*. Washington, DC: Government Printing Office.

PART IV

CONSTRAINTS IN LABOR AND
FINANCIAL MARKETS

9

Suffrage and the Terms of Labor

Robert J. Steinfeld

Great books often harbor deep tensions, which are one source of their endur-ing power. *Time on the Cross* by Robert Fogel and Stanley Engerman is a good example (Fogel and Engerman 1974). On the one hand, *Time on the Cross* argued that the economic science of Cliometrics was indispensable for a proper understanding of the past. Human beings have always been pri-marily motivated by the desire for gain, and to understand their behavior it is essential to reconstruct the economic contexts in which they acted. Some-what surprisingly, therefore, in light of the rigorous quantitative economic methodology the book adopted, the enormous labors the authors devoted to counting, measuring, and precisely assessing the profitability of slavery were all devoted, in the end, to demonstrating that economic factors *did not* explain why slavery had disappeared in the United States. Slavery had not perished because it was unprofitable. It had disappeared as the result of war and because the nation had come to a political (and moral) decision to end it, despite its continuing profitability.

And so ironically one of the principal messages of *Time on the Cross* turned out to be that economic factors could not always be invoked to explain why one set of economic practices had succeeded and another failed. Non-economic political and moral factors and the legal rules they generated often played determinative roles in the fate of economic institutions, includ-ing the fate of labor systems.

At about the same time that *Time on the Cross* appeared, another group of economic historians began to disseminate a similar message. Legal (and customary) rules were crucial for understanding why economic institutions had evolved in the ways they had (North 1981). The new institutional economists took their inspiration from the ground breaking work of Ronald Coase, who had shown that, in an economic universe without transaction costs, legal (and customary rules) would *not* have mattered. But in the world in which we actually lived, a world full of transaction costs, rules did matter, because they operated to reduce or increase the costs of transacting, and in that way either facilitated, impeded, or distorted the course of economic activity (Coase 1960). In a world with transaction costs, property and contract rules were an important component of markets, and the performance of any particular market could not be completely understood apart from the detailed rules that structured it.

It was clear to the new institutional economists, just as it was clear to the authors of *Time on the Cross*, that the legal (and customary) rules that governed economic life were not always put into place to promote efficiency. Rules were adopted for a variety of reasons, often having little to do with their capacity to reduce transaction costs. Indeed, in many cases, rules adopted for other reasons had the effect of increasing the costs of transacting and in the process reducing or choking off otherwise profitable activity.

The focus on transaction costs and on rules led institutional economists to undertake at least two kinds of inquiries. In the first kind, they sought to identify the types of transaction costs that might arise in particular types of economic exchange. What kinds of transaction costs, for example, typically arise in the course of exchange in labor markets, and what kinds of rules might serve to reduce those transaction costs in order to facilitate exchange at lower cost? Do existing rules minimize transaction costs or do they promote inefficiently high transaction costs? In a second kind of investigation, they sought to develop a deeper understanding of the processes by which rules came to be adopted or changed in the first place.

The following essay attempts to utilize the insights of *Time on the Cross* and the new institutionalism in an effort to critique and begin to revise the traditional master historical narrative of the rise of free wage labor in Anglo-America. *Time on the Cross* definitively changed the way most historians saw the history of slavery. They no longer imagined slavery to have been an economically outmoded practice that was doomed to extinction in the competition with vastly more efficient free labor. But there was another side to the argument of *Time on the Cross*, a side which had implications for the history of free labor itself. In the United States, Southern employers had not spontaneously embraced free labor because they found it more profitable than slavery. Free labor was imposed on the South following a bloody civil war. Southern employers did not abandon labor coercion because they no longer found it to be economically advantageous. They were compelled to give it up by the Federal Government. Indeed, long after slavery had been abolished, Southern states continued to rely on penal sanctions to coerce the performance of labor (Novak 1978; Schmidt 1982).

Time on the Cross largely succeeded in rewriting the master historical narrative of slavery. It did not, however, have much of an impact on the master narrative of the rise of free wage labor. And this is a little surprising given that that narrative continues to rely so heavily on the assumption that wage labor has been free simply because employers found coercion unprofitable.

The economic logic that underlies the free labor narrative is the same logic that *Time on the Cross* discredited as a basis for understanding the history of slavery. Slavery did not disappear because coercion proved unprofitable in extracting labor services. Slavery disappeared because the nation compelled slave employers to give it up. Yet while the slavery narrative has been transformed, the traditional free labor narrative endures.

Most historians, I think, continue to subscribe to the view that wage labor has been free in England and America simply because the market, rather than other more direct means of coercion, satisfied the economic needs of employers. Depending upon one's political perspective, market incentives or market pressures are thought to have worked perfectly well to supply employers with cheap, efficient wage labor. Indeed, direct compulsion is assumed to have been costly and to have produced sullen, inefficient workers. The free labor narrative with its underlying assumption about the economic inefficiency of bodily coercion has a long history dating back in its modern form to the eighteenth century (Coats 1958). During the last decade of that century, for example, Joseph Townsend wrote that

Legal constraint is attended with much trouble, violence and noise; creates ill will, and never can be productive of good and acceptable service; whereas hunger is not only peaceable, silent, unremitting pressure, but, as the most natural motive to industry and labor, it calls forth the most powerful exertions; . . . The slave must be compelled to work but the free man should be left to his own judgment and discretion; should be protected in the full enjoyment of his own, be it much or little; and punished when he invades his neighbor's property. (quoted in Davis 1975, 358–59)

Adam Smith offered a more positive version of the free labor argument during the same period. Coercion gave workers little incentive to produce efficiently. "Whatever work [a slave does] can be squeezed out of him by violence only, and not by any interest of his own" (A. Smith 1976, 411–12). By contrast free workers have "a plain interest that the whole produce should be as great as possible, in order that their own proportion may be so" (A. Smith 1976, 413). Even today such views carry great weight. Recently, for example, one survey of economic literature observed that "Elementary economic reasoning suggests that in the long run the institution of slavery is inviable economically. . . . As a slave receives only a fraction of his marginal product, enough to cover productive consumption, he has fewer incentives to work hard than if he were to internalize his entire marginal product as free workers do." (Eggertsson 1990, 205).

Modern historians have produced additional arguments to show that for centuries un-coerced labor has been economically superior to coerced labor. A number of American historians, for example, have argued that American employers spontaneously turned away from indentured servitude and toward free wage labor during the late eighteenth century because they found indentured labor more costly than free labor, given that it committed them to support their indentured workers during increasingly common economic downturns (Salinger 1987, 149–52; Nash 1979, 320). Another historian has argued that serfdom was abolished in the Scottish coal mines during the last quarter of the eighteenth century because powerful mine owners wished to gain unimpeded access to the labor pool and agitated for the abolition of serfdom in order to do so (Whatley 1987).

The dominance of this kind of reasoning has left historians with little motive to look for examples of the use of bodily coercion in the history of wage labor. And by and large historians have not found what they did not go looking for. The historical picture of free wage labor today takes for granted for the most part that wage work has not traditionally been subject to direct forms of coercion, indeed it is almost considered a contradiction in terms to think that it could have been.

What is a little strange about the enduring power of the traditional free labor narrative is that historians of slavery no longer accept the proposition, by and large, that bodily coercion cannot produce highly productive labor. On the contrary, thanks in large part to Fogel and Engerman, historians of slavery are now widely agreed that direct coercion, or direct coercion combined with incentives, did produce labor that was even more productive than free labor in certain settings, and in other settings, urban artisanal work for example, at least as productive as free labor. In the United States, Southern employers clung tenaciously to coercive practices precisely because coercion was profitable.

To be certain, over the last 25 years there has been a general reassessment of the efficacy of coercion in labor relations and historians have discovered much more coerced labor in the world than they had previously thought was there. That direct coercion cannot produce highly productive, profitable labor is no longer accepted as a universal principle. But historians have been reluctant to embrace the opposite proposition, that bodily coercion might have been economically advantageous for employers in a wide variety of labor market settings. Instead, they have strained to define precisely those market conditions under which bodily coercion could prove economically advantageous and to distinguish those from the more *typical* market conditions under which employers would not have found bodily coercion beneficial. (See, for example, Domar 1970.) This is a complicated story but in general a tacit consensus has emerged that in places where labor was relatively abundant, as in the fully developed wage labor markets of metropolitan England and the United States, bodily coercion was economically unnecessary, indeed even counterproductive. As a result coerced labor has come to be viewed mainly as a phenomenon of the periphery (where labor markets were thin), or of certain forms of agricultural production (in which working conditions were particularly onerous). For all the progress that has been made in understanding how extensive the use of coerced labor has been in the world, Fogel and Engerman's principle that bodily coercion can be of great benefit in extracting labor services has generally not been seen to apply to the free wage labor of the metropolis.

This remains true, by and large, despite the fact that as long ago as 1954 Daphne Simon made clear that penal pressure was in fact used quite widely against wage workers in nineteenth England (Simon 1954). One would have thought that the discovery that wage workers could be imprisoned at hard labor for up to three months for violations of their labor agreements under English Master and Servant law in the nation that stood at the forefront of free market industrialization would have led to some rethinking of the master historical narrative of free labor. (See, for example, Statute 4 Geo. IV, c. 34, 1823.) But it did not. One important reason was that Simon herself was steeped in a Marxist version of the traditional free labor narrative. Modern capitalism relied on the dull compulsion of economic relations to extract labor services. Other forms of coercion like those authorized by the Master and Servant acts were relics of feudalism and doomed to extinction because they did not serve the economic interests of modern employers in an advanced capitalist economy. The Master and Servant acts might have been of some help to small, backward employers, but as the economy modernized the acts became less and less useful. As soon as labor began to object, the employing classes abandoned the acts, putting up only symbolic resistance. Thus Simon, who was the first to rediscover how extensive the use of penal pressure had been in English wage labor down to 1875, dismissed its economic importance, relegating it to a marginal role in the history of wage labor.

A second important reason her discovery had practically no impact on the larger narrative of free labor was that no one seemed able to say precisely what economic benefits employers derived by using penal coercion against wage workers. And without such an understanding there was no basis for attacking the long-standing economic logic of the traditional story, that wage labor had been free simply because employers found coercion unprofitable. Yet the stubborn fact remained that in the years between 1857 and 1875 English employers resorted to penal pressure against their wage workers on a regular basis. About 10,000 English workers each year on average were prosecuted for misbehavior at work or for leaving work before they were contractually free to do so (Judicial Statistics 1857–1875; Simon 1954). Until 1867, about 1,500 workers a year were imprisoned, but a large percentage of those prosecuted who were not imprisoned were ordered back to work under threat of imprisonment should they fail to work out their agreements (Judicial Statistics 1857–1875).

Recently, historians have devoted more attention to the Master and Servant acts. A number of new studies of the acts have now been published and among them a consensus has emerged that Simon's view that the acts were economically anachronistic is simply wrong (Woods 1982; Hay 1988; 1990). But none of these studies has managed to identify precisely what economic benefits employers might have derived by using penal pressure against wage workers. As a result, even though the widespread use of penal pressure in wage labor is now well documented, there has been no direct challenge to the economic logic that underlies the free labor narrative. Historians continue to subscribe to two master historical narratives of labor based on contradictory views about the economic efficacy of bodily coercion. The newer one, the slavery narrative, derived in part from *Time on the Cross*, is based on the idea that bodily coercion of labor has been of great economic benefit to employers and that they relinquished it only when the state, for political and moral reasons, compelled them to. The other older narrative holds just the opposite, that bodily coercion of labor produced sullen, inefficient workers and that smart employers avoided using it at all costs. Hence, free wage labor was the spontaneous result of the operation of employer interests in free markets rather than a product of political intervention.

But the traditional narrative does not fit very well with what we now know about the widespread use of penal pressure, a form of bodily coercion, in nineteenth century English wage labor. If it can be shown that employers used penal pressure in nineteenth century metropolitan wage labor markets because of the economic benefits they could derive, then the traditional economic logic underlying the free labor narrative would have to be completely revised. Free labor could not be understood to have been the natural outcome of the operation of employer interests in free markets. And we would be faced with the task of constructing a historical narrative of wage labor based on the idea that employers found bodily coercion of economic benefit in a variety of market settings, and relinquished non-pecuniary coercive power only when the state compelled them to. But *was* penal pressure of economic benefit to employers in metropolitan wage labor markets?

It is on this question that the institutional economists with their transaction costs perspective can be of help. Some years ago Yoram Barzel pointed out that neither hourly wages nor piece work wages completely eliminate the need for supervision (and hence supervision costs) in waged labor. He also pointed out that employers of waged labor faced supervision problems that were not completely unlike those faced by slave owners. "Owners had the choice," he wrote, "between supervising their slaves' output [as to quality], which is comparable to what employers have to do when the free workers they employ work by the piece, and supervising their effort, which is comparable to what employers have to do when they employ free workers by the hour" (Barzel 1989, 80). Because the interests of waged workers cannot be perfectly aligned with the interests of their employers, agency costs (a type of transaction cost) inevitably arise in the course of production.

These agency costs are of two kinds, costs of supervision to enforce effort or to guarantee quality and residual costs of reduced output or low quality that cannot be eliminated through cost effective supervision. Threats of dismissal can certainly raise the costs of shirking to workers and may help to control supervision costs, but dismissal is not always a good option for employers. If the waged labor is skilled and labor markets are tight then the threat of dismissal loses a good deal of its power.

Unemployment among skilled workers in England has been estimated to have been below 4% in 11 of the 15 years between 1860 and 1875 (Beveridge 1960, Appendix A; Pigou 1929, Appendix Table 1). Suppose now that sloppiness or loafing at work can bring a prison term at hard labor, and that the law makes an inexpensive, summary process available to enforce that penalty. The prospect of prison at hard labor would seem to increase the expected costs of shirking to workers at little additional cost to employers, yielding less shirking with lower supervision costs overall. At a time when supervision strategies in many industries were not well developed, these advantages could have been substantial. This is a difficult proposition to prove definitively, but there are numerous examples in nineteenth century England of employers prosecuting workers who failed to work as hard or continuously as was expected. "George Heywood of West Bromwich," for example,

was a bundler at the furnace of an iron works with both puddlers and millmen dependent upon him. Because he left his labour for a few hours, "the work was very much in arrears and other men were idle." He was given the option of paying £5 damages or having two months in prison and remarked that "he would have to have the two months." (Woods 1982, 105)

A puddler working the night shift at an iron works in Walsall, Stafford-shire left iron in the furnace overnight where it spoiled, causing his employer substantial damage. He was given a twenty-one day sentence (Woods 1982, 105). George Odger, a shoemaker in the putting out system, testified during the 1860s that

Any decent man . . . is apt to be terrified with the thought that his employer would feel disposed to have him before a magistrate for [a] breach of contract. . . . I think it would be about two months ago . . . I went over the time [for returning finished work], the first time I ever did in my life; [my employer] called at my house when I was out and threatened that if he had not the work in a given time he would proceed against me in the ordinary way for breach of contract. I went home and then went to the workshop and worked nearly all night to get the work to him the next day, which embarrassed me a good deal because I had been at work all the day before. I do not know whether he would have carried out his threat or not, but I was within his clutches if I did not make the boots. (Parliamentary Papers 1866, XIII, Q 1813)

A summary criminal penalty for contract breach might have helped employers lower other types of transaction costs as well. Turnover costs are the costs an employer bears when a worker departs. One of the most significant elements of turnover costs is often the cost of lost output between the departure of a worker and his subsequent replacement. But an employer must also frequently bear search costs and training costs. Turnover is far from costless in the case of skilled labor, even in thick labor markets, and may be especially high when markets are tight. In England in the years between 1857 and 1875, employers prosecuted workers under the Master and Servant acts much more frequently when unemployment was low than when it was high, and as noted it was often very low in this period (Steinfeld 2001, 75–77). There is abundant evidence from the period that employers commonly used contracts of a fortnight or a month to regulate turnover, to prevent workers from leaving suddenly, possibly disrupting production, and to give themselves time to locate replacement workers. If a worker was not free to leave immediately but was required to give two weeks' or a month's notice, by the time he *was* free to leave, other offers of employment might no longer remain open and in those cases turnover costs might be avoided altogether.

In addition, a well-timed policy of signing skilled workers to criminally enforceable labor contracts of a year or several years, which employers commonly did in this period, might have helped to lower labor costs in another way, by slowing the rate of wage increases during periods of low unemployment. Workers bound by a criminally enforceable contract were obligated to work for the wages they had originally agreed upon even if a tight labor market began to drive wages up. Unemployment was extremely low, for example, in 1864 and 1865, and employers in the pottery trade began to try to impose annual contracts on their workmen. One potter complained that "seeing that trade is now in a prosperous state, that long period of agreement takes from the workman the power of raising the price of his labour" (Parliamentary Papers 1866, XIII, Q. 1410). In June, 1865 a skilled artisan named Clarke signed a two-year contract to work for a cutlery manufacturer. In November, Clarke left and Unwin, his employer, prosecuted him for contract breach. Clarke answered that "he had applied to [his employer] to make an advance in his wages in the same manner that the large majority of the cutlery manufacturers in Sheffield had recently done to their hired workmen, which the appellants had refused to do, and in consequence thereof he had felt himself justified in refusing to work for them at the low rate of wages" (Parliamentary Papers 1866, 1 L.R. 417, 418). In 1865 unemployment among skilled workers hovered around 2% (Beveridge 1960, Appendix A; Pigou 1929, Appendix Table 1). The magistrates warned Clarke that the contract prices could not be raised except by mutual consent, that Unwin was unwilling to agree to an increase, and that Clarke must return to work at the old prices or be imprisoned. Clarke answered that he would rather go to prison than return to work at the original prices. The justices obliged, sentencing Clarke to 21 days at hard labor. When he was released, he returned to Unwin to retrieve his tools, but Unwin insisted that Clarke must still work out his contract at the original prices. Clarke refused and was prosecuted again. The court ruled that he could be imprisoned a second time, and at this point Clarke had had enough, deciding to return to work on the original terms (Parliamentary Papers 1866, XIII, Q. 864, 1 L.R. 417, 418–19).

It is true that this system of criminally enforceable labor contracts held disadvantages as well as advantages for employers. In tight labor markets this system might make it more difficult for an employer to obtain skilled labor. In slack labor markets s/he might have to worry about contractual obligations to workers s/he had undertaken in more prosperous times. But taken all together employers derived considerable economic benefits from their power criminally to enforce the performance of the labor agreements of various lengths under which almost all skilled English workers were employed.

These economic benefits explain why employers continued to prosecute workers under the Master and Servant acts with great enthusiasm up until almost the moment the acts were repealed. In 1871 unemployment among skilled workers fell to 1.6%, in 1872 to 0.9%. In 1873 it rose slightly to 1.2% and in 1874 to 1.7% (Beveridge 1960, Appendix A; Pigou 1929, Appendix Table 1). During the year 1870, employers prosecuted 8,670 workers in England and Wales for offences under the Master and Servant acts. But in 1871 as unemployment plunged, they prosecuted 10,810 workers and in 1872 prosecutions soared to 17,082 and then came down slightly in 1873 to 16,230. But in 1875, the very year the Master and Servant acts were repealed, prosecutions were still at a level of 14,353 (Judicial Statistics 1857–1875).

These are large numbers, but they represent only a small percentage of the laboring population and it is impossible definitively to answer the question of whether prosecutions were actually effective in accomplishing employers' goals. (For a discussion of this problem see Steinfeld 2001, 72–82.) But we do have some evidence bearing on the issue. One justice of the peace who was an employer testified that he had not brought very many prosecutions under the Master and Servant acts because "the moral effect of having the power is often sufficient" (Parliamentary Papers 1866, XIII, Q. 1441). We also know that local newspapers throughout the country reported these prosecutions in their daily and weekly crime columns bringing them to the attention of local workmen. At the very least, the acts loomed large enough in the lives of working people to induce them to persevere in a decade and a half long campaign to have the acts reformed.

Taken all together the economic benefits employers likely derived by using coercive pressures also help to explain why ruling elites did not give up the Master and Servant Acts without a long struggle. It took organized British labor almost 15 years of campaigning before the acts were repealed, and over this period the system of penal coercion was defended tenaciously in Parliament. Concessions were made only grudgingly and a great deal of effort was expended to preserve the core practices of the old system for as long as possible. (For an extended discussion of these Parliamentary battles see Steinfeld 2001, Ch. 6.) English employers clearly believed that they profited by the use of penal pressure in wage labor, used such pressure regularly in their dealings with wage workers, and resisted efforts to deprive them of the power. A transaction costs perspective, focusing on the ways in which penal coercion could lower supervision and turnover costs, and keep wages in check while labor markets were tight, clarifies why employers would have acted in this way. A compelling economic logic existed for the continued use of non-pecuniary pressure in wage labor long after the advent of industrial capitalism.

In the traditional narrative of free labor, employer interests provide the driving force behind the rejection of coercion. But if employer interests actually pointed toward the retention of forms of bodily coercion in wage labor, the driving force behind the rejection of coercion must be sought somewhere else, given that bodily coercion *was* ultimately eliminated. In the first instance, it was an act of political intervention that ended, for all intents and purposes, the use of penal pressure in English wage labor. Parliament repealed the Master and Servant acts in 1875, compelling employers to relinquish this form of coercive power that they had continued to use against wage workers with great enthusiasm almost until the last moment. This act of political intervention, however, itself requires an explanation. How was it possible for such a fundamental ground rule of labor relations to have been changed in opposition to employer interests? The answer is a complicated one but it is to be sought in the realm of political struggle.

In 1867 Parliament passed the Second Reform Act, which greatly expanded the suffrage. In the United Kingdom as a whole the number of people enfranchised nearly doubled, from about 1.3 million to about 2.4 million (F. B. Smith 1966, 236). In many towns the new suffrage gave artisans and laborers a majority of the vote (Webb 1970, 326; F. B. Smith 1966, 225).

Whatever meaning is attached to the phrase 'working-class,' the potential working-class electorate in English and Welsh boroughs in the period immediately after 1867 was probably about *five times* the size of the working-class electorate in these boroughs before, and over a half their total electorate. (Cowling 1967, 46)

There is a strong case to be made that the expanded suffrage played a critical role in bringing about the end of the old Master and Servant regime in 1875, eliminating the right of employers to seek penal sanctions to pressure their workers into performing labor. But before we discuss the role of the suffrage in this fundamental change in the terms of waged labor, it is necessary to say something about why ruling elites would have expanded the suffrage in the first place.

The best modern authorities reject the Whig interpretation of the passage of suffrage reform. Neither free market industrialization nor liberal ideas made an enlarged suffrage inevitable in England.

[Whig historians] see mid-Victorian parliamentary politics as Liberal politics. They see Liberalism as a doctrine rather than a political party, and Radicalism as truth rather than ideology. They see industrial change on the one hand and political change on the other, and assume a simple, one-way relationship between them. They bypass, ignore or explain away both the hostility to change and the power to resist it which analysis of society at large suggests might be found, not just on one side of the House of Commons but in most parts of both.

They assume, moreover, a straight progression from the reforms of the 1830s to the reforms of the 1870s, neglecting the recession in progressive feeling.... The death of Chartism, the mid-Victorian boom and the hints given, alongside a militant trade unionism, of a contented, loyal and royalist working class in some of the larger cities, produced a sense of political stability and distrust of Radical motion which impregnated the social attitude of a great part of the House of Commons. If the Reform bill of 1867 symbolized the beginning of a period of rapid political change, it did so in a parliament which not only thought of itself as the ruling assembly of a highly stable society but was also in strong reaction against any suggestion that it should be otherwise. (Cowling 1967, 1–2)

During the 1850s and early 1860s a number of attempts to pass suffrage reform failed to make any headway in Parliament. Indeed, in 1866, just a year before the Second Reform Bill passed, a much less radical reform bill brought to the floor by Gladstone and the Liberal Party went down to defeat in Parliament (F. B. Smith 1966, 110). Ultimately a combination of factors led to electoral reform in 1867, the most important of which seems to have been the widespread desire among ruling elites to reach a limited political settlement with the increasingly well organized and restive working classes, and a political competition between Gladstone and Disraeli and the Liberal and Conservative Parties for electoral advantage in the near term future (F. B. Smith 1966, 229). The Reform Bill of 1867 was brought forward and passed by a Conservative government. While it cannot be claimed that the working classes "compelled" Parliament to enact the Reform Bill, it is nevertheless the case that as a result of the defeat of the Liberal suffrage reform bill in 1866, trade unionists and middle class radicals launched and sustained an out-of-doors agitation for suffrage reform that lasted nearly a year until "the borough suffrage provisions of the Conservative Bill were transformed and safe" (F. B. Smith 1966, 229). During this long period, mass demonstrations were held in nearly every major English city sometimes drawing as many as 150,000 people (F. B. Smith 1966, 139–40).

The expanded suffrage played a critical role in determining the ultimate fate of bodily coercion in English wage labor. It is possible to assess the impact of suffrage reform by comparing the very different results of two efforts to reform the Master and Servant acts that were undertaken within a few years of each other, the first before suffrage reform and the second after. During the early 1860s, trade unionists launched a campaign to reform the Master and Servant acts. In 1867, almost at the same time that the Second

Reform Bill was making its way through Parliament, Parliament was also considering reform of the Master and Servant acts. In August of that year Parliament did pass a Master and Servant reform act. But this first reform act was passed by a Parliament that had been elected under the old, unreformed suffrage and it did not free working people from the penal pressures to which they had long been subject in their work.

Lord Elcho, a conservative Whig, introduced the bill which ultimately became the first Master and Servant reform act. In 1866 Elcho had voted against Gladstone's suffrage bill because he thought that it did not go far enough to secure a durable political and economic settlement with the working classes. Thinking that the Tories would reward him for his role in defeating Gladstone's bill the previous year, he pressed the new Tory government in 1867 to bring forward a Master and Servant act reform bill. But the government refused and Elcho, thinking that reform was necessary immediately if social peace was to be maintained, introduced his own member's bill.

During the previous session, Elcho had been appointed chairman of the parliamentary committee established to study the problem of the Master and Servant acts. Elcho had been chosen in part because of his relationship to trade unionists. As an old-fashioned paternalist he hoped to introduce just enough reform to stabilize old hierarchies. The trade unionist agitation of the previous years had convinced him that the Master and Servant acts had to be reformed and his bill went some distance toward meeting unionist complaints. The chief complaint was that criminal compulsion violated the principle of equal treatment under law. Employers were not subject to similar criminal penalties for breaches of their side of labor agreements. Moreover, trade unionists contended, criminal penalties to enforce private agreements represented a complete anomaly in contract law. Breaches of contract ordinarily gave rise to civil actions for damages not to criminal prosecutions. The Master and Servant acts were intolerable examples of class legislation.

Elcho's bill attempted to meet some of these objections by making proceedings under the Master and Servant law as nearly civil in nature as seemed politically possible under the circumstances. In an apparent effort to preserve the civil nature of proceedings under a new Master and Servant act, Elcho's bill established an entirely separate procedure for criminal prosecutions and indicated that such prosecutions should be based only on acts that were already criminal under the general criminal law. Nevertheless, from a modern perspective, Elcho's bill was far from ideal. It continued to give employers the power to seek specific performance of labor agreements (a civil remedy), and it by no means entirely abolished the continued possibility of criminal prosecution for contract breach.

When the Elcho bill was introduced into parliament, nevertheless, it ran into stiff opposition. Most of the members who spoke thought that reform of Master and Servant law was necessary but that Elcho's bill simply went too far. Mr. Alderman Salomons, for example, said that

he must express his approval of the Bill. It was founded on reciprocity of principle between master and servant. By the present law, the master was responsible civilly – the servant criminally. [Nevertheless] [i]n all cases where, by the Act of the servant, any injury was inflicted upon the master which could not be compensated by fine, an option of imprisonment... ought still to be left. (Debate over Lord Elcho's bill, Hansard's Parliamentary Debates 1867, CLXXXVII, col. 1607, June 4)

A smaller group in parliament spoke out against even the principle of reform. Mr. Liddell said that he

could not agree that the House would do well to adopt the whole principle of the present Bill. That principle was the abandonment of the punitive process against the workmen and the doing away with the deterrent effect of the present law. (Hansard's Parliamentary Debates 1867, col. 1606, June 4)

Mr. Jackson added,

Was a man, having charge of an engine at a pit's mouth, who got drunk and ran away to be dealt with merely as a debtor, though he might leave 400 or 500 fellow workmen below in enforced idleness and in cruel uncertainty for six or seven hours? It was the knowledge that under the existing law he would be dealt with very differently which kept such a man from getting drunk and running away. (Hansard's Parliamentary Debates 1867, col. 1611, June 4)

The weight of opinion in Parliament seems to have been that the principle that masters and men should stand on a plane of equality had to be conceded, but that the details of any new legislation should preserve as much of the old penal system as possible. Lord Elcho's bill was heavily amended in the course of parliamentary deliberations. When it emerged from committee and was enacted into law as the 1867 Master and Servant Reform Act, the new act retained much more of the traditional law than had Lord Elcho's original bill. Employers could still seek immediate imprisonment for "aggravated" breaches of contract however those might be defined by the magistrates, and for "ordinary" breaches of contract they could now seek an order requiring a worker to perform his agreement. Given that employers had traditionally used the Master and Servant acts to force workers back to work more often than to imprison them, this was not a large concession.

Just eight years later, in 1875, a Tory government introduced a new bill to reform Master and Servant law and in a Parliament elected under the reformed suffrage the bill received an entirely different reception than had Lord Elcho's bill in 1867. Following suffrage reform, labor had begun to take a more active role in electoral politics. For a number of reasons trade unionists had grown deeply disaffected with the Liberal government by the time the general election of 1874 was called. During the election campaign many Tory candidates played to this antipathy in an effort to win over

newly enfranchised workers (Webb and Webb 1920, 287). The results of
the election of 1874 were somewhat of a surprise: the Tories won by a wide
margin and one factor in their victory seems to have been the active hostility
of organized labor toward the Liberal Party (Webb and Webb 1920, 286;
Blake 1967, 536). To redeem its electoral pledges the Tory government
introduced in 1875 a bill to further reform Master and Servant law.

The Tory bill was similar in its terms to the one that Lord Elcho had
introduced in 1867 but that had been rejected by Parliament as too radical. In 1875, however, the dominant reaction in Parliament was that the
government bill failed to go far enough. Apparently, once the Conservative government made the decision to place reform on the agenda, it set in
motion a process that carried the bill further and further along in the direction of abolishing penal sanctions for labor contract breaches altogether.
Liberal members competed with Tory members to outdo one another in
currying favor with newly enfranchised working class voters. The Liberal
member Robert Lowe, who in 1866 had played a large role in the defeat of
Gladstone's bill to reform the suffrage, now objected that the government
bill unjustifiably preserved a number of penal features of the old law. And
he was joined in these objections by Lord Montagu. If an act is a crime, they
argued, it should be a crime whether or not the person is under contract
and regardless of his status in life. Criminal law should impose broad legal
duties. Making breach of a labor contract an element of a crime smacked of
class legislation, singling workers out for degrading treatment just as in the
past. Lord Montagu observed that

to break a civil contract was a civil act, and we had no right to inquire into intention.
In the case of a minute contract [employment at will], a man at the pumping engine
of a mine might walk away without notice, immense damage might be done to
property, and yet the act would not be a criminal one. But if there was a contract
for a week, the man who should do the same act would commit a crime... [If
an act is a crime it should be a crime regardless of whether the person is serving
under a labor contract]. (Hansard's Parliamentary Debates 1875, CCXXV, col. 656,
June 28)

In the course of parliamentary deliberations the government bill was
heavily amended pushing the legislation further and further in the direction
of completely eliminating the penal aspects of the old Master and Servant
law. The Employers and Workmen Act of 1875 profoundly changed the
basic terms of English waged labor.

A broadened suffrage, of course, was not the only factor in the passage of
the 1875 act. The state of labor's trade union organization and its increasingly active role in electoral politics were also factors. Other factors also
played roles. Certain members of parliament had become increasingly concerned that labor would refuse to enter into any labor contract other than a
contract determinable at will unless Master and Servant law was changed.

But an expanded suffrage was the critical factor in this alteration of the basic ground rules of English wage labor, ground rules that henceforth eliminated, for all practical purposes, the use of penal pressure in wage labor.

This change in basic rules was the result of almost 15 years of political struggle by organized labor, a struggle that until almost the last moment was met with great resistance. English ruling elites did not spontaneously abandon the use of penal pressure because it was proving unprofitable. In 1875 employers prosecuted 14,353 workers for various offences under the old Master and Servant law just as the new law was about to take effect (Judicial Statistics, England and Wales, 1875). Employers did not abandon bodily coercion because it had proved unprofitable. Parliament eliminated them as the result of a complicated set of political circumstances. The logic of the rejection of bodily coercion in English wage labor was a political not an economic logic. If the English case is generalizable, it may well turn out that the story of the abolition of slavery and the story of the emergence of modern free labor are not based on such different logics after all.

To test the hypothesis that political factors – the scope of the suffrage in particular – were often important determinants of whether waged laborers would be subject to forms of penal coercion in a particular state, we might begin by comparing wage labor regimes in England and in the United States. By contrast to England, in America by the eighteenth century, wage workers were not in general subject to having their labor agreements enforced through penal sanctions (Tomlins 2004). Might political factors account for these fundamental differences between the terms on which English and American wage workers served?

Differences in the scope of the suffrage in the two countries, I would argue, account for much of the divergence between wage labor regimes in the two countries. It has been estimated that during the eighteenth century only between 15% and 20% of English male heads of household were qualified to vote for members of the one house of Parliament that was elected (Dinkin 1977, 49; Lindert 2004, 72). These percentages did not increase significantly until the First Reform Bill was enacted in 1832. Even then, until the Second Reform Act was passed in 1867 the overwhelming majority of working people continued to be excluded from the British suffrage. It was within a relative handful of years after a significant number of English working people had been admitted to the suffrage that we find penal sanctions, which had endured for centuries, being eliminated from English wage labor.

Even before the American Revolution the suffrage in America was already much broader than in England. By the middle of the eighteenth century, a majority of adult men were entitled to vote for members of their popular assemblies in the American colonies; in a number of colonies the suffrage was even wider (Dinkin 1977, 49). During the years following the American Revolution, the right to vote was extended further. By 1790, depending upon the state, between 60% and 90% of adult white males were entitled to vote (Dinkin 1982, 39). Representatives elected under this suffrage regime never attempted to pass legislation that would have imposed penal sanctions on ordinary white wage workers.

The scope of the suffrage turns out to be a quite reliable predictor of which categories of workers were and were not subject to penal enforcement of their labor obligations in colonial and post-colonial America. By the eighteenth century, only native born minors serving apprenticeships and imported indentured servants were subject, by and large, to having their labor agreements enforced through penal sanctions, and neither minors nor foreigners enjoyed full membership in the American polity. Neither would have been entitled to vote. By the 1830s white indentured servitude had largely disappeared in the United States, as a result in part of the solidarity white American workers began to show in the 1820s with their foreign counterparts, who had been imported into the country under indenture (Montgomery 1993, 13–39).

After the 1830s and until the Civil War, only free African Americans and sailors appear to have had their labor obligations enforced through penal sanctions and then only in small numbers in a few states (Morris 1948; Harris 1904, 50–55). Here again, it would seem, the scope of the suffrage helps to explain this state of affairs. During the Antebellum period, and as late as 1860, the overwhelming majority of states either did not permit free African Americans to vote or did not permit them to vote on the same terms as white Americans. Only in New England were equal suffrage rights extended to free African Americans (Litwack 1961, 91).

After the Civil War, the Southern States began to pass laws that empowered employers to enforce the labor obligations of their now free African American workers through penal sanctions. In the main, these laws were passed only after African Americans had been stripped of their voting rights as the result of the adoption of literacy tests and poll taxes, and the intensification of white violence against the African American population. Despite the sporadic efforts of the federal government and the federal courts to eliminate these laws and to bring an end to these practices, this coercive Southern labor regime, aimed at disfranchised African Americans, continued to operate until World War II. It was finally eliminated only as a result of the Civil Rights movement of the 1950s and 60s and the voting rights revolution that followed.

We must be grateful to Fogel and Engerman (1974) for their compelling demonstration that bodily coercion in American slavery served the economic interests of masters in extracting labor services cheaply and efficiently, and that slavery in the United States was finally abolished only as a result of political and moral developments. The argument advanced in this chapter is that Fogel and Engerman's insight is generalizable beyond the case of slavery: that the development of free wage labor must also be understood to have been the result of political and moral developments rather than an inevitable by-product of the free play of market forces.

References

Barzel, Yoram. 1989. *Economic Analysis of Property Rights.* New York: Cambridge University Press.

Beveridge, William. 1960. *Full Employment in a Free Society,* Second ed. New York: Norton.

Blake, Robert. 1967. *Disraeli.* London: Oxford University Press.

Coase, Ronald. 1960. "The Problem of Social Cost." *Journal of Law and Economics* 3: 1–44.

Coats, A. W. 1958. "Changing Attitudes to Labour in the Mid-Eighteenth Century." *Economic History Review* 11: 35–51.

Cowling, Maurice. 1967. *1867, Disraeli, Gladstone and Revolution: The Passing of the Second Reform Bill.* London: Cambridge University Press.

Davis, David Brion. 1975. *The Problem of Slavery in the Age of Revolution, 1770–1823.* Ithaca, NY: Cornell University Press.

Dinkin, Robert J. 1977. *Voting in Provincial America: A Study of Elections in the Thirteen Colonies, 1689–1776.* Westport, CT: Greenwood Press.

Dinkin, Robert J. 1982. *Voting in Revolutionary America: A Study of Elections in the Original Thirteen States, 1776–1789.* Westport, CT: Greenwood Press.

Domar, Evsey. 1970. "The Causes of Slavery or Serfdom: A Hypothesis." *Journal of Economic History* 30: 18–32.

Eggertsson, Thrainn. 1990. *Economic Behavior and Institutions.* New York: Cambridge University Press.

Fogel, Robert and Engerman, Stanley. 1974. *Time on the Cross: The Economics of American Negro Slavery.* Boston: Little Brown.

Hansard. *Parliamentary Debates.*

Harris, N. Dwight. 1904. *The History of Negro Servitude in Illinois and of the Slavery Agitation in That State, 1779–1864.*

Hay, Douglas. 1988. "Master, Servants, Justices and Judges." Unpublished manuscript.

Hay, Douglas. 1990. "Penal Sanctions, Masters and Servants." Unpublished manuscript. *Judicial Statistics, England and Wales, 1857–1875* (19 Vols.). London: HMSO.

Lindert, Peter. 2004. *Growing Public: Social Spending and Economic Growth Since the 18th Century.* New York: Cambridge University Press.

Litwack, Leon. 1961. *North of Slavery: The Negro in the Free States, 1790–1860.* Chicago: University of Chicago Press.

Montgomery, David. 1993. *Citizen Worker: The Experience of Workers in the United States with Democracy and the Free Market during the Nineteenth Century.* New York: Cambridge University Press.

Morris, Richard. 1948. "Labor Controls in Maryland in the Nineteenth Century." *Journal of Southern History* 14: 385–400.

Nash, Gary. 1979. *The Urban Crucible.* Cambridge, MA: Harvard University Press.

North, Douglass. 1981. *Structure and Change in Economic History.* New York: W.W. Norton.

Novak, Daniel. 1978. *The Wheel of Servitude: Black Forced Labor After Slavery.* Lexington: University Press of Kentucky.

Parliamentary Papers. 1866. XIII. *Select Committee on the Master and Servant Act.*

Pigou, A. C. 1929. *Industrial Fluctuations,* Second ed. London: Macmillan.

Salinger, Sharon. 1987. *'To Serve Well and Faithfully,' Labor and Indentured Servants in Pennsylvania, 1682–1800.* New York: Cambridge University Press.

Schmidt, Benno C., Jr. 1982. "Principle and Prejudice: The Supreme Court and Race in the Progressive Era. Part 2. The 'Peonage Cases'." *Columbia Law Review* 82: 646–718.

Simon, Daphne. 1954. "Master and Servant." In John Saville, ed. *Democracy and the Labour Movement: Essays in Honour of Dona Torr.* London: Lawrence and Wishart.

Smith, Adam. 1976. *The Wealth of Nations,* edited by Edwin Cannan. London: Methuen.

Smith, F. B. 1966. *The Making of the Second Reform Bill.* Carlton: Melbourne University Press.

Statute U.K. 1823. 4 Geo. IV, c. 34.

Steinfeld, Robert. 2001. *Coercion, Contract and Free Labor in the Nineteenth Century.* New York: Cambridge University Press.

Tomlins, Christopher. 2004. "Early British America, 1585–1830: Freedom Bound." In Douglas Hay and Paul Craven, eds. *Masters, Servants, and Magistrates in Britain and the Empire, 1562–1955.* Chapel Hill: University of North Carolina Press.

Unwin v. Clarke. 1866. 1 *The Law Reports* 417. London.

Webb, R. K. 1970. *Modern England.* New York: Dodd, Mead.

Webb, Sidney and Webb, Beatrice. 1920. *The History of Trade Unionism.* New York: Longmans, Green.

Whatley, Christopher. 1987. "'The Fettering Bonds of Brotherhood': Combination and Labour Relations in the Scottish Coal-Mining Industry, c. 1690–1775." *Social History* 12: 139–54.

Woods, D. C. 1982. "The Operation of the Master and Servants Act in the Black Country, 1858–1875." *Midlands History* 7: 93–118.

10

Prodigals and Projectors: An Economic History of Usury Laws in the United States from Colonial Times to 1900

Hugh Rockoff

I. WHY SHOULD ECONOMIC HISTORIANS STUDY USURY LAWS?[1]

With a few notable exceptions, such as Friedman (1963) and Glaeser and Scheinkman (1998), historians and economists writing about the financial history of the United States have ignored usury laws. Many of the classic financial histories of the United States do not even mention them. Yet there are several good reasons for studying usury laws. For one thing usury laws have been, arguably, the most common form of economic regulation. Usury is mentioned in the Bible and the Koran. There were usury laws in ancient Rome, although not in classical Athens (Finley 1953). And, the medieval canonists developed a detailed theory of usury. Usury laws have not been confined to countries influenced by European cultural traditions. In India, during the Buddhist period, it was recommended that interest be limited to 15 percent per year on secured loans and to 60 percent per year on unsecured loans (Seth 1955, 6). In traditional China the maximum rate was 3 percent per month, and the penalty for charging more was 40 to 100 blows with the light cane (Alabaster 1899, 550–51). Usury laws, moreover, have been the subject of classic works of literature, such as *The Merchant of Venice*. The usury laws in England were repealed in 1854 (although legislation protecting borrowers was reinstated at the turn of the century), but in the United States they were continued in many U.S. states down to the present day.

Usury laws, unlike most other forms of economic regulation, are relatively easy to quantify. During the period of concern here, from colonial times to 1900, they usually took the form of a maximum rate, a round number:

[1] I wish to thank Eugene White for sharing his Bank of A. Levy data and Zorina Khan for helping me get started on the court cases on usury. They, along with Howard Bodenhorn, Michael Bordo, Ira Gang, and Frank Lewis also made a number of helpful suggestions for improving a previous draft. I am also grateful for the chance to present the paper at a seminar at Rutgers and at the seminar in honor of Stanley L. Engerman held at the University of Rochester.

0, 6, 10, etc. The penalties for evading the usury laws, moreover, although often neglected in discussions of the law, are easily quantified. The penalty was typically forfeiture of interest and principal, forfeiture of interest alone, or something similar. By positing a standard loan contract we can reduce these disparate penalties to a common denominator. To be sure, usury laws sometimes included provisions that are not easily quantified. The maximum legal rate, for example, might differ among lenders or by type of loan, and criminal penalties might be imposed. But for the most part, the usury laws can be quantified, allowing us to draw a long-run picture of the history of usury laws, and to make generalizations about what determined the history of usury laws that may carry over to less easily quantified forms of regulation.

The level of the usury rate, moreover, provides some insight into the typical rate of interest for times and places when market quotations are scarce. Indeed, in some cases, the usury rate may be a more accurate reflection of the market rate than the quotations normally relied upon, which are often the rates on government bonds or other atypical borrowing instruments. The usefulness of the usury rate as a proxy for the market rate of interest would depend on how usury rates were determined in relation to the bulk of credit transactions. So an understanding of the political economy of maximum rates can contribute to their usefulness as a record of rates.

The main reason economic historians neglect usury laws is the conviction that they were easily evaded and therefore had almost no effect. Suppose a borrower and lender want to contract a loan at 30 percent interest when the legal maximum is 10 percent. What is to stop the borrower from signing a bond that says that 10 percent is to be paid on $100 (a legal contract), while in fact receiving only $85 in cash, or perhaps paying a "fee" of $15 for the services of arranging the loan?[2] The answer is nothing. The suggestion, then, is that the legal maximum has minimal effect.

Alternative means of evading the laws, moreover, are legion. Perhaps one of the most frequently used ways of evading usury laws is by claiming that a usurious payment is a charge for late payment. One of the earliest cases I have seen of this form of evasion in the United States is said to have occurred in Virginia in 1760. The legal maximum was 5 percent. However, interest at 10 percent could be charged on a bill of exchange that was refused. A "gentlemen of some means," it is said, agreed to draw a bill on a firm in London that he did not know so that his banker could charge 10 percent. Unfortunately, the firm on which the bill was drawn recognized the name of the drawer, assumed that he intended to open a relationship, and so accepted the bill. The banker complained that he had been tricked by being given a good bill instead of a bad one! (Kirkland 1865, vol. 1, 217).[3]

---

[2] This tactic known was known as "note shaving" in nineteenth-century America.
[3] The use of protested bills to evade Virginia's usury laws is also mentioned in Farnam (1938, 91).

Although these devices provide a good deal of protection for the lender against the risk that a contract will be found to be usurious in the event that the lender is forced to sue – courts are generally unwilling to set aside a signed contract, unless they have a strong motive for doing so – evasive devices do not reduce a lender's risk to zero. True, the lender has, as Shylock says, his bond. Should a borrower refuse to pay and offer usury as a defense, however, a judge is always in a position to find for the borrower, as Shylock found when he finally had his day in court. The risk that the borrower will escape paying by claiming that the loan was usurious – a risk that cannot be eliminated as long as the law is on the books – is bound to have some effect on the behavior of borrowers and lenders.

The usury laws of the colonial period and the early part of the nineteenth century that applied rigid limits and strict penalties to a wide range of trans-actions are now gone, and for that reason we tend to neglect them. Strict usury laws, however, may have been an important influence by forcing sav-ings into safer channels: low-risk financial investments and human capital. Usury laws, moreover, are still important mainly for protecting vulnerable consumers. The laws at issue in the current controversy over the extremely high rates charged for "payday loans" – small loans typically due at the next payday and secured by a postdated check or by an agreement that permits a bank to deduct principal and interest from a paycheck – have their roots in the usury laws discussed below.[4]

The remainder of the paper is structured as follows. Section 2 discusses the history of thought about usury laws through the period of liberalization in the nineteenth century. Changing ideas, I show, had a good deal to do with the liberalization of the usury laws. Section 3 discusses the repeal of the British laws, an important precedent for the United States. Section 4 examines the changes in U.S. usury laws in the nineteenth century from a quantitative perspective. Section 5 focuses on the debate over the usury provision of the National Banking Act. This debate in the financial press and in Congress throws a good deal of light on the factors driving liberalization of the usury laws. Section 6 summarizes some of the evidence that suggests that the economic historian's working assumption that the usury laws had no effect needs rethinking. Section 7 draws some conclusions. The narrative is written as if two factors – changing ideas about the efficacy of usury laws and competition among states for capital – explain the changing structure of the usury laws. But the evidence for correlation between changes in ideas about usury and an increase in competition among states for capital, on the

---

[4] Payday loans are discussed in "Risky Business: Exploiting a Loophole, Banks Skirt State Laws on High Interest Rates," by Paul Beckett, *Wall Street Journal*. Friday, May 25, 2001, 1+. Some lenders rely on national banks for their capital because national banks can charge interest rates based on the law of the state where the bank is located rather than where the borrower is located. The origin of this arrangement is discussed in Section 5.

one hand, and liberalization of the usury laws, on the other, is much stronger than the evidence for causation. Perhaps what follows is best regarded as a listing of the candidate hypotheses.

II. THE CHANGING INTELLECTUAL CLIMATE

The evolution of usury laws paralleled, and I believe to some extent was produced by, changes in ideas about usury. A brief sketch of the history of the "high theory" of usury laws will therefore be a useful way of setting the stage for the history U.S. usury laws that follows, and of describing one of the explanatory factors.

Broadly speaking we can distinguish two strands of support for usury laws: moral arguments that can be traced in the West to the Bible and to the ancient Greek philosophers, and economic arguments that can be traced to the mercantilists and (of all people) Adam Smith. The erosion of support for these arguments for usury laws coincided with a liberalization of the usury laws.

The evolution of religious and philosophical ideas about usury could fill many volumes.[5] Here I will simply summarize some of the ideas that seem to have influenced American lawmakers. The Old Testament, as it was usually interpreted, prohibited interest taking among the Jews, although not between Jews and non-Jews. There are three passages. In two, the prohibition on taking interest follows admonitions to be charitable toward the poor, and so seems connected mainly with charity toward the poor. But the most famous passage, Deuteronomy 23:20–21, appears to apply in all circumstances: "You shall not lend upon interest to your brother: interest on money, interest of victuals, interest on anything that is lent for interest. Unto a foreigner you mayest lend upon interest; but unto thy brother thou shalt not lend upon interest. . . . "[6] This passage became the basis for the belief of the early Christians and the medieval church that the prohibition on usury should be extended to all Christians. And it left the way open for the Jews living among Christians to become moneylenders. The New Testament also contains passages that seem to prohibit lending at interest, particularly Luke 6:35: "Lend freely, hoping nothing thereby." It has been suggested by Taeusch (1942, 313) that the survival of usury restrictions in the United States, although as we will see in a greatly attenuated form as opposed to their repeal in Britain, can be traced to the greater influence of biblical fundamentalism in the United States.

---

[5] Glaeser and Scheinkman (1998, 23–36) provide a wide-ranging summary.

[6] The quotation is from the version of the Holy Scriptures published by the Jewish Publication Society of America in 1917. Sometimes the passage is translated differently. Using the word "usury" instead of "interest" would imply greater tolerance for lending.

The tension between the stark religious doctrine that the lending of money among brothers is immoral and the needs of a commercial economy for credit led to the development of a complex usury doctrine that legitimized interest under several guises.[7] Thomas Aquinas thought that compensation for actual loss (*damnum emergens*) was permissible, and he discussed, although with hesitation, compensation for the cessation of gain (*lucrum cessans*). Other exceptions included compensation for damage caused by the failure to return payment at the agreed time (*poena conventionalis*). According to Cunningham (1905, vol. 1, 258) this exception, an obvious way of evading the usury prohibition, took a prominent place in medieval transactions.

The struggle over the morality of interest taking changed abruptly with the Protestant Reformation (Nelson 1969). Although some of the preaching of the reformers was opposed to taking interest, the reformers ultimately abandoned the idea of creating a "New Jerusalem" – with the implication that Christians would be forced to follow the ancient prohibition against lending at interest. Nelson sees Calvin as the key figure because he clearly stated that the rules about taking interest that bound the ancient Israelites, although perhaps right for their time and place, were not binding in a modern society. Religious thought had progressed, in the apt subtitle of Nelson's book, *From Tribal Brotherhood to Universal Otherhood*.[8]

The other tradition that left a residual in nineteenth-century thinking was that of the ancient Greek philosophers. Aristotle and Plato believed that money was barren. With other forms of capital, cattle for example, we can see the natural multiplication, but not with money. The taking of interest, therefore, was unnatural, and to be prohibited. Centuries later Alfred Marshall (1961, I, 584–86) was still devoting space in his *Principles of Economics* to refuting this argument. Marshall explains at length why lending a horse (a form of capital that is naturally productive) is no different than lending money.

Secular thinking about usury laws (in the English speaking world) can be traced in a trajectory of key contributions reaching from mercantilist writers, in particular Sir Josiah Child, who strongly endorsed usury laws, to John Stuart Mill, who denounced them as a religious superstition. To mercantilist writers such as Child (1668) it made good sense for the state to control the rate of interest. Child believed that low interest rates were the soul of trade. He noted that interest rates were low in prosperous Holland. And he argued that much good had come from the official lowering of the rate of interest in England from 10 to 8 per cent in 1623, and from 8 to 6 per cent in 1660. (See Table 10.1 for the English rates.) The argument was that lowering interest rates prevented the "dissipating class," usually men of

---

[7] I have relied mainly on Noonan (1957) and Nelson (1969).
[8] George (1957) vigorously challenged Nelson's emphasis on Calvin.

TABLE 10.1. *A Chronology of British Usury Laws*

Date	Maximum Rate	Penalties/Comment
Before 1545	0%	Lending at interest was practiced, however, often by members of groups that were not restricted by the usual social norms. From the time of Richard I the law recognized, usually, although not continuously, that Jews were lending at interest and regulated the rate. In 1233, for example, Henry III set the maximum rate that could be charged by Jews at two pence per pound per week, a simple rate of about 43 percent, or about 54 percent when compounded. The Jews were expelled in 1290.
1545	10%	Forfeiture of three times the principal and interest, fines, imprisonment, and ransom at the King's pleasure.
1552	0%	Forfeiture of principal and interest and fines, imprisonment, and ransom at the King's pleasure.
1571	10%	Forfeiture of three times the principal and interest and fines, imprisonment, and ransom at the King's pleasure. Courts would not enforce recovery of more than the principal.
1624	8%	Forfeiture of three times the principal and interest.
1660	6%	Forfeiture of three times the principal and interest.
1713	5%	Forfeiture of three times the principal and interest.
1833		Usury limits removed for bills of exchange with 3 months or less to run; part of the Bank Charter Act. This law frees the Bank of England to raise its discount rate.
1854		Final repeal of the Usury laws. By this time, only limits on rates charged on mortgages secured by land remained on the books.
1900		Moneylenders Act restores the defense of usury.

Sources and Notes: This table has been compiled from various secondary sources, such as Smith (1979 [1776], 106), Holdsworth (1903, volume 8, 110–13), Robinson and Nugent (1935, 28–29), and Jones (1989). It is intended merely to provide a broad-brush picture of the liberalization of the British laws.

property who could borrow on the security of their land, from competing with the merchant class. The King, Child noted, would have to pay a higher rate than the merchant class, because the lending to the King was risky, but lowering rates for the merchant class would lower rates for the King as well.

Child's analysis was not universally accepted (Ryan 1924, 46–47). Sir William Petty wrote a tract opposed to Child's stand on usury laws. And John Locke attacked Child's position as well. Locke pointed out that there were no usury laws in Holland and that low interest rates there were the result rather than the cause of prosperity. Locke did note, however, that usury laws might be useful in preventing the indolent from dissipating their fortunes – a wealthy landowner, for example, could fall into the hands of the usurers and end up losing his estate – a point taken up by later supporters of usury laws. Nevertheless, Child's essay showed that there was a mercantilist as well as moral case to be made for usury laws, and Child's essay appears to have influenced later writers.

Sir James Steuart discussed Child's ideas in his magnum opus, *Inquiry into the Principles of Political Oeconomy* published in 1767. Steuart agreed with Child that regulating the rate of interest and thereby channeling funds to the merchant class was a good idea. However, he objected to a sudden and violent pulling down of the official rate, of the sort that had happened in 1623 and 1660. All sorts of problems would be created if this was tried again, especially if the rate was forced below the rate in rival countries, notably the Netherlands. Instead, Steuart recommended a rate sufficiently above the conventional commercial rate "so as to leave a reasonable latitude for gentle fluctuations above it."

Adam Smith, although critical of much in Steuart, famously took a similar position on the rate of interest.[9] Too restrictive an interest ceiling would be a mistake; but a ceiling that was above, but not too much above, the market rate would prove beneficial. For the underlying reasoning, we can do no better than to quote Smith (1979 [1776], 357).

The legal rate, it is to be observed, though it ought to be above, ought not to be much above the lowest market rate. If the legal rate of interest in Great Britain, for example, was fixed so high as eight or ten per cent, the greater part of the money which was to be lent, would be lent to prodigals and projectors, who alone would be willing to give this high interest. Sober people, who will give for the use of money no more than part of what they are likely to make by the use of it, would not venture into the competition. A great part of the capital of the country would thus be kept out of the hands which were most likely to make a profitable and advantageous use of it, and thrown into those which were most likely to waste and destroy it. Where the legal rate of interest, on the contrary, is fixed but a very little above the lowest market rate, sober people are universally preferred as borrowers, to prodigals and projectors.

---

[9] Although Steuart was Smith's bête noire, it is one of Smith's affectations that he never cites Steuart by name.

By "prodigals" Smith meant people who had the wherewithal to borrow large sums of money for consumption purposes, perhaps the dissipated son of a rich landlord.[10] And by "projectors" he meant entrepreneurs raising money for wild and improbable schemes. Smith does not say what examples he has in mind when he speaks of projectors. Steuart mentioned the Mississippi and South Sea bubbles in this context, and presumably Smith would have included them in a list of foolish schemes touted by projectors, although it would have been typical of Smith to have more current examples in mind as well.[11]

The point in time when economic opinion swung decisively against usury laws can be dated with accuracy: the publication of Jeremy Bentham's *Defense of Usury*. Cast as a series of letters, the first was postmarked *Crichoff, in White Russia, January 1787*. It was a tour de force – passionate, detailed, logical, and filled with rhetorical flourishes. Bentham covered most of the points that would be covered in a modern textbook: (1) Usury laws prevent mutually beneficial trades among informed adults, (2) usury laws force desperate borrowers into the hands of unscrupulous lenders where the borrowers pay higher rates than they would in an unfettered market, rates that insure against the risk of nonpayment occasioned by the usury laws themselves, (3) the usury laws are often evaded in ways that add to the costs of doing business, and so on.

Bentham recognized that no argument against usury laws could succeed that did not take on Adam Smith, and so the last of his letters was addressed to Smith. Bentham thought it unlikely that prodigals would be affected by the lifting of usury laws. As long as a prodigal still had property to offer as collateral he could borrow on the same terms as others. Once his capital was exhausted, he could only rely on friends and on the delivery of goods by tradesmen; borrowing money would be nearly impossible at any rate of interest. It was on the issue of projectors that Bentham worked the hardest. Smith favored usury laws because they kept money out of the hands of foolish projectors. Progress, Bentham asserted, had been the result of smart projectors. Where would we be, Bentham asks, what would our living standards be today, if it had not been for the projectors in the past?

---

[10] Richard Brinsley Sheridan's classic, *The School for Scandal*, a play about a prodigal son, complete with Jewish moneylender, was first produced on Drury Lane in 1777.

[11] Smith's departure from Laissez Faire in this case, as in similar cases, has continued to attract the attention of economists and historians of economic thought. See, for example, Blitz and Long (1965), Jadlow (1977), and Stiglitz and Weiss (1981). The latter provide a rationale for usury laws similar to Smith's. These and other interpretations are discussed in Paganelli (2003), who argues that although modern economists have sympathized with Smith, they have not really understood him because Smith was willing to stipulate permanent misperceptions of reality, an assumption at variance with modern economic thinking. In the present case, the willingness of prodigals and projectors to enter into contracts that reduce their wealth is a case in point.

On the latter issue, Bentham attempted to quote Smith against himself. In the *Wealth of Nations* (1979 [1776], 131) Smith argued that wages would be higher in industries in which new firms were established frequently because in those industries *projectors* would have to entice workers away from existing firms by offering higher wages, and there would be some inertia of wages paid at the existing firms. To illustrate his point Smith contrasted Birmingham, which specialized in industries where demand arose from fashion and fancy, and wages were high, with Sheffield, which specialized in industries where demand arose from necessity, and wages were low. To Bentham this meant that Smith had labeled Birmingham a "projecting" town and Sheffield an "unprojecting" town. Bentham then argued that projecting must be a good thing because Birmingham was more prosperous and growing faster than Sheffield, and therefore on his own evidence Smith should concede that laws designed to reduce projecting were a mistake. Smith might well have replied that since Birmingham's industries had developed under the existing usury law, Birmingham's affluence was evidence that moderate usury laws did not discourage sound projectors.

John Stuart Mill, in his *Principles of Political Economy* (1940 [1871, 1848], 926–30, 1004), describes the laws as having "originated in a religious prejudice against receiving interest on money" and notes that "this restriction though approved by Adam Smith, has been condemned by all enlightened persons since the triumphant onslaught made upon it by Bentham in his *Letters on Usury*." Thus between Adam Smith and John Stuart Mill, "weighty" opinion had turned 180 degrees against the usury laws. This period, as we will see in the next section, also witnessed the abolition of usury laws in Britain, and the liberalization of usury laws in the United States.

Mill was the last of the great British economists of the nineteenth century to devote considerable space in his textbook to the discussion of usury laws. In part this was because the repeal of the usury laws in 1854 made discussion of them a moot point. Marshall's *Principles*, as we noted above, deals with the notion that there is something different about lending a horse from lending money, but does not deal with Smith's arguments. Arthur Cecil Pigou's *The Economics of Welfare* does not even mention usury laws.

What lay behind the change in opinion about usury laws? To some extent, the change in thinking about usury laws was simply a part of a much broader intellectual revolution that was reflected in economics in the rise of Laissez Faire, and in politics in increased concern for democracy and personal liberty. In other words, the fall of the usury laws in England, and their liberalization in the United States, was part of the same wave of trust in Laissez Faire that helped bring down the Corn Laws, and eliminate other restrictions such as those on the price of bread, the export of machinery, and the emigration of skilled labor.

Were there economic changes that lay behind the change in thinking? According to Keynes, *The General Theory* (1965 [1936], 351–53), keeping the rate of interest low was good policy prior to the nineteenth century because, in Keynes's terminology, the "marginal efficiency of investment" was low. The industrial revolution raised the marginal efficiency of investment and changed the balance of costs and benefits of usury laws. More worthwhile investment opportunities existed. One can see this in the examples used to support or oppose usury laws. Sir James Steuart reached back to the South Sea and Mississippi bubbles to show how dangerous projectors could be, and why it would be a good idea to keep money out of their hands. John Stuart Mill (1920 [1871, 1848], 930) pointed to George Stephenson, the railway entrepreneur, who could not have brought his plans to completion, Mill claims, without the ability to borrow at high interest rates. In Keynes's phrase, when we read Bentham's letter to Smith we may be "hearing the voice of the nineteenth century speaking to the eighteenth century."

Today, we casually accept the idea that the government should regulate the rate of interest indirectly through the operations of a central bank. Yet the idea that the government should regulate interest rates directly through usury laws seems foreign. Prior to the nineteenth century, however, monies were as much international as national, and the ability of government banks, such as the Bank of England, to influence interest rates was extremely limited. In such a world the main national instrument for regulating the rate of interest was the usury rate. The rise of national currencies controlled by national banks created an alternative mechanism for controlling interest rates. It was now possible to eliminate usury laws without giving up all governmental control over interest. And the new institutions would have maximum influence if their efforts to raise interest rates were not inhibited by usury rates. In the United States, as we will see below, the decisive pressure to liberalize the usury laws did not come so much from the eastern projectors of new industrial firms as from the western projectors of new agricultural settlements.

The *Defense of Usury* was an immediate and long lasting hit.[12] In England it received favorable reviews and was endorsed by important political figures. Potentially, the most important was Adam Smith. It was reported to Bentham that Smith had told a friend that the "*Defense of Usury* was the work of a very superior man" and that Smith had *seemed* to admit that Bentham was right. Bentham wrote to Smith trying to draw a formal concession. But Smith, who by then was very ill, did no more than send Bentham a copy of the *Wealth of Nations*. Smith's recantation never became a reality.

We cannot know for certain whether if Smith had been in better health, he would have changed his mind on usury laws, or what the effect would have been. Bentham himself (1952–54 [1787], 189) in his letter to Smith

---

[12] The reception of the *Defense of Usury* is described in Stark's introduction to the economic writings of Jeremy Bentham (1952–54, 26–33).

thought that a declaration by Smith against usury laws, especially considering Smith's earlier support of them, would be worth many votes. "We should have the Irish Chancellor of the Exchequer abjuring his annual motion [to reduce the rate of interest in Ireland] in the face of the House, and L[or]d Hawkesbury who, it has been said, is Mr. Pitt's tutor in this wise business, quietly and silently putting his papers and calculations into the fire." A similar conjecture is not out of place for the United States. Banking and interest regulation were debated repeatedly in the United States over the coming century. As influential as Bentham's arguments were, the weight of Adam Smith remained on the side of those who would maintain controls on interest rates. Liberalization of the usury laws might have moved further and faster if the name of Adam Smith could have been enlisted in the cause.

The positive reception of *Defense of Usury* was international. In France, the *Defense* was translated by someone in Mirabeau's circle, and may have influenced the debate over French usury laws then in progress (Bentham 1952-54, 28–29), although the French economists had already made known their opposition to usury laws. Bentham's tract also seems to have been widely read in Dublin in 1788 when a reduction in the usury rate in Ireland from 6 percent to 5 percent was under debate.

Bentham was also influential in the United States, although the extent of his influence is difficult to measure. Bentham received a letter (Stark 1952, 30–31) that reported that "The influence of your writings has already been extensively felt in the United States." The letter went on to catalog attempts to repeal the usury laws in Mississippi, Alabama, Virginia, and New Hampshire as evidence of the triumph of Bentham's principles.[13]

Morton J. Horwitz (1977, 237–45) investigated the legal literature of the period 1780–1850. He found that the attacks on usury laws that were written during this period reflected Bentham's ideas, and often mention Bentham explicitly. Horwitz (1977, 242) observes, for example, that Thomas Cooper's notes to his 1837 edition of the *Statutes of South Carolina* comment that "The public notions on the subject of usury have been totally changed by Jeremy Bentham's brief treatise on the subject...." The defenses of usury laws that Horwitz examined, on the other hand, appear to have gone back to moral, just-price considerations rather than the mercantilist defense. As we will see below, however, hints of the mercantilist doctrine can be seen in the Civil War debate over the usury provision of the National Banking Act.

Most of the economic writers covered in Joseph Dorfman's (1946) classic survey of the antebellum era appear to have been disciples of the British economists, and were opposed to usury laws. The Reverend John McVickar,

---

[13] Usury laws were actually repealed only in Alabama and Mississippi, and then only for a time.

who published his *Outlines of Political Economy*, a commentary on J. R. McCulloch, in 1825, was strongly opposed to usury laws. Langton Byllesby, whom Dorfman (1946, 640) identifies as a Ricardian Socialist, published in 1826 his *Observations on the Sources and Effects of Unequal Wealth*, which includes a statement condemning usury laws. Stephen Simpson published his *Working Man's Manual: A New Theory of Political Economy* in 1831, which argued that "usury laws are reprehensible." The Reverend Francis Wayland, President of Brown University, published perhaps the first free trade textbook in the United States, in 1837, and included a condemnation of usury laws (Dorfman 1946, 760). Jacob Newton Cardozo, editor of the *Southern Patriot*, whom Dorfman (1946, 857) called the South's ablest economic thinker, opposed usury laws and called for "freedom of banking." George Opdyke's *Treatise on Political Economy* was published in 1851. Opdyke was an enthusiastic follower of John Stuart Mill, and followed Mill in denouncing usury laws (Dorfman 1946, 755–58). In 1864 Arthur Latham Perry, a follower of Bastiat, wrote a series of articles on political economy for the *Springfield* [Massachusetts] *Republican*, which Dorfman (1946, 981) identified as an influential paper. Perry thought usury laws were a mistake, and he was especially critical of the attempt then under consideration to limit National Banks to 7 percent, an episode that will be considered in more detail below. Perry's articles were published a short time before Massachusetts repealed its usury laws.

Indeed, all the antebellum American authors discussed by Dorfman, with the exception of Alexander Bryan Johnson (who thought that low interest rates brought about by usury laws would be good for labor), were strongly opposed to usury laws. It is not surprising, perhaps, to find the usury laws being liberalized during a period in which weighty opinion was so opposed. Weighty opinion by itself, of course, is often insufficient to change a law; economists have often united, for example, in their opposition to high tariffs or other restrictions on international trade to little effect. Below I will turn to another force at work: the effort by western states to attract financial capital. First, however, I will look at the similar liberalization of the usury laws that was taking place in Britain.

III. THE LIBERALIZATION OF THE BRITISH USURY LAWS

It is important to note that British laws underwent a similar liberalization at about the same time, and that the liberalization in Britain has been attributed partly to ideological and intellectual developments. Table 10.1, which I have compiled from various sources, summarizes the history of British usury laws. The modern history of British usury laws began in 1545 when a maximum rate of 10 percent was set. Although the law was couched in terms of the old exceptions to the church's prohibition of interest taking, it seemed to recognize a new economic reality (Cunningham 1905, 152).

Interest was again prohibited in 1551, a law that Adam Smith (1979 [1776], 106) attributed to "religious zeal." But this prohibition was soon reversed, and in 1571 the maximum rate of 10 percent was restored.

As suggested by the reversals in the law, there was considerable debate in England during the sixteenth century about the morality of interest taking (Tawney 1925). Shakespeare's exploration of the economics and morality of usury, *The Merchant of Venice*, was written in 1596.[14] Although disagreements about the morality of interest taking were intense during the sixteenth century, Cunningham (1905–7, 159) concludes that by 1604 "the revolution in public opinion was complete, and that the practice of lending money for moderate interest was at last regarded as entirely reputable."

As shown in Table 10.1 the maximum rate was lowered to 8 percent in 1624, to 6 percent in 1660, and to 5 percent in 1713. Adam Smith (1979 [1776], 106) thought that these reductions had been made "with great propriety," and that the changes seem to "have followed and not to have gone before the market rate of interest." This is where things stood when Bentham wrote his case against the usury laws: a maximum rate of 5 percent and a penalty of three times the principal and interest.

The next major change appears to have occurred in 1833 when usury limits were eliminated on bills of exchange with less than three months to run. This break may have been due to the problems created by the 5 percent rule for bill brokers during the crisis of 1825. The usury laws were finally repealed in 1854. The need for the Bank of England to raise its discount rate in times of crisis, a need that became increasingly clear as the Bank's operating procedures took their classic nineteenth century form, may have played a role in the repeal. The development of the joint stock company – limited liability was introduced in 1855 – may also have been a factor. Bond issues would have been more difficult if companies were legally barred from paying more than 5 percent. The transition from regulated credit markets to unregulated (or at least indirectly regulated) markets, moreover, cannot be divorced from the general movement toward Laissez Faire in England, as manifested by the famous repeal of the Corn Laws in 1848.

The English example, as Louis Robinson and Rolf Nugent (1935, 29) point out, was soon followed by the repeal of the usury laws in a number of European countries: Denmark (1855); Spain (1856); Sardinia, Holland, Norway, and Geneva (1857); and Saxony and Sweden (1864). Canada also followed in 1858. Robinson and Nugent attribute all of these repeals to the

---

[14] Kish-Goodling (1998) provides a superb overview of the economic meaning of the play, and a number of suggestions for using the play as a tool for teaching monetary economics. Shakespeare's father John, it turns out, had been prosecuted for usury in 1570, the last year of the prohibition, a not uncommon occurrence in those days (Thomas and Evans 1984). In one of two cases he was fined 40 shillings. It is not certain how the other case was resolved; Shakespeare's father may have settled with his informer. Peter Levi (1988, 18–20) attributes the prosecution to John Shakespeare's political enemies.

spread of Laissez Faire in general and to Benthamite ideas about usury in particular, and to the example of Britain. Perhaps the international repeal movement also owed something to the fear that a country that did not follow suit would risk losing capital to Britain and to the countries that had repealed. The repeal movement in the United States occurred during a similar period, and the fear that capital would move to regions with liberal usury laws, as well as the ideological pressures cited by Robinson and Nugent, seems to have been at work.

IV. THE LIBERALIZATION OF U.S. USURY LAWS

The basic sources for the usury laws to 1890 are George K. Holmes (1892), and Holmes and John S. Lord (1895), which summarize the legal history of the usury laws in the United States to that date. Where I have been able to check these accounts against studies of individual states, or tables presented in legal journals, Holmes and Lord appears accurate, although slight discrepancies in dating do emerge. Where I found discrepancies I have followed Holmes and Lord, to provide a consistent set of estimates.

Figure 10.1 plots the average maximum rate of interest in the United States as a whole, and in the 13 original colonies, from 1750 to 1890. The averages are simple unweighted means: Massachusetts and Rhode Island count as equal observations. The number of states is steadily growing so that the population on which the national average is based is continually changing. Some laws distinguished between the maximum rate permitted when no rate was specified in the contract, and the maximum rate when the rate was stated explicitly. The data plotted here reflect the latter. A complication is that some states, such as California, permitted any rate so long as the rate was specified in the contract, and some states repealed their laws altogether. My convention was to use 13 percent as the rate for these states when computing the national average. Twelve percent was the highest maximum among most states, although rates as high as 20 percent were permitted under certain laws, so this convention assigns a rate 1 percent above a relatively high rate to those states that repealed their usury laws. Figure 10.1 also shows the average excluding states that repealed.

Evidently, there is a good deal of inertia in these rates. Massachusetts, to take an extreme example, established a rate of 8 percent in 1641. This was lowered to 6 percent in 1693 where it remained until the usury laws were repealed in 1867, a period of 174 years![15] Nevertheless, there is a clear picture of change when we take the long view and look at the national average. Maximum rates began to trend upward after the Revolution, peaked in the 1870s, and then trended downward toward the end of the century. There

---

[15] Colonial usury laws are discussed in Farnam (1938, 88–91).

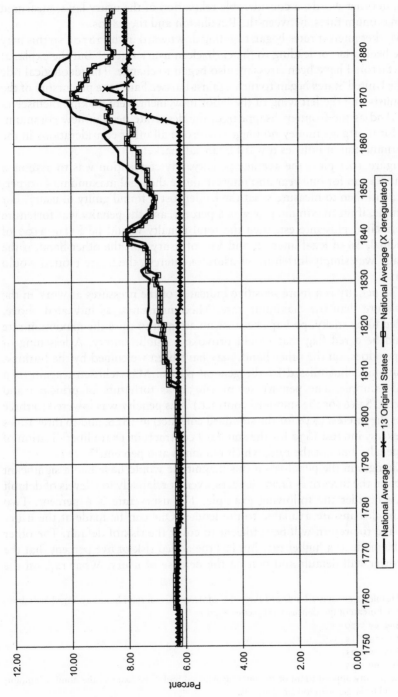

FIGURE 10.1. Average Maximum Rate of Interest, 1750–1890.

National Average   X 13 Original States   National Average
   National Average (X deregulated)

was, in other words, a considerable relaxation of the usury laws, measured by maximum rates, between the Revolution and the 1870s.

Market interest rates began trending downward in the 1870s, so this may have been a factor leading to the cutback in usury rates.[16] But the explanatory factors I have been stressing also began to change. The ideological tide in the United States began to turn against Laissez Faire; the precursors of the Populists and the left wing of the labor movement were making themselves felt. And as the frontier disappeared, the desperate need in new communities for mortgage money no longer overrode all other considerations in the determination of policies toward financial markets.

Figure 10.2 plots the average penalty. My convention was to assume a loan of $100 for one year and interest above the legal maximum of 10 percent; and then to measure what the lender lost if found guilty of usury. For example, if the maximum rate was 6 percent, and the penalty was forfeiture of principal plus interest, then the total penalty would be $116: $100 of principal, $6 of legal interest, and $10 of usury. On the other hand, if the penalty was simply forfeiture of usurious interest, the figure plotted would be $10.

The penalty is a more sensitive indicator of the pressures at work in the legislature than the maximum rate. Maximum rates, as indicated above, tended to be sticky, perhaps because an attempt to raise the maximum rate would be a red flag that would provoke a public outcry. A lessening of the penalties, on the other hand, may have been welcomed by the business community, but missed by the general public. Massachusetts, again, is a good example. The penalty set in 1693 was forfeiture of principal and interest ($116 for the standard contract.) This penalty was lowered to three times the interest ($48 for the standard contract) in 1826, and to three times the excess interest ($30 for the standard contract) in 1846: liberalization of the penalty but not the rate, which remained at 6 percent.[17]

Changes in the penalties of this magnitude would have had a significant effect on the incentives facing lenders, even at relatively low levels of default risk. Consider the following example. The usury rate is 6 percent. Two potential loans are available to the lender. One can be made at the usury rate and the return will be sufficient to cover the risk of default. The other can be made at a higher rate but has the added risk of five percent that the borrower will default and win on the defense of usury. What rate on the

---

[16] Macauley's unadjusted index of the yields of American railroad bonds averaged as follows (U.S. Bureau of the Census 1975, series X476):

1860–69 7.70
1870–79 7.14
1880–89 4.95
1890–99 4.35

[17] The penalty applied to all of the interest incurred under the loan, so the nominal amount would be larger with longer contracts.

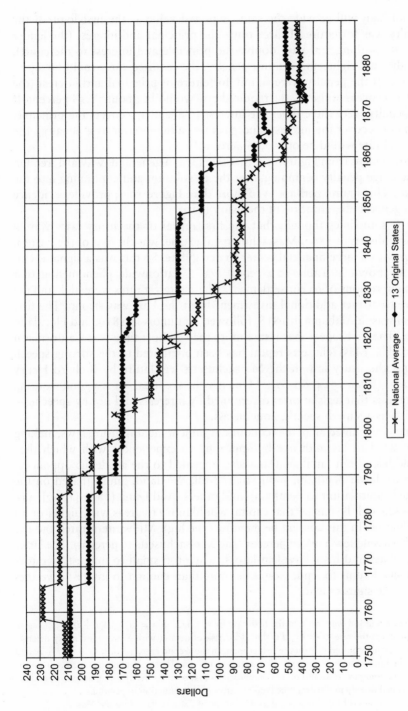

FIGURE 10.2. Average Penalty, 1750–1890 ($ penalty if $10 usury is charged on a $100 loan).

second loan will provide the same expected value as the first loan? If the penalty was forfeiture of three times the principal and interest (the lender recovers nothing and pays double the principle and interest to the court), a traditional eighteenth century penalty, the required rate would be 24.71 percent. If the penalty were simply forfeiture of principal and interest (the lender recovers nothing), the required rate would be about 11.58 percent. If the penalty were three times the interest (the lender recovers the principle, does not recover the interest, and pays twice the interest as a penalty), the required rate would be only 7.06 percent.[18]

It is evident from Figure 10.2 that there was a general downward trend in the average penalty beginning after the Revolution and continuing into the 1870s. This figure, perhaps even more than Figure 10.1, provides evidence for a general liberalization of the usury laws.

It is sometimes thought that the first repeal of the usury laws was in Massachusetts in 1867. Massachusetts, it is true, was the first of the Eastern states with a large financial center to deregulate. So this was a signal event. But as shown in Table 10.2 repeal was a nationwide phenomenon that began in regions of recent settlement, where interest rates were high and the desire to attract additional investment from the East was strong. The first repeal was in Alabama in 1818, followed by Illinois in 1819, and Florida in 1822. The first repeal that lasted more than a short time was California in 1850. The Massachusetts repeal has been attributed to the stirring speech against the usury law in the Massachusetts legislature by Richard Henry Dana Jr. (Ryan 1924, 60–62).[19] One may be skeptical – it is a good working hypothesis that legislation is determined by interests and not by speeches – but it was a superb speech, nonetheless.

Dana recounted all of the economic arguments against usury laws, making them vivid to his audience by appealing to experiences with which they would have been familiar. Dana also appealed to the academic opponents of usury laws: Bentham, John Stuart Mill, Wayland, Smith (based on the alleged capitulation to Bentham), and others. And Dana (1881 [1867], 51–52) discussed the danger that capital would move to areas with higher or no maximums. In this context he mentions the high Midwestern rates and the gap between New York (7 percent) and Massachusetts (6 percent). The latter gap, he assured his fellow legislators, while too small to interest investors with small sums to lend, would be more than enough to interest investors with large sums to lend.

---

[18] The calculation was made in the first case by setting $1 + u = (1 - d)(1 + i) - 2d(1 + i)$, where u is the rate of usury, d is the added risk of default with a successful usury defense, and i is the required rate on the riskier loan. In the second case, $1 + u = (1 - d)(1 + i)$; and in the third case, $1 + u = (1 - d)(1 + i) + d(1 - 2i)$. These calculations abstract from the cost of going to court and other complications that would affect lending decisions, and are intended merely to illustrate the consequences of the reduction in penalties.

[19] Today, Dana is best remembered as the author of *Two Years before the Mast*.

TABLE 10.2. *Chronological History of the Repeal of U.S. Usury Laws in the Nineteenth Century*

Year in which the Usury Law was Repealed	State
1818–1818	Alabama
1818–1821	Mississippi
1819–1832	Illinois
1822–1829	Florida
1831–1832	Indiana
1832–1832	Florida
1849–1851	Wisconsin
1850	California
1851–1852	Iowa
1851–1859	Minnesota
1852–1881	New Mexico
1854–1862	Oregon
1854	Washington
1855–1860	Nebraska
1859–1859	Kansas
1860	Louisiana
1861	Nevada
1862	Colorado
1864–1870	Idaho
1865	Arizona
1865	Montana
1865	North Dakota
1865	Rhode Island
1866	Florida
1866–1876	South Carolina
1867	Massachusetts
1868–73	Arkansas
1869	Utah
1869	Wyoming
1870	Maine
1870–75	Texas
1872–1872	Connecticut
1873–1874	Georgia
1873–1874	Mississippi
1877	Connecticut
1881	North Dakota

Source and Notes: (Holmes 1892, 436–42). The table includes states in which there existed a maximum rate when no rate was specified explicitly in the contract. If a range of years is shown, the repeal was subsequently reversed prior to 1890.

Under the 1850 California law, as under several similar statutes, as noted above, no limit was imposed on contracts in which the rate of interest was explicitly stated. If no rate was specified in the contract, however, the maximum interest allowed was 10 percent. The penalty in the latter case, if more than 10 percent was charged, was relatively light. The borrower could, however, refuse to pay more than 10 percent, and the lender could not sue to recover the excess. Once the interest was paid, however, the borrower could not sue to recover the amount in excess of 10 percent. This law retained some measure of protection for the unwary while generally freeing commercial transactions from restrictions. Indeed, by specifically sanctioning any rate that the parties agreed to, the law preempted an attempt by a borrower to invoke a common-law anti-usury tradition, and so provided lenders with more protection than if no law was in place.

Although the trend toward deregulation shown in Figures 10.1 and 10.2 is clear, individual states sometimes, as shown in Table 10.2, reversed course, depending on current economic circumstances. Lawrence Friedman's (1963) study of Wisconsin tells a story that was probably typical, at least for the areas of recent settlement. During the territorial period Michigan's maximum of 7 percent applied. The land boom of the late 1830s led to dissatisfaction with this rate. Potential farmers were anxious to acquire land even if it meant borrowing at rates above 7 percent. The result was an increase in the legal rate to 12 percent if the rate was explicitly stated in the contract. The rate was still 7 percent if no rate was stated explicitly. In 1849 the usury law was repealed. Any rate was legal so long as it was stated explicitly. A land boom, and hence the need for mortgage money, once more was the driving force. Repeal, however, lasted only two years. Low wheat prices and the drain of labor to California resulting from the Gold Rush put farmers in a bad mood. In 1851 the legislature, looking for a way to respond to widespread discontent, reinstated the 12 percent maximum, and imposed a stiff penalty. Usurious contracts were void and the lender had to return three times the excess interest. In 1856, in the midst of a long economic expansion, the penalties were reduced. Now only the excess interest was voided, and the borrower had to make a tender of the principal before the usury defense could be invoked. In 1862 hard times occasioned by the outbreak of the Civil War and the resultant closing of the Mississippi produced a reduction of the maximum rate to 7 percent. In 1866 a postwar land boom led the legislature to increase the rate to 10 percent where it remained for the rest of the century.[20]

Samuel Rezneck (1950, 505) noticed a similar phenomenon in the east. A financial panic, such as the panic of 1857, hardened attitudes. When

[20] One might conjecture that the Civil War inflation (prices about doubled) would have produced higher market rates and adjustments in the usury rates. However, higher nominal rates did not materialize in the North during the war, and usury law ceilings were not adjusted.

the market rate pushed through interest ceilings, merchants and bankers demanded their repeal. But opponents of high interest rates also mobilized, and in some cases were successful in defeating attempts to repeal the usury laws.

What had undone the usury laws? One factor I believe, as I argued above, was the spread of confidence in Laissez-Faire in general, and Bentham's critique of usury laws in particular. It was hard to argue for usury laws when all the best economic authorities starting with Bentham and Mill opposed them, and when Britain, the most advanced nation, was eliminating them.

In addition, there was the competition among the states for capital. One piece of evidence for the role of interstate competition is shown in Figures 10.1 and 10.2 The 13 original states lagged behind newer regions in the process of liberalization both in terms of raising rates and in terms of reducing penalties. Figure 10.3, which shows maximum rates by regions, illustrates the point in another way. Liberalization began in the South and Midwest. New England eventually liberalized after the Civil War, but the Middle Atlantic States held to their tough usury maximums.[21]

The liberalization did not end with the complete disappearance of the usury laws. Instead, the pattern was, typically, one of relatively light penalties and usury ceilings that reflected conditions in local markets. The pattern of usury ceilings for the post-bellum period thus ended up similar to the pattern of regional rates made famous in Davis (1965), at least in terms of the ordering of the regions.[22]

Friedman (1963, 517) documents several cases in which the fear of a capital drain to states with more liberal usury laws was brought up in legislative debates. For example a legislative committee in Connecticut in 1871 "painted a picture of money fleeing to Massachusetts," where the usury law had been repealed in 1867. The following year Connecticut repealed its usury law, although repeal proved to be short lived. The desire to promote expansion of the capital market will also show up when we look at the debate over the usury provision of the National Banking Act in Section 5.

It would be natural to conjecture, along the lines of Keynes's discussion of Bentham, that the liberalization of the usury laws in the United States was a response to industrialization and deepening financial development. Financiers would be strongly opposed to usury laws and their influence would increasingly win out against the interests of debtors. The influence of finance can be seen at various points in our story. But if this were a major factor, we would observe the liberalization occurring first in the Eastern financial centers. New York would be leading the way. But this was not the case. The political economy of the New York usury law has been traced

---

[21] In 1882 New York removed the ceiling for "demand loans" over $5,000 and secured by collateral. This was probably a response to the growth of the call loan market.

[22] Causation might well have run in both directions, from market rates to usury rates and from usury rates to market rates.

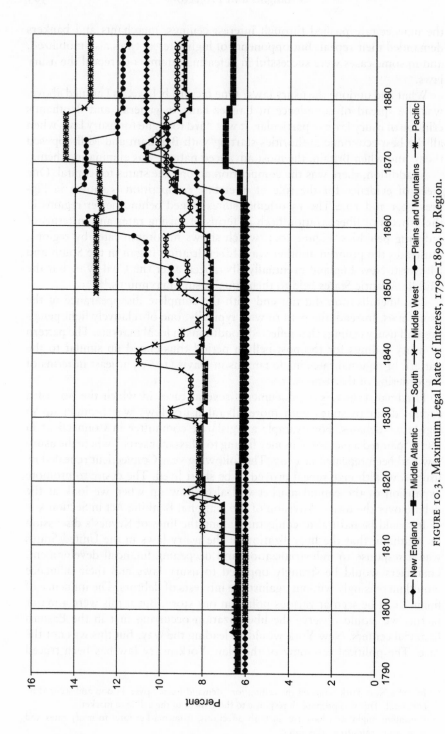

FIGURE 10.3. Maximum Legal Rate of Interest, 1790–1890, by Region.

New England ◆   Middle Atlantic ■   South ▲   Plains and Mountains ●   Middle West ✳   Pacific ✳

by Mary Ann Romano (1989, 163–210). In 1837 New York had passed a fairly stiff law that included possible criminal penalties (a fine and imprisonment) as well as the civil penalties (loss of principal and interest) that were typical and on which I have been focusing. In subsequent years the business community steadily pushed for a repeal, or at least a liberalization, of the law. But it was not until the 1880s that they had any real success.[23] The opposition came from rural areas of the state that believed that funds would move toward New York if it were not for the leveling effect of the usury law. There is a clear contrast here between the interests of the settled agricultural regions of New York, which could offer collateral with well-established values and could therefore benefit from usury laws, and the interests of the newly settled agricultural regions that could compete for capital only by offering to pay high rates. Liberalization of the usury laws, in short, was mainly the result of western boosterism, a way of attracting capital to the frontier, rather than a response to the growing needs of the business or industrial communities.

At the end of the nineteenth century, enthusiasm for further liberalization waned, and a new concern arose: the small household loan. Although pawn broking was an ancient phenomenon, Robinson and Nugent (1934, 40–42) show (based on their reading of advertisements in newspapers) that this market grew in urban areas after the Civil War.[24] These were small loans taken out by the urban poor and secured by furniture or salaries. Extraordinarily high rates of interest were common. Rates of 10 percent per month were considered "reasonable." Usury laws, if applicable, were ignored. The loan sharks, as they were known, drew the attention of reformers. Newspapers ran stories detailing the evils of the small loan market. Philanthropic organizations were set up to address the problem by making low interest loans and by becoming involved in cases where lenders were pressing borrowers for repayment.

It was obvious to the reformers that traditional usury laws that limited rates on all loans would be inappropriate to deal with the small loan problem. The solution, it was felt, was a law that licensed firms making small loans and limited them to rates that assured reasonable profits. An 1895 statute in New York was regarded as a model. Only chartered lenders could make small (less than $200) loans. On these loans lenders were limited to

---

[23] In a famous case in New York in the late 1840s the New York Dry Dock Bank refused to pay a loan of about $225,000 that was due the American Life Insurance and Trust Company on the grounds that the loan was usurious. The courts upheld Dry Dock's refusal. As a result the New York legislature passed a law in 1850 preventing corporations from interposing the usury defense. Although on the surface this looks like an anti-usury law, it is if anything an anti-bank law (Ryan 1924, 58–60).

[24] The next two paragraphs are based on Robinson and Nugent (1934), which summarized the material developed in a number of Russell Sage foundation publications on the small loan problem.

3 percent per month for the first two months, and 2 percent per month thereafter. Violation of the law was made a criminal act. After all, the lender was not an ordinary businessman, but rather a "loan shark." Under the New York law a reward of $250 could be paid for evidence of a violation. By 1911 twenty-two states had passed small loan legislation, although the Russell Sage Foundation, which had been active in promoting reform, doubted how effective these laws really were. The small loan laws reflected the moral justification for usury laws, and conceded the broad range of interest rates to the market. Although we have not tested the maximum rates in the small loan laws, it seems likely that they would reflect the pattern described by Glaeser and Scheinkman (1998): a more unequal distribution of income would imply a more restrictive usury law.

V. THE USURY PROVISION OF THE NATIONAL BANKING ACT

In general the usury laws, then as now, were state laws. The question of rate restriction did come up, however, when the Federal government chartered the First and Second Banks of the United States, and when it established the National Banking System. Alexander Hamilton recommended a maximum rate of 6 percent for the First Bank of the United States, and this limit was included in the charter. His argument was mercantilist: low rates were good. A violent reduction of rates would do more harm than good, but a gentle nudging of rates downward would help (Miller 1924, 319). The Second Bank also was limited to 6 percent (Krooss 1969, 311, 469).[25] The Bank of England at that time was limited by the British usury laws to 5 percent, and the authority of the British model may have influenced the Americans.[26]

The issue of usury laws at the Federal level came up again during the Civil War when the United States set up the National Banking System. The debate that ensued over usury restrictions for the national banks opens a window on the mix of ideas and interests that were shaping usury laws.

At the outbreak of the Civil War the federal government created the famous greenback dollar. It proved to be surprisingly popular with the general public because it provided a uniform currency (a bill that had the same value no matter where it was spent) and with the government because it provided revenue. The commercial banking system that had produced the paper money before the war, moreover, was in disarray in the Western states because banks there had circulated notes backed with bonds

---

[25] It is not obvious, however, from reading the charter what if any penalty Congress intended if the Banks should charge a higher rate. The Supreme Court eventually dealt with the issue.

[26] David Ricardo later criticized the application of the usury restriction to the Bank of England because it prevented the Bank from limiting credit expansion by raising the discount rate. This was part of his criticism of the Bank's excessive issue of paper money during the restriction of specie payments that accompanied the Napoleonic wars.

issued by southern states, and these were now of doubtful value. The problem before the Congress, then, was how to create a currency that would have the benefits of the greenback – uniformity, safety, and seignorage for the government – that would at the same time be the basis after the war for a private currency backed by gold. The answer was the National Currency Act of 1863, creating the National Banking System.

In creating the National system Congress had to face the question of what, if any, usury restrictions would be placed on the banks. One might assume that since the Republican Party was a pro-business, pro-creditor party it would have opposed lending restrictions. After all, in the post-bellum era the Republican Party would be the defender of gold standard orthodoxy. The National Currency Act, however, contained a tough usury provision. The law of 1863 provided that the maximum rate that could be charged by a national bank would be "such rate of interest or discount as is at the time the established rate of interest for delay in the payment of money, in the absence of contract between the parties, by the laws of the several states in which the banks are located." The penalty was "forfeiture of the debt."

This was a strict usury provision on two counts. First, many usury laws in the western states set a lower rate when no rate was specified in the contract than when the rate was named explicitly, presumably to protect the unwary borrower. In Illinois the maximum was 6 percent when no rate was specified; 10 percent when the rate was specified. Iowa was the same as Illinois. In Michigan the maximum was 7 percent when no rate was specified; 10 percent when the rate was specified. California called for 10 percent when no rate was specified but permitted any rate so long as it was named in the contract. Forfeiture of the whole debt was also strict. Many western states had much lower penalties. In Illinois the penalty was forfeiture of the whole interest, but not the principal. In Indiana the penalty was simply the return of the "usury," the interest over the maximum. In Iowa the interest over 6 percent went to the School Fund.

How did this provision get into law? The National Banking System as a whole was the brainchild of Salmon P. Chase, the first Secretary of the Treasury under Lincoln. Chase recommended the system in general terms in the *Treasury Report* issued in December 1861. He argued for the new system partly on practical grounds – it would give additional support to the market for federal bonds and additional flexibility in arranging federal payments, and also on idealistic grounds – it was a permanent reform that would establish a uniform currency without the danger of inflation from a paper currency. Indeed, Andrew McFarland Davis in his classic account of the National Banking Act concludes that the establishment of a permanent uniform national currency was Chase's primary motive.[27] He had expressed

---

[27] Davis (1910, 106–12). Hammond (1970) provides an overview of the political and economic forces that led to the establishment of the National Banking System.

his desire for such a reform as early as his inaugural address as governor of Ohio 1856. Chase's report was forwarded to the House of Ways and Means Committee where several hands, in particular Congressmen E.G. Spaulding of New York and Samuel Hooper of Massachusetts, seem to have worked on turning Chase's suggestion into law.[28]

Exactly which of these men wrote the tough and complex usury section is not known. However, the evidence seems to point to Hooper. Hooper was a banking theorist as well as banker and Congressmen. He had written articles comparing banking legislation in different states, and would have been aware of the inclusion of separate interest maximums for contracts in which no explicit mention of a rate was made, and of different types of penalties. Hooper also favored strict usury laws. Fritz Redlich in his classic *Molding of American Banking* (1951, 212) also attributes the usury provision to Hooper. Redlich, however, fails to distinguish between the hybrid 1863 usury provision, and the provision calling for a uniform 7 percent which Hooper (as we shall see) incorporated in his amended 1864 bill. This mistake led Redlich to deduce that the usury provision had simply been copied from New York's free banking law, which was not the case.

The Spaulding-Hooper bill was not introduced in the House, however, because of the opposition of Thadeus Stevens who preferred the greenback as a way of establishing a uniform currency. The bill eventually became law after being introduced in the Senate by John Sherman. The debate over the bill was intense, but the usury provision, per se, was not discussed. This is hardly surprising. At issue, or so it seemed, was the future monetary system of the United States. In this context the usury provision was a secondary issue. But once the National Currency Act became law in June 1863 the shortcomings of the usury provision were felt.

The usury provision of the National Currency Act of 1863 was criticized along two conflicting lines. (1) The law was inequitable across national banks in different states. It permitted a national bank in a state with a high usury ceiling such as California to charge a higher rate than a national bank in a state with a lower ceiling such as Maine. Critics who stressed this point generally favored a uniform rate of six or seven percent that would apply to national banks in all states. (2) The law was inequitable across state and national banks within a state. A state bank in, say, Illinois could charge as much as 10 percent (if the rate was stipulated in the contract) and the penalty if they charged more was merely forfeiture of the interest. A national bank in the same state was restricted to 6 percent, the rate in Illinois when no rate was specified in the contract, and the national bank was subject to the loss of both principal and interest if the law was violated. Critics of the law of 1863 who stressed this point generally preferred making the national banks subject to state rules on usury.

---

[28] Davis (1910, 55–62).

Hugh McCulloch, the widely respected former president of the State Bank of Indiana, became the first Comptroller of the Currency – head of the National Banking System.[29] He stressed the first criticism of the usury provision in his First *Annual Report.* Instead of the current provision he suggested a maximum rate of 7 percent for all national banks, and a penalty of forfeiture of the interest.[30] McCulloch also acknowledged the second criticism that a uniform rate across national banks would work to the disadvantage of national banks in the high interest rate regions of the West. But he took the view that high rates often encouraged reckless banking. McCulloch, believed that the success of the State Bank of Indiana, where he had risen to prominence, was the result, partly, of its charter, which included a limit of 6 percent on the interest the bank could charge (Harding 1895, 118). McCulloch noted, moreover, the peculiar property of the usury provision of 1863 that it left the setting of the usury rate in the hands of the state, but left the penalty in the hands of the federal statute. He recommended as a second best solution that if the state was allowed to fix the rate of interest, it also be allowed to fix the penalty.[31]

McCulloch's reason for supporting usury laws is evidently the same as Adam Smith's: usury laws keep the money away from prodigals and projectors. The similarity of their views does not necessarily mean that McCulloch was influenced directly by Smith. Smith's views probably reflected a working tradition among bankers to which McCulloch was also an heir. Nevertheless, McCulloch's position suggests that the mercantilist case for usury laws was still far from dead, even at mid-century.

What seems to have done in the strict usury provision in the 1863 Act, and the milder, but still tough, alternatives proposed by McCulloch, wasn't Bentham's arguments, but rather a more practical problem: getting banks to convert from state to national status. The problem was pointed out in the lead article in *Bankers Magazine* (Ketchum 1863) published a few months before Congress began debating a revised version of the Banking Act. The author, Hiram Ketchum, stressed an important practical consequence of the different treatment afforded state and national banks under the usury provision in the 1863 act: state banks, particularly in the West, were reluctant to join the national system, because they could charge higher rates as state banks. Ketchum's recommendation was that national banks be permitted to charge the highest rate allowed in any state, or be free of all controls.

An important piece of evidence supporting Ketchum's claim that western state banks would not convert until they could compete on the same basis

---

[29] He would soon be appointed Secretary of the Treasury.
[30] *First Annual Report of the Comptroller of the Currency,* as reported in *Banker's Magazine,* New Series XIII (Feb. 1864), 621–24.
[31] *First Annual Report of the Comptroller of the Currency,* as reported in *Bankers Magazine,* New Series XIII (Feb. 1864), 621.

as state banks that didn't convert, or other intermediaries, comes from a report made by one of Jay Cooke's bond salesmen. Cooke was the Treasury Department's chief agent in the sale of government bonds during the Civil War. In November 1863 he received a letter from his agent in Michigan outlining the reasons for the slow sale of government bonds to potential national banks. In part the agent described the problem:

> The low rate of interest permitted – seven per cent only in Michigan, whereas state law permits 10 per cent. (by contract) and throughout the greater portion of the state the actual rate is 1 $\frac{1}{2}$ to 2 per cent. a month.... Quite a large amount of 5–20's [a federal bond, 5 percent per year for 20 years] are now held by bankers and others in interior towns of Michigan and still more will be purchased for the use in banking under the Act ... the hope being strong that the coming Congress will allow interest to be charged on loans in accordance with state enactments ... Oberholtzer. (1907, 357)

McCulloch's recommendation of a flat 7 percent for all national banks, however, was far from dead. He was strongly supported by a committee of bankers from New York who lobbied McCulloch and the House Ways and Means Committee, probably in the first weeks of March 1864.[32] The interest of the New York bankers in a national 7 percent maximum is clear. New York's state usury law set a maximum of 7 percent. State banks and national banks would be on a par in New York, and conversion to the national system would be unimpeded. In the west, however, bankers would prefer the state system, and access to state usury laws. The national banks of New York would come to dominate the system. And if note issue were confined to national banks, it would be the notes of the New York national banks that would circulate throughout the country.

Although I have seen no explicit evidence, it is likely that the committee of bankers also lobbied for a clause permitting the Secretary of the Treasury, or some similar authority, to suspend the usury laws in major financial centers during a crisis, a policy that McCulloch supported.[33] Such flexibility would have been important for bankers who could still remember the levels reached by interest rates during the Panic of 1857.

In any event McCulloch's recommendation of a uniform 7 percent interest rate ceiling was incorporated in the bill introduced in the House by Samuel Hooper in April 1864.[34] Here it was strongly criticized by Congressmen from the Western states who emphasized the inequality between state and national banks that would develop in their states if a uniform rate were adopted. Blaine (of Maine!) offered an amendment substituting the language

---

[32] *Merchant's Magazine*, vol. L (April 1864), 309.

[33] *First Annual Report of the Comptroller of the Currency*, 623–24.

[34] The high rate of inflation during the war would have turned a 7 percent nominal rate into a negative real rate. But the legislators were probably thinking in terms of a long run characterized by return to the gold standard and stable prices.

"[the maximum rate of interest] established by law in the state where the bank is located" for the uniform rate. Blaine's purpose was actually to restrict the national banks in Maine to the state interest ceiling of 6 percent. But he was strongly seconded by Cole of California who argued that there would be a great disparity between the then current rate in California of 2 percent or more per month and the uniform 7 percent rate in the House bill. Cole finished his speech by endorsing Blaine's proposal:

Mr. Cole... "In New England the rate of interest is six percent; but it is not so in the western states. In Iowa it is different; and there is no reason for creating this discord by establishing a rate of interest for States different from what prevails there by their own laws. Therefore I am in favor of striking out the section [providing for a uniform rate], thereby leaving the matter entirely under the control of the several States. That is the proposition of the gentleman from Maine. He proposes to leave it to the local legislation of the several States entirely." (Mr. Blaine. "Entirely.")[35]

Other Congressman supported Cole's point that a uniform rate would discourage conversion to national status or the settling up of national banks in high interest rate states. Higby of California went so far as to claim that no national banks would be set up in his state where high rates of interest were the norm. He himself was paying two percent per month at that very moment![36] Blaine's amendment was adopted, but as it turns out it did not provide the actual text of the law of 1864. In a peculiar turn of events a second amendment limiting the rate of interest to 6 percent was adopted leaving the usury section in a confused state. This version of the Currency Act was later tabled, and a second bill, again incorporating a uniform rate, was introduced in the House.

The actual source of the usury formula in the Act of 1864 was a Senate amendment proposed by the Senate Finance Committee. I have not seen any direct references to what happened in the Finance Committee. But we do know that in January 1864 Jay Cooke dispatched his brother Henry to talk with John Sherman, the chairman of the Finance Committee, and Salmon Chase, the Secretary of the Treasury, about needed revisions in the law. And the next month Sherman's Finance Committee reported out a series of amendments to the 1863 law including the language of the 1864 usury section, which allowed the national banks to follow the usury law of the state where the bank was located. It may be that the Finance Committee

---

[35] *The Congressional Globe*, 38th Cong., 1st sess., 1353.

[36] Ibid, 1374. Statements such as these are, I must admit, somewhat inconsistent with the picture of an integrated antebellum capital market painted in Bodenhorn and Rockoff (1992). We did, however, qualify our argument by pointing to the frontier and arguing that beyond the frontier rates did seem to be higher, reflecting uncertainty surrounding investment in regions of new settlement. So at least to some extent, these statements can be reconciled with the evidence for integrated markets within the East that we presented.

rejected the uniform rate in favor of a rate to be determined by state law partly as a result of Cooke's lobbying effort.[37]

This amendment was debated in the Senate on May 5 with the Senators going over much of the same ground as the Representatives had earlier. Grimes of Iowa complained that national banks in one state could end up charging more than national banks in neighboring states.[38] But Trumbull of Illinois argued that state banks would not convert unless given equal freedom to lend under the national charters. He told the Senate that leading bankers from Chicago had made this point to him.[39]

Senator Henderson of Iowa then raised the point that in his state note-issuing banks were under a lower interest rate ceiling than private lenders.[40] Several attempts were made to amend the usury section to make the rate applying to state banks the relevant rate. But there were objections. Some states, for example, did not create banks of issue. Perhaps most telling was the brief interjection by Lane of Kansas who pointed out that, in his state, private bankers took advantage of the higher ceiling for private lenders and yet issued notes that circulated as money.[41] Evidently, limiting the national banks to the rate permitted under state law for incorporated banks of issue would discourage entrepreneurs from setting up national banks in Kansas because they could not offer investors the same return as private bankers.

It is possible that his remark rang a bell with Sherman. In 1850 Ohio (Sherman's state) had passed the so-called "ten percent interest law" that allowed private lenders 10 percent while banks of issue were limited to 6 percent. The law produced several unfortunate consequences (Huntington 1915). For one thing state chartered banks largely abandoned discounting home paper and concentrated on bills of exchange payable out of state because fees for "exchange" were not easily attacked under the usury laws. More important for our purpose, the ten percent law discouraged investment in banks of issue. Investors in Ohio preferred putting their capital into private banks or banks chartered in other states. The result was that the currency in Ohio contained a large admixture of notes issued by private bankers and by banks in other states. Indeed, the ten percent law was the major cause of the lack of uniformity in Ohio's currency that Chase complained of during his inaugural address as Governor of Ohio in 1856, the position he held before becoming Secretary of the Treasury (Huntington 1915, 450). The ten percent law was abandoned in 1859.

---

[37] Oberholtzer (1907, 358). The only insight into the work of the Finance Committee that I have found is a remark by Sherman in the Senate. He said that he initially favored a flat maximum rate but the committee found that it would "create so many disputes and rivalries and troubles" that he was forced to yield.

[38] *The Congressional Globe*, 38th Cong., 1st sess., 2123.

[39] Ibid.

[40] Ibid., 2126. Banks of issue were public banks in the sense that they operated under charters providing for limited liability and other privileges granted by the state legislature.

[41] Ibid.

In the end, Fessenden of Maine, another key member of the Finance Committee, cut the debate short by offering to fix up the amendment. When Sherman reported the new wording two days later it contained the phrase, "except that where by the laws of any State a different rate is limited for banks of issue organized under State laws, the rate so limited shall be allowed for associations organized in any such State under this act." The effect of Fessenden's rewording, on close reading, was to give the national banks favored status. They could take the rate permitted private investors if that rate was higher, or use the rate allowed to banks of issue if that was higher. Nothing like the disaster that had occurred under Ohio's ten percent law could now occur under the National Banking Act. This wording was adopted without further debate.[42] Evidently, the desire to get capital flowing into the National Banking System in the Western states had triumphed over any lingering regard for usury laws.

VI. DID LIBERALIZING THE USURY LAWS HAVE ANY IMPACT?

I have been concerned so far with the usury laws as a case study in the causes of economic regulation. It is natural to ask whether the liberalization of the usury laws had any impact on the economy. The conventional wisdom among economic historians, as noted above, seems to be that usury laws had no significant effect because they were easily evaded. The borrower and lender simply wrote a contract that hid the usury. However, the history of the usury laws developed above and other evidence developed by economic historians makes me skeptical of the conventional wisdom.

(1) Usury laws are inherently popular because they speak to fundamental ethical concerns. Why liberalize them if they have no economic effect? Why, in other words, should legislators have risked the wrath of a large segment of the public who believed that usury was immoral by raising maximum rates or lowering penalties if the only savings to the business community was the ink on loan contracts? Yet as we have seen, legislators persistently made the effort to liberalize the laws.

(2) The conventional wisdom assumes that judges cannot or will not see beyond the legal document placed in front of them. Judges do put a lot of weight on signed documents. Nevertheless, there must be some risk when a usury law is on the books that a judge will be sympathetic to the borrower rather than the lender, and willing to believe whatever proofs of usury the borrower can muster.

(3) In most circumstances, the effects of liberalizing moderate usury laws are likely to be hard to see: the reallocation of some capital from lower risk to higher risk investments and less investment in human capital and more in financial and physical capital. However, when abrupt

---

[42] *The Congressional Globe*, 38th Cong., 1st sess., 2143.

and far-ranging changes are made in the usury laws the results will
be visible. Two examples from our narrative are the difficulties that
arose from the Ohio ten percent law and from the attempt to establish
a uniform rate in the National Currency Act.

(4) Leslie Pressnell's classic study, *Country Banking in the Industrial Revolution* (1956), shows that British usury laws appear to have had an
important effect on country banks in England during the eighteenth
and early nineteenth centuries, although Pressnell is careful not to go
beyond his evidence and make too strong a claim (Pressnell 1956,
285–88, 316–21, and *passim*). Rather than change their lending rate
when equilibrium interest rates rose above the usury rate, and thus risk
writing contracts that could not be enforced, country banks responded
by changing the length of loans.[43] Pressnell (1956, 321) concludes that
"The relaxation of the usury laws in fact introduced into the money
market a flexibility much greater than is immediately visible: against
higher rates of interest, bankers could discount longer bills, or allow
clients to draw for shorter periods than had hitherto been possible."
Clapham (1970, vol. 2, 15), writing about the period before 1833,
says that while bill brokers might have circumvented the usury law
by charging a commission, and private bankers might have done so
by requiring compensating balances, "that was not for the Bank [of
England]; and so it suffered."

(5) Lance Davis's classic study of the financing of the New England textile
mills argued that the usury laws in Massachusetts were "fairly well
observed, at least by the major institutional lenders, until the mid
1850s" (Davis 1960, 3). The tendency, that Davis observed, for the
usury laws to lose their effect as mid-century approached may have
been due to the reduction in the penalties in Massachusetts discussed
above. Similarly, Barry Eichengreen's study of the mortgage rates at
the end of the nineteenth century (1984) found some impact from
usury limits, when the limits were relatively low, on mortgage rates.
And Ken Snowden (1988) found additional evidence of an impact on
mortgage rates in urban markets.[44] It seems likely that the impact
of usury limits would have been larger earlier in the century when
penalties were higher.[45]

(6) Eugene White generously gave me access to the data for his study of
the California Bank of A. Levy (White 2001). Levy was lending money

---

[43] This is another instance of the Smith effect. If lenders are unable to charge long-term
borrowers a premium, lenders will allocate more of their funds to the short-term market.

[44] Initially, Snowden seems to have been a bit skeptical about the potential impact of usury
laws. See Snowden (1987) and Eichengreen (1987).

[45] Recent works by John Munro (2001) and Elaine Tan (2002) in different ways have questioned the assumption that the medieval usury laws were a dead letter.

in a state that permitted any rate so long as it was stated explicitly in the contract. A rate of 10 percent applied when no rate was stated explicitly. It turns out in White's sample that if, say, 10 percent had been made the maximum rate, then 15.4 percent of Levy's loans by count and 30.7 percent by value would have been illegal. Would Levy have continued to place such a large fraction of his funds in loans that could be challenged in court, or would he have reacted as Adam Smith suggested, and lent a larger proportion to lower-risk borrowers at a lower rate? Economic historians have become increasingly aware of the importance of the law when it comes to other forms of property rights – bankruptcy law, the law of negotiable instruments, and so forth – why should usury laws have been an exception?

(7) The most visible sign of an impact from the usury laws would be in the courts. And here one must concede the evidence is mixed. Robert Wright (2001, 29–41) undertook an exhaustive examination of colonial records and found no evidence of the usury defense. His unequivocal conclusion is that the colonial usury laws were a dead letter. On the other hand, there is evidence from the nineteenth century that the usury defense was invoked from time to time, and that the courts took the law of usury seriously.[46]

I looked at the Supreme Court Cases involving usury in the nineteenth century. There were simply too many cases to read if one looked at lower courts, and the Supreme Court would reflect the national picture. There were about 60 cases before the Supreme Court between 1800 and 1900 in which usury laws played a significant role. There were many additional cases in which the law of usury was cited in the course of the argument by way of analogy. The number of cases fluctuated somewhat from period to period. The 1830s (10 cases), the 1870s (also 10 cases), and the 1890s (14 cases) stand out. These were periods of economic distress, and hence periods when loan defaults were high.

The amounts involved were substantial in today's money. *Dundas v. Hitchcock* (1851) began with a bond for $620,530.96 written in 1838 ($11,700,000 in 2001 using a Consumer Price Index). In *the Bank of the United States v. Herbert G. Waggener, George Wagley and Alexander Miller* (1835) the case arose from a $5,000 obligation paying 6 percent purchased by the Bank of the United States in 1822, but paid for with notes of the Bank of Kentucky, which were then depreciated from 30 to 40 percent in the market ($75,000 in 2001 using a Consumer Price Index – and ignoring

---

[46] I searched the papers of George Washington for evidence that the usury laws might have influenced him in his business dealings. There was nothing from the colonial period. There was, however, a letter to George Ball (1797) in which Washington reacted angrily to the suggestion that he had violated the usury laws, and some evidence that Washington understood the usury law and had taken it into account.

the depreciation of the notes). *Levy v. Gadsby* (1805) began with a note for $1,436.62 created in 1797 ($20,000 in 2001 using a Consumer Price Index).

The Supreme Court, as might be imagined, was asked to settle a variety of thorny legal issues. In a few cases these were simply technical legal questions that could have arisen under other laws, for example the proper instruction of juries. Most of the cases, however, involved interpreting the law of usury. In several cases the old question of whether various devices constituted prohibited attempts to evade the usury laws played a prominent role. In *the United States v. Waggener* (1835) the loan made by the Bank of the United States was legal on the face of it (6 percent as required by the bank's charter), but usurious when the depreciated market value of the Bank of Kentucky notes was taken into account. Reading between the lines, there seems to be a suggestion that the borrowers may have had the usury defense in mind when they insisted on the Bank of Kentucky notes. In *United States Mortgage Company v. Sperry* (1891) the issue was whether unpaid interest added to the principal could in some way render the original loan usurious. In *Cockle et al. v. Flack et al.* (1876) the case involved a meat packer in Peoria who had borrowed from a merchant in Baltimore who also charged a commission for selling the final product. The commission was charged whether or not the product was sold. The question was whether those commissions were a dodge for evading the usury law. In *Call v. Palmer* (1885) the issue was whether an agent who exacted a separate commission could render the contract between the principal and the borrower usurious. In *Wheeler v. National Bank* (1877) the case revolved around a bill of exchange on which it was alleged the bank had charged an excessive amount for exchange to evade the usury law.

As might be imagined, conflicts among usury laws in different states had to be resolved. In *Tilden v. Blair* (1874), for example, the case centered on a bill that was drawn in one state on the resident of another. The bill was accepted in the second state and returned to the first state where it was negotiated for a price that would have implied usurious interest in the second state but not in the first. The creation of federal institutions also created the need for Supreme Court interpretations. *Fleckner v. the President, Directors, and Company of the Bank of the United States* (1823) addressed the six percent usury provision of the charter of the Bank of the United States. Several cases, including *Tiffany v. National Bank of Missouri* (1872) and *National Bank v. Johnson* (1881), were aimed at settling the interpretation of the usury provision of the National Banking Act and its amendments.[47] The willingness of the Supreme Court to hear these cases shows that it took the proper structuring of the usury laws seriously.

---

[47] The latter cases have been cited in recent court cases concerning the charging of credit card interest by national banks.

VII. CONCLUSIONS

Usury laws provide a good case study of how the interaction of economic ideas and economic conditions shaped economic regulation. During the colonial era, the colonies that were to become the United States, heavily influenced by traditional religious thinking, had strict usury laws. Maximum rates appear relatively low to a modern eye, and penalties for violating the laws appear tough. During the antebellum period, however, these laws were gradually liberalized or repealed, although the system was never completely abandoned.

Part of the explanation for the liberalization of the usury laws was the rising faith in Laissez Faire in general, and in Bentham's case against the usury laws in particular. The influence of ideas on legislation is always difficult to prove; but it seems plausible that at the margin the strong consensus among American economists and economic opinion makers that Bentham had won his argument with Adam Smith and other supporters of usury laws must have had an impact. As one dogged supporter of usury laws in Wisconsin was forced to admit, he "did not believe in the principle of free trade in money – not because he could reply to the arguments of those who were in favor of it – they had all the arguments in their favor" but because "experience has taught us that it is unjust" (quoted in Friedman 1963, 556).

Ideas, however, were not the whole story. Competition among the states for capital was also important. Typically, loan rates were higher in the West. This was partly a matter of resources – the West was resource-rich and credit-poor – but it was also a function of risk and uncertainty. Loan rates were higher in regions of new settlement because lenders did not have the experience on which to base assessments of risk. Low and uniform rates of usury would have made it difficult to attract the financial capital needed for economic development.

The liberalization of the usury laws was part of a larger process by which developing states in the West attempted to attract the capital – financial capital, physical capital, and human capital – they needed for economic development. One important tool for attracting human capital to the West (and other regions of new settlement), as Stanley L. Engerman and Kenneth L. Sokoloff (2005) have argued, was liberalizing voting restrictions: the right to vote attracted settlers. Interest rate restrictions in the West were eased for similar reasons: the right to charge high interest rates attracted financial capital. Credit, even at high rates, was needed so that settlers could buy land, equipment, and supplies, and so that merchants could start new businesses. Just as the liberalization of voting rights in the West put pressure on the East to follow suit, the liberalization of usury laws in the West also put pressure on the East to follow suit. The fear that capital would leave a state that maintained tough usury laws proved to be a powerful argument in the hands of those who favored an unfettered capital market.

The next question about the usury laws will be harder to answer: by how much did the change in the usury laws influence the course of economic development? Liberalizing the usury laws encouraged lenders to choose "prodigals and projectors," in Adam Smith's terms, over "sober people." Liberalizing the usury laws, moreover, encouraged savers to turn away from investments, such as investments in human capital, which yielded returns that could not be challenged under the usury laws, and toward financial markets. These effects are subtle and will be hard to measure. Nevertheless, understanding them may well provide an important insight into the nature of American capitalism in the nineteenth century.

References

Alabaster, Ernest. 1899. *Notes and Commentaries on Chinese Criminal Law, and Cognate Topics*. London: Luzac & Co.

Bentham, Jeremy. 1952–54. *Jeremy Bentham's Economic Writings*. Critical edition based on his printed works and unprinted mss., ed. W. Stark. London: Allen & Unwin, for the Royal Economic Society.

Blitz, Rudolph C., and Millard F. Long. 1965. "The Economics of Usury Regulation." *Journal of Political Economy* 73 (Dec.): 608–619.

Bodenhorn, Howard, and Hugh Rockoff. 1992. "Regional Interest Rates in Antebellum America." In *Strategic Factors in Nineteenth Century American Economic History: A Volume to Honor Robert W. Fogel*, eds. Claudia Goldin and Hugh Rockoff. Chicago: University of Chicago Press for the NBER, pp. 159–87.

Clapham, Sir John. 1970. *The Bank of England: A History*. Cambridge: Cambridge University Press.

Child, Josiah. 1668. *Brief Observations Concerning Trade and Interest of Money*. London: Printed for Elizabeth Calvert at the Black-spread Eagle in Barbican, and Henry Mortlock at the Sign of the White-Heart in Westminster Hall. [McMaster University Archive for the History of Economic Thought, http://socserv2.socsci.mcmaster.ca:80/~econ/ugcm/3ll3/index.html].

Cunningham, William. 1905–07. *The Growth of English Industry and Commerce*. 4th ed. Cambridge: Cambridge University Press.

Dana Richard H. Jr., David A. Wells, and others. 1881. *Usury laws: Their Nature, Expediency, and Influence*. New York: The Society for Political Education.

Davis, Andrew McFarland. 1910. *The Origin of the National Banking System*. Washington, DC: GPO.

Davis, Lance E. 1960. "The New England Textile Mills and the Capital Markets: A Study of Industrial Borrowing 1840–1860." *Journal of Economic History* 20 (March): 1–30.

Davis, Lance E. 1965. "The Investment Market, 1870–1914: The Evolution of a National Market." *Journal of Economic History* 25 (Sep.): 355–99.

Dorfman, Joseph. 1946. *The Economic Mind in American Civilization. Volume 2, 1606–1865*. New York: Viking Press.

Eichengreen, Barry. 1984. "Mortgage Interest Rates in the Populist Era." *American Economic Review* 74 (Dec.): 995–1015.

Eichengreen, Barry. 1987. "Agricultural Mortgages in the Populist Era: Reply to Snowden." *Journal of Economic History* 47 (Sep.): 757–60.

Engerman, Stanley L., and Kenneth L. Sokoloff. 2005. "The Evolution of Suffrage Institutions in the New World." *Journal of Economic History* 65 (Dec.): 891–921.

Farnam, Henry W. 1938. *Chapters in the History of Social Legislation in the United States to 1860*, ed. Clive Day. Washington, DC: Carnegie Institution of Washington.

Finley, M. I. 1953. "Land, Debt, and the Man of Property in Classical Athens." *Political Science Quarterly* 68 (June): 249–68.

Friedman, Lawrence M. 1963. "The Usury Laws of Wisconsin: A Study in Legal and Social History." *Wisconsin Law Review* (July): 515–65.

George, Charles H. 1957. "English Calvinist Opinion on Usury, 1600–1640." *Journal of the History of Ideas* 18 (Oct.): 455–474.

Glaeser, Edward L., and Jose Scheinkman. 1998. "Neither a Borrower nor a Lender Be: An Economic Analysis of Interest Restrictions and Usury Laws." *Journal of Law and Economics* 41 (April): 1–36.

Hammond, Bray. 1970. *Sovereignty and an Empty Purse: Banks and Politics in the Civil War*. Princeton: Princeton University Press.

Harding, William F. 1895. "The State Bank of Indiana." *Journal of Political Economy* 4 (Dec.): 1–36; "Appendix: Tables Relating to the State Bank of Indiana," 109–38.

Holdsworth, William Searle. 1903. *A History of English Law*. London: Methuen.

Holmes, George K. 1892. "Usury in Law, in Practice and in Psychology." *Political Science Quarterly* (Sep.): 431–67.

Holmes, George K., and John S. Lord. 1895. "Report on real estate mortgages in the United States at the eleventh census, 1890." Reports of the eleventh census of the United States, 1890, v. 12. Washington, DC: G.P.O.

Horwitz, Morton J. 1977. *The Transformation of American Law: 1780–1860*. Cambridge, MA: Harvard University Press.

Huntington, C.C. 1915. "A History of Banking and Currency in Ohio before the Civil War." *Ohio Archaeological and Historical Publications* XXIV: 442–50.

Jadlow, Joseph M. 1977. "Adam Smith on Usury Laws." *Journal of Finance* 32 (Sep.): 1195–200.

Jones, Norman L. 1989. *God and the Money Lenders: Usury and the Law in Early Modern England*. Oxford, UK: Basil Blackwell.

Ketchum, Hiram, Jr. 1863. "The Usury Laws and the National Banking System." *Bankers Magazine*, New Series, 12: 161–66.

Keynes, John Maynard. 1965 [1936]. *The General Theory of Employment, Interest, and Money*. New York: Harcourt, Brace & World.

Kirkland, Frazar. 1865. *Cyclopedia of Commercial and Business Anecdotes*. New York: D. Appleton.

Kish-Goodling, Donna M. 1998. "Using the Merchant of Venice in Teaching Monetary Economics." *Journal of Economic Education* 29 (Fall): 330–39.

Krooss, Herman E. 1969. *Documentary History of Banking and Currency in the United States*. 4 volumes. New York: Chelsea House.

Levi, Peter. 1988. *The Life and Times of William Shakespeare*. New York: Random House.

Marshall, Alfred. 1961. *Principles of Economics.* 9th (variorum), ed. C. W. Guille-baud. London, New York: Macmillan for the Royal Economic Society.

Mill, John Stuart. *Principles of Political Economy,* edited by W. J. Ashley. London: Longman's Green and Co., 1940. The first edition appeared in 1848; the seventh edition, the last revised by Mill, was published in 1871.

Miller, Harry E. 1924. "Earlier Theories of Crises and Cycles in the United States." *Quarterly Journal of Economics* 38 (Feb.): 294–329.

Munro, John. 2001. "The Origins of the Modern Financial Revolution: Responses to Impediments from Church and State in Western Europe, 1200–1600." University of Toronto, Department of Economics, Working Paper, 2001–02.

Nelson, Benjamin. 1969. *The Idea of Usury: From Tribal Brotherhood to Universal Otherhood.* Chicago: University of Chicago Press.

Noonan, John T., Jr. 1957. *The Scholastic Analysis of Usury.* Cambridge, MA: Harvard University Press.

Oberholtzer, Ellis Paxson. 1907. *Jay Cooke: Financier of the Civil War.* Philadelphia: George W. Jacobs.

Paganelli, Maria Pia. 2003. "*In Medio Stat Virtus*: An Alternative View of Usury in Adam Smith's Thinking." *History of Political Economy* 35 (Spring): 21–48.

Pressnell, Leslie S. 1956. *Country Banking in the Industrial Revolution.* Oxford, UK: Clarendon Press.

Redlich, Fritz. 1947–51. *The Molding of American Banking: Men and Ideas.* New York: Hafner.

Rezneck, Samuel. 1950. "Distress, Relief, and Discontent in the United States during the Depression of 1873–78." *Journal of Political Economy* 58 (Dec.): 494–512.

Robinson, Louis Newton, and Rolf Nugent. 1935. *Regulation of the Small Loan Business.* New York: Russell Sage Foundation.

Romano, Mary Ann Florence. 1989. *Law, Politics, and the Economy: Changing Patterns of Growth in Debtor-Creditor Laws, New York State, 1785–1860.* PhD dissertation, New York University.

Ryan, Franklin Winton. 1924. *Usury and Usury Laws: A Juristic-Economic Study of the Effects of State Statutory Maximums for Loan Charges upon Lending Operations in the United States.* Boston and New York: Houghton Mifflin.

Seth, M. L. 1955. "Indian Money-Lender in Pre-British Times." *The Research Bulletin (Arts), University of Panjab* (Nov.), XV Economics I. Hoshiarpur, India: Vishveshvaranand Book Agency.

Smith, Adam. 1979 [1776]. *An Enquiry Into the Nature and Causes of the Wealth of Nations.* Glasgow edition of the Works of Adam Smith, general eds. R. H. Campbell and A. S. Skinner. Oxford: Oxford University Press.

Snowden, Kenneth A. 1987. "Mortgage Rates and American Capital Market Development in the Late Nineteenth Century." *Journal of Economic History* 47 (Sep.): 671–91.

Snowden, Kenneth A. 1988. "Mortgage Lending and American Urbanization, 1880–1890." *Journal of Economic History* 48 (June): 273–85.

Steuart, Sir James. 1998 [1767]. *Inquiry into the Principles of Political Oeconomy,* edited by Andrew Skinner; contributing editors, Noboru Kobayashi and Hiroshi Mizuta. Brookfield, VT: Pickering & Chatto.

Stiglitz, Joseph E., and Andrew Weiss. 1981. "Credit Rationing in Markets with Imperfect Information." *American Economic Review* 71 (June): 393–410.

Taeusch, Carl F. 1942. "The Concept of 'Usury': the History of an Idea." *Journal of the History of Ideas* 3 (June): 291–318.

Tan, Elaine S. 2002. "An Empty Shell? Rethinking the Usury Laws in Medieval Europe." *Journal of Legal History* 23 (Dec.): 77–96.

Tawney, R.H. 1925. "Introduction" to *A Discourse Upon Usury by Way of Dialogue and Orations* by Thomas Wilson (1572), 1–172. New York: Harcourt Brace.

Thomas, David L., and Norman E. Evans. 1984. "John Shakespeare in the Exchequer." *Shakespeare Quarterly* 35 (Autumn): 315–18.

U.S. Bureau of the Census. 1975. *Historical Statistics of the United States, Colonial Times to 1970.* Bicentennial Edition. Washington, DC: Government Printing Office.

U.S. Comptroller of the Currency. 1864. *Annual Report.*

Washington, George. 1797. "Letter to George Ball, May 7." The George Washington Papers at the Library of Congress, http://memory.loc.gov/ammem/gwhtml/gwhome.html.

White, Eugene N. 2001. "California Banking in the Nineteenth Century: The Art and Method of the Bank of A. Levy." *Business History Review* 75 (Summer): 297–324.

Wright, Robert E. 2001. *A Financial Interpretation of Early U.S. History.* Mimeo, University of Virginia.

Index